Do Good to All People as You Have the Opportunity

Reformed Academic Dissertations

A Series

Series Editor
John J. Hughes

Do Good to All People as You Have the Opportunity

A Biblical Theology of the Good Deeds
Mission of the New Covenant Community

John Anthony Wind

P&R
PUBLISHING
P.O. BOX 817 • PHILLIPSBURG • NEW JERSEY 08865-0817

Do Good to All People as You Have the Opportunity: A Biblical Theology of the Good Deeds Mission of the New Covenant Community. John Anthony Wind, Adv. M.Div., Ph. D., The Southern Baptist Theological Seminary. Submitted to The Southern Baptist Theological Seminary, 2015, for the degree of Ph.D. Supervisor: M. David Sills.

Printed in the United States of America

ISBN: 978-1-62995-461-5 (pbk)

"John Wind has provided us with a deeply researched study of evangelism and good deeds in world missions. Beginning in Genesis 1–3, he considers what it means to be created in the image of God, our purpose, and how sin affects this. Then taking us through Scripture, he applies contemporary research on missions to the important questions concerning the kingdom and the gospel. I especially benefited as I thought through the debate about otherworldly dualism and the role of good deeds in this life. This is an engaging book about the work of missions and raises the important questions about good deeds and lasting fruit."
—**Owen Anderson**, Professor of Philosophy and Religious Studies, Arizona State University

"How we connect the gospel to the way we live the Great Commission to the Great Commandment is one of the most important theological issues today. Those who are concerned that any 'good deeds' mission for the church must inevitably displace the 'good news' should read this clear and careful study. John Wind builds methodically on the covenantal structure of Scripture to show how we can prioritize the redemptive mission of good news without leaving behind the life-giving mission of good works."
—**Greg Forster**, Director, Oikonomia Network, Trinity International University

"As evangelicals, we need to think clearly about cultural and political realities and how they relate to the gospel, to the kingdom, and to evangelism. John Wind has thought carefully and deeply about these matters, and in this clearly written work he points a way forward that should be considered by all."
—**Thomas R. Schreiner**, James Buchanan Harrison Professor of New Testament Interpretation, Associate Dean, The Southern Baptist Theological Seminary

"John Wind offers here a thorough biblical-theological study of 'the good-deeds mission of the covenant community' framed entirely by the categorical distinction between common grace and special grace. Christian good deeds in the world are, as he explains, to promote 'common-grace justice' and 'penultimate human flourishing' insofar as those outside the Christian community are enabled by God's grace to flourish in this age. The priority for Christians, however, remains its evangelistic, special-grace mission to the world."

—**James W. Skillen**, former president, Center for Public Justice

"Verbal proclamation and social action: which is more important in the church's mission? In his book *Do Good to All People As You Have the Opportunity*, John Wind helpfully surveys a very important debate in the church and creatively shows how the two sides of mission fit together. He also gives us a timely admonition to use our words carefully lest we dilute the gospel."

—**Donald W. Sweeting**, President, Colorado Christian University

"John Wind has taken up a controversial subject with a host of practical implications for the life of the church. He's provided readers with a thorough, insightful, and charitable study that makes a wonderful contribution to these important debates. By focusing his study on the biblical covenants, he invites and compels us to think about these issues according to the whole counsel of God, as we should. This work will be a blessing to the church as it pursues the mission that Christ has given it."

—**David VanDrunen**, Robert B. Strimple Professor of Systematic Theology and Christian Ethics, Westminster Seminary California

To Rachel,
A wife whose life and character beautify the gospel

Contents

CONTENTS

Series Introduction

P&R Publishing has a long and distinguished history of publishing carefully selected, high-value theological books in the Reformed tradition. Many theological books begin as dissertations, but many dissertations are worthy of publication in their own right. Realizing this, P&R has launched the Reformed Academic Dissertation (RAD) program to publish top-tier dissertations (Ph.D., Th.D., D.Min., and Th.M.) that advance biblical and theological scholarship by making distinctive contributions in the areas of theology, ethics, biblical studies, apologetics, and counseling.

Dissertations in the RAD series are *curated*, which means that they are carefully selected, on the basis of strong recommendations by the authors' supervisors and examiners and by our internal readers, to be part of our collection. Each selected dissertation will provide clear, fresh, and engaging insights about significant theological issues.

A number of theological institutions have partnered with us to recommend dissertations that they believe worthy of publication in the RAD series. Not only does this provide increased visibility for participating institutions, it also makes outstanding dissertations available to a broad range of readers, while helping to introduce promising authors to the publishing world.

We look forward to seeing the RAD program grow into a large collection of curated dissertations that will help to advance Reformed scholarship and learning.

John J. Hughes
Series Editor

Foreword

What is the mission of the church? Given that the church is God's new covenant community—God's elect people whom our Lord Jesus Christ has secured and built by his glorious person and work—this question is vitally important to answer correctly. If we, as the church, are confused regarding who we are as Christ's people and what our mission is in the world, we will inevitably fail to live out what the Lord of the church has called us to be and do.

No doubt, the question regarding the church's mission is not new. For centuries, Protestants and now evangelicals have debated it, especially regarding the relative priority of the responsibilities of evangelism and social action. No one wants to dichotomize these responsibilities too much, and both are needed; yet it is crucial to think through which one has priority. Otherwise, our focus may blur, practical decisions regarding the church's allocation of time and resources may go awry, and, most significantly, the gospel may be redefined.

If this question has been debated for centuries, then why another book on it? Many reasons could be given, but probably the best is that although the debate about the church's mission is not new, in recent days it has returned in full force. In the last decade, in various books, at conferences, and on social media a debate is raging once again over the mission of the church, much of it cast in terms of "social justice." Is social justice the gospel or an entailment of it? Is the church's primary calling evangelism and discipleship, or is it to see society "transformed" by our evangelism and to take on various social causes? Are we to bring God's "kingdom" to this world by our social and political involvement in the world? In light of these recent developments, centuries-old questions are here again, requiring careful thought, reflection, and a return to Scripture. As in any other era, especially today we need a renewed look at what exactly the church *is* and *how* we ought to fulfill our mission as the church in a growing post-Christian, secular world, especially we who live in the West.

For this reason, *this* book is so greatly needed today. As serious questions are being asked about the church's mission, we need to return again to Scripture to answer the questions of the day in light of God's Word. What is unique about John Wind's book, and why I commend it so highly, is that John answers the crucial question about the mission of the church from Scripture, but not in a piecemeal way. This is not to say that previous books on the subject have been selective in their use of Scripture. Yet it is to say that what has often been missing in previous discussions of the subject is a larger biblical theology of the church, her mission, and how we ought to live in the world as God's new covenant people. The volume's subtitle nicely signals what the book is about and why it is so important: "A Biblical Theology of the Good Deeds Mission of the New Covenant Community." But what exactly does John mean by *biblical theology*, and why is it important?

In recent years, biblical theology as a discipline has grown in evangelical theology, but the term *biblical theology* is still misunderstood. At the popular level, most Christians think of biblical theology as being "true to the Bible," which obviously is vitally important! Yet this is not what biblical theology is in the disciplinary sense of the word *biblical*. So what is it? To best grasp the concept, it may be helpful to see how *biblical theology* has been understood since the Reformation, especially contrasting a nonevangelical use of the term with an evangelical, orthodox use.

In and after the Reformation, biblical theology was often identified with systematic theology as the church sought to understand the entirety of Scripture and to grasp how the whole canon is put together in light of the person and work of our Lord Jesus Christ. Nevertheless, there was a tendency to read Scripture in more logical and atemporal categories rather than to think carefully through the Bible's developing covenantal storyline. With the rise of the Enlightenment, however, biblical theology began to emerge as a distinct discipline. Yet it is crucial to distinguish the emergence of biblical theology at this time along two different paths: one an illegitimate path tied to Enlightenment presuppositions, and the other a legitimate path tied to the Bible's own self-attestation and presentation of itself.

Regarding the illegitimate path, there was a growing tendency to read Scripture *critically* and uncoupled from historic Christianity. The Bible was approached "as any other book," subservient to historical-critical methods that operated within the confines of a *methodological* naturalism. The Bible was not approached on its own terms, i.e., as God's Word written. In fact, the idea that Scripture was God-breathed through human authors—a text that authoritatively and accurately unfolds God's redemptive plan centered in Christ—was rejected. The end result of this approach was a denial of Scripture's authority and an increasingly fragmented reading of Scripture, given that the practitioners of this view did not believe Scripture to be a unified, true revelation. Biblical theology as a discipline became merely "descriptive" and governed by *critical* methods and unbiblical theological assumptions. Ultimately, as a discipline, it failed to help the church because at its heart, it denied biblical authority.

Contrary to the Enlightenment approach, a legitimate approach to biblical theology emerged. It was grounded in orthodox Christian theology, a high view of Scripture, and reading Scripture along its unfolding covenantal storyline. Probably the best-known twentieth-century pioneer of this approach was Geerhardus Vos, who developed biblical theology at Princeton Seminary in the early part of the century. Vos sought to do biblical theology with a firm commitment to the authority of Scripture. In contrast to the Enlightenment view, Vos argued that biblical theology, as an exegetical discipline, not only must begin with the biblical text but also must view Scripture as God's own self-attesting Word, fully authoritative and reliable.

Furthermore, as one exegetes Scripture, Vos argued, biblical theology seeks to trace out the Bible's unity and multiformity and find its consummation in the coming of Christ and the inauguration of the new covenant era. Biblical theology must follow a method that reads the Bible on its own terms, following the Bible's own internal contours and shape, in order to discover God's unified plan as it is disclosed to us over time. The path that Vos blazed was foundational for an evangelical understanding of biblical theology in the disciplinary sense.

So what, then, is biblical theology in this understanding? Biblical theology is the hermeneutical discipline that seeks to do justice to what Scripture claims to be and what it actually is. Regarding its claim, Scripture is *God's* Word written, and as such, it is a unified revelation of his gracious plan of redemption. In terms of how it has come to us, God has given us his Word over time, as a *progressive* unfolding of his plan, rooted in history, and unpacked along a specific redemptive-historical plotline primarily demarcated by the biblical covenants. As a discipline, biblical theology attempts to exegete texts in their own context and then, in light of the entire canon, to examine the unfolding nature of God's plan and carefully think through the relationship between *before* and *after* in that plan, which culminates in Christ. Thus, biblical theology provides the basis for understanding how texts in one part of the Bible relate to all other texts so that they will be read correctly, according to God's intention, which is discovered through human authors but ultimately at the canonical level. Biblical theology, then, is the attempt to grasp the "whole counsel of God" and "to think God's thoughts after him."

Now, it is *this* understanding of biblical theology that *this* book follows to answer the crucial question about the mission of the church. Why is this significant? Because ultimately we cannot answer the question in a biblical way apart from thinking through the entire canon of Scripture according to the Bible's own covenantal progression. Biblical theology is the discipline that allows us to grasp all that Scripture says, and therefore it is the basis, underpinning, and warrant for our theological conclusions from Scripture.

To answer the question "What is the mission of the church?" is to give a theological answer. But to give a correct theological answer, we must first think through the biblical-theological framework of Scripture as unpacked by the progression of the biblical covenants. Only after we have done so will we be able to answer the question in a biblical way from the entirety of Scripture.

We can state it another way: a biblical missiology (the focus of this book) is really a systematic theology in practice. But for it to be fully warranted missiology from Scripture, its theological proposal must be warranted not only from all that Scripture says but also in the way that Scripture says it. This is what John Wind's study aims to do and, in my view, he does masterfully. By carefully working from Genesis to Revelation, by especially following the Bible's own intrasystematic structures—namely, the progression of the covenants—John clarifies what it means for the church, as God's new covenant people, to be the church in our place in redemptive history. In this careful work of biblical theology, John labors hard to understand texts in their context and then place these texts in their covenantal location, before he draws theological conclusions about what it means for the church to be the church today. After John is done, he has not only answered the question regarding the church's mission, but also painted a beautiful portrait of what the church is as God's new covenant community in Christ, and how we ought to live as God's redeemed image-bearers and sons as we await the glorious return of our Lord Jesus Christ and the consummation of the ages.

In my view, the church (especially in the West) is struggling to know who she is and how she ought to live in the world. So this book is greatly needed today. If read, understood, and applied, it will help the church to be all that we are called to be as Christ's people, for the glory of our great Redeemer, for the good of his people, and indeed for the benefit of those outside the church as we learn anew to do good to all people as we have opportunity.

Stephen J. Wellum

Preface

As I reflect back upon the journey of this book, the dominant theme of my heart is thanksgiving. Thank you to my supervisor, David Sills, for seminars and colloquiums filled with academic insight and for helping guide this project to completion. Thank you to my other committee members, Steve Wellum and George Martin, whose seminars, at the beginning and end, respectively, of my classroom program, providentially helped first to set me on the course of this book and then brought my research to its final focus. Thank you to Tim Beougher, Greg Allison, and Jim Hamilton, each of whose seminar also left a significant mark on the structure of this book. Thank you to Ken Magnuson for your leadership of The Commonweal Project on Faith, Work, and Human Flourishing, which not only provided me a job but which also stimulated so much of my thinking as represented in the book that follows. Thank you to Tom Schreiner for your generous encouragement of my writing and for your ongoing inspiration as a model of Christian scholarship. Thank you also to John Sailhamer (1946–2017) for your seminal influence on how I both trust and read the Bible.

Thank you to my colleagues at Colorado Christian University who, after the completion of my formal academic studies, have continued to stimulate my ongoing education in all matters biblical and theological. It is my distinct honor and pleasure to labor with you in the work of academic ministry. Thank you to President Don Sweeting for your wise leadership of our institution, including keeping clearly before us the vision of uniting our academic research with cultural engagement. Thank you to Dean of the School of Theology

David Kotter for your mentoring of me as a rookie teacher, including your own steady example of combining scholarly depth with pastoral concern. Thank you to my other colleagues in the School of Theology, David Bosworth, Ian Clary, Megan DeVore, Matt Jones, Michael Plato, Seth Rodriguez, and Kevin Turner, for your friendship in Christ and for your partnership in the ministry of the Word.

Thank you also to John Hughes for your interest in bringing my research and writing to a wider audience. Thanks for shepherding me through the publishing process. May the Lord Jesus continue to use P&R Publishing to equip his church and to advance his kingdom.

Thank you to my father and mother, Charles (1924–94) and Ann Wind, whose foundational love, training, and example is intimately connected to all I have ever accomplished, including this book. Thank you to my parents-in-law, Jim and Jan Roelofs, for your love and kind support over the last quarter century (and for allowing me to marry your daughter!) To my dear wife, Rachel, and to our five daughters, Clara Anne, Chloe, Christin, Charis, and Catherine, I owe a whole different level of gratitude. You have each happily borne the impact of my research and writing on our family over the course of producing this book, providing unfailing encouragement and faithful love. Each of you is woven into the fabric of this book in a way more profound than the words on the page or the arguments presented. Finally, I offer up this book to my Lord Jesus Christ as a sacrifice of praise: may it serve your church and glorify your name.

John Wind
Lakewood, Colorado
February 2019

1

Introduction

Debating the Mission of the Church

Evangelicals[1] have debated the relative priority of the responsibilities of verbal proclamation and social action in the church's mission for centuries.[2] In the 1800s, urban poverty in Europe and

[1] The term "evangelical" is an increasingly disputed designation today. See Andrew David Naselli and Collin Hansen, eds., *Four Views on the Spectrum of Evangelicalism* (Grand Rapids: Zondervan, 2011). Traditionally, the term "evangelical" was used to describe those who (among other things) shared a commitment to the centrality of the Scripture, the importance of proclaiming the gospel message in evangelism, and the necessity of individuals being born again by the Spirit. This book presupposes these "evangelical" convictions and speaks primarily to those who share them. See Richard Lints, *The Fabric of Theology: A Prolegomenon to Evangelical Theology* (Grand Rapids: Eerdmans, 1993), 49, for a slightly expanded list of six evangelical core doctrines.

[2] One early, post-Reformation individual who might (anachronistically) be labeled an "evangelical" missionary is seventeenth-century New England pastor and missionary to the Algonquian Indians, John Eliot (1604–90). He generally followed the understanding of his day that the Native Americans first needed to be "civilized" before they could be "christianized." Though different in many ways from the present verbal proclamation versus social action debate, in other ways the debate over the relative priority of the civilizing mission versus the christianizing mission is the analogous debate within that time and place. Jon Hinkson, "Mission among Puritans and Pietists," in *The Great Commission: Evangelicals and the History of World Missions*, eds. Martin I. Klauber and Scott M. Manetsch (Nashville: B&H Academic, 2008), 25–29. During the

America (accompanying the onset of the Industrial Revolution
and rapid urbanization), as well as Protestant missions expansion into impoverished lands abroad, prompted evangelicals to
debate this question with new intensity. Some in missions, like
Rufus Anderson (1796–1880), head of the American Board of
Commissioners for Foreign Missions for forty years, believed that
the church's primary responsibility is verbal proclamation and the
planting of churches.[3] Others, like John R. Mott (1865–1955), a
leader in the Student Volunteer Movement and a national sec-
retary for the YMCA for fifty years, held that the church has a
more equal responsibility for both verbal proclamation and social
action.[4] With the growing prominence of the "social gospel" in the
early 1900s, followed by the outbreak of the fundamentalist-mod-
ernist controversy in the 1920s, the evangelistic priority side of
the debate became solidly fundamentalist in its theology and the
equal priority side increasingly embraced the modernist theology
of the social gospel. After World War II, theologian Carl F. H.
Henry, in his book *The Uneasy Conscience of Modern Fundamentalism*, began questioning fundamentalists' (some began to prefer the
title "evangelicals") lack of engagement in social action along with
their evangelism.[5] Yet, even as some evangelicals answered Henry's call to become more socially involved in the post-war period,

---

eighteenth century, the revivals of the First Great Awakening challenged the
chronological priority of the civilizing mission over the christianizing mission,
with "the flames of revivalism demonstrat[ing] from that 'civilization' need not
precede salvation, but rather could proceed out of it," (ibid., 32). This same
debate continued within the Scottish church between the years 1750 to 1835.
Ian Douglas Maxwell, "Civilization or Christianity? The Scottish Debate on
Mission Method, 1750–1835," in *Christian Missions and the Enlightenment*, ed.
Brian Stanley (Grand Rapids: Eerdmans, 2001), 123–40.

[3] Fred W. Beuttler, "Evangelical Missions in Modern America," in *The Great
Commission: Evangelicals and the History of World Missions* (Nashville: B&H
Academic, 2008), 114.

[4] Ibid., 116.

[5] Carl F. H. Henry, *The Uneasy Conscience of Modern Fundamentalism* (Grand
Rapids: Eerdmans, 2003).

the mainstream of evangelicalism continued to give priority to the task of verbal proclamation, as evidenced by the reaffirmation of evangelism as "the supreme task of the church" at the 1966 Berlin World Congress on Evangelism.[6]

The 1974 International Congress on World Evangelization in Lausanne, Switzerland marked something of a turning point in this ongoing debate within evangelicalism. The "Lausanne Covenant" that emerged from the congress affirmed the "Christian social responsibility" to "share [God's] concern for justice and reconciliation throughout human society and for the liberation of men and women from every kind of oppression. . . . express[ing] penitence both for our neglect and for having sometimes regarded evangelism and social concern as mutually exclusive," when in fact they are "both part of our Christian duty."[7] Yet, even in affirming the duty of social action, the covenant continued to assert that "evangelism is primary" in the church's mission.[8] The chair of the drafting committee for the Lausanne Covenant, John Stott, who as recently as the 1966 Berlin Congress had held an "evangelism only" position concerning the church's mission, was the key influence behind this recognition of the church's social action responsibility.[9] Some within

---

[6] Quoted in Charles Van Engen, *Mission on the Way: Issues in Mission Theology* (Grand Rapids: Baker Books, 1996), 134.

[7] International Congress on World Evangelization, "The Lausanne Covenant," in *Making Christ Known: Historic Mission Documents from the Lausanne Movement, 1974–1989*, ed. John R. W. Stott (Grand Rapids: Eerdmans, 1997), 24.

[8] Ibid., 28. This book likewise presupposes that both tasks are legitimate Christian responsibilities. Concerning social action, Tennent observes, "It is difficult to find evangelicals who do not acknowledge the importance of social action." Timothy C. Tennent, *Invitation to World Missions: A Trinitarian Missiology for the Twenty-First Century* (Grand Rapids: Kregel, 2010), 391. Concerning the ongoing responsibility of Christians to proclaim the verbal message, see Robert L. Plummer, *Paul's Understanding of the Church's Mission: Did the Apostle Paul Expect the Early Christian Communities to Evangelize?* (Waynesboro, GA: Paternoster, 2006).

[9] John R. W. Stott, *Christian Mission in the Modern World* (Downers Grove,

the Lausanne Movement were still unhappy with the covenant's language designating evangelism as "primary," leading Stott to convene the 1982 International Consultation on the Relationship between Evangelism and Social Responsibility in Grand Rapids, Michigan. The report produced by this consultation sought further to clarify the relationship between evangelism and social responsibility, agreeing that evangelism has a "logical" priority in that people must first become Christians before they can become socially responsible Christians and that evangelism has an eternal priority since "a person's eternal, spiritual salvation is of greater importance than his or her temporal and material well-being." But the paper also claimed that "seldom if ever should we have to choose between" these two responsibilities, as "the choice . . . is largely conceptual," with the dual responsibilities inseparable in practice.[10]

While the second International Congress on World Evangelism in Manila in 1989 ("Lausanne II") continued explicitly to affirm the primacy of evangelism in "The Manila Manifesto," the Third Lausanne Congress on World Evangelism in 2010 in Cape Town, South Africa, conspicuously avoided any overt affirmation of evangelistic priority in "The Cape Town Commitment"—though the document began with a claim to "remain committed to" and to "stand by" the Lausanne Covenant and the Manila Manifesto. In spite of the claim, the Cape Town Commitment is best seen as promoting an equal priority between evangelism and social action, a position referred to in the document as "integral mission" (also known as "holistic mission").[11] Christopher Wright, the chair of the

---

IL: IVP, 2008), 37.

[10] International Consultation on the Relationship between Evangelism and Social Responsibility, "The Grand Rapids Report on Evangelism and Social Responsibility: An Evangelical Commitment," in *Making Christ Known: Historic Mission Documents from the Lausanne Movement, 1974–1989*, ed. John R. W. Stott (Grand Rapids: Eerdmans, 1997), 183.

[11] Rose Dowsett, *The Capetown Commitment: A Confession of Faith and a Call to Action—Study Edition* (Peabody, MA: Hendrickson, 2012), 1, 43.

working group that drafted the Cape Town Commitment (notably, a protégé of John Stott as well as the International Ministries Director at an organization founded by Stott, Langham Partnership), is in fact perhaps the most prominent contemporary *opponent* of the evangelistic priority position and *proponent* of integral or holistic mission. Wright believes that the evangelism and social action responsibilities have equal priority and "should never have been separated in the first place," nor one given priority over the other.[12]

David Hesselgrave characterizes the position held by Wright as "revisionist holism," making "evangelism and social action full and equal partners."[13] Hesselgrave labels the original position of the Lausanne Covenant as "restrained holism," which "attempts to preserve the traditional priority for evangelism, while elevating social action," making evangelism and social action "more or less equal partners."[14] Hesselgrave himself holds to evangelistic priority, the position he labels "traditional prioritism."[15] This position affirms the legitimacy and necessity of a broad range of social action by Christians while preserving a distinct, operational priority for evangelism and church planting by the institutional church. These differing positions demonstrate that in spite of decades of discussion, the debate over the relative priority of the responsibilities of evangelism and social action remains unresolved, as "evangelicals committed to the primacy of proclamation in Christian mission have been accused of 'reductionism' by their counterparts, whereas the latter have been charged with 'expansionism' by the former."[16] Kevin DeYoung and Greg Gilbert describe this debate as "the most confusing, most

---

[12] Christopher J. H. Wright, *The Mission of God's People: A Biblical Theology of the Church's Mission* (Grand Rapids: Zondervan, 2010), 276.

[13] David J. Hesselgrave, *Paradigms in Conflict: 10 Key Questions in Christian Missions Today* (Grand Rapids: Kregel, 2005), 120.

[14] Ibid., 121.

[15] Ibid.

[16] Christopher R. Little, "What Makes Mission Christian?" *International Journal of Frontier Missiology* 25, no. 2 (Summer 2008): 66.

discussed, most energizing, and most potentially divisive issue in the evangelical church today."[17] Perhaps now is the time to end this divisive discussion since nothing more remains to be said? On the contrary, Hesselgrave believes "it is imperative that discussions such as this one continue."[18] In fact, Hesselgrave is convinced that "nothing could be more obvious than the fact that the entire future of Evangelical missions/missiology rests upon" correctly answering the question, "What is the mission of the church?"[19]

While the existing literature in both missiology and biblical theology contains numerous biblical-theological arguments supporting either the evangelistic priority or the equal priority side of the debate, one crucial interpretive issue within the larger discussion is the question of the proper biblical-theological framework for examining the relevant biblical data. More specifically, this book will explore how one's conception of the overall covenantal macro-structure of Scripture impacts one's answer to this debated question.[20] As Peter Gentry and Stephen Wellum argue, "Every loci

[17] Kevin DeYoung and Greg Gilbert, *What Is the Mission of the Church? Making Sense of Social Justice, Shalom, and the Great Commission* (Wheaton, IL: Crossway, 2011), 25.

[18] David J. Hesselgrave, "Conclusion: A Scientific Postscript—Grist for the Missiological Mills of the Future," in *Missionshift: Global Mission Issues in the Third Millennium*, eds. David J. Hesselgrave and Ed Stetzer (Nashville: B&H Academic, 2010), 293.

[19] Ibid., 272.

[20] The covenantal framework of the biblical story is crucial for determining *where* believing readers are within the storyline (i.e., what time is it within the story) and, therefore, what is the readers' proper mission in response. Vanhoozer calls this storyline the "theodrama," within which believing readers must take up their role by answering key questions: "1. Where are we in the theodrama? What kind of scene are we playing? 2. Who are we? In what kind of plot are our lives entangled? 3. What time is it? What act and scene of the drama of redemption are we playing? 4. What is happening? What is God doing? 5. What should we say or do? Together, these five add up to a single, comprehensive question: Why are we, the church, here? The answer to that question takes the form of a mission statement: we are here to participate rightly in God's triune mission to the world." Kevin Vanhoozer, "A Drama

of theology is affected by one's understanding of the relationship between the biblical covenants, given the fact that the covenants form the backbone of Scripture's story line."[21] While Gentry and Wellum explore the impact of one's covenantal framework on theology proper, Christology, ecclesiology, and eschatology, this book will further explore its impact on missiology.[22]

Wright, in arguing for the equal priority position, also recognizes the crucial role of one's larger biblical-theological framework, seeing his own overall academic project as "develop[ing] an approach to biblical hermeneutics that sees the mission of God (and the participation in it of God's people) as a framework within which we can read the whole Bible."[23] Timothy Tennent, another proponent of the equal priority position, agrees with Wright's emphasis: "It is important . . . that the relationship between [evangelism and social action] are [sic] clearly understood by those in missiological training and flow [sic] out of a proper biblical and theological framework."[24] Mark

---

of Redemption Model," in *Four Views on Moving Beyond the Bible to Theology*, ed. Gary T. Meadors (Grand Rapids: Zondervan, 2009), 162–63. One way to describe the purpose of this book is as an attempt to discern the parameters of how God's people are to participate rightly in God's triune mission through doing good deeds on behalf of those outside the New Covenant.

[21] Peter J. Gentry and Stephen J. Wellum, *Kingdom through Covenant: A Biblical-Theological Understanding of the Covenants* (Wheaton, IL: Crossway, 2012), 653. According to Gentry and Wellum, "[C]rucial theological differences within Christian theology, and the resolution of those differences, are directly tied to one's understanding of how the biblical covenants unfold and relate to each other . . . . correctly 'putting together' the biblical covenants is central to the doing of biblical and systematic theology and thus to the theological conclusions we draw from Scripture in many doctrinal areas. If we are going to make progress in resolving disagreements within Christian theology . . . then how we understand the nature of the biblical covenants and their relationship to each other much be faced head on and *not* simply assumed" (ibid., 21, 23) [original emphasis].

[22] Ibid., 653–716.

[23] Christopher J. H. Wright, *The Mission of God: Unlocking the Bible's Grand Narrative* (Downers Grove, IL: IVP Academic, 2006), 17.

[24] Tennent, *Invitation to World Missions*, 393.

Russell sounds a similar note, stating, "Much of my contention with missiologists who support the priority of proclamation is with the framework they use to draw their conclusions."[25] Russell believes, "As long as our framework is wrong, the longstanding debate will not come to an end and unfruitful debates will continue *ad nauseum*."[26] Those on the other side of the debate, such as DeYoung and Gilbert, agree that consensus can only be achieved by first addressing fundamental, structural questions, such as identifying "the right categories and the right building blocks" for building a biblical theology of mission.[27]

As this book's literature review in chapters 2 and 3 will demonstrate more fully, many evangelicals have already addressed the question of what this book is calling the "good deeds"[28] mission of the church. Some of the more recent biblical-theological works which include a treatment of the good deeds mission while both arguing for an equal priority position and also addressing to some degree the covenantal structure of Scripture are Christopher Wright (*The Mission of God: Unlocking the Bible's Grand Narrative*, 2006), Arthur Glasser (*Announcing the Kingdom: The Story of God's Mission in the Bible*, 2003), Roger Hedlund (*The Mission of the Church in the World: A Biblical Theology*, 1985), and William Dyrness (*Let the Earth Rejoice!: A Biblical Theology of Holistic Mission*, 1983). But each book falls short of a more comprehensive analysis

---

[25] Mark L. Russell, "A Brief Apology for Holistic Mission: My Response to 'The Universal Priority of Proclamation' by Kurt Nelson," *Occasional Bulletin* 20, no. 3 (Fall 2007): 3.

[26] Ibid., 4.

[27] DeYoung and Gilbert, *What Is the Mission of the Church?*, 16.

[28] Two phrases in the Greek NT can be translated as "good deeds": καλος εργον and αγαθος εργον. Matthew uses καλος εργον in Matt. 5:16, Peter uses it in 1 Peter 2:12, and the author of Hebrews uses it in Heb. 10:24. Luke uses αγαθος εργον in Acts 9:36, and Paul uses it in Eph. 2:10. Paul uses these two phrases interchangeably in 1 Tim. 2:10; 5:10, 25; 6:18 and in Titus 1:16; 2:7, 14; 3:1, 8, 14; demonstrating that in general usage, these two phrases are synonymous.

of the covenantal structure and its impact on our understanding of the good deeds mission.

From the evangelistic priority side, DeYoung and Gilbert (*What Is the Mission of the Church? Making Sense of Social Justice, Shalom, and the Great Commission*, 2011) provide detailed biblical argumentation written at a popular level supporting their position but spend limited time either examining the covenantal structure of Scripture or developing a positive vision of the church's good deeds mission. Writing at a more academic level, the authors of a collection of essays, edited by William Larkin and Joel Williams (*Mission in the New Testament: An Evangelical Approach*, 1998), also advocate evangelistic priority while only giving passing attention to issues of covenantal structure (or to the Old Testament [OT] as a whole) and leave the good deeds mandate largely unaddressed. This same critique applies to works of biblical theology by Andreas Köstenberger and Peter O'Brien (*Salvation to the Ends of the Earth: A Biblical Theology of Mission*, 2001) and by Eckhard Schnabel (*Early Christian Mission*, 2004). Two older works of biblical theology by George Peters (*A Biblical Theology of Missions*, 1972) and by J. Herbert Kane (*Christian Missions in Biblical Perspective*, 1976) likewise give scant attention to either covenantal structure or the good deeds mission. A more recent collection of essays edited by Bruce Riley Ashford (*Theology and Practice of Mission: God, the Church, and the Nations*, 2011) takes a distinctly biblical-theological approach to examining the church's mission, spending significant time developing a vision of the church's good deeds mission. Nonetheless, while highlighting the creation-fall-redemption structure of Scripture and prioritizing evangelism, the essays do not give focused attention to issues of covenantal structure. Books by Michael Horton (*The Gospel Commission: Recovering God's Strategy for Making Disciples*, 2011) and David VanDrunen (*Living in God's Two Kingdoms: A Biblical Vision for Christianity and Culture*, 2010) emphasize Scripture's covenantal structure and address the good deeds responsibility, all while promoting evangelistic priority in the church's mission—though neither book is focused more narrowly on the question of the church's good deeds mission.

Good Deeds Mission Proposal

As this book will exhibit more comprehensively in the literature review, both the missiological and the biblical-theological literature lack a thorough and focused treatment exploring how one's conception of the overall covenantal macro-structure of Scripture impacts one's interpretation of the good deeds mission of the church, including its relationship to the church's evangelism responsibility. As well, while those taking an equal priority position have written more extensively about the church's need to do good deeds, those who have argued for an evangelistic priority position have tended to neglect the development of their own detailed, alternative proposal for rightly understanding the good deeds mission of the church. Also, though much has been written on this topic, a review of the literature demonstrates that much disagreement and lack of clarity remains within the discussion, highlighting the need for additional contributions which aim further to clarify the fundamental issues of the debate and thereby potentially produce a greater resolution in the ongoing disagreement. Since evangelicals generally agree that theological debates are to be resolved by reference to the authoritative text of Scripture, a study taking a distinctly biblical-theological approach[29] and narrowly focusing on an examination of Scripture's positive portrayal of the church's good deed's responsibility is a needed contribution to the debate. And yet, as briefly noted above and as more comprehensively demonstrated in the literature review of chapters 2 and 3, no such narrowly-focused study presently exists.

Therefore, this book will propose a biblical theology narrowly focused on the "good deeds" mission of the church. In particular,

---

[29] This book's specific "biblical-theological approach" will be examined in detail below in the "Presuppositions for Doing Biblical Theology" section.

this book will explore the impact of one's conception of the overall covenantal macro-structure of Scripture upon how one interprets the Bible's good deeds mandate, demonstrating that covenantal framework heavily determines one's conclusions concerning this mandate. This book will also remedy the lack of a more comprehensive, affirmative portrayal of the church's good deeds mission from the evangelistic priority side of the debate, seeking to present accurately Scripture's positive mandate for Christians to "do good to all people as you have opportunity" (Gal. 6:10).[30] In doing so, this book will also seek to clarify the fundamental issues of disagreement in the larger debate by providing an overall template for exploring the key biblical-theological questions that each evangelical must address when developing his or her own biblical theology of the good deeds mission of the church. Beyond clarifying the impact of macro concerns of covenantal structure, this book will also seek to explore additional micro questions about the good deeds mission, such as: How extensive is this responsibility? What are the purposes of the good deeds mission? Are good deeds inherently glorifying to God, regardless of their connection to verbal proclamation? What goals and expectations should Christians have for their good deeds mission? Should the institutional church carry out this responsibility or is it merely the responsibility of individual Christians? If the good deeds mission is the institutional church's responsibility, how much of its limited resources should the church allocate to this mission?

Defining Terms

Because of the complex, and at times contentious, nature of the debate over the good deeds mission, precision in defining key terms used in this book's argument is crucial. The terms in particular need of definition include *biblical theology*, *mission*, *good deeds mission*,

---

[30] Author's translation.

verbal proclamation mission, evangelistic priority, equal priority, and *New Covenant community*.

Biblical theology can be defined in various ways.[31] The detailed working definition of *biblical theology* for this book is borrowed from Gentry and Wellum:

> [T]he hermeneutical discipline which seeks to do justice to what Scripture claims to be and what it actually is. In terms of its claim, Scripture is nothing less than God's Word written, and as such, it is a unified revelation of his gracious plan of redemption. In terms of what Scripture actually is, it is a progressive unfolding of God's plan, rooted in history, and unpacked along a specific redemptive-historical plot line primarily demarcated by covenants. Biblical theology as a hermeneutical discipline attempts to exegete texts in their own context and then, in light of the entire Canon, to examine the unfolding nature of God's plan and carefully think through the relationship before and after in that plan which culminates in Christ. As such, biblical theology provides the basis for understanding how texts in one part of the Bible relate to all other texts, so that they will be read correctly, according to God's intention, which is discovered through the individual human authors but ultimately at the canonical level. In the end, biblical theology is the attempt to unpack the "whole counsel of God" and "to think God's thoughts after him," and it provides the basis and underpinning for all theology and doctrine.[32]

Some of the key elements of this definition include hermeneutical discipline, unified revelation, progressive unfolding,

---

[31] For one recent attempt to categorize different versions of "biblical theology," see Edward W. Klink and Darian R. Lockett, *Understanding Biblical Theology: A Comparison of Theory and Practice* (Grand Rapids: Zondervan, 2012).

[32] Gentry and Wellum, *Kingdom through Covenant*, 33–34.

demarcated by covenants, divine and human authorial intent, and underpinning for all theology and doctrine. These and other aspects of this book's approach to *biblical theology* will be described in greater detail in the "Presuppositions for Doing Biblical Theology" section below.

Missiologists have debated the term *mission* extensively in the last fifty years, a term typically distinguished from the plural *missions*. As a result of these discussions, *mission* is often used to denote everything that God is doing in the world and *missions* signifies the varied human expressions of their participation in God's larger *mission*.[33] While recognizing the conceptual value of this distinction, this book will use *mission* more narrowly than either of these usages, instead designating this term as signifying the responsibilities of Christians, members of the New Covenant community, toward those who are not members of the New Covenant. Describing the church's responsibilities out to the world as a *mission* in no way implies that this narrower *mission* is equivalent to the fullness of God's own *mission*. As well, the New Testament (NT) also clearly portrays God giving an internal *mission* to the church, mutual responsibilities *within* the church, likewise a legitimate use of the term *mission*.[34] Nonetheless, within this book, *mission* will refer to the responsibilities entrusted by God to the New Covenant community toward those *outside* the New Covenant.

The *good deeds mission* will refer to a wide range of acts of love by Christians, not including the act of verbally proclaiming the gospel message,[35] an act which this book will label the *verbal proclamation*

[33] Craig Ott and Stephen J. Strauss, *Encountering Theology of Mission: Biblical Foundations, Historical Developments, and Contemporary Issues* (Grand Rapids: Baker Academic, 2010), xv.

[34] For a book helpfully arguing that the Great Commission responsibility of the church includes a mission of both verbal proclamation to non-Christians ("reaching") and ongoing training of disciples ("teaching"), see M. David Sills, *Reaching and Teaching: A Call to Great Commission Obedience* (Chicago: Moody, 2010).

[35] In chap. 7, this book will further examine the definition of "gospel" and

mission. The *good deeds mission* describes much of what this book referred to above as *social action, holistic mission* or *integral mission,* encompassing the mission of meeting human needs and promoting general human flourishing through relief ministry, community and cultural development, and working for structural transformation in society, in particular on behalf of those who are weak, exploited, and marginalized.[36] This book will use the term *good deeds* rather than *holistic* since *holistic* is not an explicitly biblical term, is typically associated with the equal priority position, and includes an unhelpful polemical connation (i.e., those who do not embrace the positive label, *holistic*, are instead categorized under the negative label, *dualistic*). As an explicitly NT term and category, the phrase *good deeds* overcomes some of the weaknesses of the term *holistic*, including the avoidance of biased terminology (though some would argue that even the act of clearly distinguishing the two missions inevitably leads to the prioritization of *verbal proclamation*).[37] Though this book will employ the term *good deeds mission,* alternative phrases also rooted solidly in NT categories include the *Great Commandment mission* (distinguished from the *Great Commission mission*), *mercy*

---

whether the biblical term should be defined as strictly a verbal message or if the meaning of the term also includes the results of the verbal message (i.e., the "gospel" *is both* the verbal message about what Christ does *and* the transforming actions that Christians do in response). One's answer to this definitional question is one of the issues that often divides the equal priority and evangelistic priority positions.

[36] Christians certainly have a "good deeds mission" and responsibility toward those *within* the New Covenant community, but "good deeds mission" here will refer exclusively to the good deeds that those *within* the New Covenant community perform towards those *outside* the New Covenant community. Of course, many of those good deeds done out to the world will also have positive benefit for those within the New Covenant community. In this sense, many broader good deeds done by Christians out to the world can be understood as being done for "society" or the "human community"—which includes New Covenant members—rather than just being done for non-New Covenant members.

[37] For example, see Tennent, *Invitation to World Missions,* 393.

mission, and the *common* or *universal grace mission* (distinguished from the *special* or *particular grace mission*).

In distinguishing the verbal proclamation mission from the good deeds mission, the question of whether either mandate has relative priority inevitably arises (as discussed above). *Evangelistic priority* will refer to the position that gives the verbal proclamation mission operational priority over the good deeds mission in the institutional church's allocation of resources of personnel, time, prayer, money, and other capital. *Equal priority* will refer to the position that attempts to give equal operational priority to the verbal proclamation and good deeds responsibilities, including those who would acknowledge a "conceptual" or "logical" priority for verbal proclamation even while making no significant distinction of priority in the church's actual practice (such as Hesselgrave's category of "restrained holism").

This book will use the term *New Covenant community* as synonymous and interchangeable with the word *church*. Since some also use *church* to refer to the OT people of God and since this book emphasizes the missiological significance of the overall covenantal structure of Scripture, including the impact of covenantal shifts (such as from the OT to the NT), using the phrase *New Covenant community* clarifies the argument of this book by explicitly describing its goal as a biblical theology of the good deeds mission of the *New Covenant community*. This distinction implies recognition that the good deeds mission of the *New Covenant community* is not necessarily the same thing as the good deeds mission of the *Old Covenant community*. Though this book will use the terms *New Covenant community* and *church* interchangeably, using *New Covenant community* helps clarify the intended meaning of *church*.

Scope of Research

As mentioned at the outset, in one form or another, the debate over this mandate has been taking place for centuries. Surveying the whole of this historical debate is beyond the scope of this book. Instead, the literature review in chapters 2 and 3 will be limited to written works from 1974 to 2014. While representing a somewhat arbitrary starting point in the midst of an already long-standing conversation, 1974, as the year of the International Congress on World Evangelization in Lausanne, Switzerland, does mark a significant point in the modern debate among evangelicals. Beginning with the first Lausanne meeting and exploring all the literature stimulated by it provides a forty year window within which to orient this book to the contemporary debate.

Because of its limited length, this book will not attempt to interact exhaustively with all the data of Scripture or of Scripture's extra-textual historical backgrounds but will necessarily select and focus on the parts of the Bible and the interpretive questions which this book identifies as most crucial in constructing a biblical theology of the good deeds mission of the New Covenant community. This book will give particular attention to the parts of Scripture that reveal the Bible's over-arching covenantal structure.

Finally, the scope of this book will be restricted by the presuppositions upon which it will build its biblical-theological proposal. Different presuppositions in theological method inevitably lead to different theological conclusions. Rather than focusing on the debate over the proper presuppositions for doing biblical theology, this book will instead state its presuppositions for biblical theology up front and then quickly proceed to do biblical theology within those confines. This approach will necessarily limit this book's interaction with those who approach Scripture with fundamentally different presuppositions.

Presuppositions for Doing Biblical Theology

This book will take a distinctly biblical-theological approach that agrees with Kösterberger that "the church's mission—in both belief and practice—should be grounded in the biblical theology of mission."[38] Most self-identified evangelicals would affirm this statement. The more debated question among evangelicals is "Which approach to biblical theology?" Ed Stetzer responds to Köstenberger's own arguments for a particular biblical-theological understanding of the mission of the church by noting that other evangelicals disagree with Köstenberger because they have different "method[s] for biblical theology" and varying approaches to "how [one] applies and integrates [the] discipline of biblical theology with another discipline, such as missiology."[39] Stetzer correctly recognizes that one's presuppositions and methodology for doing biblical theology have a determinative effect on the missiological conclusions one reaches. While such differing fundamental assumptions in theological method cannot easily be overcome when seeking to reach theological consensus, this book will nonetheless seek clearly to identify its own biblical-theological presuppositions and methodology in advance. Those who disagree significantly with this book's biblical-theological presuppositions and methodology will understandably have greater cause to disagree with this book's conclusions. Even so, increased and explicit "epistemological self-consciousness" for all participants in this ongoing debate is necessary in order to help clarify the areas of fundamental disagreement, even if those disagreements continue.[40]

Theological method in general can be understood as "the entire range of assumptions that control the way in which theological conclusions are reached."[41] As well, "hermeneutics" is essentially

---

[38] Andreas J. Köstenberger, "Twelve Theses on the Church's Mission in the Twenty-First Century: In Interaction with Charles Van Engen, Keith Eitel, and Enoch Wan," in *Missionshift: Global Mission Issues in the Third Millennium*, eds. David J. Hesselgrave and Ed Stetzer (Nashville: B&H Academic, 2010), 63.

[39] Ed Stetzer, "Responding to '"Mission" Defined and Described' and the Four Responders," in *Missionshift: Global Mission Issues in the Third Millennium*, eds. David J. Hesselgrave and Ed Stetzer (Nashville: B&H Academic, 2010), 76.

[40] Gentry and Wellum, *Kingdom through Covenant*, 24.

[41] Don J. Payne, *The Theology of the Christian Life in J. I. Packer's Thought:*

"synonymous with theological method" for those who understand the biblical text as the ultimate source and authority for formulating theology.[42] Biblical theology is a fundamentally hermeneutical discipline, and the roots of the divide between the evangelistic priority and equal priority sides of the good deeds mission debate are hermeneutical in nature.[43] In addressing this same debate forty years

---

Theological Anthropology, Theological Method, and the Doctrine of Sanctification (Bletchey, UK: Paternoster, 2006), 9. Goldsworthy says, "How we refine our definition of biblical theology and develop our practice will largely depend on the doctrinal assumptions we make about the Bible. For this reason we need to be aware of our presuppositions and how we have arrived at them." Graeme Goldsworthy, *Christ-Centered Biblical Theology: Hermeneutical Foundations and Principles* (Downers Grove, IL: IVP Academic, 2012), 38.

[42] Payne, *The Theology of the Christian Life in J. I. Packer's Thought*, 9. Sailhamer agrees, "Far from being the mere starting point or presupposition of a [biblical] theology, hermeneutics and hermeneutical decisions are the material out of which it is made." John Sailhamer, *Introduction to Old Testament Theology: A Canonical Approach* (Grand Rapids: Zondervan, 1995), 17. Tate also states that every hermeneutical approach is "anchored to a set of underlying presuppositions that determine the questions to be put to the text; and the answers are those expected in advance." W. Randolph Tate, *Biblical Interpretation: An Integrated Approach* (Peabody, MA: Hendrickson, 1991), 173. Klein, Blomberg, and Hubbard likewise declare, "No interpretation begins without presupposition. As evangelical interpreters we approach the Bible with commitments. We affirm the Bible's uniqueness, and we acknowledge this commitment before we begin the process of interpretation." William W. Klein, Craig Blomberg, and Robert L. Hubbard, Jr., *Introduction to Biblical Interpretation* (Dallas: Word, 1993), 96. Vanhoozer similarly posits, "The serious student of Scripture needs to develop an epistemology (theory of knowledge) and hermeneutic (theory of interpretation)." Kevin J. Vanhoozer, *Is There a Meaning in This Text? The Bible, the Reader, and the Morality of Literary Knowledge* (Grand Rapids: Zondervan, 1998), 9.

[43] Important to note is that both sides of the debate seem to recognize the hermeneutical orientation of the differences between the two sides. For example, one who recognizes the hermeneutical root of the debate from the equal priority side is Christopher Wright, "Christ and the Mosaic of Pluralisms," in *Global Missiology For The 21st Century: The Iguassu Dialogue*, ed. William D. Taylor (Grand Rapids: Baker Academic, 2000), 75. An example from the evangelistic priority side of someone who identifies theological method as determinative in the debate is J. Robertson McQuilkin, "An Evangelical Assessment of Mission Theology of the Kingdom of God," in *The Good News of the Kingdom:*

ago, Donald McGavran posited that progress in the debate is only possible if it begins with

> A clear statement of whether or not the speakers believe in the inspiration and authority of the Scriptures. But more must be said than this. Most Christians claim to believe in the inspiration and authority of the Bible, but they believe it in different ways. Consequently, their clear statement must also describe *the way in which* [emphasis added] they believe in the Bible. Their doctrines of revelation and inspiration must be stated before their pronouncements can be evaluated.[44]

John Stott agrees that the "greatest need" in the debate is to "find an agreed biblical hermeneutic, for without this, a broader consensus on the meaning and obligation of 'mission' is unlikely ever to be reached."[45] Hesselgrave likewise recognizes the relationship between the different "understandings of the nature of revelation [and] hermeneutics" and the different positions in this debate.[46] Keith Eitel concurs, "Theological methodologies are of utmost importance. Presuppositions regarding the integrity and reliability of the biblical text set in motion interpretive mechanisms that build one's theology into a set of strategic initiatives and practices."[47]

This section will therefore seek clearly to lay out this book's methodological presuppositions for biblical theology, expressed in ten propositions: first, God's revelation is the locus of authority for doctrinal truth; second, the inspired and unique locus of

---

Mission Theology for the Third Millennium, eds. Charles Van Engen, Dean S. Gilliland, and Paul Pierson (Maryknoll, NY: Orbis, 1993), 175.

[44] Donald A. McGavran, *The Clash between Christianity and Cultures* (Washington, DC: Canon, 1974), 52.

[45] Stott, *Christian Mission in the Modern World*, 17.

[46] Hesselgrave, *Paradigms in Conflict*, 334.

[47] Keith E. Eitel, "On Becoming Missional: Interacting with Charles Van Engen," in *Missionshift: Global Mission Issues in the Third Millennium*, eds. David J. Hesselgrave and Ed Stetzer (Nashville: B&H Academic, 2010), 37.

God's revelation is the written text of Scripture; third, the inspired written text is the canonical text; fourth, the locus of inspired and authoritative canonical textual meaning is author-encoded meaning and significance; fifth, the larger canonical structures of the Bible reflect both divine and human authorial intention; sixth, interpreters can know author-encoded textual meaning and significance with increasing (though always limited and imperfect) clarity on the basis of a "Christian critical realist" epistemology (and the enlightening work of the Holy Spirit); seventh, biblical theology is the foundation, authority, and guide for systematic theology; eighth, biblical theology is a universally-valid revelation of divine truth while systematic theology is a contextualized expression and application of universal biblical truth, including some aspects of application that are only valid in certain contexts; ninth, biblical theology begins with a careful description of the diachronic diversity of Scripture (paying special attention to textual forms and genres) but also includes a synthesis which recognizes the synchronic unity of Scripture; and tenth, themes in biblical theology (such as the good deeds mission of the New Covenant community) must be traced out along the progressively unfolding covenantal structure of the canon. Together, these ten methodological presuppositions set the stage for the possibility of developing a sufficiently clear, unified, and authoritative biblical-theological understanding of the good deeds mission of the New Covenant community which applies at all times and in all places.[48]

First, God's revelation is the locus of authority for doctrinal truth. As Richard Lints notes, "The evangelical theological vision begins with God's revelation."[49] This book therefore first presupposes

[48] Lints discusses the concept of "plausibility structures." Lints, *The Fabric of Theology*, 117–21. In some sense, these ten propositions for doing biblical theology can be called the "plausibility structures" within which the particular focus and conclusions of this book will be most persuasive. One implication is that the more a reader embraces these same "plausibility structures," the more "plausible" or convincing the book's conclusions are likely to be.

[49] Ibid., 65.

God's self-revelation—God has spoken. The task of this book is not merely creative human thought but an attempt carefully to listen, correctly to understand, and accurately to communicate what God has authoritatively revealed concerning the good deeds mission of the New Covenant community. Though this presupposition is embraced by most self-identified evangelicals, we must nevertheless begin by stating with Köstenberger, "Reflections on the church's mission should be predicated on the affirmation of the full and sole authority of Scripture."[50]

Second, the inspired and unique locus of God's revelation is the written text of Scripture. Not only does this book presuppose that God has authoritatively spoken, it also presupposes that he has spoken in a unique way in the written text of Scripture. Though this book affirms that God did reveal himself in the events of history, the written text is the only authoritative access to and interpretation of those events which God has given. The written text is therefore "text-revelation" (in contrast to "event-revelation"), a written revelation which alone the NT describes as "breathed out by God" (2 Tim. 3:16). To repeat, this presupposition in no way denies the reality and importance of God's event-revelation, fully embracing the fact that the Bible is what it claims to be, a true and trustworthy record of historical events.[51] As theologians informed by "speech-act theory" often emphasize, God's speaking in history is always connected with God's acting in history.[52] Nonetheless, our only inspired access to God's event-actions and speech-actions in history are the

[50] Köstenberger, "Twelve Theses on the Church's Mission in the Twenty-First Century," 64.

[51] Even though the task of biblical theology here proposed is a pursuit of text-revelation rather than event-revelation, this text-oriented approach still must use the tools of the historical method, in particular, the methods of textual criticism and philology. See Sailhamer, *Introduction to Old Testament Theology*, 225.

[52] Gentry and Wellum, *Kingdom through Covenant*, 88. Also see, Michael S. Horton, *Covenant and Eschatology: The Divine Drama* (Louisville: Westminster John Knox, 2002), 126–39.

written text-actions of Scripture.[53] Therefore, this book presupposes that the written text of Scripture is the inspired and unique locus of God's revelation.[54] One implication for the methodology of this book is a primary focus on explicit textual data in developing a biblical theology of the good deeds mission and not on extra-biblical historical data.[55]

[53] For one of the earliest and best treatments of the distinction between text and event, see Hans W. Frei, *The Eclipse of Biblical Narrative: A Study in Eighteenth and Nineteenth Century Hermeneutics* (New Haven, CT: Yale, 1974). For two more recent cases made for the fundamental importance of this distinction for biblical theology, see Sailhamer, *Introduction to Old Testament Theology* and Robert H. Stein, *Playing by the Rules: A Basic Guide to Interpreting the Bible* (Grand Rapids: Baker, 1994). In the pre-critical era of biblical studies (roughly, pre-1750), Protestants typically took the text at face value as an accurate and trustworthy presentation of historical events. Later, Protestants who accepted the Enlightenment-influenced presuppositions and conclusions of historical criticism began to doubt the simple connection between text and event, doubting the historical reality of miracles. But how could a "historically embellished text" function as authoritative special revelation? In response, some, like Schleiermacher, responded with an understanding of authority not in the textual meaning but in the reader's religious experience. Authority moved from text to experience, from author to reader. Others moved authority from text to historical event, with the fallible text merely being a witness to God's authoritative revelation in historical events (see Karl Barth and Neo-orthodoxy for a similar view of revelation). According to Scalise, in emphasizing event-revelation instead of text-revelation, "The Bible formally preserves its authority, but its relation to revelation changes." Charles J. Scalise, *Hermeneutics as Theological Prolegomena: A Canonical Approach* (Macon, GA: Mercer, 1994), 11. Schleiermacher moved authoritative revelation "in front of the text" (reader's experience), others moved authoritative revelation "behind the text" (historical events).

[54] Schnabel argues (as many have) that the uniqueness of Scripture requires us to approach it with unique presuppositions: "The inspiration of Scripture forces us to recognize that theology is a discipline *sui generis* in which humans can participate only on the basis of adequate presuppositions. This implies that a specific *hermeneutica sacra* is necessary for the interpretation of Scripture." Eckhard J. Schnabel, "Scripture," in *New Dictionary of Biblical Theology*, ed. T. Desmond Alexander et al. (Downers Grove, IL: IVP, 2000), 41.

[55] According to Richard Hays, "Extrabiblical sources stand in a hermeneutical relation to the New Testament; they are not independent, counter-balancing

Third, the inspired written text is the canonical text. Related to the previous proposition concerning the locus of revelation in event or text, this proposition answers the question, "Which text?" In other words, even if one believes the locus of revelation is in the text, one must still decide whether this text is the canonical text or a critically-reconstructed version of the text(s) at an earlier point in textual history before the consolidation of the canon.[56] This book presupposes that the canonical text is the inspired text, and the biblical theology developed here will make no attempt to interact with or speculate about a reconstructed, pre-canonical text.[57]

Fourth, the locus of inspired and authoritative canonical textual meaning is author-encoded meaning and significance. Even if one agrees that the canonical text is the inspired locus of God's revelation, still debated is whether inspired textual meaning is found in the author's intent, the reader's response, or a combination of the two, with some doubting that these two aspects of "meaning" can even be distinguished. (As in the previous proposition, some also believe authoritative meaning is found in the historical event itself or in the interplay between text and event.) This book will adopt E. D.

---

sources of authority. In other words, the Bible's perspective is privileged, not ours." Richard B. Hays, *The Moral Vision of the New Testament: Community, Cross, New Creation* (San Francisco: HarperSanFrancisco, 1996), 296.

[56] For an extensive discussion of this issue, see Sailhamer, *Introduction to Old Testament Theology*, 86–113.

[57] Some recent books which grapple with the canon's process of development include Timothy H. Lim, *The Formation of the Jewish Canon* (New Haven, CT: Yale, 2013); Lee Martin McDonald, *Formation of the Bible: The Story of the Church's Canon* (Peabody, MA: Hendrickson, 2012); Christopher R. Seitz, *The Goodly Fellowship of the Prophets: The Achievement of Association in Canon Formation* (Grand Rapids: Baker Academic, 2009); Craig A. Evans and Emanuel Tov, eds., *Exploring the Origins of the Bible: Canon Formation in Historical, Literary, and Theological Perspective* (Grand Rapids: Baker Academic, 2008); Roger Beckwith, *The Old Testament Canon of the New Testament Church* (Eugene, OR: Wipf & Stock, 2008); Craig D. Allert, *A High View of Scripture? The Authority of the Bible and the Formation of the New Testament Canon* (Grand Rapids: Baker Academic, 2007).

Hirsch's distinction between the categories of meaning and significance when interpreting texts.[58] In this view, textual meaning is an unchanging, determinate reality as intended by the author.[59] Significance, on the other hand, is changing and indeterminate, depending upon the particular response of a particular reader(s).[60] This book uses the term "author-encoded meaning" instead of the more commonly used "author-intended meaning" in order to distinguished between the author's intent as explicitly encoded in the text and the author's intent as speculatively imagined behind the text (a view labeled the "intentional fallacy"[61]). As well, the author-encoded textual meaning includes both author-encoded textual concepts and author-encoded textual significance, both what the author says and how the author intends for his readers to respond. But author-encoded textual concepts must be differentiated from reader-understood textual concepts, and author-encoded textual significance must be differentiated from reader-responded personal significance. A reader may or may not understand (or understand the fullness of) the conceptual meaning encoded by the author, and a reader may or may not respond personally in a way consistent with the author-encoded textual

---

[58] E. D. Hirsch, *Validity in Interpretation* (New Haven, CT: Yale, 1967).

[59] This book presupposes that the category "biblical authors" includes both inspired original authors and, in the case of the OT, inspired later author-editors who amplified and extended the meaning of the original authors but in no way contradicted their original meaning.

[60] Hirsch later nuanced this distinction by describing "implications" that are also rightly understood as part of textual meaning, even if they go beyond what the author consciously intended. This is because these implications are in keeping with and fall legitimately under the umbrella of the author's intended meaning and therefore are not merely a part of the reader's personal significance but ought to still be understood as part of textual meaning. See E. D. Hirsch, "Meaning and Significance Reinterpreted," *Critical Inquiry* 11, no. 2 (December 1984): 202–25; idem, "Coming with Terms to Meaning," *Critical Inquiry* 12, no. 3 (Spring 1986): 627–30; idem, "Transhistorical Intentions and the Persistence of Allegory," *New Literary History* 25, no. 3 (Summer 1994): 549–67.

[61] Stein, *Playing by the Rules*, 23–24.

significance. But regardless of the reader's personal, contextualized response, the author-encoded textual concepts and intended significance remain unchanged, determinate, and universal.[62] Biblical theology as framed by this book seeks to understand and communicate the author-encoded textual meaning (both intended concepts and intended significance)—an unchanging reality as originally intended by the author(s) and communicated via the text.

A significant implication of this presupposition for a biblical theology of the good deeds mission concerns where one looks for a divinely authoritative answer to the question, "What good deeds mission has God given to the New Covenant community?" Christopher Wright believes that Christians "need a broader understanding of revelation."[63] As well, he argues, Christians should embrace a more flexible and "dynamic understanding of the authority and role of the Bible in a post-modern world."[64] Wright is convinced that the church exhibits a "misleading tendency to equate the terms 'revealed and authoritative' too exclusively with the category of command."[65] Wright wants to expand the idea of biblical authority "beyond merely direct, positive textual commands."[66] Instead of biblical authority attached more strictly to author-encoded textual meaning, Wright

---

[62] This understanding can also be correlated with Vanhoozer's work using speech-act theory, allowing us to understand author-encoded textual meaning as roughly equivalent to "locution," author-encoded textual significance as equivalent to "illocution," and reader-responded contextual significance as equivalent to "perlocution." See Vanhoozer, *Is There a Meaning in This Text?* for further consideration of speech-act theory. Another author who upholds the necessity of a distinction between the author's meaning and the reader's response is Hays who calls the idea that "texts do have determinate ranges of semantic possibility" and that "a text's world of signification can be meaningfully distinguished from the tradition's construal of it" a "commonsense acknowledgment." Hays, *The Moral Vision of the New Testament*, 8.

[63] Christopher J. H. Wright, *Old Testament Ethics for the People of God* (Downers Grove, IL: IVP, 2004), 451.

[64] Wright, "Christ and the Mosaic of Pluralisms," 76.

[65] Wright, *Old Testament Ethics for the People of God*, 450.

[66] Wright, *The Mission of God*, 52.

argues, "The authority of the Bible is that it brings us into contact with reality—primarily the reality of God himself"—as well as other realities.[67] These realities, portrayed in the text but also transcending the text, in turn "generate authority that governs our responsive behavior."[68] So, for example, even if a clear NT command for Christians to be responsible for environmental stewardship is lacking, the historical reality of OT Israel's responsibilities toward their covenant land "authorizes" the Christian responsibility for creation care. But Wright subtly shifts the locus of authoritative meaning from strictly the author-encoded textual meaning to a mixture of textual meaning and the actual historical realities referred to in the text. This broadened understanding of the Bible's authoritative meaning allows Wright to claim biblical warrant and authority for greatly expanding the church's mission into a broad range of good deeds. This book's presupposition that the locus of inspired and authoritative textual meaning is more strictly limited to author-encoded textual meaning (including both intended concepts and significance) means that this book will answer the question "what good deeds mission has God given to the New Covenant community?" in a more limited and cautious way than Wright, believing that "only what is directly taught in Scripture is binding on the conscience."[69]

Fifth, the larger canonical structures of the Bible reflect both divine and human authorial intention. This book presupposes that author-encoded textual meaning is not only available at the level of individual books (often associated with one author) but is also available at the macro-level of canonical structures. Many evangelicals agree that canonical level meaning is intended by the divine author, but this book also presupposes that (at least some) canonical level meaning is simultaneously intended by the divine author *and* human authors—including later inspired editor-authors whose editorial

---

[67] Ibid., 53.

[68] Wright, *Old Testament Ethics for the People of God*, 469.

[69] Walter C. Kaiser and Moisés Silva, *An Introduction to Biblical Hermeneutics: The Search for Meaning* (Grand Rapids: Zondervan, 1994), 204.

work was responsible for the shape of the OT canon as it existed in Jesus' day.[70] Understanding God's work of inspiration as operative throughout the compositional process, including the development of canonical macro-structures, only further undergirds the importance of considering those structures (in particular, covenantal structures) when developing biblical theology. A biblical theology of the good deeds mission must seek author-encoded textual meaning not only at the micro-level of exegesis but also at the macro-level of canonical framework.

Sixth, interpreters can know author-encoded textual meaning and significance with increasing (though always limited and imperfect) clarity on the basis of a "Christian critical realist" epistemology (and the enlightening work of the Holy Spirit). Even if one accepts textual meaning as an unchanging reality intentionally embedded by human authors at both the micro and macro levels of the biblical text, is clear knowledge of that textual meaning possible for sinful and finite humans, particularly across the "ugly ditch" of time and culture that separate contemporary readers from the biblical authors? This question rightly captures two key obstacles to human knowing and to communication of that knowledge between persons—our finitude and our fallenness. These two obstacles were not always recognized adequately by Enlightenment and modernist theologians, who were instead characterized by a "non-critical" and "naively realist" epistemology, approaching the Bible with "historical positivism." Post-modern theologians reacted with an epistemology of "non-realism" and "radical skepticism," ultimately approaching Scripture with epistemologically relativistic presuppositions. Today among believing biblical scholars, both the modern and post-modern voices are acknowledged, with many scholars finding epistemological consensus around some form of "critical realism."[71] Lints describes this

---

[70] For further development of this argument, see Sailhamer, *Introduction to Old Testament Theology*, 239–52.

[71] D. A. Carson calls this position a uniting of a "chastened modernism" and a "soft postmodernism." D. A. Carson, *Christ and Culture Revisited* (Grand

perspective by speaking of both the "realism principle" and the "bias principle." The realism principle affirms the genuine possibility of attaining and communicating true knowledge (revealed by God through both general and special revelation). The bias principle recognizes the inescapable prejudice embedded in human knowing resulting from our creaturely finitude and our sinfulness, a reality requiring us to acknowledge the limits of our understanding and the deception of our hearts.[72] Though God has revealed true knowledge to humanity and has designed us with adequate (though fallen) epistemological tools to receive this revelation, our knowledge is always finally, at best, analogical to God's perfect knowledge.

But is critical realism when studying science and the natural world (general revelation) no different than critical realism when studying the Bible (special revelation), meaning we approach both realms with an equal expectation of certainty and clarity? Millard Erickson cautions us against an "uncritical, superficial transfer of the realism of science to religious belief and to theology."[73] This book therefore presupposes that the verbal and more explicit revelation of Scripture gives us access to a comparatively *greater* certainty and clarity in the areas of knowledge which biblical authors address.[74] This epistemological position is promoted by Wayne Grudem, who believes "it is appropriate for us to be more certain about the truths we read in Scripture than about any other knowledge we have. If we are to talk about degrees of certainty of knowledge we have, then the knowledge we attain from Scripture would have the highest

---

Rapids: Eerdmans, 2008), 90. Stewart Kelly describes the position as a form of "modest objectivity." Stewart E. Kelly, *Truth Considered and Applied: Examining Postmodernism, History, and Christian Faith* (Nashville: B&H Academic, 2011), 112. Vanhoozer calls it a "middle way between absolutism and relativism." Vanhoozer, *Is There a Meaning in This Text?*, 334.

[72] Lints, *The Fabric of Theology*, 20–26.

[73] Millard J. Erickson, "Foundationalism: Dead or Alive?" *Southern Baptist Journal of Theology* 5, no. 2 (Summer 2001): 25.

[74] This position is in keeping with the Protestant Reformers' view of the perspicuity of Scripture.

degree of certainty."[75] Wellum calls this general position "Christian critical realism."[76] Christian critical realism not only embraces the unique revelation of Scripture but also the illuminating work of the Spirit in revealing truth to readers of the text, both factors providing an extra level of epistemological clarity on certain questions of truth which God has revealed in Scripture.[77] Therefore, this book begins with a cautious expectation of epistemological clarity when seeking to understand the good deeds mission of the New Covenant community.[78]

Seventh, biblical theology is the foundation, authority, and guide for systematic theology. This commonly accepted proposition is a basic but important one. In addition, this point lays necessary groundwork for the next proposition.

Eighth, biblical theology is a universally-valid revelation of divine truth while systematic theology is a contextualized expression and application of universal biblical truth, including some aspects of application that are only valid in certain contexts. Proposition four argued that biblical theology seeks to understand and communicate

---

[75] Wayne A. Grudem, *Bible Doctrine: Essential Teachings of the Christian Faith*, ed. Jeff Purswell (Grand Rapids: Zondervan, 1999), 56.

[76] Stephen J. Wellum, unpublished class notes for *Contemporary Issues in Evangelical Theological Formulation*, Spring 2013.

[77] Christian critical realism also embraces the process of the "hermeneutical spiral," a concept recognizing the possibility of a progressively clearer and fuller understanding of the author-encoded textual meaning. Furthermore, Christian critical realism recognizes the importance of a "hermeneutical community" within which this progressively emerging understanding takes place. While an individual reader can legitimately experience a hermeneutical spiral in textual understanding, this process is enriched, accelerated, and regulated by reading the Bible together as a community.

[78] This epistemological expectation differs from David Bosch, who resists even offering a definition of "mission" since he believes, "Ultimately, mission remains undefinable; it should never be incarcerated in the narrow confines of our own predilections. The most we can hope for is to formulate some approximations of what missions is all about." David J. Bosch, *Transforming Mission: Paradigm Shifts in Theology of Mission* (Maryknoll, NY: Orbis Books, 1991), 9.

the author-encoded textual meaning—a reality that remains unchanged over time or in different cultures. Systematic theology, on the other hand, is a reader's response which applies and contextualizes the unchanging author-encoded textual meaning within a certain time and culture. Norman Geisler seems to agree with this distinction when he states that "there is some truth to [the idea that theology reflects the culture of the theologian], especially in regard to systematic theology, biblical theology is supracultural. It transcends culture."[79] Gentry and Wellum also concur that systematic theology is the application of the right interpretation of Scripture to all areas of life within specific historical and cultural contexts.[80] In making this contextualized application, systematic theology "must stay true to the Bible's own framework, structure, and categories as she draws theological conclusions and constructs a Christian worldview."[81] The importance of maintaining biblical categories is one reason why this book uses the clearly NT category of a "good deeds" mission rather than the biblically ambiguous category of a "holistic" mission. According to this distinction between biblical theology and systematic theology, in doing biblical theology this book will seek to reach conclusions which are universally valid biblical truths rather than merely applications of this truth that may be relevant in only some historical and cultural contexts.

Ninth, biblical theology begins with a careful description of the diachronic diversity of Scripture (paying special attention to textual forms and genres) but also includes a synthesis which recognizes the synchronic unity of Scripture. A diachronic ("through time" or historical) hermeneutical method "approaches the OT in terms of each

[79] Norman L. Geisler, "A Response to Paul G. Hiebert 'The Gospel in Human Contexts: Changing Perceptions of Contextualization' and to Darrell Whiteman and Michael Pocock," in *Missionshift: Global Mission Issues in the Third Millennium*, eds. David J. Hesselgrave and Ed Stetzer (Nashville: B&H Academic, 2010), 141.

[80] Gentry and Wellum, *Kingdom through Covenant*, 35.

[81] Ibid., 34–36.

of its parts rather than attempting to view it as a whole."[82] In contrast, a synchronic ("at one point in time" or ahistorical) hermeneutical method "attempts to view the whole of the OT as a unit, rather than looking only at the parts."[83] A diachronic approach is more inductive and organic in methodology; a synchronic approach, more deductive and synthetic. Put another way, "Biblical theology is characterized by two distinct but related activities which may be broadly described as analysis and synthesis."[84] Therefore, not only systematic theology involves synthesis, but biblical theology also includes an appropriate level of canonical synthesis.[85] This book will combine diachronic and synchronic approaches, letting the parts interpret the whole and letting the whole interpret the parts. This combination is consistent with the Reformation principle of the "analogy of faith" (*analogia fidei*) which recognizes that Scripture must be allowed to interpret Scripture since the canon is uniquely inspired, authoritative, and unified in diversity. Since diachronic attention to Scripture's diversity includes sensitivity to textual forms and genres, biblical theology in this book will seek to interpret Scripture in keeping with its chronological, historical, and narratival forms and to recognize the importance of identifying and properly interpreting the various literary genres within the text.[86] One specific application of proposition nine to this book is allowing the various parts of Scripture to inform our understanding of the covenantal macro-structure and allowing the covenantal macro-structure to inform our understanding of the various parts.

---

[82] Sailhamer, *Introduction to Old Testament Theology*, 33.

[83] Ibid., 32.

[84] Brian S. Rosner, "Biblical Theology," in *New Dictionary of Biblical Theology*, ed. T. Desmond Alexander et al. (Downers Grove, IL: IVP, 2000), 6.

[85] D. A. Carson, "Unity and Diversity in the New Testament: The Possibility of Systematic Theology," in *Scripture and Truth*, eds. D. A. Carson and John D. Woodbridge (Grand Rapids: Baker, 1992), 70, 90.

[86] See Vanhoozer, *Is There a Meaning in This Text?* for one interpreter who emphasizes the importance of interpreting literary genres in Scripture carefully.

Tenth, themes in biblical theology (such as the good deeds mission of the New Covenant community) must be traced out along the progressively unfolding covenantal structure of the canon. In particular, this book will highlight both the continuity and discontinuity between the various covenants of Scripture and how a careful recognition of both continuity and discontinuity impacts our understanding of the good deeds mission.

Overview of Argument

The last proposition—tracing the good deeds mission along the covenantal structure—describes concisely the approach this book will use in developing a biblical theology of the good deeds mission. After the literature review of chapters 2 and 3, chapters 4 and 5 will propose a biblical-theological understanding of the good deeds responsibility of all humanity first revealed in Genesis 1–11 in both the Creation Covenant of Genesis 1–2 and the Fallen Creation Covenant of Genesis 9, outlining the good deeds task given to all humanity. Next, chapter 6 will argue for a particular interpretation of the good deeds mandate given to Abraham and his descendants during the wandering period before the Mosaic Covenant, during the Mosaic Covenant while possessing the covenant land before exile, and during the Mosaic Covenant after exile and before Christ, concluding by exploring how the good deeds mission of the Old Covenant community relates to the good deeds responsibility of all humanity. Then, chapters 7 and 8 will present a biblical-theological reading of the good deeds mission of the New Covenant community, examining this mission during Jesus' earthly ministry before the inauguration of the New Covenant, during the present Inaugurated New Covenant age, and during the future Consummated New Covenant age. Chapter 8 will also inspect the relationship between the good deeds mission of the New Covenant community and the good deeds responsibility of all humanity. Finally, chapter 9 will summarize the results of the study and explore applications for today.

2

Review of Equal Priority
Literature Since 1974

The primary purpose of this two-chapter literature review is to clarify and collect in one place all of the main biblical-theological arguments that were made between 1974 and 2014 in arguing for either the equal priority or evangelistic priority position. Doing so will also further demonstrate the need for the contribution which this book seeks to make. This literature review will not attempt to be an exhaustive examination of *every* work which has argued for either equal priority or evangelistic priority between 1974 and 2014 but will instead be a representative sample of the literature in this debate. While the debate has taken place in a variety of books, journal and magazine articles, and unpublished conference papers, because of the wide scope of material, this literature review will limit itself to surveying the biblical-theological arguments published only in books—works which sufficiently cover the main lines of argumentation used in other sources such as journals. The review will be conducted in two chapters, this chapter exploring books arguing for equal priority and chapter 3 books arguing for evangelistic priority, with each part proceeding chronologically. The review will not comprehensively examine the content of any of the books, but will instead narrowly focus on the biblical-theological arguments each book makes in support of one of the positions in the debate. Additionally, since the key goal of the review is to develop a composite picture of the overall argument used by each side, once a particular supporting point has been noted in the review, that same point will not be restated (though variations of it may be), even if it is also used in one or more chronologically later works included in the review. Furthermore, identifying a particular argument with a certain book in no way implies that the rationale offered is original with that author. Rather than assigning credit for originality of argument, the purpose of the literature review is primarily to demonstrate the scope of different arguments employed in service of the two perspectives. Finally, though each supporting point of the composite picture is put forward by at least one author in the review, no author necessarily holds to each point represented in the composite picture.

Equal Priority Arguments Since 1974

In *The Church and Its Mission: A Shattering Critique from the Third World* (1974), Orlando E. Costas clearly rejects "the primacy of proclamation" within the church's mission.[1] Instead, he believes the church is called, simultaneously and without distinction of priority, to both verbal proclamation and good deeds, with good deeds themselves "proclaim[ing] . . . the good news of this new order of life [God's kingdom] in the multitudinous structures of society—family and government, business and neighborhood, religion and education. . . . stand[ing] in solidarity with the poor and the oppressed. . . . engag[ing] actively in their struggle for life and fulfillment."[2] Since communication always involves both verbal and non-verbal elements, for Costas, the "gospel" must be understood as both words and deeds.[3] As well, we cannot understand the written or spoken words of the biblical "gospel" apart from our personal encounter with and application of those words within our particular

---

[1] Orlando E. Costas, *The Church and Its Mission: A Shattering Critique from the Third World* (Wheaton, IL: Tyndale, 1974), 199.

[2] Ibid., 309.

[3] Ibid., 140.

context. Therefore, the verbal "gospel" message cannot be primary in our definition of "gospel" while our contextual applications (deeds) are merely secondary.[4] Instead, the biblical word and our deeds in response are equal in priority in defining "gospel."[5] The "salvation" offered in the gospel then includes a comprehensive "humanization" which begins in this life for the believer but also includes broader "progress, development, and social change. . . . [and the] active commitment [by believers] toward world peace, understood in the broadest terms—as *shalom*—and equally strong commitment to the struggles of justice," since "political, economic, and social structures . . . too must be redeemed by the liberating power of the gospel."[6] At the same time, Costas acknowledges that we must maintain a tension between the already and the not yet of Christ's kingdom, a tension which does not "absolutely identify" progress in society with "salvation."[7] Likewise, the church[8] is "a sign of the kingdom," "a new order that irrupts on the old," but not the kingdom itself, and the church's humanizing works in broader society are opportunities "where the gospel can be dramatically demonstrated," as these works are "legitimate manifestations (glimpses, if you wish) of salvation."[9] According to Costas, even God's direct, providential work of bringing a measure of progress in a society apart from

[4] Note how Costas' understanding of "gospel" is affected by his understanding of the relationship between the author-encoded meaning/significance of the biblical text and the reader(s)' personal, contextualized response, with his definition of "gospel" giving equal priority to text and response. In contrast, this book presupposes (see chap. 1) the priority and unique authority of the author-encoded meaning and significance of the text, even while in no way diminishing the importance and necessity of the reader's response.

[5] Costas, *The Church and Its Mission*, 193.

[6] Ibid., 195, 203, 69.

[7] Ibid., 69, 203.

[8] In Costas' use of "church," he makes no distinction between the church in its "gathered," institutionalized work and the church's more informal work through its members "scattered" throughout society.

[9] Costas, *The Church and Its Mission*, 70, 66, 205.

the work of believers is a sign and manifestation of "God's coming salvation."[10]

Rich Christians in an Age of Hunger: A Biblical Study (4th ed.; 1997) by Ronald J. Sider focuses more narrowly on the question of the Christian responsibilities to help the poor, to be generous, and to address global hunger rather than on Christians' good deeds mission more broadly considered. Sider notes the frequency of God's identification with and concern for the poor throughout Scripture and the direct commands for "believers to imitate God's special concern for the poor and oppressed."[11] In the 1977 edition, Sider talks about "the poor" and "the rich" in general, with God on the side of the poor and against the rich since, in Sider's view, the rich usually "become wealthy by oppressing the poor and . . . [by] fail[ing] to feed the hungry."[12] In 1997, Sider adjusts his argument to only refer to the poor "who are economically impoverished due to calamity or exploitation" and to the rich "when they become wealthy by oppressing the poor; or when they fail to share with the needy," rather than assuming that unjust riches and poverty are the exclusive or normative reality.[13] Whereas in 1977, Sider uses Matthew 25:31–46 as unqualified warrant for a Christian responsibility to care for all poor people,[14] in 1997 he acknowledges that direct responsibility in the passage may only refer to responsibility for poor Christians while still having secondary application to all poor people.[15] Sider also talks extensively about the responsibility of Christians to care for one another's physical needs, an internal church responsibility that this book fully affirms while also placing it outside the parameters

---

[10] Ibid., 298.

[11] Ronald J. Sider, *Rich Christians in an Age of Hunger: A Biblical Study* (New York: Paulist Press, 1977), 79.

[12] Ibid., 73, 84.

[13] Ronald J. Sider, *Rich Christians in an Age of Hunger: Moving from Affluence to Generosity*, 20th anniversary ed. (Dallas: Word, 1997), 42, 53.

[14] Ibid., 66, 83.

[15] Ibid., 60–61.

of what this book labels "missions." In considering this responsibility within the New Covenant community, Sider examines the OT principles of "jubilee," "sabbatical year," and "tithing and gleaning," recognizing that these laws are not binding on the New Covenant community but do contain "underlying principles" which we should try to apply within the church.[16] While Sider never directly addresses the question of equal priority versus evangelistic priority in this book, in a book published jointly with John R. W. Stott in 1977, *Evangelism, Salvation and Social Justice*, the same year as the first edition of *Rich Christians*, Sider argues that "evangelism and social action are equally important, but quite distinct aspects of the total mission of the church" and goes on to proclaim that "the time has come for all biblical Christians to refuse to use the sentence: 'The primary task of the Church is . . .'. . . [since] evangelism and social action are distinct and also . . . inseparable and interrelated in life."[17] Sider's main biblical warrant for his equal priority position is that Jesus, "our only perfect model," gave equal priority to preaching and healing in his earthly ministry.[18] Sider also understands the Pauline "principalities and powers," already triumphed over by Christ (Col. 2:15), as a concept which includes a reference to human institutions and structures of thought, thereby providing warrant and demand for Christians to express in this age the lordship of Christ in human institutions and societal spheres beyond the institutional church.[19]

In *Bring Forth Justice: A Contemporary Perspective on Mission* (1980), Waldron Scott argues for equal priority by claiming that the "biblical understanding of mission" should be understood as "the establishment of justice," which he defines as the "rectification" of our relationship with God, other individuals, society, and nature.[20]

---

[16] Ibid., 88–95.

[17] Ronald J. Sider, "Evangelism, Salvation and Social Justice," in *Evangelism, Salvation and Social Justice* (Nottingham, UK: Grove Books, 1977), 17–18.

[18] Ibid., 17.

[19] Ibid., 9–10.

[20] Waldron Scott, *Bring Forth Justice: A Contemporary Perspective on Mission*

Since rectification of each relationship is crucial to establishing justice, equal priority must be maintained—though at the end of the book, Scott recognizes that he has so emphasized the necessity of the church's mission of establishing justice in society that he feels the need to correct any misconception that he actually prioritizes *horizontal* rectification over *vertical* rectification, when in fact he gives them equal priority (259–60). Scott believes that justice as the mission of the New Covenant people is supported by the mission of Abraham and his descendants (the Old Covenant people) to "keep the way of the LORD by doing righteousness and justice" (Genesis 18:19), which Scott interprets as "blessing the nations . . . [by] the restoration of social justice"—though Scott never defines exactly what he means by "social justice" (49–50). Scott recognizes some discontinuity between the mission of the Old Covenant people and the New Covenant people, but he believes that the "restoration of justice" is an element of continuity between the two missions (86). For example, the Old Testament word for "compassion" (*hesed*) is "intimately linked with social justice," and when we think of Jesus' expressions of "compassion" in the Gospels, we should also think of the Old Testament connotation of social justice (123). According to Scott, the "essential characteristic" of the inaugurated new creation in Christ is "justice" (97). Therefore, "true evangelism" must include a component of "social action" (98). As well, Peter's description of how Jesus "went about doing good and healing all that were oppressed by the devil" (Acts 10:38) demonstrates that Christians must "attempt to bring *shalom*—wholeness and well-being—to individuals and communities" (168). In Scott's interpretation, Scriptures which require Christians to pursue "distributive justice" *within* the New Covenant community (such as 1 John 3:17–18) also require this economic redistribution in the broader human community (154).

The conference papers of *The Church in Response to Human Need* (1983), convened by the World Evangelical Fellowship at Wheaton

---

(Grand Rapids: Eerdmans, 1980), xv.

College, cumulatively promote an equal priority position. Vinay Samuel and Chris Sugden, in "God's Intention for the World," support equal priority by defining the "kingdom of God" in broader and more general terms as a partially present "reality attacking evil, driving out demons, healing the sick, and forging new relationships of trust between alienated groups."[21] Using this broadened definition, God's "kingdom building activity" is not limited to the church but also includes his work "in the history of all the nations and human society."[22] Therefore, the church's "kingdom" work must include both the church and general society. Samuel and Sugden not only reject a sacred/secular divide in the church's work but also reject a sacred/secular divide in their understanding of history, since God is at work in all of history. On this basis, they also do not limit God's special revelation to "his activities with either Israel or the church" because they believe that "such an assumption is not biblical" since "God used historical events at Sodom and Gomorrah, Nineveh, Babylon, Assyria, and Rome to reveal himself."[23] According to Samuel and Sugden, God's kingdom work in history is expressed in "many activities, structures, and movements in the world" where God graciously brings a measure of "transformation" to people's lives (even if that "transformation" does not include "salvation" or personal submission to Christ as Lord).[24] Social transformation such as "chang[ing] the

---

[21] Vinay Samuel and Chris Sugden, "God's Intention for the World," in *The Church in Response to Human Need*, eds. Vinay Samuel and Chris Sugden (Grand Rapids: Eerdmans, 1987), 132.

[22] Ibid., 135.

[23] Ibid., 136. In contrast to this book's presuppositions for biblical theology, Samuel and Sugden do not make a distinction between "text-revelation" and "event-revelation" (see chap. 1). Therefore, since God uses a multitude of means for "event-revelation," Samuel and Sugden conclude that special revelation is not confined to God's work with Israel and the church. But this blurs the distinction between special revelation in a text and special revelation in an event. If our only access to God's special revelation in events is the canonical text of Scripture, we should be more hesitant to adopt the broadened understanding of special revelation that Samuel and Sugden promote.

[24] Ibid., 141.

status of women and other oppressed groups in society" is "the fruit of the kingdom" and a "part of God's work of breaking down the dividing wall of hostility between separated groups, of creating in himself one new humanity in Christ in which there is neither male nor female"—even if those people have not become Christians.[25] Likewise, God's non-salvific work outside the church can also be labeled "redemption."[26] A final argument Samuel and Sugden make for equal priority is that because of Christ's resurrection, any present deed of love, "in any sphere of life, be it social, political, economic, or religious, will remain [in the consummated kingdom] if it is marked by the love of the new order," being fulfilled and transformed in the new age and making our work in society eternally important.[27] The concluding statement of the conference, "Transformation: The Church in Response to Human Need—The Wheaton '83 Statement," echoes Samuel and Sugden's expanded understanding of the kingdom of God when it states that a part of the church's kingdom work now "means striving to bring peace among individuals, races, and nations by overcoming prejudices, fears, and preconceived ideas about others. . . . sharing basic resources like food, water, the means of healing, and knowledge."[28] The statement goes on to argue that believers' identity as salt and light (Matt. 5:13–16) is a call to "work with God in the transformation of our societies . . . [and] to bring people and their cultures under the Lordship of Christ."[29] As well, Christ's call to love our enemies (Matt. 5:43–48) shows that "our ministry of justice and healing is not limited to fellow Christians. . . . Our economic and political action is inseparable from evangelism."[30]

[25] Ibid., 141–42.

[26] Ibid., 153.

[27] Ibid., 145.

[28] World Evangelical Fellowship Consultation on the Church in Response to Human Need, "Transformation: The Church in Response to Human Need—The Wheaton '83 Statement," in *The Church in Response to Human Need*, eds. Vinay Samuel and Chris Sudgen (Grand Rapids: Eerdmans, 1987), 258.

[29] Ibid., 260.

[30] Ibid., 261.

The Good News of the Kingdom Coming: The Marriage of Evangelism and Social Responsibility (1983) by Andrew Kirk also posits that any view that "give[s] priority to one aspect of the Church's mission arises from too narrow an understanding of evangelism."[31] Kirk believes that this narrow view is rooted in the false idea that separates the material world from the spiritual world and elevates the spiritual over the material. Rather, "the fully biblical position" understands "evangelism" as including social responsibility.[32] The "gospel" can be proclaimed both verbally and visually, which means that "by being the Church the people of God are automatically 'spreading abroad the good news.'"[33]

In *Let the Earth Rejoice! A Biblical Theology of Holistic Mission* (1983), while recognizing discontinuity and progression between the biblical covenants, William A. Dyrness' biblical theology stresses overall continuity.[34] Therefore, both Genesis 1–2 and OT Israel's covenant instructions have direct bearing on the mission of the New Covenant community out to the world. For instance, the requirements of the Old Covenant were to "assist [Israel] in regaining the dominion over creation that they had lost at the fall" and in "the restoration of the created order" (62, 64). As well, OT Israel and her God-designed social structures in the covenant land were a particular expression of "God's desire that structures exist that will correct the imbalance that enters into human relationships" and are "a token of what God intends for all his creation" (66, 79). Additionally, "The lesson of the monarchy was that God wished to be honored in the political and economic spheres as well as in the social and religious" (95). Since Christ as cosmic Lord has fulfilled the Old Covenant, "no human structure can now lie outside the sphere of his authority

---

[31] Andrew Kirk, *The Good News of the Kingdom Coming: The Marriage of Evangelism and Social Responsibility* (Downers Grove, IL: IVP, 1983), 57.

[32] Ibid., 105.

[33] Ibid., 104.

[34] William A. Dyrness, *Let the Earth Rejoice! A Biblical Theology of Holistic Mission* (Westchester, IL: Crossway, 1983), 61.

41

or remain indifferent to his purposes" (188). Therefore, Christians must seek to do justice in society "because Christ's Lordship is to be reflected in all human authorities" (197). Christians who "care lovingly for creation" are "reflect[ing] God's restorative purposes" for the natural world (148). Dyrness is convinced that "Christ's death and resurrection . . . has made possible a whole new level of peace in the created order as well," such that, even now, "no purpose or promise of creation . . . is not fulfilled in principle in the reign of Jesus Christ" (136, 147). Dyrness undergirds his case for equal priority not only by emphasizing continuity between the OT and the NT but also by arguing for continuity between the present inaugurated New Covenant age and the future consummated New Covenant age. As textual support, Dyrness interprets 2 Peter 3:10–11 as portraying a renewal which preserves "the essential qualities of the earth" rather than a picture of complete discontinuity between the present earth and the future new earth (179). Furthermore, Dyrness sees the bringing of the glory of the nations into the New Jerusalem in Rev 21:24, 26 as implying that the future consummation of God's kingdom "brings with it the perfection and salvation of all that is good and perfect" in this age (182). This enables us to "invest ourselves in the seemingly hopeless work of making our society and its institutions more just because by faith we see through them to the heavenly Jerusalem" (183). The comprehensive scope of the future consummated kingdom necessarily increases "the scope of our [present] responsibility to this world . . . and the breadth of our mission" (173). The result is that all dimensions of human life—"economic, political, social and cultural"—must be "incorporated integrally and holistically into the essence of evangelism and the substance of salvation" (189). As well, "all genuine development" in the various spheres of life, even if it has "no connection with the Church," is nonetheless a "reflection and fruit of the gospel" and are realities that Christ "claims . . . for his kingdom" (196).

Ministries of Mercy: The Call of the Jericho Road (1989) by Timothy J. Keller notes that in the Good Samaritan parable of Luke

10:25–37, "Jesus commands us to provide shelter, finances, medical care, and friendship to people who lack them."[35] Keller believes this parable "shatters" any attempts to prioritize evangelism over "social relief work" in the mission of the New Covenant community.[36] Keller holds that it is "inappropriate to ask whether evangelism or social concern is more important" since together they "constitute a whole that should not be divided."[37] The Christian ministry of mercy must extend to non-Christians because the parable of the Good Samaritan expands the definition of "neighbor" to include anyone in need. Three other reasons Keller gives that support a Christian responsibility of good deeds to non-Christians are that OT Israel was commanded to show mercy to the non-covenant sojourners living among them, Christians are commanded to "love . . . all men" (1 Thess. 3:12), and God shows mercy to his enemies and so must we.[38]

In *The Mission of the Church in the World: A Biblical Theology* (1991), Roger E. Hedlund promotes a covenant-based understanding of the church's mission in which the "cultural mandate" of Genesis 1–2 and the "missionary mandate" of Matthew 28:16–20 are both covenant mandates and are both equally a part of the church's responsibility.[39] Hedlund describes the OT provisions within the covenant people for alleviating poverty, addressing unjust government, caring for the covenant land, and promoting "social justice" and argues that Christians ought to apply these principles, in some measure, in broader society today.[40] According to Hedlund, "Social concern does not diminish redemptive concern when kept in biblical balance. . . . God's redemptive mission aims at social justice."[41] Hedlund also

---

[35] Timothy J. Keller, *Ministries of Mercy: The Call of the Jericho Road*, 2nd ed. (Phillipsburg, NJ: P&R Publishing, 1997), 11.

[36] Ibid., 38.

[37] Ibid., 109.

[38] Ibid., 83–85.

[39] Roger E. Hedlund, *The Mission of the Church in the World: A Biblical Theology* (Grand Rapids: Baker, 1991), 63.

[40] Ibid., 76–79.

[41] Ibid., 79.

employs NT commands for the display of mercy (Rom. 12:8) and care for the poor (James 2:14–17) *within* the New Covenant community as proper warrant for a mission of social action *beyond* the New Covenant community.[42] These verses "demand . . . action on behalf of the oppressed" and "work[ing] for justice in the world."[43]

In *Transforming Mission: Paradigm Shifts in Theology of Mission* (1991), David J. Bosch rejects any significant distinction between God's salvific activities and God's providential activities and believes such a distinction leads to evangelistic ministries wrongly being given priority over social service ministries.[44] Instead, our understanding of "salvation" needs to include "concern for humaneness, for the conquering of famine, illness, and meaninglessness."[45] In Bosch's view, when Christians "introduce change" into such broken situations, they "mediate salvation."[46] For Bosch, designating evangelism as primary and good deeds as secondary, "implies that the one is essential, the other optional."[47]

God's Missionary People: Rethinking the Purpose of the Local Church (1991) by Charles Van Engen supports equal priority by first postulating "the work and role of Jesus Christ as a pattern for the Church in the world."[48] Then, Van Engen argues that Christ's ministry is expressed in five roles: prophet, priest, king, healer, and liberator, roles which the church must now continue in its ministry (121–26). In its prophetic role, the church will be "calling for and working toward justice, toward *shalom*, toward righteousness and peace in human relationships and social structures." In its priestly role, the church will be a "sacramental presence" in the world "call[ing] for

---

[42] Ibid., 244, 254–56.

[43] Ibid., 256.

[44] David J. Bosch, *Transforming Mission: Paradigm Shifts in Theology of Mission* (Maryknoll, NY: Orbis Books, 1991), 394.

[45] Ibid., 397.

[46] Ibid., 400.

[47] Ibid., 405.

[48] Charles E. Van Engen, *God's Missionary People: Rethinking the Purpose of the Local Church* (Grand Rapids: Baker, 1991), 120.

reconciliation of people with God, each other, and themselves." In its kingly role, the church will "take seriously its role in nation building, in bringing harmony to chaos, in calling for government which cares for its people, and in organizing itself for the proclamation of the gospel of freedom and grace in Jesus Christ" (124). The church's healing role "is one of the most important functions which the church can exercise in the world" and includes "healing of body, of mind, of psychological stress, or of spiritual illness" (125). Finally, in following Christ's model as liberator, "spiritual, emotional, personal, political, economic, and social liberation is . . . an essential part of the Church's role in the world" (126).

In *Walking with the Poor: Principles and Practices of Transformational Development* (1999), Bryant L. Myers advocates equal priority by defining the Christian calling to be a "witness" as the "declaration of the gospel by life, word, and deed."[49] Christians witness by their lives because they "are the message," by word because the story must be proclaimed, and by deed because Christians must be "engaged with the world . . . seeking to make it more for life and for the enjoyment of life."[50] In addition, both Christian witness and "transformational development" fit under the larger umbrella and broad scope of the kingdom of God. Transformational development refers to Christian efforts "seeking positive change in the whole of human life materially, socially, and spiritually."[51] Since God is "working to redeem and restore the whole of creation, human beings, all living things, and the creation itself . . . transformational development is part of God's redemptive work in the world" and should be part of our work as well.[52] Though transformational development focuses more broadly on "four critical relationships: with self, community, others, and our environment" and Christian witness focuses more

---

[49] Bryant L. Myers, *Walking with the Poor: Principles and Practices of Transformational Development* (Maryknoll, NY: Orbis, 1999), 4.

[50] Ibid.

[51] Ibid., 3.

[52] Ibid., 47.

narrowly on our relationship with God, nonetheless, their goals are the same: "changed people and changed relationships."[53]

James F. Engel and William A. Dyrness in *Changing the Mind of Missions: Where Have We Gone Wrong?* (2000) assert that a distinction between evangelism and social transformation is "a specious dichotomy."[54] Instead, Jesus tells us his mission statement in Luke 4:18–19, declaring "a bold mandate to combine faith with action to overcome injustice and oppression," holistic responsibilities that define his agenda and "also must define ours," as Jesus makes clear that "the essence of the good news is liberation, justice and shalom."[55] As well, Christians are called to "incarnate the reality of God, even as Jesus himself did," therefore our mission must be "the extension of the mighty work that Christ embodied as he restored God's reign on earth," a mission which is "sensitive to the breadth of God's activities from creation to consummation."[56] All authority has been given to Jesus (Matt. 28:18), meaning that now "all lesser authority (political, cultural and economic) has been called to account in light of this new ruler, the King of Kings."[57]

Announcing the Kingdom: The Story of God's Mission in the Bible (2003) by Arthur F. Glasser describes an OT distinction between God's "universal kingdom" and his "special covenantal" rule over Israel. God administered his universal kingdom by "exercis[ing] a loving and providential care over his creation." God's special covenantal kingdom by contrast consisted of his redeemed people, though these two rulerships also had an "intimate correlation."[58] All humanity in the universal kingdom was given a "cultural mandate"

[53] Ibid., 212, 211.

[54] James F. Engel and William A. Dyrness, *Changing the Mind of Missions: Where Have We Gone Wrong?* (Downers Grove, IL: IVP, 2000), 63.

[55] Ibid., 23, 95.

[56] Ibid., 35, 37.

[57] Ibid., 32.

[58] Arthur F. Glasser, *Announcing the Kingdom: The Story of God's Mission in the Bible* (Grand Rapids: Baker Academic, 2003), 22.

regarding "family and community, law and order, culture and civilization, and ecological concern."[59] After the fall, this mandate was "clearly distinguished" from the redemptive mandate given in God's OT covenantal kingdom. But, according to Glasser, "When Jesus inaugurates the Kingdom of God, these two mandates will fuse into one fundamental task. The New Testament does not separate evangelism from social responsibility."[60] Since these two mandates have fused, the OT responsibility for the "stranger within the gates" no longer applies merely within the covenant community but now requires the mission of the church to "give priority to the needs of all minority and immigrant peoples."[61] As well, Christians should be those "dominated by a heightened concern for social justice and the poor."[62] Furthermore, the NT *diakonia* consists of ministry both internally within the covenant community and externally outside the covenant. The external *diakonia* includes evangelism, "ministry to those in special need," and working for "justice and concord among people and nations and within their separate cultures."[63]

Michael E. Wittmer, *Heaven Is a Place on Earth: Why Everything You Do Matters to God* (2004), claims that Christians are broadly responsible to be "agents of shalom," an OT word which he defines as "absence of conflict [in relationships and] . . . the deep satisfaction and security that arise from such open and mutually enriching relationships. . . . the sense of well-being and wholeness people feel when all is right with the world."[64] Christians "must seek to increase the net gain of shalom in the world," which includes everything from simple politeness and friendliness to being involved in "confront[ing] and solv[ing] the significant social issues of our

[59] Ibid., 38.
[60] Ibid., 39.
[61] Ibid., 87.
[62] Ibid., 118.
[63] Ibid., 309.
[64] Michael E. Wittmer, *Heaven Is a Place on Earth: Why Everything You Do Matters to God* (Grand Rapids: Zondervan, 2004), 116, 105.

day," including "larger, global opportunities to restore flourishing and delight to those in need."[65] Wittmer believes Christians today should apply the command given to the Jewish exiles in Babylon to "seek the peace and prosperity [shalom] of the city" (Jer. 29:7) by "remembering that all people have been endowed by their Creator with certain inalienable rights, such as the right to earn a living wage, dwell in safe neighborhoods, freely participate in society, and access clean drinking water and basic medical care. Wherever basic rights are denied, shalom is broken and God's image in the world is sullied."[66] By carrying out these responsibilities, Christians are "redeeming society" and "human culture," work which Wittmer describes as "joining the upward climb from the pristine garden of Genesis 2 to the organized city of Revelation 21."[67]

In *The Heavenly Good of Earthly Work* (2006), Darrell Cosden begins his argument by proposing that all human work, including our good works in society, has "eternal value and meaning . . . [because all human work] in some way actually adds to (though it does not cause, determine, or bring about) the ultimate shape of eternity—the new creation."[68] Stated another way, Cosden believes that not only the human person but also human work itself must be understood as "an object of God's final salvation," a created reality which is "open to the possibility of salvation" (31, 32). If this is *not* true, according to Cosden, then human work cannot be "*in itself* ultimately meaningful . . . [but only] spiritually meaningful to a limited degree" (31, original emphasis), with no "intrinsic value" (2) and no "solid theological basis for experiencing a 'spiritual' dimension in our work" (46) but instead only "spiritual frustration" without "the vision and motivation we need to live now according to God's kingdom values" (114). Cosden provides five points of biblical support

[65] Ibid., 113–15.

[66] Ibid., 116.

[67] Ibid., 189, 196, 199.

[68] Darrell Cosden, *The Heavenly Good of Earthly Work* (Peabody, MA: Hendrickson, 2006), 2.

for his claims. First, Jesus' post-resurrection and eternal body still contains the scars of his suffering, the effect of human work upon it (albeit evil work). This suggests that the result of human work carries over into eternity (59). Second, in Christ's future cosmic rule, he will bring "everything under his feet" (1 Cor. 15:27), which Cosden believes means a "transformation of all realities," including "purifying" human work and other so-called "secular realities" (65). Third, the incarnation requires such continuity between this age and the next since "through his incarnation, Jesus unites fully (and thus saves) that which is spirit and that which is matter—all things secular, or earthly, and all things religious, or heavenly" (67). Fourth, Cosden proposes that Romans 8:19–22 teaches that "non-human reality is also the object of God's final salvation and will be vindicated and thus *justified* in being ultimately valuable. . . . [creation has a] genuine right to salvation" (70, original emphasis). In like manner, all human work can be "justified" and "saved" eternally. Lastly, Revelation 21:24–26 reveals that the New Jerusalem will "include the best of human culture" (75). Embracing Cosden's claims requires a broadened understanding of the saving work of God's kingdom and our corresponding mission responsibilities. Our mission should not be understood as exclusively "Christian" with "the church, at the center" but instead as a calling possessed by "all people, whether Christian or not," allowing even non-Christians to "find a place in work within God's mission" (139).

The Mission of God: Unlocking the Bible's Grand Narrative (2006) and *The Mission of God's People: A Biblical Theology of the Church's Mission* (2010) by Christopher J. H. Wright both aim to connect the New Covenant community's understanding of its mission closely to the biblical picture of God's own mission, with the first book "lay[ing] the foundation" for the second.[69] Both books reject the language of "primacy" for evangelism in the church's mission since

---

[69] Christopher J. H. Wright, *The Mission of God's People: A Biblical Theology of the Church's Mission* (Grand Rapids: Zondervan, 2010), 17.

evangelism and social action "should never have been separated in the first place."[70] According to Wright, prioritizing evangelism over social action makes no more sense in practice than prioritizing breathing over drinking water.[71] Wright notes that the Bible begins with God's pronouncement of blessing on his creatures, and Christians are likewise to be instruments of blessing. Wright translates the end of Genesis 12:2 as a command to Abraham to "be a blessing," expressing a "limitless mission," as agents of God's redemption.[72] God's redemption is comprehensive, addressing political, economic, social, and spiritual realities, as demonstrated in Israel's exodus from Egypt, "God's model redemption."[73] Therefore, God's "exodus-shaped redemption demands exodus-shaped mission" from his people today.[74] Since there is an "organic continuity between Old and New Testament" and since Old Covenant Israel has "paradigmatic significance" for the New Covenant community, the mission of the church must also holistically address political, economic, social, and spiritual realities.[75] In like manner, Wright presents OT Israel's jubilee institution described in Leviticus 25 as a paradigm and model for "restoration"—a jubilee-shaped restoration which likewise extends the mission of the church beyond the spiritual into the economic, social, and political spheres.[76] As well, since God's holistic redemption includes the whole created world, Christian mission is "not truly holistic if it includes only human beings" but must also include creation care as Christians doing "ecological projects are engaged in

[70] Ibid., 276.

[71] Ibid., 277. Though Wright's underlying point is that you cannot determine a priority between two actions which are determined to be equally necessary, the limitation of Wright's analogy is revealed by the fact that, at least in the short-term, one *must* prioritize breathing over drinking water.

[72] Christopher J. H. Wright, *The Mission of God: Unlocking the Bible's Grand Narrative* (Downers Grove, IL: IVP Academic, 2006), 207, 212.

[73] Ibid., 268–71, 273.

[74] Ibid., 275.

[75] Ibid., 279, 281.

[76] Ibid., 289–98.

a specialized form of mission that has its rightful place within the broad framework of all that God's mission has as its goal."[77] Wright offers Hosea 4:1–3, which describes God's curses upon the covenant land because of OT Israel's unfaithfulness, as "the most direct [biblical] example" of the "strong moral link between how humans behave on earth and the state of the earth itself—for good or ill."[78]

On the basis of Jesus' command to his disciples in Luke 10:1–9 to both preach and heal, Charles Fielding, *Preach and Heal: A Biblical Model for Missions* (2008), argues that preaching and healing ought to be the New Covenant community's model for missions today. In Jesus' own earthly ministry, he "was able to maintain a perfect balance between preaching and healing."[79] As well, Fielding believes this model is "to be learned and practiced by every disciple and taught to everyone who is not already utilizing it," since even after Christ's ascension, this model "became the standard practice of the disciples "[80] On this basis, Fielding embraces an equal priority position, likening it to "a two-handled plow," requiring that "both handles must be held with equal pressure and commitment . . . [for] if priority is given to one handle or the other, the furrow will go off at an angle and spoil the field."[81] Recognizing that Jesus' and the early church's healing ministries were strictly miraculous rather than medical, Fielding encourages his readers to consider the ongoing validity of a miraculous healing mission model.[82] But whether or not his readers embrace a miraculous healing ministry, Fielding believes that medical mission strategies are also a legitimate "variation of the Luke 10 strategy" and thereby fulfill the demand to both preach and heal.[83]

---

[77] Ibid., 416.

[78] Wright, *The Mission of God's People*, 55.

[79] Charles Fielding, *Preach and Heal: A Biblical Model for Missions* (Richmond, VA: International Mission Board, 2008), 15.

[80] Ibid., 102, 20.

[81] Ibid., 31.

[82] Ibid., 103–4.

[83] Ibid., 127.

The Cape Town Commitment (2010) promotes equal priority "framed in the language of love," which is "the language of covenant," a covenant love which embodies the "whole gospel" as "God's glorious good news in Christ, for every dimension of his creation."[84] Since "The mission of God's people flows from our love for God and for all that God loves" and since "God's love extends over all his creation," therefore the church is "commanded to love in ways that reflect the love of God in all those same dimensions."[85] Love compels God's people to address "individual persons . . . society and creation. All three are broken and suffering because of sin; all three are included in the redeeming love and mission of God; all three must be part of the comprehensive mission of God's people."[86] As an expression of "our commitment to seeking justice and *shalom* for the oppressed and poor," the New Covenant community should "fight the evil of human trafficking," embrace the United Nations Millennium Development Goals, and challenge "excessive wealth and greed."[87] Likewise, we should address "the threat of climate change . . . [with] urgency" by pressing developed nations toward "rapidly reducing their own carbon emissions and to share their wealth and skills with developing countries to enable them to adapt to climate change and build sustainable economies."[88]

[84] Rose Dowsett, *The Capetown Commitment: A Confession of Faith and a Call to Action—Study Edition* (Peabody, MA: Hendrickson, 2012), 3.

[85] Ibid., 6.

[86] Ibid., 29.

[87] Ibid., 74–75.

[88] Ibid., 82.

3

Review of Evangelistic Priority Literature Since 1974

The Lausanne Covenant (1974), as noted in chapter one, affirms that "evangelism and socio-political involvement are both part of our Christian duty."[1] Yet, while recognizing both responsibilities as part of "the church's mission of sacrificial service" out to the world, the document also clearly states that "evangelism is primary" and socio-political involvement is secondary—though the covenant provides no further clarification of the relationship between the two tasks (28). The covenant defines "gospel" according to 1 Corinthians 15:3–4 and Acts 2:32–39 as a message revealed by Scripture concerning Jesus' death for our sins, resurrection, present reign as universal Lord, offer of forgiveness, reconciliation with God, and the gift of the Spirit, a message which each person must respond to personally with repentance and faith (20). "Evangelism" then only refers to the proclamation of this message, seeking to persuade hearers to repent and believe, not also referring to social action (20, 24). These two tasks must be distinguished, even though they are not "mutually exclusive" (24). According to the document, while the salvation offered through trusting in Christ "should be

[1] International Congress on World Evangelization, "The Lausanne Covenant," in *Making Christ Known: Historic Mission Documents from the Lausanne Movement, 1974–1989*, ed. John R. W. Stott (Grand Rapids: Eerdmans, 1997), 24.

transforming us in the totality of our personal and social responsibilities," salvation is not itself an offer of "political liberation" in this life (28). The church, understood as "the community of God's people" (which results from evangelism) "rather than [as] an institution" (20), must nonetheless be faithful in "responsible service in the world" because God is concerned about matters of justice and oppression in broader society, because all humanity has "intrinsic dignity" as those made in the image of God, and because Jesus commands love of neighbor (24).

Byang H. Kato in *Theological Pitfalls in Africa* (1975) briefly offers reasons why evangelism must retain priority in the church's task. First, Kato, in agreement with the Lausanne Covenant, understands "gospel" in the Bible as referring to the salvation of individuals, while the possible transformation of society in this age is not itself part of the "gospel" but only a secondary result of transformed individuals influencing society. According to Kato, defining "gospel" to include the transformation of a present society makes it "no longer the gospel of Jesus Christ."[2] While Christ came to serve, his primary service was "the atonement made possible on the cross (Mark 10:45)."[3] The responsibility of believers to minister to the needs of the hungry, thirsty, homeless, unclothed, sick, and imprisoned (Matt. 25:31–46), a responsibility crucial for determining who are true and who are false believers, is a clear responsibility toward "these brothers of [Christ]" (25:40), not toward all humanity.[4] As well, though Christ "cured the sick and fed the hungry" in conjunction with his preaching, he also asked, "For what does it profit a man to gain the whole world, and forfeit his soul?" (Mark 8:36), giving ultimate priority to people's eternal needs, not their temporal needs.[5] Therefore, for Kato, the church's mandate is to "show

---

[2] Byang H. Kato, *Theological Pitfalls in Africa* (Kisumu, Kenya: Evangel, 1975), 142.

[3] Ibid., 153.

[4] Ibid., 154.

[5] Ibid., 179.

concern in social action but bear in mind at all times that the primary goal of the church is the presentation of personal salvation."[6]

Christian Mission in the Modern World (1975) is John Stott's elaboration of the argument of his opening address at the Lausanne Congress.[7] Stott affirms the evangelistic priority position of the Lausanne Covenant (largely crafted by Stott himself) while further clarifying some of the key theological distinctions contained within the covenant. According to Stott, not to distinguish social action and evangelism is to "mix what Scripture keeps distinct—God the Creator and God the Redeemer, the God of the cosmos and the God of the covenant, the world and the church, common grace and saving grace, justice and justification, the reformation of society and the regeneration of men" (142). By maintaining these distinctions, evangelism and social action, as legitimate expressions of Christian love, can then each potentially stand alone as "an end in itself" (43). As well, though each Christian has both a verbal proclamation and a good deeds responsibility, the particular mixture of these two responsibilities within an individual's life will depend upon his or her unique gifting and vocation (49–51). An additional distinction of terms that Stott makes is that "the biblical categories of *shalom*, the new humanity and the kingdom of God are not to be identified with social renewal" in broader society during this age but only with God's New Covenant people (30–31). According to Stott, Christians should do good deeds not to establish the kingdom of God in society but to express love of neighbor (Matt. 22:39) and to serve by being "the salt of the earth" and "the light of the world" (Matt. 5:13–16) (46–48). Stott also supports a Christian responsibility to love non-Christians by reference to some texts which only explicitly refer to the responsibility of Christians to love one another (1 John 3:17–18; Acts 6:1–3) (44–45). While we are to love our neighbors

---

[6] Ibid., 183.

[7] John R. W. Stott, *Christian Mission in the Modern World* (Downers Grove, IL: IVP, 2008), 16.

by caring for their physical needs, in Stott's interpretation, Jesus' "works of physical rescue (from disease, drowning and death) were intentional signs of his salvation" (131) from sin rather than an establishment of a ministry model for Christians which prioritizes "psychophysical health" in this life (126). Likewise, Jesus' use of Isaiah 61:1–2 in Luke 4:18–19 to describe his ministry is, according to Stott, primarily a reference to the alleviation of spiritual rather than physical poverty, captivity, and blindness in this life and is "hardly [to] be taken as an instruction to us to perform similar miraculous cures today" or to empty prisons (147). In Stott's response to Ronald J. Sider in *Evangelism, Salvation and Social Justice* (1977), Stott also rejects the claim that Christ's victory over "principalities and powers" in Paul is a victory over "structures of thought, tradition and society" in this age, thereby providing some biblical warrant for transformation of social structures as part of the mission of the New Covenant community. Rather, "principalities and powers" refers strictly to personal agents (angels and demons) rather than impersonal structures.[8]

Christian Missions in Biblical Perspective (1976) by J. Herbert Kane attempts a thorough re-examination of the Scriptures to "see what they have to say concerning the *unchanging* aspects of the Christian mission."[9] Though Kane gives only a brief treatment of the OT or the topic of covenant, he does note issues of discontinuity and distinction when examining the question of mission responsibilities throughout the biblical storyline. In considering OT Israel's mission responsibilities, Kane separately considers Israel's mission before the captivity and during exile (26–33). He also identifies the radical impact of the incarnation, the cross, the resurrection, and Pentecost on the mission of God's people, recognizing important discontinuities (such as Jesus' earthly ministry being almost exclusively to

---

[8] John R. W. Stott, "The Response," in *Evangelism, Salvation and Social Justice* (Nottingham, UK: Grove Books, 1977), 24.

[9] J. Herbert Kane, *Christian Missions in Biblical Perspective* (Grand Rapids: Baker, 1976), 10. Original emphasis.

God's covenant people in contrast to the disciple's post-Pentecost ministry to both Jews and Gentiles) even while recognizing continuities between these historical eras (34, 41–42, 227). One important area of continuity which Kane recognizes across Scripture is the responsibility of God's covenant people to address the whole person, displaying the "indiscriminate love of God" toward all people (44–45, 123). Even as Jesus himself "went about doing good" (Acts 10:38), so are believers to do good to all people (Gal. 6:10) (191). But Kane qualifies this recognition of continuity by noting that Jesus' (and the apostles') miraculous and compassionate alleviation of human suffering was also intended to "authenticate" both Jesus' messianic claims and the apostles' message as well as to demonstrate supernatural power which would "inculcate faith in the individual" and "induce . . . repentance" (302–3). In contrast, non-miraculous healing through medical missions today rightly alleviates human suffering but lacks the demonstration of power which characterized Jesus' and the apostles' ministries (312–13). Therefore, while Kane believes that non-miraculous medical missions are a good deed which Christians should embrace, where governments are able to provide those services, the missionary "should rejoice that he is now being set free for the spiritual work that *only he can perform*" (153, original emphasis), since the church is "the one institution to which Jesus Christ delegated the responsibility for the evangelization of the world" (265). Therefore, while affirming the importance and necessity of Christian good deeds of love, Kane identifies "the church's chief task [as] to preach the gospel, to beseech men to be reconciled to God" (210).

In *Church Growth and the Whole Gospel: A Biblical Mandate* (1981), C. Peter Wagner agrees with Arthur Glasser in speaking of the mission of the church in terms of two mandates: the cultural mandate and the evangelistic mandate.[10] Unlike Glasser,

---

[10] C. Peter Wagner, *Church Growth and the Whole Gospel: A Biblical Mandate* (New York: Harper & Row, 1981), 91.

Wagner believes these two mandates remain distinct rather than becoming fused into one mandate at Christ's first coming. For Wagner, to "confuse the cultural mandate with the evangelistic mandate" tends toward the designation of cultural mandate work *as* evangelism (55). As well, though both mandates are obligatory for Christians, Wagner gives priority to the evangelistic over the cultural since "the Scriptures have a bias toward the evangelistic mandate" (115). This biblical emphasis on evangelism over culture work requires maintaining a distinction between the two mandates since such a distinction is "indispensable to recognizing the priority of the evangelistic mandate" (97). According to Wagner, evangelistic priority is not only a reflection of the Bible's own emphasis but also an appropriate expression of the Bible's prioritizing of eternal consequences over temporal consequences. On a related question, Wagner does not believe that our cultural work itself will last into eternity (100). Even though upholding the priority of evangelism, Wagner acknowledges that at times "the cultural mandate may take priority" in the church's work in places which Wagner labels as "social disaster area[s]," situations which require the church to prioritize meeting immediate human need. Wagner sees the Good Samaritan parable as exemplifying just such a circumstance (111). Wagner understands the cultural mandate as a command rooted in Genesis 1–2 and as including human responsibilities such as the "distribution of wealth, the balance of nature, marriage and the family, human government, keeping the peace, cultural integrity, liberation of the oppressed," requiring individual Christians "to live lives that will promote *shalom* to the greatest extent possible" and obligating "every church [to] contribute in some way to the effective fulfillment of the cultural mandate" (13). Wagner also divides cultural mandate responsibilities into two categories: "social service" and "social action" (35). By social service, Wagner refers to two tasks often termed "relief and development." By social action, Wagner refers to "social justice" or work "geared toward changing social structures. . . . [which]

involves socio-political changes" (36). While Wagner believes social action is a theologically legitimate (and even required) extension of the cultural mandate, he does not see clear biblical evidence that such work in the world is "specifically and explicitly mandated by Jesus for his disciples" (37). So, even in the church's cultural mandate work, social service should be prioritized over social action. As well, only the church's work should be seen as "kingdom work" since, "no other agency in the world . . . has been designated by God as the interpreter of the kingdom to this present generation" (9–10). Wagner identifies the presence of God's kingdom "only where Jesus is openly and consciously declared to be Lord." Even though, "In a cosmic sense Christ reigns over all creation . . . this reign is not actualized until persons have submitted to it in faith, trust, and obedience. . . . Personal submission to the king, Jesus Christ, is the chief characteristic of the kingdom" (5). But while Wagner classifies only the church as a legitimate instrument of "kingdom work," he also recognizes the church in both its congregational structure (local church—Ralph Winter's "modality") and its mission structure (parachurch—Ralph Winter's "sodality") as valid avenues for church work (186–87). Concerning cultural mandate work, Wagner advises that the less clearly the Bible assigns a particular cultural task to the local church and the more a task moves from the realm of social service to the realm of social action, the more likely that the task is best carried out by a mission structure rather than a congregational structure (191–93). Finally, Wagner agrees with Stott that Luke 4:18–19 and Luke 10:1–9 do not provide direct textual warrant for a church mission of ameliorating poverty, freeing slaves, providing healthcare, or pursuing socio-political liberation (17–19). Unlike Stott, Wagner believes that the supernatural signs of the kingdom described in those texts can (and perhaps ought to) provide a model for Christian mission today, miraculous signs which will "draw public attention to the power of God in order to open unsaved people's hearts to the message of the gospel" (17).

The papers and final report of the *Consultation on the*

Relationship between Evangelism and Social Responsibility (1982), co-sponsored in Grand Rapids by the Lausanne Committee for World Evangelism and the World Evangelical Fellowship, together promote a nuanced position of evangelistic priority, though some papers presented at the consultation also advocate the equal priority position, with the final report maintaining a carefully constructed view of evangelistic priority. The consultation was both a recognition that the precise relationship between the duties of evangelism and social responsibility had not been clarified in *The Lausanne Covenant* and an attempt to offer further definition to this relationship.[11] After affirming the necessary interrelationship between the two tasks (along with necessary distinction), the final report nevertheless affirms that each task is intrinsically legitimate and can "exist in independence of the other." To illustrate, neither can the Good Samaritan be "blamed for tending the wounds of the brigands' victim and failing to preach to him," nor can Philip be "blamed for preaching the Gospel to the Ethiopian eunuch in his chariot and failing to enquire into his social needs" (180). As well, the priority of evangelism over good deeds is not an "invariable temporal priority" but instead both a "logical" priority (since the existence of "Christian social responsibility presupposes socially responsible Christians") and a durational priority (since "a person's eternal, spiritual salvation is of greater importance than his or her temporal or material well-being)" (183). Additionally, in societies with limited political freedom, any Christian responsibility for socio-political involvement or public preaching will be correspondingly lessened (200–209). But particularly in freer societies, the final report goes on to claim that in practice, "Seldom if ever should we have to choose between satisfying physical hunger and spiritual

---

[11] International Consultation on the Relationship between Evangelism and Social Responsibility, "The Grand Rapids Report on Evangelism and Social Responsibility: An Evangelical Commitment," in *Making Christ Known: Historic Mission Documents from the Lausanne Movement, 1974–1989*, ed. John R. W. Stott (Grand Rapids: Eerdmans, 1997), 171.

hunger, or between healing bodies and saving souls" (183). Though the report affirms a measure of continuity between human bodies in this age and the next, best illustrated by Jesus' own resurrected body, the report is hesitant to embrace the claim that the Bible teaches that "our present works will be carried over into eternity," thus providing motivation for good deeds (194–95). But this additional motivation for good deeds is not necessary since "the Gospel demands both to be preached and to be lived. Once we have come to know it, we are obliged to share it with others and to 'adorn' it by good deeds (Titus 2:10)" (185). According to the final report, the distinction of priority between evangelism and other good deeds is also rooted in a necessary recognition that Christ rules believers in this age (as confessed Lord) differently than he rules non-believers (as cosmic Lord). The report labels this distinction using the legal terms "de facto" (in practice) and "de jure" (formally and technically, even if not in practice): "over his redeemed people Jesus is King *de facto*, while it is only *de jure* that he is presently King over the world, his right being still challenged by the usurper." Because of this important distinction and in order to "maintain the tension between what Christ rules *de facto* and *de jure*," the report suggests that it is best to "reserve the expression 'the kingdom of God' for the acknowledged rule of Christ" and to use "the sovereignty of God" to describe Christ's present cosmic rule over all things (188–89). In support of this, "How Broad is Salvation in Scripture?," a paper presented at the consultation by Ronald J. Sider and James Parker III, notes that "absolutely none of the scores of New Testament texts on the Kingdom of God speak of the presence of the Kingdom apart from conscious confession of Jesus Christ. . . . [and therefore there is] no warrant in the New Testament for talking about the coming of the Kingdom of God via societal change apart from confession of Christ."[12] According to the final report, the church alone then is

[12] Ronald J. Sider and James Parker III, "How Broad Is Salvation in Scripture?" in *In Word and Deed: Evangelism and Social Responsibility*, ed. Bruce J.

"the kingdom community . . . [whose] values and ideals, its moral standards and relationships, its sacrificial lifestyle, its love, joy and peace" are "signs of the kingdom" which "present the world with a radically alternative society" and whose values may at times "spill over into society as a whole, so that [the society's] industry, commerce, legislation and institutions become to some degree imbued with kingdom values." In spite of that influence, such a society is "not the kingdom of God," though it does "owe a debt to the kingdom which is often unrecognized."[13] As cosmic Lord, Christ is "directly at work in his world, apart from the agency of his people," providing "common grace" to his whole creation, including mankind's imperfect "appreciation of justice, freedom, beauty, dignity, and peace"—but such work is "not what Jesus meant by his kingdom."[14] Not only does the final report advocate a narrower, more restricted use of the language of the "kingdom of God," the report also states that most consultation participants believe that it is "more prudent and biblical to reserve the vocabulary of salvation for the experience of reconciliation with God through Christ and its direct consequences," rather than using it also "to refer to the emergence of justice and peace in the wider community."[15] The paper by Sider and Parker also significantly undergirds this definition for "salvation" as adopted by the final report. Sider and Parker argue that salvation in the OT is "clearly social and corporate and includes every aspect of life" but that the OT also "does not speak of God's salvation as present apart from his covenant with his chosen people where he is consciously confessed as Lord."[16] Likewise in the Gospels, even though "the 'salvation' word-group" is also "used to describe physical healing where Christ brings persons to physical wholeness and well-being," such healing is "always in a specifically Christological

---

Nicholls (Grand Rapids: Eerdmans, 1986), 104.

[13] International Consultation, "The Grand Rapid Report," 189.

[14] Ibid., 190.

[15] Ibid., 185–86.

[16] Sider and Parker, "How Broad Is Salvation in Scripture?" 92.

context," meaning that following the biblical pattern requires only using "salvation" in "a specifically and distinctively Christological/ Christocentric context" (98). Furthermore, in Romans 8:19–24, though "both persons and the whole created order groan in anticipation of the final redemption of all things," according to Paul, only Christians and *not* the created order "already have the 'first fruits' of the Spirit" (v. 23) and already "have been saved in the hope of the final eschaton" (v. 24), meaning that these verses provide "no support at all for using salvation language today to refer to environmental or socio-economic improvements in secular society." In Sider and Parker's view, the only possible NT support for a broader use of salvation language is Colossians 1:20 where "reconciliation"—"one of the important terms in Paul's salvation word group"—is used in the past tense in reference to all creation (102). But, "the overwhelming volume of biblical usage points towards the narrower usage of salvation language" (105). Interestingly, Sider acknowledges that he has changed his view on the usage of salvation language in the five years since the publication of *Evangelism, Salvation and Social Justice* (1977), co-authored with John Stott (107).

The essays collected in *Mission in the New Testament: An Evangelical Approach* (1998), edited by William J. Larkin Jr. and Joel F. Williams, are intended to fill a perceived void in evangelical NT scholarship concerning the study of missions since "all comprehensive work by evangelicals in this area has come from missiologists" rather than NT scholars.[17] They also aim to establish "the priority of proclamation" in the New Covenant community's mission, even while fully embracing a secondary responsibility to "care for the poor and serve a broken world."[18] John D. Harvey, in "Mission in Jesus'

---

[17] William J. Larkin Jr., "Introduction," in *Mission in the New Testament: An Evangelical Approach*, eds. William J. Larkin Jr. and Joel F. Williams (Maryknoll, NY: Orbis, 1998), 2.

[18] Joel F. Williams, "Conclusion," in *Mission in the New Testament: An Evangelical Approach*, eds. William J. Larkin Jr. and Joel F. Williams (Maryknoll, NY: Orbis, 1998), 244.

Teaching," observes that "prior to the resurrection, the disciples' mission was identical to and an extension of Jesus' mission," while after the resurrection, there was "a significant change both to Jesus' role in mission and to the disciples' actual mission."[19] Jesus' ministry involved both preaching and healing, but Jesus himself "declared that his primary activity would be preaching" when he stated that "I must preach (*euangelisasthai*) the kingdom of God to the other cities also, for I was sent (*apestalen*) for this purpose" (Luke 4:43), Luke further emphasizing that Jesus "kept on preaching (*en kerusson*) in the synagogues of Judea" (Luke 4:44). As well, Jesus "limited his mission to the Jewish people" (37). Pre-resurrection, the task of the disciples was "identical to that of Jesus," as they were "given the same authority . . . carried out the same activities . . . preached the same message . . . target[ed the same] group . . . [and experienced the same] results" (43). But Christ's resurrection "marked a turning point in Jesus' teaching on mission. His own mission was completed, and his role changed from sent one to sender" (44). For the disciples as well, the scope of their mission is now universal rather than strictly Jewish, and, whereas in Jesus' previous commission they were authorized "both to preach and heal," in the post-resurrection commission, "the emphasis falls heavily on the preaching/teaching dimension of their task," with miracles being simply "signs that accompany them as they proclaim the good news" (45, 47). Likewise, the message proclaimed changes from "the kingdom of God is at hand" to the message of Christ's death, resurrection, and the corresponding call to "repentance for forgiveness of sins" (47). This discontinuity between the pre-resurrection ministry of Jesus/his disciples and the post-resurrection ministry of the disciples therefore calls into question the legitimacy of arguing for equal priority simply on the basis of the model of Jesus' pre-resurrection ministry of

---

[19] John D. Harvey, "Mission in Jesus' Teaching," in *Mission in the New Testament: An Evangelical Approach*, eds. William J. Larkin Jr. and Joel F. Williams (Maryknoll, NY: Orbis, 1998), 31.

preaching and healing. In "Mission in Acts," William J. Larkin Jr. offers additional support for Harvey's argument by observing concerning the disciples post-resurrection ministry that "spiritual salvation . . . is Luke's consistent focus throughout Acts . . . [while] the preaching of Acts lacks an equal focus on salvation as liberation in socio-economic circumstances."[20]

Andreas J. Köstenberger in *The Mission of Jesus and the Disciples according to the Fourth Gospel: With Implications for the Fourth Gospel's Purpose and the Mission of the Contemporary Church* (1998) likewise highlights the discontinuity between the ministry of Jesus and the ministry of the church, as demonstrated in the Gospel of John. Köstenberger traces John's portrayal of Jesus' "ontological uniqueness . . . [a] fundamental dissimilarity in person, role, and function" between Jesus and his disciples.[21] One way John expresses this dissimilarity is by presenting Jesus' miraculous "signs" ("public works . . . with symbolic significance designed to lead others to faith in Jesus as the true representative of God") as "uniquely Jesus'," the disciples not participating in "the 'signs' portion of Jesus' mission" (73). According to Köstenberger, this "crucial element of dissimilarity" also demonstrates that John "appears to conceive of 'signs' as confined to the historical point in time prior to Jesus' glorification." One reason for this is that in John the "signs" are "significantly linked . . . to the expectations related to [Jesus'] Messianic identity," making it inappropriate to assign the working of Messianic "signs" to the disciples, who are instead assigned the "more humble task . . . of witnessing to Jesus" (170). Additionally, the disciples' task in John is also characterized as "sent to harvest (4:38) . . . appointed to go and bear fruit (15:16) . . . testify

---

[20] William J. Larkin Jr., "Mission in Acts," in *Mission in the New Testament: An Evangelical Approach*, eds. William J. Larkin Jr. and Joel F. Williams (Maryknoll, NY: Orbis, 1998), 179.

[21] Andreas J. Köstenberger, *The Mission of Jesus and the Disciples according to the Fourth Gospel: With Implications for the Fourth Gospel's Purpose and the Mission of the Contemporary Church* (Grand Rapids: Eerdmans, 1998), 74.

(15:27) . . . forgive others their sins (20:23)" (169). In summary, "both the revelatory and redemptive aspects of Jesus' work . . . are tied to the unique personal characteristics of Jesus to such an extent that the disciples can be said to participate in these only in a secondary sense" (81). Because of this, Köstenberger argues that even the disciples' "greater works" which Jesus describes in John 14:12 are "not simply more works, nor are they merely more spectacular or more supernatural works or 'miracles,'" but they are greater because of "their eschatological dimension." Such later works are not possible until Jesus has died, rose, and ascended and therefore are "constrained by salvation-historical realities" (172). Only when "the age of the Spirit" has arrived will "the disciples help gather the eschatological harvest and thus perform 'greater works' even than Jesus," works that are greater "because they will take place in a different, more advanced phase of God's economy of salvation" and will be accomplished by "the exalted Christ through believers" (173, 175). An additional observation that Köstenberger makes in favor of the evangelistic priority position is that in John, "A focus on human service and on human need . . . is not presented . . . as the primary purpose of either Jesus' or the disciples' mission" (215). Furthermore, while the equal priority position is also often argued for on the basis of the model of Christ's incarnation, Köstenberger believes that incarnational language should be reserved for Jesus uniquely. Rather than imitating Jesus in his incarnational mission, the disciples are to imitate "the nature of Jesus' relationship with his sender" (the Father) by displaying "obedience and utter dependence" toward their sender (the Son) (217).

In another work that illustrates the development of Ron Sider's position in the evangelistic/equal priority debate, *Good News and Good Works: A Theology for the Whole Gospel* (1999), though still clearly advocating "both personal and social sin, both personal conversion and structural change, both evangelism and social action, both personal and social salvation [within the church], both Jesus as moral example and Jesus as vicarious substitute, both orthodox theology and ethical obedience," nonetheless also affirms key arguments for evangelistic priority.[22] Sider continues to uphold a clear distinction between evangelism and social action since it is "confusing and misleading to call [social action] evangelism" as only individual persons can repent and be saved (159). Sider also agrees with *The Grand Rapids Report* that evangelism has a logical priority since Christian social responsibility first requires the existence of Christians (166). As well, Sider affirms that eternal life has priority over our temporal circumstances, calling this aspect "ontological" priority (166–67). Furthermore, "if we had unlimited resources," Sider would prefer for the church to use its "time, money, and personnel" equally between evangelism and social action (168). But since "our resources, alas, are very limited," Sider acknowledges the legitimacy of a position prioritizing resources for evangelism in the church's work out to the world, even though he himself aims toward "devoting approximately equal amounts to both evangelism and social action" (168–70). Additionally, Sider continues to maintain the importance of the distinction between God's work of creation and God's work of redemption for understanding correctly the relationship between social action and evangelism. He rejects the idea that upholding this proper dualism between creation and redemption "necessarily leads to other misconceived and damaging dualisms . . . [such as] a platonic body-soul dualism . . . [or] a spiritual-secular dualism" (203). Sider also now rejects the possibility that Paul's use of salvation language in Colossians 1:20 refers to cosmic reconciliation as *already* having taken place since the "aorist tense . . . does not tell us *when* [all things] are actually reconciled. It rather tells us that God's decisive action that makes that reconciliation possible has already occurred" (206). Finally, at a personal level, Sider understands his own "special call" from God to be "in the area of biblically shaped social action;" however, in reflecting on thirty years of ministry, he wishes he had

---

[22] Ronald J. Sider, *Good News and Good Works: A Theology for the Whole Gospel* (Grand Rapids: Baker, 1999), 10.

done "more personal evangelism" and plans a greater emphasis on evangelism in his future ministry (121).

Andreas J. Köstenberger and Peter T. O'Brien, in *Salvation to the Ends of the Earth: A Biblical Theology of Mission* (2001), though never directly addressing the question of evangelistic versus equal priority, do provide exegetical arguments that lend support to the evangelistic priority position. For example, Köstenberger and O'Brien argue that Jesus' fundamental mission in Luke 4:18–19 is to "preach good news" rather than social action, with "the poor" referring to "the eschatological community, the suffering exiles or faithful in Israel, who have been spiritually oppressed" rather than "the poor," broadly defined, and with "release" referring to "first and foremost, the forgiveness of sins," as it does "throughout the rest of Luke-Acts," rather than socio-political liberation.[23] As well, in general, Köstenberger and O'Brien argue for a greater level of discontinuity between the earthly ministry of Jesus and the ministry of the New Covenant community. While Köstenberger and O'Brien emphasize the crucial need for each local church to vibrantly display New Covenant holiness out to the world, "adorn[ing] their verbal message with the witness of a godly life and proper relationships," for the most part, their biblical theology of mission appears to find scant textual warrant for a church focus on social action in its ministry out to the world.[24]

Early Christian Mission (2004–2 volumes) by Eckhard J. Schnabel, like Köstenberger and O'Brien's work, only addresses the relationship between evangelism and social action in passing. For instance, Schnabel does not see God's cosmic redemption described in Colossians 1:18–20 as directly "linked with the missionary activity of the disciples," making it inappropriate to "describe the missionary work of the church as fulfillment of the divine commission

---

[23] Andreas J. Köstenberger and Peter T. O'Brien, *Salvation to the Ends of the Earth: A Biblical Theology of Mission* (Downers Grove, IL: IVP, 2001), 116, 117, 158, 157.

[24] Ibid., 227.

given to Adam and to Israel to subjugate the earth as God's viceroy" since the church "subdues neither people nor the world but rather serves people and the world unselfishly and sacrificially."[25] Rather than an expanded understanding of the kingdom of God as partially manifest in broader human society today, "the reality of the kingdom of God, as the reality of the new creation, increasingly and visibly takes shape in the communities of believers and in individual Christians."[26] In describing the Apostle Paul's ministry, Schnabel notes "the primacy of the proclamation of the word" as "the central action of missionary work."[27] Paired with the primacy of proclamation, Schnabel also stresses that for the church to "be effective in mission and evangelism" requires that "God's love is realized in their midst, and . . . in the life of every believer," including "the love of one's enemies."[28] While Paul seeks to "establish churches and lead believers to spiritual maturity and moral integrity," the term "evangelism" implies "primarily the active oral proclamation of the gospel."[29] Schnabel's close examination of the church's mission in the NT, even more comprehensively than Köstenberger and O'Brien's volume, displays little indication of social action as an equal priority among the church's responsibilities.

Timothy Keller, *Generous Justice: How God's Grace Makes Us Just* (2010), like Ron Sider, evidences the development of his position in comparison to his earlier-published works, such as *Ministries of Mercy: The Call of the Jericho Road* (1989). Whereas in 1989, Keller rejected any prioritization of evangelism over social justice in the church's mission, in 2010 he proposes that, although these two elements of mission are "inseparable," the relationship between them

---

[25] Eckhard J. Schnabel, *Jesus and the Twelve*, vol. 1 of *Early Christian Mission* (Downers Grove, IL: IVP, 2004), 535, 536.

[26] Ibid., 536.

[27] Eckhard J. Schnabel, *Paul and the Early Church*, vol. 2 of *Early Christian Mission* (Downers Grove, IL: IVP, 2004), 972, 977.

[28] Ibid., 1475.

[29] Ibid., 1549.

is nonetheless "asymmetrical" because of the fact that "evangelism is the most basic and radical ministry possible to a human being," since "the eternal is more important than the temporal."[30] These two tasks must be kept distinct in order to maintain the priority of evangelism, which is "the single most unique service that Christians can offer the world."[31] As one expression of his concern for evangelistic priority in the institutional church's mission, Keller thinks it wiser for believers working for social justice to do this work "through associations and organizations rather than through the local church," since churches which "try to take on all the levels of doing justice often find that the work of community renewal and social justice overwhelms the work of preaching, teaching, and nurturing the congregation."[32] A textual reason that undergirds Keller's concern for maintaining evangelistic priority is his hesitancy to apply "the social legislation of Old Testament Israel . . . to our society at large . . . [because] the laws of social justice in Israel were principles for relationships primarily between believers" living within a theocracy, which is "not the situation of our society today," even if Israel's civil laws have "some abiding validity" in an "inferential" way.[33] Another example of Keller's concern for establishing sufficient textual warrant in determining mission responsibilities is his recognition that "most examples of generosity in the New Testament are of care for the poor within the church, such as the support for widows (Acts 6:1–7; 1 Timothy 5:3–16)."[34] While Keller observes the unmistakable NT requirement for believers to care for one another in need, he distinguishes between the greater weight of this responsibility and the lesser weight given in the NT to the responsibility to care for the needs of those outside the New Covenant community.

---

[30] Timothy Keller, *Generous Justice: How God's Grace Makes Us Just* (New York: Dutton, 2010), 139.

[31] Ibid., 141.

[32] Ibid., 146.

[33] Ibid., 23, 24, 31.

[34] Ibid., 60.

In *Living in God's Two Kingdoms: A Biblical Vision for Christianity and Culture* (2010), David VanDrunen, like Keller, distinguishes between the mission of "the church as a community or institution" and "the work and life of individual believers (or groups of believers) as they make their way in this world."[35] According to VanDrunen, the institutional church is limited in its "ministerial authority" to "only one simple but profound responsibility: ministering the Word of God" (152). Individual Christians "should be active in human culture . . . accountable to God in every activity . . . seek[ing] to live out the implications of their faith in their daily vocation" (14–15). But such Christian good deeds within the broader culture are not part of the mission of the institutional church. VanDrunen advocates a "two kingdoms" view in which Christ now rules over all things by two separate administrative structures or kingdoms. The membership of the "common kingdom" includes all people, including Christians. The membership of the "redemptive kingdom" includes only Christians. Therefore Christians live in two kingdoms simultaneously, one kingdom (the common kingdom) rooted in creation and expressing God's providential, common grace bestowed on both Christians and non-Christians alike, the other kingdom (the redemptive kingdom) rooted in salvation and clarifying the radical spiritual anti-thesis between believers and unbelievers. VanDrunen argues that each kingdom is administered by God through a covenant, the Noahic covenant administering the common kingdom, the special grace covenants (Abrahamic, Mosaic, Davidic, and New) administering the redemptive kingdom (29). Concerning the applicability of Genesis 1–2 to the mission of the church today, VanDrunen states that Christians are not called to take up Adam's task but that Christ alone fulfilled Adam's task and is "the last Adam," with the mandate of the Noahic covenant not being equivalent to Adam's Genesis 1–2 task (50). Concerning the applicability of OT Israel's social ethics to

---

[35] David VanDrunen, *Living in God's Two Kingdoms: A Biblical Vision for Christianity and Culture* (Wheaton, IL: Crossway, 2010), 117.

broader society today, VanDrunen asserts that Israel in the land is not a model for believers' shared life with non-believers today, since Israel lived only in one kingdom, a theocracy, with the "cultural commonality among believers and unbelievers ordained in the Noahic covenant . . . suspended for Israel within the borders of the Promised Land" (89). Instead, Abraham the sojourner and Israel in exile in Babylon are the proper OT models for Christians living in the world today, a model for living in two kingdoms by both "remaining radically separate from the world in [our] religious faith and worship but simultaneously engaging in a range of cultural activities in common with [our] pagan neighbors" (85, 92). Christians today are "living in Babylon, striving for justice and excellence in their cultural labors, out of love for Christ and their neighbor, as sojourners and exiles in a land that is not their lasting home" (15). Therefore, rather than identifying our work and good deeds in broader society with God's kingdom, "the New Testament teaches that the redemptive kingdom finds its present manifestation and penultimate fulfillment in the church, and the church alone" (106). VanDrunen also rejects as "speculation beyond Scripture" the idea that our cultural products "will be transformed and taken up into the world-to-come" (66).

VanDrunen's Westminster Seminary California colleague, Michael S. Horton, expresses similar conclusions in *The Gospel Commission: Recovering God's Strategy for Making Disciples* (2011). According to Horton, "the most crucial vocation of the church in this present age is the proclamation of gospel," and "the kingdom of God in this present phase is primarily *audible* not visible."[36] The "cultural mandate" of Genesis 1–2 was unique in that it required a fusing of "worship and cultural labors," a fusing which is no longer possible in a fallen world, meaning that the "Great Commission is not the 'cultural mandate'" (63). Because Christ alone has fulfilled Adam's original mandate, the application of this mandate

---

[36] Michael Horton, *The Gospel Commission: Recovering God's Strategy for Making Disciples* (Grand Rapids: Baker, 2011), 67. Original emphasis.

to the New Covenant community during the age of the inaugurated kingdom is not cultural work in broader society but instead fruitful multiplication "by the Spirit through the raising of a worldwide spiritual family, the true offspring of Abraham" (69). At the same time, Christians do have "an obligation to active love and service of their neighbors, but this is different from the Great Commission that Christ has entrusted to the church's official ministry" (213). The kingdom of God is only "identified with the delivery of Christ in the gospel," even though "the kingdom's effect will be evident in the good works of the saints" (248). Likewise, the "gospel" in Scripture refers "exclusively" to "something that is proclaimed," rather than something that is "lived." While some verses command believers to live "*in view of* the gospel, in a manner *worthy of* the gospel, and bearing the *fruit of* the gospel," Horton observes that "no passage . . . says that we are to *live the gospel*" (269). Finally, Horton calls into question the assumption that whatever good deed is "worthwhile for a Christian (or group of Christians) to invest in" is necessarily a proper task for "the church as an official activity," noting not only the institutional church's more limited commission in Scripture but also its limited "competence" in addressing a broad range of economic, health, legal and business issues (225).

Similar to others holding an evangelistic priority position, Kevin DeYoung and Greg Gilbert in *What is the Mission of the Church? Making Sense of Social Justice, Shalom, and the Great Commission* (2011) stress the Christian responsibility to do all sorts of good deeds even while noting the danger of commending these "good behaviors . . . in the wrong categories."[37] According to DeYoung and Gilbert, one incorrect category for understanding Christian good deeds is as an expression of the command in Genesis 12:2 to Abraham to "be a blessing" to the nations, as argued by Christopher

---

[37] Kevin DeYoung and Greg Gilbert, *What Is the Mission of the Church? Making Sense of Social Justice, Shalom, and the Great Commission* (Wheaton, IL: Crossway, 2011), 21.

Wright and others. Instead, DeYoung and Gilbert see "no evidence Abraham ever takes his call in chapter 12 as a commission to go find ways to bless the nations. . . . The call of Abram is not about a community blessing program. . . . [but] about God's unilateral promise . . . to bless the nations through faith in the promised Seed" (33). Another invalid category for good deeds put forward by DeYoung and Gilbert is as an embodiment of the holistic mission of God, assuming that whatever Scripture reveals God as doing necessarily determines the church's mission agenda as well (42). Other biblically-unwarranted categories for classifying Christian good deeds as identified by DeYoung and Gilbert include the unique mission of Jesus, the internal life of the early church, social justice, and shalom. They examine twelve passages of Scripture often used to argue for a church mission of "social justice" outside the covenant community and question the validity of the exegetical claims made by "social justice" advocates on the basis of these verses (142–71). Lastly, DeYoung and Gilbert distinguish between two different ways that the OT uses the term "shalom." Some passages, such as Jeremiah 29:7's command to the exiles of Israel in Babylon, speak of a "less-than-ultimate shalom" which is not the same as a command to "seek the ultimate, eternal peace of Babylon" (201). But many other OT uses of "shalom" are referring to "a situation in which God's authority and rule are absolute, where his creations—including human beings—exist in right relationship with him and with each other, and where there is no separation between God and man because of sin" (197). DeYoung and Gilbert argue that the church's mission to the world is primarily concerned with this ultimate and eternal shalom and consequently with preaching the gospel message (197–203). Associating Christian good deeds with the pursuit of "shalom"—without further qualification and explanation—is easily misunderstood or misused in drawing theological conclusions.

In *Center Church: Doing Balanced, Gospel-Centered Ministry in Your City* (2012), Timothy Keller agrees with DeYoung and Gilbert that the "shalom" of the city of Babylon that the Old Covenant people were called to seek in Jeremiah 29:6, while important, was not directly an expression of God's "plan of salvation," Jewish good works in Babylon not being God's primary mission concern.[38] This distinction (though not separation) between God's work of salvation and believers' good works illustrates Keller's contention that "the gospel is not the results of the gospel," in the same way that "faith and works must not be separated or confused."[39] By extension, the gospel, which is "preeminently a report about the work of Christ on our behalf," can only be spread by preaching, not "by the doing of justice."[40]

Duane Litfin in *Word versus Deed: Resetting the Scales to a Biblical Balance* (2012) also declares that "the gospel simply cannot be preached by our deeds."[41] Litfin surveys the biblical references to the good deeds of believers. He organizes the differing arenas of these good deeds into five concentric circles, beginning in one's private life as an individual (including the hidden motives of the heart) and moving outward into the spheres of "family, God's people, society at large and the natural world."[42] According to Litfin, "the vast majority of the Bible's instructions concerning the believer's social obligations" are located within the first three arenas: private life, family life, and church life.[43] Neither good deeds toward society at large nor toward the natural world "receive detailed attention in the Bible," as the OT concentrates on social ethics "within God's theocratic community" and the NT "focus[es] heavily on life within the church."[44]

Scot McKnight notes in *Kingdom Conspiracy: Returning to the Radical Mission of the Local Church* (2014) that he had previously

[38] Timothy Keller, *Center Church: Doing Balanced, Gospel-Centered Ministry in Your City* (Grand Rapids: Zondervan, 2012), 142–43.

[39] Ibid., 30.

[40] Ibid., 31.

[41] Duane Litfin, *Word versus Deed: Resetting the Scales to a Biblical Balance* (Wheaton, IL: Crossway, 2012), 45.

[42] Ibid., 83.

[43] Ibid., 86.

[44] Ibid., 98, 91.

advocated a broadened understanding of the "kingdom of God" in this age.[45] Now, McKnight believes Christians should "never use the word 'kingdom' for what we do in the 'world,'" since there is "no kingdom outside the church" (18, 81). He is convinced that defining words and concepts with precision and clarity is crucial to the task of biblical theology and attempts to achieve this goal in regard to the biblical use of "kingdom" (19). One implication of McKnight's study is his support for "the primacy of evangelism" in the church's mission (153). McKnight argues that the OT reveals three aspects of God's kingship: "the universal kingship of God, the covenant kingship of God with Israel, and a future universal rule," aspects that are interconnected but which must be distinguished and cannot be collapsed into one another (45). McKnight also rejects the common argument that defines "kingdom" only as "the dynamic of ruling" and not also as the people being ruled, with the resulting claim that the kingdom cannot be equated with the church (73). While he agrees that the church is not equivalent to the kingdom in its *future*, consummated state or to God's present universal rule, he believes the church *is* equivalent to the inaugurated, covenant kingdom since "kingdom" in Scripture primarily refers to "a people governed by a king" (74). Since God's present universal rule is not delegated to believers in this age, "all true kingdom mission" today "is church mission, church mission is kingdom mission, and there is no kingdom mission that is not church mission" (96). Consequently, the justice and peace of the kingdom are found currently only (though imperfectly) within the church, not within larger society. McKnight affirms that the Bible expects Christians to do "good deeds in the public sector for the common good" (i.e., 1 Peter 2:13–3:12), but such deeds should not be described with the adjective "kingdom" (111–15). Good deeds have their own legitimacy, apart from "assigning the word 'kingdom' to such actions in order to render that action sacred or to justify that

---

[45] Scot McKnight, *Kingdom Conspiracy: Returning to the Radical Mission of the Local Church* (Grand Rapids: Brazos, 2014), 14–15.

action as supernatural or to give one the sense that what she or he is doing is ultimately significant" (115).

Conclusion

The parameters of each of the composite arguments aggregated in chapters 2 and 3 are determined in part by the definitions authors use for certain key terms, such as: gospel, evangelism, salvation, redemption, the poor, principalities and powers, justice, shalom, and the kingdom. Another dividing line between the two positions is how each side understands the relationship between Christians' good deeds in society today and what various sections of Scripture seem to portray or command. Specifically, each side defines good deeds differently in relation to Genesis 1–2, Abraham's call in Genesis 12, Israel's prescribed social ethic for life in the covenant land, Israel's responsibility toward Babylon while living there in exile, the Gospels' presentation of Jesus' and his disciples' pre-resurrection ministries, the NT's picture of the life and mission of the post-resurrection church, and the future, consummated kingdom of God. While some authors above integrate a treatment of the biblical covenants into their overall biblical-theological argument, none (with the exception of David VanDrunen) focus their attention on how one's conception of the covenantal structure of Scripture is determinative in developing one's position on the good deeds mission of the church. (While VanDrunen's work is more oriented toward current debates over issues such as Neo-Calvinism and natural law, this book will display a greater orientation toward contemporary missiological literature.)

This book will demonstrate how an examination of the Bible's covenantal macro-structure provides a means to integrate all of the disputed definitions and interpretations highlighted in the literature review. This examination will by no means end the disputes, but it will provide a covenantal template which clarifies the key interpretive questions which each evangelical must address when constructing a biblical theology of the good deeds mission of the New Covenant community. This book's covenantal examination will seek to present each interpretive issue fairly, even if in the end favoring an evangelistic priority interpretation of the biblical data. The result will be a thorough, biblical-theological treatment focused narrowly on a positive portrayal of the good deeds mission of the New Covenant community from an evangelistic priority perspective—something presently lacking in the literature.

4

The Good Deeds Responsibility
of Humanity in Genesis 1–2

As just surveyed, the debate between the equal priority and evangelistic priority positions has received considerable attention within evangelical literature in recent decades. Even with this focus on the precise relationship *between* evangelism and good deeds, the good deeds mission of the New Covenant community *itself* has not received equally extensive, stand-alone treatment—in particular from the evangelistic priority side of the debate. But, in seeking to develop more fully a biblical theology of the good deeds mission of the New Covenant community, this book must first address a prior question: What good deeds responsibility has God assigned to all humanity? To answer this question, this chapter and the next will examine Genesis 1–11, along with a brief look at additional OT texts which confirm the conclusions drawn from Genesis 1–11. Since this book is using the term "mission" to refer strictly to the duties of those within the covenant community toward those outside the covenant, the topic of this chapter will be mankind's good deeds "responsibility" rather than the covenant community's good deeds "mission," maintaining a necessary distinction between these two categories. Chapter 6 includes a treatment of the relationship between humanity's good deeds responsibility and the Old Covenant community's good deeds mission, while chapter 8 considers how the universal good deeds mandate relates to the New Covenant community's good deeds mission.

In considering the good deeds responsibility given to humanity in Genesis 1 and 2, one must first establish the literary relationship between the two chapters. Genesis 1 and 2 consist of two discernible sections with the division happening either between verses 2:3 and 2:4 or verses 2:4a and 2:4b.[1] Though some see two distinct and largely unrelated accounts of creation, others see clear signs of unity between the two in elements such as "the numerical symmetry based on the number seven that we find in [chapter 2] just as we encountered it in [chapter 1]."[2] This book, as established in its first chapter, presupposes canonical unity when interpreting the text and therefore agrees with those who see Genesis 1 and 2 "function[ing] together to provide the canonical picture of creation."[3] Therefore a proper understanding of the good deeds responsibility of humanity as revealed in Genesis 1 and 2 must be discovered from both chapters treated as a literary whole. Concerning this literary interrelationship, Sailhamer further argues that chapter 2 is "intentionally embedded in chapter 1 so that [chapter 2] serves as a kind of excursus to chapter 1."[4] Those who also see chapter 2 as elaborating on chapter 1 often identify the "image of God" in chapter 1 as the key theme upon which chapter 2 expands and which unifies the two chapters thematically.[5]

---

[1] This book will presuppose a literary break between Gen. 2:4a and 2:4b and will refer to Gen. 1:1–2:4a as "chapter 1" and Gen. 2:4b–25 as "chapter 2."

[2] Umberto Cassuto, *A Commentary on the Book of Genesis: Part 1, From Adam to Noah* (Jerusalem: Magnes, 1961), 94.

[3] Terence E. Fretheim, *The Book of Genesis: Introduction, Commentary, and Reflections*, in vol. 1 of *The New Interpreter's Bible*, ed. Leander E. Keck (Nashville: Abingdon Press, 1994), 340.

[4] John H. Sailhamer, *Genesis*, in vol. 1 of *The Expositor's Bible Commentary*, eds. Tremper Longman III and David E. Garland, rev. ed. (Grand Rapids: Zondervan, 2008), 72.

[5] For example, Gentry states, "Therefore, 2:4–3:24 is, in fact, devoted to further development of the topics broached in the sixth paragraph of the 'first account' and so adds to the significance of the creation of mankind." Peter J. Gentry, "Kingdom through Covenant: Humanity as the Divine Image," *Southern Baptist Journal of Theology* 12, no. 1 (Spring 2008): 22. See also Sailhamer, *Genesis*, 73; Fretheim, *The Book of Genesis*, 349; Kenneth A. Mathews, *Genesis*

An alternative theme that unites the two chapters (and encompasses the image of God theme) is the seventh day of creation. Concerning the number seven, in the Old Testament it is "generally seen as a number which symbolizes 'completeness,' 'wholeness,' 'perfection' and 'satisfaction.'"[6] Following this numerical symbolism, the seventh day, rather than the creation of humanity, seems more clearly presented as God's culminating work of creation.[7] Gerhard Hasel agrees that the seventh day is "the final goal of Creation," even while still designating humanity as "the crown of Creation."[8] Harold Dressler counters that "the crown of creation is not man" but instead argues that the seventh day alone crowns creation as "all creative activities of God flow into a universal rest period."[9] While not seeking to create a false dichotomy, in interpreting the text one must decide whether the author intends to present the creation of man or the establishment of the seventh day as ultimate in creation. In this case, the text seems most clearly to point to the seventh day as creation's supreme focus, while in no way diminishing the importance of mankind's creation.[10]

1–11:26, The New American Commentary, vol. 1A (Nashville: B&H, 1996), 189; W. J. Dumbrell, *Covenant and Creation: A Theology of the Old Testament Covenants* (Carlisle, UK: Paternoster, 2000), 35.

[6] Gnana Robinson, *The Origin and Development of the Old Testament Sabbath* (Frankfurt: Peter Lang, 1987), 110.

[7] Alexander notes, "Most readers of Genesis 1 concentrate on the six days of creation. However, the opening section of Genesis comes to a climax with the seventh day." T. Desmond Alexander, *From Paradise to the Promised Land: An Introduction to the Pentateuch*, 3rd ed. (Grand Rapids: Baker Academic, 2012), 122.

[8] Gerhard Hasel, "Sabbath in the Pentateuch," in *The Sabbath in Scripture and History*, ed. Kenneth A. Strand (Washington, DC: Review and Herald, 1982), 23. Blocher concurs, "The creation of mankind crowns the work, but the sabbath is its supreme goal." Henri Blocher, *In the Beginning: The Opening Chapters of Genesis* (Downers Grove, IL: IVP, 1984), 57.

[9] Harold H. P. Dressler, "The Sabbath in the Old Testament," in *From Sabbath to Lord's Day*, ed. D. A. Carson (Grand Rapids: Zondervan, 1982), 29.

[10] Mathews observes, "The literary pattern of six plus one (6+1) is designed to highlight the seventh and culminating member in the seven-item arrangement." Mathews, *Genesis 1–11:26*, 176.

In support of this conclusion, others describe the seventh day as "a consummation of all that has gone before,"[11] "the *telos* of creation,"[12] "last in creation, first in intention,"[13] and conclude that "the entire creation story of ch. 1 focuses on the sanctification of the seventh day."[14] Creation is presented not as anthropocentric, but instead as 'seventh-daycentric' and thereby as theocentric.

The text displays the seventh day as set apart from the first six days in that God has completed creation, ceases from his work, does not speak, and sanctifies the day. The seventh day is also set apart in that "unlike the previous days, the seventh day is simply announced. There is no mention of morning or evening, no mention of a beginning or an ending."[15] Gerhard Von Rad believes that this omission, "like everything else in this chapter, is intentional" and is intended to communicate that the seventh day "is not limited."[16] Samuel Balentine suggests that the seventh day "exists in perpetuity."[17] Kenneth Mathews is convinced that "theologically the absence of the refrain [of morning and evening] implies that creation was intended to enjoy a perpetual rest provided by God, although that rest was disturbed by sin."[18] Henri Blocher notes that Augustine also interprets the seventh day as eternal, and Blocher believes this is the "most

---

[11] S. Dean McBride Jr., "Divine Protocol: Genesis 1:1–2:3 as Prologue to the Pentateuch," in *God Who Creates: Essays in Honor of W. Sibley Towner*, eds. William P. Brown and S. Dean McBride Jr. (Grand Rapids: Eerdmans, 2000), 14.

[12] E. Carson Brisson, "The Gates of Dawn: Reflections on Genesis 1:1–10; 2:1–4a," in *God Who Creates: Essays in Honor of W. Sibley Towner*, eds. William P. Brown and S. Dean McBride Jr. (Grand Rapids: Eerdmans, 2000), 57.

[13] Abraham J. Heschel, *The Sabbath: Its Meaning for Modern Man* (New York: Farrar, Straus & Giroux, 1951), 14.

[14] Brevard S. Childs, *The Book of Exodus: A Critical, Theological Commentary* (Philadelphia: Westminster, 1974), 416.

[15] Samuel E. Balentine, *The Torah's Vision of Worship* (Minneapolis: Fortress, 1999), 93.

[16] Gerhard Von Rad, *Genesis* (London: SCM Press, 1961), 61.

[17] Balentine, *The Torah's Vision*, 93.

[18] Mathews, *Genesis 1–11:26*, 176.

simple and natural conclusion."[19] Following this interpretation, the text presents God not only as creating the seventh day as the goal of creation but also as intending this seventh day state of existence to be creation's perpetual condition—the eternal seventh day.

Genesis 2:2 portrays God himself as entering into the rest of the eternal seventh day. God enters not as a tired worker needing a brief rest or time of inactivity but as a conquering king "resting in kingdom sovereignty"[20]—a never-ending rulership over all creation. This entrance is depicted as "an enthronement," with the Creator assuming "his rightful position as Lord of the world."[21] Having demonstrated his wisdom and might during six days of creative work, God's "kingly rest" now "further reveal[s] his sovereign power,"[22] indicating that the "pomp and majesty of the six days simply subserves the revelation of the ultimate and absolute dominion celebrated in the seventh day."[23]

While most interpreters seem to see the rest inaugurated on the seventh day as a goal for all creation, in dispute is whether the text portrays this as a goal also achieved by humanity only after a time of testing or whether "creation simply moves into the Seventh Day by default," immediately joining God in his rest.[24] The delayed entry view is common within the Reformed tradition, positing a "probationary" period for Adam and Eve during which their faithful obedience would eventually earn them entrance into the rest of the eternal seventh day.[25] While there are some weighty theological reasons in

[19] Blocher, *In the Beginning*, 56.

[20] Meredith G. Kline, *Kingdom Prologue: Genesis Foundations for a Covenantal Worldview* (Overland Park, KS: Two Age Press, 2000), 35.

[21] Ibid., 19.

[22] G. K. Beale, *The Temple and the Church's Mission: A Biblical Theology of the Dwelling Place of God* (Downers Grove, IL: IVP, 2004), 62.

[23] Kline, *Kingdom Prologue*, 39.

[24] A. G. Shead, "Sabbath," in *New Dictionary of Biblical Theology*, ed. T. Desmond Alexander et al. (Downers Grove, IL: IVP, 2000), 746.

[25] For one recent proponent of this traditional Reformed position, see David VanDrunen, *Divine Covenants and Moral Order: A Biblical Theology of Natural Law* (Grand Rapids: Eerdmans, 2014), 69–74.

favor of this position, such as the biblical correspondence between Adam and Christ, this view appears nonetheless to go beyond the explicit textual data of Genesis 1–2.[26] Therefore, the better interpretation is that Adam and Eve immediately "enjoyed the rest God initiated on the seventh day of creation."[27] God creates humanity as images who reflect his own kingly glory, meaning that "Genesis 1 rest is designed not only for the deity, but also for humanity as an imitation of the deity."[28] Adam and Eve are "perfectly formed as potential partners for fellowship with God" and for rulership over creation in the eternal seventh day.[29]

If indeed the theme of Genesis 1:1–2:4a is the entrance of God, humanity, and all creation into God's eternal seventh day rest and if Genesis 2:4b–25 is an elaboration of this theme, then the "unending seventh day provides the context in which the ideal life of the garden is to take place and is to be perpetuated in human experience."[30] Genesis 2 is thus a window into life within the eternal seventh day. Within this setting, God gives mankind a mandate, responsibilities which flow from Adam and Eve's identity as the image of God. Throughout the interpretive history of the phrase "image of God" in Genesis 1:26–28, many have taken an "atomizing and reductionist approach to the passage, in which attention is focused on a single phrase or clause, severing it from its immediate context and from

---

[26] Blocher asks, "Should we think that God was merely establishing a temporary system, in order to raise mankind later if he passed his examination? Such speculation is manifestly a long way from the text, and we share G. C. Berkouwer's reticence in this matter: 'there is reason to question whether the term "probationary command" is actually a correct expression of that which Scripture means to tell us in the Genesis account.'" Blocher, *In the Beginning*, 133.

[27] Scott J. Hafemann, *The God of Promise and the Life of Faith: Understanding the Heart of the Bible* (Wheaton, IL: Crossway, 2001), 62.

[28] Mark S. Smith, *The Priestly Vision of Genesis 1* (Minneapolis: Fortress, 2010), 106.

[29] R. R. Reno, *Genesis* (Grand Rapids: Brazos, 2010), 67.

[30] William J. Dumbrell, *Covenant and Creation: An Old Testament Covenant Theology* (Carlisle, UK: Paternoster, 2013), 37.

its context within the larger composition."[31] Seeking to avoid this error, we will now examine the meaning of mankind's creation as the image of God based upon a unified reading of the two chapters, all in order to understand accurately the mandate of Genesis 1–2 and any good deeds responsibility that it includes.

Man as the Image of God

Regarding the image of God in Genesis 1:26–28, many interpretations have been suggested, sometimes organized into three categories: substantive, relational, and functional.[32] The view of the image argued below will incorporate aspects of all three categories. Scott Hafemann proposes that the image is a "description not primarily of our nature but of our function. We were created in the 'image of God' not primarily to possess certain capabilities but to fulfill a certain calling *in relationship to God*."[33] Blocher agrees that image "does not speak firstly of the nature of the human creature (although a secondary interest in it cannot be excluded). It defines our *constitutive relationships*."[34] In contrast, Peter Gentry argues for a definition of the image which is fundamentally ontological (substantive) rather than relational or functional. He notes, "The grammar reveals that man rules as a result of being made as the divine image; ruling is not the essence of the image itself. . . . Man is the divine image."[35] Clines likewise advocates for an ontological understanding.[36]

---

[31] Phyllis A. Bird, "Male and Female He Created Them: Genesis 1:27b in the Context of the Priestly Account of Creation," in *I Studied Inscriptions from before The Flood: Ancient Near Eastern, Literary, and Linguistic Approaches to Genesis 1–11*, eds. Richard S. Hess and David Toshio Tsumura (Winona Lake, IN: Eisenbrauns, 1994), 330.

[32] Millard J. Erickson, *Christian Theology*, 2nd ed. (Grand Rapids: Baker, 1998), 517–36.

[33] Hafemann, *The God of Promise and the Life of Faith*, 24. Original emphasis.

[34] Blocher, *In the Beginning*, 85. Original emphasis.

[35] Gentry, "Kingdom through Covenant," 32.

[36] D. J. A. Clines, "The Image of God in Man," *Tyndale Bulletin* 19 (1968): 81.

Clines states, "Man is the flesh-and-blood image of the invisible God. . . . the representation of the one who is imaged in a place where he is not."[37] Genesis 1:26 can then be translated, "Let us make man *as* our image . . . *so that* they may rule," the function of the image resulting from its nature.[38] Put another way, function follows nature. This book will adopt a definition of image which is first of all ontological and only secondarily (but necessarily) relational and functional.[39] In the world of the eternal seventh day, humanity *is*, by nature, God's visible representative in the created order, designed to live in right relationship to God and one another, carrying out faithfully their assigned responsibilities.[40] Fulfilling these responsibilities within the eternal seventh day *is* the mandate of Genesis 1–2 for humanity.

The Responsibilities of the Image

The five imperatives spoken by God in Genesis 1:28 ("be fruitful," "multiply," "fill," "subdue," and "have dominion over") are usually recognized as crucial for understanding the responsibilities of the image.[41] But Sailhamer argues that these imperatives should "not be understood as commands" since within the verse itself they are identified as a "blessing" and since the Hebrew form of "the imperative, along with the jussive, is the common mood of the blessing (cf. Gen. 27:19)."[42] According to Sailhamer, God's blessing upon

---

[37] Ibid., 86–87.

[38] Gentry, "Kingdom through Covenant," 25, 31.

[39] Clines, "The Image of God," 87. See also Anthony A. Hoekema, *Created in God's Image* (Grand Rapids: Eerdmans, 1986), 13; Dumbrell, *Covenant and Creation* (2000), 34.

[40] According to Clines, "Though man's rulership over the animals is not itself the image of God, no definition of the image is complete which does not refer to this function of rulership." Clines, "The Image of God," 97.

[41] When directly quoting from the Bible in English, the text of the *English Standard Version* (esv) will be used unless otherwise noted.

[42] John Sailhamer, *The Pentateuch as Narrative: A Biblical-Theological*

humanity (and earlier upon animals) is neither a future endowment received upon completion of assigned tasks nor is it the assigned tasks themselves but is instead "a present gift to be enjoyed by God's creatures."[43] But others, like Beale, believe that this verse is "a blessing that includes a mandate or command," a more traditional interpretation for which Beale cites numerous supporters.[44] While acknowledging Sailhamer's grammatical argument, this book accepts the view that this verse contains at least an implied command for humanity.[45] However, this command must be kept situated in the context of God's act of blessing, a word of blessing which was "bound to have its effects and to confer the beneficial power whereby man would be enabled to fulfill the potential for which he had been created."[46] God's blessing within the eternal seventh day context empowers humanity to fulfill four essential responsibilities: representational rulership, image multiplication, dependent sonship, and priestly worship in God's presence.

Representational Rulership

As God's representative, man is ruler over creation. William Dumbrell observes, "In Genesis 1 the concept of man's rulership is connected in the strongest possible way with the idea of the image."[47] The term "image of God" is "a royal designation, the precondition or requisite for rule."[48] The word translated "image" was often used in other Ancient Near Eastern (ANE) cultures to refer to statues

---

Commentary (Grand Rapids: Zondervan, 1992), 96.

[43] John H. Sailhamer, The Meaning of the Pentateuch: Revelation, Composition, and Interpretation (Downers Grove, IL: IVP Academic, 2009), 432.

[44] Beale, The Temple and the Church's Mission, 86n13.

[45] The grammatical question marks surrounding the status of the imperatival force of this verse should add extra caution to any efforts to apply this verse as a command for Christians to obey today.

[46] Dumbrell, Covenant and Creation (2000), 68.

[47] Ibid., 95.

[48] Bird, "Male and Female He Created Them," 341.

which represented a god's visible presence and protection within the community, allowing "public access to divine power."[49] These ANE cultures would also categorize their human king as an "image"— though by contrast the Bible designates all humanity as the "image," thereby "democratiz[ing] the royalistic and exclusivistic concepts of the nations that surrounded Israel."[50] According to Genesis 1, all humanity would "closely represent God in image . . . represent[ing] his rule in the world."[51] Within the eternal seventh day, "man is thus not simply master of the animals, but king of the earth."[52] As the image of God, Adam and Eve are given a mandate to display the kingly rulership of God, a responsibility for "performing the justice and enacting the sovereign will of God."[53]

---

[49] W. Randall Garr, *In His Own Image and Likeness: Humanity, Divinity, and Monotheism* (Boston: Brill, 2003), 144.

[50] Victor P. Hamilton, *The Book of Genesis: Chapters 1–17* (Grand Rapids: Eerdmans, 1990), 135.

[51] Gentry, "Kingdom through Covenant," 31. See also Stephen G. Dempster, *Dominion and Dynasty: A Biblical Theology of the Hebrew Bible* (Downers Grove, IL: IVP, 2003), 61–62.

[52] Clines, "The Image of God," 99. Gentry observes, "The term 'to rule' (*rādâ*) in Gen. 1:26, 28 is particularly true of kings as Ps. 72:8 illustrates. Also the term 'to subdue' especially speaks of the work of a king (e.g., 2 Sam. 8:11)." Gentry, "Kingdom through Covenant," 29. According to Waltke, these two verbs "entail respectively repressing and subduing/subjugating someone or something who/that resist and opposes as an enemy the exercise of authority." Bruce K. Waltke, *An Old Testament Theology: An Exegetical, Canonical, and Thematic Approach* (Grand Rapids: Zondervan, 2007), 220.

[53] Garr, *In His Own Image*, 219. Another thought-provoking interpretation of this ruling mandate is put forward by Seth D. Postell, *Adam as Israel: Genesis 1–3 as the Introduction to the Torah and Tanakh* (Eugene, OR: Wipf & Stock, 2011). Postell states, "God's mandate to Adam and Eve to conquer the land and its inhabitant (the serpent) foreshadows God's mandate to Israel to conquer the land and its inhabitants (the Canaanites), thus establishing a link between the land God gives to Adam and Eve and the land God gives to Abraham and his descendants" (100). Furthermore, "The militaristic overtones of the creation mandate, therefore, make sense only when understood as the prototypical mandate to conquer the Promised Land. The purpose of the militaristic terminology is not to give license for the exploitation of the natural

One aspect of this representational rulership within the setting of the eternal seventh day is oversight over the animals and the rest of the natural world. In Genesis 1:28, God blesses and commands Adam and Eve to "subdue [the earth]" and "have dominion over" the animals. Many interpreters identify creation care as the clearest and perhaps weightiest and most comprehensive human responsibility in Genesis 1–2.[54] This book recognizes stewardship of the natural world as one significant expression of humanity's representational rulership within the eternal seventh day but argues that the four responsibilities highlighted within this section (representational rulership, image multiplication, dependent sonship, and priestly worship in God's presence) are the most fundamental and essential human responsibilities portrayed in Genesis 1–2. Additionally, this chapter will address below how humanity's representational rulership (including creation stewardship) and other original responsibilities transfer (or do not transfer) from the world of the eternal seventh day to the world after sin's entrance.

In displaying God's rule, the image is required to display God's character, for "ethical-spiritual stipulations . . . were integral to the

---

resources in the world. Rather, it prepares the reader for understanding what should have been Adam and Eve's response to the serpent in Gen. 3, and also supplies Israel with their marching orders in the remainder of the Pentateuch (and in the Tanakh). . . . The royal terminology used in the creation mandate suggests that Adam is the prototypical king who is called to conquer the Promised Land" (102).

[54] Wright believes that Gen 1–2 teaches creation care as "the first great responsibility that God laid on the human race." Christopher J. H. Wright, *Old Testament Ethics for the People of God* (Downers Grove, IL: IVP, 2004), 127. See also Michael A. Bullmore, "The Four Most Important Biblical Passages for a Christian Environmentalism," *Trinity Journal* 19, no. 2 (Fall 1998): 153; Sandra Richter, "A Biblical Theology of Creation Care," *The Asbury Journal* 62, no. 1 (Spring 2007): 69; Steven Bouma-Prediger, *For the Beauty of the Earth: A Christian Vision for Creation Care*, 2nd ed. (Grand Rapids: Baker Academic, 2010), 64; Richard Bauckham, *The Bible and Ecology: Rediscovering the Community of Creation* (Waco, TX: Baylor, 2010), 18; Richard Bauckham, *Living with Other Creatures: Green Exegesis and Theology* (Waco, TX: Baylor, 2011).

divine mandate."[55] According to Gentry, this understanding of the image is common in ANE literature, where "the behavior of the king reflects the behavior of the god. The image reflects the characteristics of the god. The image reflects the essential notions of the god."[56] The character of the human ruler is intended to represent the character of God—a representational rulership.[57] Therefore, being the image "entails the obligation to understand the nature of the relationship [with God] and the duty to maintain it by exercising a God-centered life."[58] Adam and Eve must be holy like the holy God who rules in the sanctified eternal seventh day.[59] The image is not required merely to rule *for* God but to rule *like* God.[60] In doing so, the image displays and reflects the glory of God,[61] as "the visual metaphor of the image of God in humankind is that of a polished mirror with no cracks."[62] The perfect display of God's glory in his mirror-images is the ultimate purpose of mankind's mandate to be representational rulers.[63]

---

[55] Kline, *Kingdom Prologue*, 189.

[56] Gentry, "Kingdom through Covenant," 27.

[57] Ibid., 32. Routledge concurs that Genesis 1 teaches that "all human beings are called to reflect the character of the one in whose likeness they have been made." Robin Routledge, *Old Testament Theology: A Thematic Approach* (Downers Grove, IL: IVP Academic, 2008), 248.

[58] Dumbrell, *Covenant and Creation* (2000), 36.

[59] For a later, but parallel, ethical responsibility for OT Israel (and subsequently the NT church), see Lev. 11:44 "Be holy, for I am holy." Also see Lev. 19:2; 20:7, 26.

[60] Wright makes this same point, "Whatever way this human dominion is to be exercised, it must reflect the character and values of God's own kingship." Christopher J. H. Wright, *The Mission of God: Unlocking the Bible's Grand Narrative* (Downers Grove, IL: IVP Academic, 2006), 426.

[61] Meredith G. Kline, *Images of the Spirit* (Eugene, OR: Wipf & Stock, 1999), 61.

[62] W. Sibley Towner, *Genesis* (Louisville: Westminster John Knox, 2001), 27. See also Kline, *Kingdom Prologue*, 63.

[63] As Beale states, "God's ultimate goal in creation was to magnify his glory throughout the earth by means of his faithful image-bearers inhabiting the world." Beale, *The Temple and the Church's Mission*, 82.

Image Multiplication

Man is not just king, but both king and queen, for "God created man as His own image, as the image of God He created him; male and female He created them" (1:27).[64] Some suggest that the author presents the duality of male and female as the image of God for the purpose of revealing the duality (or even the tri-unity) of God himself.[65] Regardless of the merit of this argument, the text clearly says that mankind's position as God's image is expressed through both male and female, king and queen. Yet there is not just one king and one queen. In the next verse we read, "God blessed them; and God said to them, 'Be fruitful and multiply; and fill the earth'" (1:28). It appears that God intends for humanity within the eternal seventh day to become a kingdom of kings and queens, as "they cannot accomplish their . . . mandate without reproducing their kind to help them do it."[66] As well, though all will rule, there is no hint of any struggle for power. Instead, all rule together in perfect harmony and cooperation under the ultimate sovereignty of their creator. Therefore, the eternal seventh day is presented as an existence of perfect human unity and community, increasingly filled with images reflecting the glory of God. Like representational

[64] Author's translation.

[65] See Clines, "The Image of God," 68, and Sailhamer, *The Pentateuch as Narrative*, 96. Barth emphasizes a relational understanding of the image claiming, "Could anything be more obvious than to conclude . . . that the image and likeness of the being created by God signifies existence in confrontation, i.e., in this confrontation, in the juxtaposition and conjunction of man and man which is that of male and female . . . ?" Karl Barth, *Church Dogmatics*, eds. G. W. Bromiley and T. F. Torrance, in vol. 3 of *The Doctrine of Creation*, pt. 1, trans. J. W. Edwards, O. Bussey, and H. Knight (London: T&T Clark International, 2004), 195.

[66] Dempster, *Dominion and Dynasty*, 61. Fesko agrees that humanity was responsible to "multiply the image of God through procreation [and] fill[ing] the earth with the image of God." J. V. Fesko, *Last Things First: Unlocking Genesis 1–2 with the Christ of Eschatology* (Fearn, Scotland: Christian Focus Publications, 2007), 101.

rulership, image multiplication is a fundamental responsibility given to Adam and Eve.

As argued above, original humanity's responsibility to steward the natural world was an important manifestation of their representational rulership but was nonetheless not the essence of mankind's responsibility before God. Similarly, many interpreters conclude that the responsibility to develop the institutions, products, and practices of human culture and society is implied in the command to "be fruitful and multiply; and fill the earth" (as well as in the commands to "subdue [the earth]" and "have dominion over" the animals). One celebrated proponent of this "cultural mandate," Abraham Kuyper, understands it as "a precept 'to preserve and cultivate the material world'. . . [by] apply[ing] human abilities ([such as] art [and] craftsmanship) to nature . . . [in order] to enable and perfect [nature].'"[67] According to John Frame, this mandate "includes science, the arts, agriculture, politics—everything we associate with culture."[68] While acknowledging the legitimacy of this implied mandate to construct human culture within the eternal seventh day, this book proposes that the tasks of cultural development and natural resource management are secondary expressions of the more fundamental responsibilities of mankind to be images who rightly represent God's character and who multiply and fill the earth with additional God-reflecting images.

Dependent Sonship

Rulership and multiplication are commonly identified as essential to the human responsibilities of Genesis 1–2, but the image of God is "broader than kingship, comprehending such further benefits as sonship."[69] In fact, Gentry argues that in Genesis 1–2, "the

[67] James E. McGoldrick, *Abraham Kuyper: God's Renaissance Man* (Auburn, MA: Evangelical Press, 2000), 82.

[68] John M. Frame, *Salvation Belongs to the Lord: An Introduction to Systematic Theology* (Phillipsburg, NJ: P&R Publishing, 2006), 98.

[69] Kline, *Kingdom Prologue*, 42.

relationship between humans and God is best captured by the term sonship."[70] In the broader world of the ANE, "rulership" epitomized the relationship of the image to the realm he ruled and "sonship" described the relationship of the image to the god he represented.[71] Likewise in Genesis 1–2, Adam is the son of God, and both Adam and Eve are children of God their Father.[72] This understanding of the father-son relationship in the Genesis 1–2 portrayal of the image of God is confirmed in Genesis 5:1–3 where Adam's own son Seth is called his image.[73] Stephen Dempster concisely summarizes this interpretation by observing, "As Seth is a son of Adam, so Adam is a son of God."[74]

As children of their heavenly Father, Genesis 2:17 presents Adam and Eve as those forbidden from direct access to "the tree of the knowledge of good and evil." This limitation on Adam and Eve further characterizes them as situated in a parent-child relationship toward God as later in the Pentateuch children are described

---

[70] Gentry, "Kingdom through Covenant," 32.

[71] Ibid., 27. Gentry states in another place, "Given the normal meanings of 'image' and 'likeness' in the cultural and linguistic setting of the Old Testament and the ancient Near East, 'likeness' specifies a relationship between God and humans such that *adam* can be described as the son of God, and 'image' describes a relationship between God and humans such that *adam* can be described as a servant king." Peter J. Gentry and Stephen J. Wellum, *Kingdom through Covenant: A Biblical-Theological Understanding of the Covenants* (Wheaton, IL: Crossway, 2012), 194–95. In this sense, the *likeness* relates to God as son, and the *image* relates to creation as ruler.

[72] See Kline, *Kingdom Prologue*, 45; Clines, "The Image of God," 58; Meredith G. Kline, "Creation in the Image of the Glory-spirit," *Westminster Theological Journal* 39, no. 2 (Spring 1977): 265; Gentry, "Kingdom through Covenant," 28; Blocher, *In the Beginning*, 89–90.

[73] Kline concludes, "Unmistakably, the father-son relationship of Adam and Seth is presented as a proper analogue for understanding the Creator-man relationship and clearly man's likeness to the Creator-Spirit is thus identified as the likeness of a son derived from his father." Kline, "Creation in the Image of the Glory-spirit," 260.

[74] Dempster, *Dominion and Dynasty*, 58.

as those who "have no knowledge of good or evil" (Deut. 1:39).[75] As children without the knowledge of good or evil, Adam and Eve in the eternal seventh day must depend completely upon God for wisdom and for the provision of the good. This dependence is cast in an entirely positive light as "Genesis 1 and 2 portray God as a loving father preparing the very best for his children."[76] God provides all that is good for man, only requiring mankind to "rejoice in his filial dependence and reject the mirage of a truant autonomy like that of the prodigal son."[77] After six days of "good" creation, God installs humanity as rulers, as well as provides them an abundance of food (1:29).[78] Hafemann observes that humanity in the eternal seventh day is "not called to exercise dominion in order to gain the food God gives, but because God has *already* granted the food they needed. Mankind's dominion would therefore express their dependence and their dependence would honor the One upon whom mankind depended, since the Giver gets the glory."[79] In fact, such complete dependence upon their heavenly Father is the prerequisite for Adam and Eve to exercise dominion in the way which God requires since "Only dependence on God makes dominion possible."[80] God's perfect provision of the good also includes companionship. In 2:18, God declares Adam's companionless state as "not good," and so God provides woman, an act which is presented as "an archetypal example of God's knowledge of the good."[81] In the eternal seventh day, God

---

[75] Cassuto observes, "Before they ate of the tree of knowledge, the man and his wife were like small children, who know nought of what exists around them; and it is precisely in connection with small children that we find a similar expression in Deut. 1:39 . . . ." Cassuto, *A Commentary on the Book of Genesis*, 112.

[76] Postell, *Adam as Israel*, 98.

[77] Blocher, *In the Beginning*, 133.

[78] Cassuto describes man as "like a babe of a day, who receives his food without any toil." Cassuto, *A Commentary on the Book of Genesis*, 113.

[79] Hafemann, *The God of Promise and the Life of Faith*, 29. Original emphasis.

[80] Ibid., 64.

[81] Sailhamer, *The Pentateuch as Narrative*, 101.

richly provides his children with all they need for good, including one another, only requiring humanity to depend upon and trust Him as Father.[82] Just as the mandate of Genesis 1–2 is not only a call to rulership but a call to *a certain kind of* rulership, so the call is also not merely to sonship but to *a certain kind of* sonship: dependent sonship.[83]

---

[82] Sailhamer states, "God alone knows what is good for human beings and God alone knows what is not good for them. To enjoy the 'good' we must trust God and obey him" (ibid).

[83] An argument can be made that this sonship is also presented as a Spirit-filled sonship. Gen. 2:7 says, "Then the LORD God formed the man of dust from the ground and breathed into his nostrils the breath of life, and the man became a living creature." Clines understands this verse as portraying man as filled with the Spirit of God. Man as the image of God "becomes a genuine image of the deity by the infusion of divine spirit or breath." Clines, "The Image of God," 90. Kline concurs that this "divine inbreathing . . . is to be understood in terms of the vitalizing breath of the Spirit." Kline, "Creation in the Image of the Glory-Spirit," 259. According to Clines, within the ANE, "the primary function of the image was to be the dwelling-place of spirit or fluid which derived from the being whose image it was." Clines, "The Image of God," 81. The image of the god was understood to be the place where the spirit of the god resided. Some have observed that "Genesis 2 bears many of the marks of the Mesopotamian ritual known as the *mïs pî* (the washing of the mouth) or *pït pî* (the opening of the mouth), a ritual known from various Assyrian and Babylonian tablets, which typically took place in a sacred grove beside a river (a motif echoed in the garden narrative of Genesis 2). The purpose of the ritual was to vivify the newly carved cult statue so that it would become a living entity, imbued with the spirit and presence of the deity for which it was an image." J. Richard Middleton, *A New Heaven and A New Earth: Reclaiming Biblical Eschatology* (Grand Rapids: Baker Academic, 2014), 48–49. If this practice indeed informs Gen. 1–2, then Adam and Eve may also be being presented as Spirit-filled children. By being the dwelling place of the Spirit of God, they are then empowered to be representational rulers and dependent children. Though an intriguing reading, the textual evidence is more inconclusive, and some, such as Jeffrey Niehaus, are not persuaded. See Jeffrey J. Niehaus, *The Common Grace Covenants*, vol. 1 of *Biblical Theology* (Wooster, OH: Weaver Book Company, 2014), 59–60.

Priestly Worship in God's Presence

Earlier this book noted that God's rest in the eternal seventh day presents a picture of the victorious reign of a sovereign. Gordon Wenham and others have also argued that God's rest alludes to his later "resting" in Israel's tabernacle, with "parallels in phraseology between the conclusion of the creation account in 1:1–2:3a and the tabernacle building account in Exodus 25–40."[84] In this sense, "the completion of the 'universe parallels the completion of the tabernacle.'"[85] Creation is presented as the dwelling place of God.

Not only does Genesis 1 portray God as preparing a creation-tabernacle, man is also rendered as God's priest in the tabernacle. In readying the creation-tabernacle on day four, God says, "Let there be lights in the expanse of the heavens to separate the day from the night. And let them be for signs and for seasons, and for days and years" (Gen. 1:14).[86] The lights in the heavens are assigned a

---

[84] Gordon J. Wenham, "Sanctuary Symbolism in the Garden of Eden Story," in *I Studied Inscriptions from before The Flood: Ancient Near Eastern, Literary, and Linguistic Approaches to Genesis 1–11*, eds. Richard S. Hess and David Toshio Tsumura (Winona Lake, IN: Eisenbrauns, 1994), 403. Kline also observes, "The Sabbath motif that informs Genesis 1:1–2:3 is prominent in the account of the tabernacle." Kline, *Images of the Spirit*, 38. Likewise, Mathews states, "Repetition of creation-sabbath language is found in the construction of the tabernacle." Mathews, *Genesis 1–11:26*, 177.

[85] Wenham, "Sanctuary Symbolism in the Garden of Eden Story," 403. Fesko concurs, "The tabernacle-creation parallels mean that, if the creation is part of God's cosmic temple, then the garden of Eden was the first holy of holies, the location of God's throne." Fesko, *Last Things First*, 71.

[86] Sailhamer proposes that the correct translation for 1:14 is "Let the lights in the expanse of the sky be for separating the day and the night, and let them be for signs to mark the seasons and days of the year." In Sailhamer's view, the sun, moon, and stars (along with their light) were already made "in the beginning" (1:1). Day four is therefore not a recounting of the initial creation of these astral bodies only God's designation of their assigned purpose in regulating humanity's relationship with God. John H. Sailhamer, *Genesis Unbound: A Provocative New Look at the Creation Account*, 2nd ed. (Colorado Springs, CO: Dawson Media, 2011), 137–44.

particular purpose for humanity as signs to mark "seasons . . . days and years." The author of the Pentateuch likely intends this phrase as an intertextual allusion "to the special functions of the sun and moon in the sacred seasons of the worship of Yahweh, especially as defined in Leviticus 23."[87] God prepares the heavenly lights "to serve the priestly purpose of marking the 'times' of the festivals."[88] Therefore, the kingly image of God in the creation-tabernacle of Genesis 1 is also depicted as a priest of God. This priestly aspect is further suggested when man is described as being made according to God's "likeness" (Gen. 1:26). Within ANE literature, this word is "associated with baldly petitionary language,"[89] thereby portraying man as standing before God in the "dependent and petitionary" posture of a priest.[90] Additionally, the verb used to communicate humanity's responsibility to "subdue [the earth]" in Genesis 1:28 refers to the work of priests elsewhere in the OT.[91] Finally, God's pronouncement of blessing in Genesis 2:3a is suggestive of the blessing function of the later priests of Israel.[92] As the imitative image of God in the

---

[87] Bill T. Arnold, *Genesis* (New York: Cambridge, 2009), 42. According to Smith, these appointed times were "the festivals as known from the priestly calendars in Leviticus 23 and Numbers 28–29. The same word for festivals occurs at the head of the calendar in Leviticus 23:4. This usage also fits in with the Sabbath in Leviticus 23, since it treats the calendars along the lines of the priestly Sabbath." Smith, *The Priestly Vision*, 98. See also Towner, *Genesis*, 23.

[88] Smith, *The Priestly Vision*, 98.

[89] Garr, *In His Own Image and Likeness*, 122. The term "likeness" is "cultic and votive" and within the ANE is used to portray "the Mesopotamian ruler . . . [as a] devoted worshipper" (ibid., 232).

[90] Daniel I. Block, "To Serve and to Keep: Toward a Biblical Understanding of Humanity's Responsibility in the Face of the Biodiversity Crisis," in *Keeping God's Earth: The Global Environment in Biblical Perspective*, eds. Noah J. Toly and Daniel I. Block (Downers Grove, IL: IVP Academic, 2010), 127.

[91] Smith, *The Priestly Vision*, 101. Unlike Smith, this book does not follow the historical critical presupposition that Gen. 1 was written by a Priestly writer (in contrast to Gen. 2 as written by the Yahwist). Nonetheless, Smith does point out some elements of Gen. 1 that demonstrate that the image of God is also presented as a priest of God.

[92] Ibid., 104.

eternal seventh day, this hints that mankind will likewise function as a proclaimer of priestly blessing upon creation.

The Genesis 1 literary portrayal of God preparing a tabernacle within which his image serves him as a priest is also evident in the Genesis 2 portrait of the garden. The descriptions of the garden in Genesis and of the tabernacle in Exodus show many signs of inter-textuality, including "the close similarity between the appearance and role of the garden and that of the tabernacle in Exodus 25–27."[93] Beale itemizes more than ten parallels between Eden and the taber-nacle.[94] These many parallels combine to give significant support to Beale's contention that "the Garden of Eden was the first archetypal temple in which the first man worshipped God."[95]

Like Genesis 1, man in the garden-temple of Genesis 2 is also depicted as a priest. Genesis 2:15 says "The LORD God took the man and put him in the garden of Eden to work it and keep it." While many translators seem to understand Adam's task in Genesis 2:15 as primarily an agricultural one[96]—that is, working and taking care of the garden or the ground of the garden—there are significant weak-nesses in this interpretation.

> The word translated 'work'. . . is often used of worship (Ex. 3:12). The verb and its noun derivative 'service'. . . frequently describe Levitical duties in tabernacle and temple worship. . . . 'Take care' [keep] . . . frequently [describes] . . . 'observ-ing' covenant stipulations. For priestly duties it describes the faithful carrying out of God's instructions (Lev. 8:35) and

---

[93] Sailhamer, *Genesis*, 77. Wenham likewise notes, "Many of the features of the garden may also be found in later sanctuaries particularly the tabernacle or Jerusalem temple." Wenham, "Sanctuary Symbolism in the Garden of Eden Story," 399.

[94] Beale, *The Temple and the Church's Mission*, 66–80.

[95] Ibid., 66. See also Gentry, "Kingdom through Covenant," 37–38.

[96] See, for example, Dempster, *Dominion and Dynasty*, 65; Middleton, *A New Heaven and A New Earth*, 42.

caretaking of the tabernacle (Num. 1:53; 18:5). Both terms occur together to describe the charge of the Levites for the tabernacle (Num. 3:7–8; 18:7).[97]

So while the verb translated "work" can "refer to an agricultural task when used by itself (e.g., 2:5; 3:23)," when "these two words . . . occur together in the Old Testament . . . they refer either to Israelites 'serving' God and 'guarding [keeping]' God's word . . . or to priests who 'keep' the 'service' (or 'charge') of the tabernacle."[98] In addition, in most translations, the objects of the verbs "work" and "keep" are usually interpreted as suffixed pronouns translated as "it," with implied reference to either the "garden" or the "ground." Yet, the suffixed pronoun is feminine while "garden" is masculine.[99] As well, concerning a reference to the feminine object "ground," "later in this same narrative (3:23), 'working the ground' is said to be a result of the Fall, and the narrative suggests that the author has intended such a punishment to be seen as an ironic reversal of humanity's original purpose" rather than as a continuation of humanity's initial responsibility.[100] In fact, when the verb translated "work" is used in a religious sense in other places (Ex. 3:12; Num. 3:7–10), "the object of the verb usually refers to what or whom is being worshipped (e.g., Ex. 4:23; 23:33)."[101] Since the author almost certainly does not mean that

[97] Mathews, *Genesis 1–11:26*, 209–10.

[98] Beale, *The Temple and the Church's Mission*, 67. Hamilton agrees, "The language used to describe Adam's 'working and keeping' the garden (Gen. 2:15) is used elsewhere in the Pentateuch to describe the priests' 'working and keeping' the tabernacle. And this language is used for no other purpose." James M. Hamilton Jr., *God's Glory in Salvation through Judgment: A Biblical Theology* (Wheaton, IL: Crossway, 2010), 73. See also, William J. Dumbrell, "Genesis 2:1–17: A Foreshadowing of the New Creation," in *Biblical Theology: Retrospect and Prospect*, ed. Scott J. Hafemann (Downers Grove, IL: IVP, 2001), 59.

[99] Sailhamer, *The Pentateuch as Narrative*, 100.

[100] Ibid., 101.

[101] J. H. Walton, "Eden, Garden of," in *Dictionary of the Old Testament: Pentateuch*, eds. T. Desmond Alexander and David W. Baker (Downers Grove, IL: IVP, 2003), 205–6.

God intended Adam to "worship" either the garden or the ground, then the more likely object of the verbs is God himself.[102] If God is indeed implied as the intended object of the two verbs in Genesis 2:15, then the proper translation would not be "to work [the ground]" but "to worship [God]."[103] Sailhamer advocates this interpretation and concludes, "A more suitable translation of the Hebrew text would be 'to worship and obey.' The man is put in the Garden to worship God and obey him. The man's life in the Garden was to be characterized by worship and obedience; he was to be a priest, not merely a worker and keeper of the Garden."[104] Cassuto notes that this interpretation of the two verbs has a long history within the rabbinic tradition, an interpretation which, Cassuto claims, should not be seen as merely "a homiletical exposition" but rather understood as "the actual meaning of the text."[105] But even if one prefers the more common English translation of these two verbs, the verbs nonetheless retain the priestly connotation which further supports the identification of Adam as a priest within God's tabernacle. As T. Desmond Alexander concludes, man is "appointed first and foremost as a guardian of sacred space; he was not created simply to be a gardener."[106] Therefore, a primary responsibility for humanity within the eternal seventh day is not merely to be an agricultural worker but instead to be a priestly worshipper.[107]

---

[102] In this case, according to Beale, the two verbs are translated not as "infinitives with a feminine pronominal suffix" but rather as "infinitival gerunds." Beale, *The Temple and the Church's Mission*, 67n89.

[103] After considering the textual data, Beale rejects this interpretation (ibid., 68).

[104] Sailhamer, *The Pentateuch as Narrative*, 101.

[105] Cassuto, *A Commentary on the Book of Genesis*, 123. Also see Dumbrell, "Genesis 2:1–17," 60.

[106] Alexander, *From Paradise to the Promised Land*, 124.

[107] Fesko concludes, "Adam's responsibilities in the garden are primarily priestly rather than agricultural." Fesko, *Last Things First*, 71. Fesko also observes, "Adam dwelt in the temple of God, like Samuel, who as a boy was taken to the temple 'that he may appear in the presence of the LORD and dwell there forever' (1 Sam. 1:22) and minister to him (1 Sam. 3:1)" (ibid., 75).

Genesis 2:15 provides further support for understanding Adam as a priest. The verse says that God "put" the man into the garden. The word translated as "put" is only used elsewhere within the Pentateuch in two special ways: either in reference to "God's 'rest' or 'safety,' which he gives to humanity in the land (e.g., Gen. 19:16; Deut. 3:20; 12:10; 25:19)" or in reference to "the 'dedication' of something in the Lord's presence (Ex. 16:33–34; Lev. 16:23; Num. 17:4; Deut. 26:4, 10)."[108] Combining these two aspects, "man is 'put' into the garden, where he can 'rest' and be 'safe,' and man is 'put' into the garden 'in God's presence,' where he can have fellowship with God."[109] The garden tabernacle is a true sanctuary, allowing God's priests to rest safely in his presence in order to know, worship, and obey him. The special presence of God is "the key to the garden,"[110] and God's blessing for Adam and Eve and the possibility of fulfilling their other responsibilities are inseparable from their "experience of the divine presence."[111] Meredith Kline refers to the relationship between the responsibilities of worship and rulership as the relationship between cult and culture. Kline argues that in the eternal seventh day, these two responsibilities exist in "institutional coalescence," as humanity dwells within a "theocratic" kingdom.[112] In that context, these two responsibilities are uniquely fused yet still differentiated, with priestly worship maintaining a priority since "Before man faced the world, sent into it with royal cultural commission, he was confronted with the Presence-Face of his Creator."[113] Therefore, "Priesthood is man's primary office. . . . [the result of] the teleological subordination of the kingly occupation to priest-cultic objectives. In a theocratic context, kingship is an adjunct of priesthood," and "culture was to be oriented and

---

[108] Sailhamer, *Genesis*, 79.
[109] Ibid.
[110] Walton, "Eden, Garden of," 205.
[111] Dumbrell, *Covenant and Creation* (2000), 36.
[112] Kline, *Kingdom Prologue*, 51.
[113] Ibid., 83.

subordinated to the cult."[114] Gentry and Wellum also recognize Adam's need to uphold the "priority of worship" in order to fulfill his other responsibilities since "only when the father-son relationship is nurtured through worship, fellowship, and obedient love will humankind appropriately and properly reflect and represent to the world the kind of kingship and rule intrinsic to God himself."[115] To maintain this priority, God causes man to rest within the safety of His presence in order that man might worship and obey Him.[116] As the image of God, God gives Adam and Eve the fundamental responsibility to be priestly worshippers dwelling in his presence.[117]

Covenant in Genesis 1-2

As established in chapter 1, this book will give special attention to the impact of one's understanding of the overall covenantal structure of Scripture upon how one conceives of the good deeds mission of the New Covenant community. As we consider Genesis 1-2 then, the question naturally arises, "Does Genesis 1-2 portray God as relating to humanity through a covenant relationship?" The strongest reason to answer "no" is the lack of an explicit reference in the text to a covenant. Paul Williamson is one recent interpreter

---

[114] Ibid. 87–88, 89.

[115] Gentry and Wellum, *Kingdom through Covenant*, 212, 216.

[116] Some, like Beale, argue that not only are Adam and Eve to dwell in the temple-garden of God's presence but that they are also responsible to expand the boundaries of the garden (and thereby expand the experience of God's presence in the world). Beale, *The Temple and the Church's Mission*, 82. But others, like Waltke, deny that Adam and Eve were responsible to expand the garden. Waltke, *An Old Testament Theology*, 259.

[117] In addition to man's kingly and priestly roles, Niehaus also suggests that Gen 1–2 hints at a prophetic role for humanity as well since "the man and the woman hear from God and receive instructions from him about the administration of his kingdom on earth. A person who is in such a position, and who receives such instruction (such torah) from God, is later called a prophet. . . . communicat[ing] the *substance* of a prophetic relationship . . . without yet giving that relationship a name." Niehaus, *The Common Grace Covenants*, 63.

who answers "no" because he believes "it is difficult to get past the lack of unambiguous textual warrant for the existence of a covenant between God and Adam," a terminology decision by the biblical author which "must carry considerable significance."[118] The absence of a direct mention of a covenant in Genesis 1–2 leads Williamson to insist that "the burden of proof still rests with those who maintain the existence of such a 'covenant with creation.'"[119]

In response, those who interpret Genesis 1–2 as portraying a covenant explain the lack of overt reference in various ways. One explanation is that the covenant was "established by the fact of creation itself."[120] Therefore, the standard rituals performed by the two members initiating a covenant were not possible "since what was involved was the creation of one of the parties in the relationship."[121] Instead, by his act of creation, God institutes the covenant with humanity, a covenant "requiring no further establishment or confirmation."[122] In contrast to the other biblical covenants, the creation covenant was "in this respect unique."[123] Another explanation is that though the term "covenant" is missing, the relationship outlined "appears covenantal,"[124] containing the "substance" of later biblical covenants.[125] Daniel Elazar notes that both rabbinic Judaism and patristic Christianity see an "implicit" covenant relationship between God and man in Genesis 1–2.[126] As well, in other parts of

---

[118] Paul R. Williamson, *Sealed with an Oath: Covenant in God's Unfolding Purpose* (Downers Grove, IL: IVP, 2007), 58.

[119] Paul R. Williamson, "Covenant," in *New Dictionary of Biblical Theology*, ed. T. Desmond Alexander et al. (Downers Grove, IL: IVP, 2000), 421.

[120] Dumbrell, *Covenant and Creation* (2000), 32.

[121] Gentry and Wellum, *Kingdom through Covenant*, 164.

[122] VanDrunen, *Divine Covenants and Moral Order*, 85.

[123] Kline, *Kingdom Prologue*, 59.

[124] Block, "To Serve and to Keep," 124.

[125] Kline, *Kingdom Prologue*, 15. See also Niehaus, *The Common Grace Covenants*, 37; Garr, *In His Own Image and Likeness*, 227.

[126] Daniel J. Elazar, *Covenant & Polity in Biblical Israel: Biblical Foundations & Jewish Expressions* (New Brunswick, NJ: Transaction, 1995), 111.

Scripture, covenants are referred to at times even "without actually using the word."[127] A third explanation for the lack of "covenant" recognizes that a covenant typically functions to establish a kinship relationship between non-relatives (such as in a marriage).[128] Covenants are appropriate instruments to establish "fictive kinship" in the absence of "natural kinship." So if humanity was created to be in a kinship relationship with God by nature, no covenant was necessary to establish "fictive kinship." A formal covenant is therefore required only after mankind's "natural kinship" relationship with God is altered by sin.[129] This book will adopt the position that it *is* proper to recognize an Adamic Creation Covenant in Genesis 1–2. Yet even in recognizing continuity in God's general mode of relating to humanity (through covenant) both before and after the entrance of sin, the God-directed author's decision not to use "covenant" in Genesis 1–2 should also begin to sensitize us to elements of *discontinuity* between life before and life after sin.

Good Deeds Responsibility

As just asserted, Genesis 1–2 presents all humanity as living in a covenant community of close family relationships and perfect divine provision, with no scarcity of time or material resources. As will be discussed below, the unique circumstances of the eternal seventh day should engender caution when considering any transfer of the responsibilities of that singular setting to new settings. As well, rather than commanding merely the responsibilities of creation care, culture building, and work in general, Genesis 1–2 entrusts humanity with the more fundamental responsibilities of representational rulership, image multiplication, dependent sonship, and priestly worship in God's presence.[130] Instead of an emphasis simply on working

---

[127] Gentry and Wellum, *Kingdom through Covenant*, 177.

[128] Ibid., 132–33.

[129] Sailhamer, *The Meaning of the Pentateuch*, 309.

[130] In contrast, for Ott and Strauss the essence of the human responsibilities

and having children, mankind first and foremost is commanded to dwell with God in dependence, obedience, and worship, displaying a perfectly accurate reflection of God's character to the world through an increasing number of images. If humanity's relationship with God had continued according to the original design, good deeds of love (mankind's good deeds responsibility) would have naturally, necessarily, and perfectly flowed from human to human within the sinless world of the eternal seventh day.

---

of Genesis 1–2 is "to embody and advocate such values as human dignity, family, just government, environmental stewardship, and creative expression." Craig Ott and Stephen J. Strauss, *Encountering Theology of Mission: Biblical Foundations, Historical Developments, and Contemporary Issues* (Grand Rapids: Baker Academic, 2010), 151. Likewise, Cosden claims that "just by working, a person images God." Darrell Cosden, *The Heavenly Good of Earthly Work* (Peabody, MA: Hendrickson, 2006), 141.

5

The Good Deeds Responsibility
of Humanity in Genesis 3–11

Before the entrance of sin, God created Adam and Eve to be his image, designed to live in relationship to him and function perfectly as a multiplying kingdom of worshippers, displaying God's glory to all creation. As noted above, being the image of God is mankind's ontological identity—and as such, cannot be removed. But closely tied with man's nature as the image is the intended function for which God designed his image—that is, the responsibilities of Genesis 1–2. How then did sin affect humanity's functioning as the image of God, including their good deeds responsibility?

The Effect of Sin on Humanity's Good Deeds Responsibility in Genesis 3–7

While Adam and Eve continued to be mirror-images of God by nature, the aftermath of Genesis 3 reveals a broken, distorted mirror, "an *inversion* of the true order of things."[1] Instead of ruling over the animals, the snake rules over them (3:1–5). Rather than beholding God's face and reflecting his kingly glory, Adam and Eve

---

[1] Henri Blocher, *In the Beginning: The Opening Chapters of Genesis* (Downers Grove, IL: IVP, 1984), 142.

disobey his command and hide from his presence (3:6–13).[2] Instead of displaying child-like dependence upon their Father for the knowledge of good and evil and for the provision of the good, they seek to provide the good for themselves and to pursue wisdom apart from God (3:6). Adam and Eve are ejected from the tabernacle of God's presence, barred from God's blessing and from the tree of eternal life (3:22–24). The harmony of the original covenant family becomes a power struggle within the home (3:16) as well as perpetual enmity between the two groups into which humanity is now divided (3:15). Mankind has broken God's covenant and received God's curse, with certain death looming (3:16–19).

Responsibilities Impossible as Originally Intended

After sin, can humanity still fulfill the responsibilities of Genesis 1–2? The first answer is "no." The responsibilities required Adam and Eve to dwell before God within the garden-tabernacle of the eternal seventh day, but now they are "cast out of the sanctuary of God's glorious presence and . . . [are] not able to fulfill the divine commission."[3] Priestly worship, originally the essence of humanity's responsibilities, is now impossible since they are "stripped of their priestly status."[4] East of Eden, the reflection of God's glory is radically marred in the malfunctioning of man's broken nature, such that "man cannot accomplish the work of the first Adam. He cannot

---

[2] Block describes in detail how Gen. 3 "exposes the nature and consequences of false worship." Daniel I. Block, *For the Glory of God: Recovering a Biblical Theology of Worship* (Grand Rapids: Baker Academic, 2014), 58–59.

[3] G. K. Beale, *The Temple and the Church's Mission: A Biblical Theology of the Dwelling Place of God* (Downers Grove, IL: IVP, 2004), 116. Dumbrell agrees that, barred from God's presence, humanity is "now unable to exercise proper dominion over nature." William J. Dumbrell, "Genesis 2:1–17: A Foreshadowing of the New Creation," in *Biblical Theology: Retrospect and Prospect*, ed. Scott J. Hafemann (Downers Grove, IL: IVP, 2001), 64.

[4] T. Desmond Alexander, *From Eden to the New Jerusalem: An Introduction to Biblical Theology* (Grand Rapids: Kregel, 2008), 74.

extract himself from his fallen condition."[5] Mankind lost its "original righteousness"[6] and can no longer "reproduce perfectly the character of the original theocratic-family community of Eden."[7] Fulfilling the responsibilities of Genesis 1–2 is impossible because humanity "cannot reconstruct the perfect world of Paradise, in which sin was not known,"[8] for, as Kuyper proclaims, that world "no longer exists."[9] This discontinuity between the world before sin and the world after means that people *cannot* fulfill their God-given responsibilities as originally intended.[10]

---

[5] J. V. Fesko, *Last Things First: Unlocking Genesis 1–2 with the Christ of Eschatology* (Fearn, Scotland: Christian Focus Publications, 2007), 140. As Beisner concludes, "Every aspect of the image of God in man was corrupted by the Fall." E. Calvin Beisner, *Where the Garden Meets Wilderness: Evangelical Entry into the Environmental Debate* (Grand Rapids: Eerdmans, 1997), 104.

[6] Blocher, *In the Beginning*, 93.

[7] Meredith G. Kline, *Kingdom Prologue: Genesis Foundations for a Covenantal Worldview* (Overland Park, KS: Two Age Press, 2000), 181.

[8] Henry R. Van Til, *The Calvinistic Concept of Culture* (Grand Rapids: Baker, 1959), 59.

[9] Abraham Kuyper, *The Historical Section: Part 1, Noah-Adam*, part 1 in vol. 1 of *Common Grace* (Grand Rapids: CLP Academic, 2013), 19.

[10] Another way to describe this discontinuity in mankind is with the terms "structure" and "direction." Structure corresponds to the man's nature (image) while direction corresponds to humanity's actual functioning. Before sin, Adam and Eve functioned perfectly (direction). According to Van Til, after sin, in "the structure of his creaturehood, man remained the same, but functionally he departed from his original rectitude. The direction of his life was changed; he became derailed as to his true goal in life; he no longer sought God as his chief joy." Van Til, *The Calvinistic Concept of Culture*, 57. See also Albert M. Wolters and Michael W. Goheen, *Creation Regained: Biblical Basics for a Reformational Worldview*, 2nd ed. (Grand Rapids: Eerdmans, 2005), 59. While remaining the image (structure), the fallen image cannot function as originally intended (direction). Fulfilling their original responsibilities is impossible. The traditional Reformed teaching concerning the distinction between the "covenant of works" in Gen 1–2 and the "covenant of grace" thereafter, also communicates the impossibility of man's original mandate.

Responsibilities Possible in an Altered Sense
That Ultimately Produces Judgment

The responsibilities of Genesis 1–2, though impossible as originally intended, are possible in an altered, truncated sense. Genesis 4:16–24 presents Cain and his descendants as bearing children, building cities, and developing culture, all either direct or implied responsibilities given to mankind in Genesis 1–2. Therefore, alongside a discontinuity with the Genesis 1–2 world, the world after sin also reflects a "partial continuity"[11] with the original creation, a combination of discontinuity and continuity that requires making "subtle distinctions."[12] Nonetheless, if we understand man's original responsibilities according to the more robust portrait painted in the previous chapter, then Cain and his descendants clearly fall short of being priestly worshippers dwelling as dependent children in God's presence and being representational rulers whose multiplication increasingly displays God's glory. The work entrusted to Adam and Eve in Genesis 1–2 was intended to please and honor God, but the work of Cain and his descendants is "depraved" and, in the end, produces only God's condemnation and judgment.[13] The statement of Genesis 6:5, "The LORD saw that the wickedness of man was great in the earth, and that every intention of the thoughts of his heart was only evil continually," is God's final assessment of the culture building of Cain and his descendants.[14] Rather than fulfilling the responsibilities of Genesis 1–2, Cain's culture is an effort to "establish a world system hostile and antithetical to the one God intended

---

[11] Kline, *Kingdom Prologue*, 167.

[12] Blocher, *In the Beginning*, 94.

[13] Bruce K. Waltke, *An Old Testament Theology: An Exegetical, Canonical, and Thematic Approach* (Grand Rapids: Zondervan, 2007), 268.

[14] Umberto Cassuto, *A Commentary on the Book of Genesis: Part 1, From Adam to Noah* (Jerusalem: Magnes, 1961), 301. Kaminski agrees that this statement "looks back over the human story, providing its sobering conclusion." Carol M. Kaminski, *Was Noah Good? Finding Favor in the Flood Narrative* (New York: Bloomsbury T&T Clark, 2014), 78.

at creation," a culture whose members and products would be largely destroyed by the flood.[15]

Common grace. Though Cain's culture was ultimately rejected for its wickedness, it also produces numerous goods, such as animal husbandry (4:20), music (4:21), metallurgy (4:22), and an ordered legal system (4:23–24). God's blessing, allowing humanity in spite of their sinfulness to do good and experience some areas of cultural progress in a limited, imperfect sense, is often understood under the label of God's "universal" or "common grace." Common grace is then typically distinguished from "particular" or "special grace."[16] Special grace is saving, redemptive grace, while common grace does not save but only temporarily "preserves nature,"[17] causing "the devastating effects of sin in creation [to be] restrained and counteracted."[18] While common grace "keep[s] a rein on the extreme effects of the common curse . . . restrain[ing] the expression of the evil within man," this gracious work of God "does not eliminate these evils"[19] and "will not bring heaven to earth."[20]

Kuyper was one of the first to popularize the term "common grace," noting that common grace and special grace "in former times . . . never enjoyed separate treatment."[21] Kuyper conceives of common grace as originating in creation (specifically, in Christ's

[15] Eugene H. Merrill, *Everlasting Dominion: A Theology of the Old Testament* (Nashville: B&H, 2006), 222.

[16] When examining God's love as revealed in Scripture, D. A. Carson makes a similar distinction between God's love with regard to all humanity (both his providential love and his yearning, salvific love) and God's love with regard to only some humans (both his elective love and his conditional, covenantal love). D. A. Carson, "Love," in *New Dictionary of Biblical Theology*, ed. T. Desmond Alexander et al. (Downers Grove, IL: IVP, 2000), 648.

[17] David VanDrunen, *Divine Covenants and Moral Order: A Biblical Theology of Natural Law* (Grand Rapids: Eerdmans, 2014), 34.

[18] Wolters and Goheen, *Creation Regained*, 60.

[19] Kline, *Kingdom Prologue*, 178.

[20] Michael Horton, *Introducing Covenant Theology* (Grand Rapids: Baker, 2006), 115.

[21] Kuyper, *The Historical Section*, 13.

work as the "mediator of creation"), while special grace originates in redemption (specifically in Christ's work as "mediator of redemption").[22] Kuyper's colleague, Herman Bavinck, also identifies shared human cultures in this age as "not the product of redemption or biblical revelation but a given of creation . . . a gift of divine providence."[23] Making this distinction between a creational and a redemptive orientation allows Kuyper to recognize intrinsic, stand-alone value for the developments and accomplishments of general human culture which arise from common grace, even if such cultures ultimately produce no saving benefit to their members.[24] Cultural development is therefore an inherent (though limited) good which requires no direct connection to redemption to be validated. But even if God's common grace and the human culture it produces is not itself directly salvific, it *is* "put into the service of redemption" since it "make[s] possible an interim historical environment as the theater for a program of redemption."[25] As well, this grace, though non-saving and given by God in various measure to all humanity, is nonetheless still *God's* grace, creating a realm of general human blessings which is still under God's rulership and "by no means, a neutral space."[26]

---

[22] Van Til, *The Calvinistic Concept of Culture*, 134. Van Drunen argues that, though using new terminology such as "common grace," Kuyper is largely in continuity with the traditional Reformed position in rooting social and political life in the creational rather than redemptive realm. David VanDrunen, *Natural Law and the Two Kingdoms: A Study in the Development of Reformed Social Thought* (Grand Rapids: Eerdmans, 2010), 276–315.

[23] John Bolt, *Economic Shalom: A Reformed Primer on Faith, Work, and Human Flourishing* (Grand Rapids: Christian's Library Press, 2013), 17. Kline refers to common grace as having a "creational rootage" but not a redemptive one. Kline, *Kingdom Prologue*, 157.

[24] Van Til observes that "Kuyper was not always consistent in holding to the independent and self-sufficient purpose of common grace." Van Til, *The Calvinistic Concept of Culture*, 119.

[25] Kline, *Kingdom Prologue*, 156, 155.

[26] James Davison Hunter, *To Change the World: The Irony, Tragedy, and Possibility of Christianity in the Late Modern World* (New York: Oxford, 2010),

Though the "cultural mandate" as initially instituted in Genesis 1–2 cannot be fulfilled in the world after sin's entrance and though general humanity as portrayed in Genesis 3–6 is not given specific new responsibilities from God, the common grace work of family life and building human culture as recounted in Genesis 4:17–24 may imply a "common grace cultural mandate" for mankind.[27] According to Kline, "certain functional and institutional provisions of the original mandate are resumed in the common grace order," even if these human responsibilities must still be clearly distinguished from those of Genesis 1–2 since they "now have such a different orientation, particularly as to objectives."[28] As a result, the city building of Genesis 4 produces only "the merely horizontal city of man" rather than the holy city of God which the mandate of Genesis 1–2 was intended to produce.[29] Consequently, if Genesis 3–6 implies a "common grace cultural mandate," it only includes "obligations for things that serve to preserve [human] existence and to promote a limited and penultimate flourishing within this present creation," instead of the perfect and ultimate human flourishing for which the world of Genesis 1–2 was designed.[30] This duty for fallen man to pursue a limited and penultimate human flourishing, this "common grace cultural mandate," is then essentially equivalent to what this book is labeling the "good deeds responsibility of humanity."

---

233. Horton emphasizes that God's works of creation (and preservation) and redemption are "distinct, but not separate." Michael S. Horton, *Where in the World Is the Church? A Christian View of Culture and Your Role in It* (Phillipsburg, NJ: P&R Publishing, 2002), 183.

[27] Kline, *Kingdom Prologue*, 199.

[28] Ibid., 156.

[29] Ibid., 271.

[30] VanDrunen, *Divine Covenants and Moral Order*, 35.

Responsibilities Possible in an Altered Sense That Ultimately Accompanies Salvation

The question remains, are none of the more fundamental, God-oriented responsibilities of Genesis 1–2 possible in a corrupted world? According to the text, the line of Cain is not the only line of descent existing in the world after mankind is ejected from Eden. In Genesis 4:26, Seth is presented as the start of a parallel line, one which, in contrast to Cain's line, consists of those who "call upon the name of the LORD" (the author, strikingly, using God's covenant name as later known by Israel).[31] This line includes Enoch and Noah, who both "walked with God" (Gen. 5:22, 24; 6:9). Enoch, in fact, escapes the curse of death as "God took him" (Gen. 5:24). Noah's father Lamech believes that his son will "give us rest from our work and from the toil of our hands arising from the ground which the LORD has cursed" (Gen. 5:29 NASB), bringing to mind the "rest" experienced in the eternal seventh day. Noah "found favor in the eyes of the LORD" and is "a righteous man, blameless in his generation" (Gen. 6:8–9). All of these details combine to confirm that "the distinctive characteristic of those who are listed in Genesis 5 is clearly that they are God's people."[32] Jeffrey Niehaus labels Seth as the progenitor of the "elect line" while Cain begins the "nonelect line," with Seth's descendants given "greater prominence" within the narrative than Cain's.[33]

Following the categories of Genesis 3:15, Seth's line can also be understood as the "seed of the woman," while Cain's line can be understood as the "seed of the serpent." According to Bruce Waltke, "The contrast and struggle between the two seeds is the

[31] Sailhamer states that "at least as far as the line of Seth was concerned, these men, like Abraham after them, are described as true worshippers of the covenant God." John Sailhamer, *The Pentateuch as Narrative: A Biblical-Theological Commentary* (Grand Rapids: Zondervan, 1992), 116.

[32] Kline, *Kingdom Prologue*, 190.

[33] Jeffrey J. Niehaus, *The Common Grace Covenants*, vol. 1 of *Biblical Theology* (Wooster, OH: Weaver Book Company, 2014), 125, 157.

central theme of the book of Genesis."[34] In the world of the Genesis narratives, "people are either seed of the serpent, on the side of the snake in the garden, or seed of the woman, on the side of God and trusting in his promises."[35] While Seth's line is still barred from God's Edenic presence, they nonetheless exhibit toward God the kind of trust, obedience, and ethical righteousness which was at the heart of humanity's responsibilities in Genesis 1–2. Being priestly worshippers had been sinless humanity's primary responsibility, making it noteworthy that the descriptions of Seth's line in Genesis 5–6 may imply "an organized system of worship."[36] Interestingly, the author seems to present Noah's building of the ark in Genesis 6 as parallel to "the account of Creation in Genesis 1 and the building of the tabernacle in Exodus 25–39."[37] In a sense, during the flood, Noah, with the animals under his rulership, is portrayed as dwelling in God's special presence in the tabernacle of the ark, approximating mankind's original Edenic role more fully than was possible for Cain's line and the culture which it produced.[38] Cain's culture leads only to God's final judgment in the flood, while Noah, heir of a long lineage of worshippers, experiences salvation from judgment.

Special grace. While Seth's line shares many common grace blessings with Cain's line, God's rescue of Noah and his family illustrates that they also uniquely experience God's special, saving grace.

---

[34] Waltke, *An Old Testament Theology*, 325.

[35] James M. Hamilton Jr., *God's Glory in Salvation through Judgment: A Biblical Theology* (Wheaton, IL: Crossway, 2010), 84. Waltke observes, "After the Fall, humanity is divided into two communities: the elect, who love God and pray to the one God as King over all, and the reprobate, who love self . . . and seek to dethrone God from his rightful place and usurp his authority." Waltke, *An Old Testament Theology*, 281. See also Alexander, *From Eden to the New Jerusalem*, 107.

[36] Blocher, *In the Beginning*, 208. See also Block, *For the Glory of God*, 59.

[37] Sailhamer, *The Pentateuch as Narrative*, 125.

[38] Although the fact that Noah's life later ends with the refrain "and he died" (9:29)—unlike Enoch (5:23–24), but just like the rest of his ancestors (5:5, 8, 11, 14, 17, 20, 27, 31)—illustrates that the line of Seth still lives "east of Eden."

God's rule over his creation through the dual channels of common grace and special grace corresponds to the OT's "important distinction between the sovereignty and rule of God over the entire creation and the coming of [his] *saving reign*."[39] This understanding of God's kingdom as administered through two distinct orders has traditionally been designated by the terms *regi a Deo* ("a kingdom of God in which all creation is subject to God as king") and *regnare cum Deo* ("a kingdom of God consisting only of those who willingly submit to God as king").[40] While this doctrine is sometimes referred to as "two kingdoms," Luther, for instance, spoke more precisely of "two governments (*Regimenten*), not two kingdoms (*Reichen*), showing that we are dealing not with two spheres but with two modes of the divine rule."[41] Such careful distinctions help emphasize that the common grace and special grace aspects of God's rule are distinct but connected, neither to be divorced nor confused.[42]

The demonstration of special grace in Noah's life is displayed not only in Noah's salvation from the flood but also in the "righteous" life he lives in contrast to his contemporaries (Gen. 6:9). The word translated "righteous" refers to "Noah's conduct in his relationship with God . . . [conduct which] was based upon conformity to God's way out of his commitment to God."[43] "Righteous" is one of the "crucial terms for understanding biblical ethics," a word whose usage "combines piety and ethics" and is often correlated with "justice."[44]

---

[39] Peter J. Gentry and Stephen J. Wellum, *Kingdom through Covenant: A Biblical-Theological Understanding of the Covenants* (Wheaton, IL: Crossway, 2012), 593. Original emphasis.

[40] John H. Sailhamer, *The Meaning of the Pentateuch: Revelation, Composition, and Interpretation* (Downers Grove, IL: IVP Academic, 2009), 582.

[41] Donald G. Bloesch, *The Invaded Church* (Waco, TX: Word, 1975), 59.

[42] Horton, *Introducing Covenant Theology*, 17. See also Kline, *Kingdom Prologue*, 160. VanDrunen provides a compelling historical overview of the two kingdoms doctrine within the Reformed tradition. VanDrunen, *Natural Law and the Two Kingdoms*.

[43] Gentry and Wellum, *Kingdom through Covenant*, 151.

[44] Waltke, *An Old Testament Theology*, 289.

Rather than abstract and impersonal, such righteousness "tends to be relational and concrete."[45] Within Scripture, a right relationship with God not only describes a person's relational faithfulness and God-centered moral rectitude, but is also used to speak of a right relationship between God and the whole created order, infusing the biblical concept of "righteousness" with a "creational basis . . . [which] brings with it the notion of universal norms," including verses where "the establishment of righteousness is envisaged as the renewal of the created order and its elements."[46] The standards by which Noah is judged "righteous" are ultimately the standards which apply to all humanity and which are even intended to character-ize the whole natural world. According to these standards, Noah is "blameless" (Gen. 6:9), a word which describes him as one whose life is "characterized by integrity, endowed with a strong character with the will to refrain from sin," a life whose contrast to the life-styles of the surrounding culture can only be explained by special grace.[47] Noah's special relationship with God as the explanation for his countercultural lifestyle is confirmed when the author states that "Noah walked with God" (Gen. 6:9), implying "agreement and com-munion with God" as well as "teaching by God."[48] While the original responsibilities of Genesis 1–2 still remain impossible for humanity in a fallen world, Noah's life and the line of Seth indicate that those who "walk with God," receiving his special grace, are empowered to live lives which partially and imperfectly express the God-centered life of worship, trusting obedience, and loving service for which God designed mankind.

---

[45] Mark A. Seifrid, "Righteousness, Justice, and Justification," in *New Dictionary of Biblical Theology*, ed. T. Desmond Alexander et al. (Downers Grove, IL: IVP, 2000), 740.

[46] Ibid., 741.

[47] Waltke, *An Old Testament Theology*, 289.

[48] Ibid.

The Good Deeds Responsibility of Humanity in Genesis 8–11

While the labors of Cain's line produces a faint and hollow echo of the vision originally assigned to humanity, Seth's descendants more accurately reveal a way of life with a fundamentally Godward orientation, including as seen in good deeds which manifested "righteousness." With the destruction of Cain's line in the flood and the solitary survival of Seth's line, did humanity's obligations before God, including their good deeds responsibility, change or develop in any way?

New Creation, New Adam, New Covenant with a New Mandate

God's work of causing the waters of the flood to recede from the land in Genesis 8 is presented by the author in the garb of a new creation, "a virtual second creation event."[49] Gentry asserts that both "linguistic usage" and "literary techniques such as key words, dominant ideas, parallel sequences of actions, and similar themes clearly link the Noah narrative to the creation narrative in Genesis 1 and 2."[50] In Genesis 8:1, we read, "God made a wind blow over the earth, and the waters subsided," the author apparently alluding to "the Spirit of God hover[ing] over the waters of the original chaotic deep" in Genesis 1:2.[51] Additionally, in both the portrayal of the original creation and of the post-flood re-emergence of the land, the removal of the waters is immediately followed by the appearance of vegetation (Gen. 1:11–12; 8:10–11).[52] Waltke also describes how within the Old Testament, "Adam and Noah are uniquely associated with the 'image of God,' an expression found only in Genesis

---

[49] Kline, *Kingdom Prologue*, 221.

[50] Peter J. Gentry, "Kingdom through Covenant: Humanity as the Divine Image," *Southern Baptist Journal of Theology* 12, no. 1 (Spring 2008): 21.

[51] Ibid. See also Stephen G. Dempster, *Dominion and Dynasty: A Biblical Theology of the Hebrew Bible* (Downers Grove, IL: IVP, 2003), 73.

[52] Gentry, "Kingdom through Covenant, 21.

1:26–28 and 9:6. . . . God commands both Adam and Noah to 'be fruitful and increase in number.' . . . Both Adam and Noah 'walk with God' . . . Both Adam and Noah rule the animals . . . Adam names the animals; the restored Adam saves them."[53] Through these and other parallels, the author seems to intend for the reader to see the world after the flood as a kind of new creation within which Noah is cast as a new Adam.[54]

Above, this book adopted the title "Adamic Creation Covenant" to describe how God related to humanity within the world of Genesis 1–2. Notably, God also relates to the new Adam in the new creation through a new covenant. Like the Adamic Creation Covenant, this new covenant is universal in its scope as God institutes it with all humanity (Noah and his descendants, 9:8–9) and with "every living creature" (9:10). Unlike the Adamic Creation Covenant, this new covenant is designed for a fallen world, a covenant which, in spite of mankind's ongoing sin (8:21), will continue "while the earth remains" (8:22). Gentry unequivocally states, "The covenant with Noah is in effect today. The promises and future statements made by God employ an emphatic negative 'never again' four times . . . There is no evidence anywhere in the completed canon of Scripture as a whole that this covenant has been annulled or superseded."[55] From an earlier era, Kuyper likewise places "heavy emphasis" on the "incontrovertible" truth that the covenant of Genesis 9 is still in effect for mankind.[56] Accepting this conclusion, one can see that although both covenants share a universal human and creational orientation, the covenant with Adam is no longer possible for man to fulfill, while, in contrast, the covenant with Noah is still in effect.

---

[53] Waltke, *An Old Testament Theology*, 296.

[54] Ibid. See also W. J. Dumbrell, *Covenant and Creation: A Theology of the Old Testament Covenants* (Carlisle, UK: Paternoster, 2000), 43; Kenneth A. Mathews, *Genesis 1–11:26*, The New American Commentary, vol. 1A (Nashville: B&H, 1996), 414.

[55] Gentry and Wellum, *Kingdom through Covenant*, 171.

[56] Kuyper, *The Historical Section*, 44.

Since the covenant with Noah therefore exhibits both continuity and discontinuity with the Adamic Creation Covenant, this book will employ the title "Noahic *Fallen* Creation Covenant" as a means of indicating both continuity and discontinuity.

The Relationship between Genesis 1–2 and Genesis 9

The two covenants give other indications of an interrelationship of both continuity and discontinuity. A closer look at this interrelationship is necessary, in particular because the covenant with Noah has "seldom received much scholarly attention,"[57] a reflection of "its more tenuous links with a salvation history whose primary focus is God's dealings with Israel."[58] The unmistakable continuity between the two covenants is seen in multiple aspects. First, all mankind is still the covenant partner, and all mankind is still the image of God (9:6), unique within creation in nature, relationship to God, and assigned responsibilities. Second, humanity's Noahic Fallen Creation Covenant task, like that given to Adam, includes the commands to "be fruitful and multiply and fill the earth" (9:1, 7). As the commands of Genesis 1:28 were expressed in the form of God's blessing, so "God blessed Noah" (9:1). Third, the arena within which these tasks will be discharged remains the entire created order, including mankind's continued authority over the animals (9:2).

But while it is correct to identify continuity between the covenants, it is a mistake to ignore discontinuity, thereby in any way suggesting that "the fall has had no effect upon the original dominion mandate."[59] For instance, while humanity is the partner in both covenants, at the institution of the Noahic Fallen Creation Covenant, mankind is already fallen from the sinless state originally occupied by Adam and Eve. In spite of Noah's special-grace-enabled

---

[57] Scott W. Hahn, *Kinship by Covenant: A Canonical Approach to the Fulfillment of God's Saving Promises* (New Haven, CT: Yale University, 2009), 9.

[58] Paul R. Williamson, *Sealed with an Oath: Covenant in God's Unfolding Purpose* (Downers Grove, IL: IVP, 2007), 60.

[59] Fesko, *Last Things First*, 169.

"righteousness," after the flood God confirms that the continued baseline for Noah and his descendants is the reality that "the intention of man's heart is evil from his youth" (8:21). This statement confirms that "human nature is indelibly marked by sin,"[60] such that, notwithstanding the new beginning, "human nature has not changed."[61] If, as argued above, the Adamic Creation Covenant became impossible for humanity to fulfill after sin, in part because it required a sinless covenant partner, then the radically altered covenant partner of the Noahic Fallen Creation Covenant implies that it is also a radically altered covenant, making necessary the conclusion that "Gen. 9 is not simply a replay of Gen. 1."[62]

Not only is the covenant partner changed, the covenant task entrusted to him is also no longer the same. Some, like Christopher Wright, do not appear to see this discontinuity, claiming that "the human task remains the same."[63] Gentry and Wellum also propose that "Noah is recommissioned with all of the ordinances given at creation to Adam and Eve and their family."[64] But almost immediately, Gentry and Wellum qualify this statement with a recognition of discontinuity by describing Noah's task as "Adam's mandate modified somewhat to suit the circumstances of a fallen world."[65] One modification to the task of fruitful multiplication was already revealed in Genesis 3:16 where Eve is told that the pain involved in childbearing will "multiply." While humanity is still given a multiplication mandate, "the difficulty of carrying it out has increased."[66] Additionally, as argued above, the original task of image multiplication in Eden is

---

[60] Dempster, *Dominion and Dynasty*, 73.

[61] Alexander, *From Eden to the New Jerusalem*, 29.

[62] Victor P. Hamilton, *The Book of Genesis: Chapters 1–17* (Grand Rapids: Eerdmans, 1990), 313.

[63] Christopher J. H. Wright, *The Mission of God: Unlocking the Bible's Grand Narrative* (Downers Grove, IL: IVP Academic, 2006), 327.

[64] Gentry and Wellum, *Kingdom through Covenant*, 163.

[65] Ibid., 165.

[66] Robin Routledge, *Old Testament Theology: A Thematic Approach* (Downers Grove, IL: IVP Academic, 2008), 156.

much more than mere childbearing but requires the reproduction of perfectly God-glorifying images. For Noah and his descendants, this task is impossible since "the intention of man's heart is evil from his youth" (8:21). Noah's task of multiplying sinners cannot be directly equated with Adam's task of multiplying sinless worshippers.

The dominion which God called Adam to exercise over the animal kingdom also underwent significant adjustments for Noah. Whereas in Eden, "humans and other living creatures were to live in harmony, in a peaceful hierarchy based on a common vegetarianism," man's rulership now requires God to cause animals to fear man (9:2).[67] Rather than the perfect dominion of Genesis 1–2, humanity will exert a "fearful domination" over the animals.[68] This rulership also "permit[s] mankind to be carnivorous at the expense of the creatures over which he was created to rule," a change which was among "the dreadful alterations" of the human/animal relationship.[69] Another alteration to the human rulership over the animals in the Noahic Fallen Creation Covenant is that not only may a human legitimately kill an animal for food, an animal may at times wrongly kill a human, requiring the death of that animal (9:5), all of which is "radically different from the ideal of Gen. 1."[70] As well, human dominion in the post-flood world requires "the new and necessary institution of a sword-wielding government," since man's unique status as God's image requires the retributive death of all who murder, a problem unknown in Eden.[71] Finally, while, on the one hand, humanity's dominion over animals is significantly altered in the Noahic Fallen Creation Covenant, on the other hand, the command

---

[67] Daniel J. Elazar, *Covenant & Polity in Biblical Israel: Biblical Foundations & Jewish Expressions* (New Brunswick, NJ: Transaction, 1995), 113.

[68] Kevin DeYoung and Greg Gilbert, *What Is the Mission of the Church? Making Sense of Social Justice, Shalom, and the Great Commission* (Wheaton, IL: Crossway, 2011), 211.

[69] Merrill, *Everlasting Dominion*, 240.

[70] Hamilton, *The Book of Genesis*, 314.

[71] DeYoung and Gilbert, *What Is the Mission of the Church?*, 211.

of Genesis 1:28 to "subdue [the earth]" is "entirely missing [in Genesis 9], suggesting that the task [as originally intended] has by now become impossible."[72] These textual details combine to demonstrate how, along with continuity between Adam and Noah's tasks, a substantial discontinuity exists, with the result that Noah's covenant task is "considerably muted" in comparison to Adam's.[73]

Not only do the covenant partners and their covenant tasks exhibit discontinuity, so do the arenas within which each covenant is to be lived out. The sinless creation of Genesis 1–2 is radically different from the "changed world in which [Noah] is summoned to operate."[74] Whereas God completed the work of the original creation and declared it "very good" (1:31), upon completing the work of the "new" creation in Genesis 8 and 9, God does not offer a comparable assessment of the post-flood world.[75] Even more significantly, as proposed above, the Adamic Creation Covenant required humanity to dwell in the tabernacle of God's Edenic presence. Since mankind is now forbidden from entrance to that presence (3:23–24), the arena within which the Noahic Fallen Creation Covenant is to be performed is also radically distinct from Adam's original covenant arena.

Along with a different covenant partner, tasks, and arena, the Noahic Fallen Creation Covenant has a different covenant goal. Though the need for "redemption" and "salvation" was absent in the sinless world administered by the Adamic Creation Covenant, the relationship with God which the post-fall experience of redemption and salvation provides humanity (partially in the present, fully in the future) is in many ways a reestablishment of the relationship with God which mankind enjoyed in Eden. In Genesis 1–2, God provided for all of Adam and Eve's needs, including eternal life (2:9; 3:22). Therefore, while labeling the Adamic Creation Covenant as "redemptive" is anachronistic, for the purpose of this book, we will

---

[72] Routledge, *Old Testament Theology*, 156.
[73] VanDrunen, *Divine Covenants and Moral Order*, 119.
[74] Dumbrell, *Covenant and Creation* (2000), 27.
[75] VanDrunen, *Divine Covenants and Moral Order*, 105.

categorize it as such, since it not only provided Adam and Eve with temporal provision and preservation but also with eternal "salvation" and abundant life in God's presence.

Is the Noahic Fallen Creation Covenant also both preservational and redemptive? Frame answers that "God's covenant with Noah is an administration of God's redemptive grace, religious through and through."[76] Dumbrell agrees and offers two reasons why he believes this covenant includes both goals. First, he believes that the biblical portrait of God's future redemption as a new creation indicates a close connection between creation and redemption. Second, since 1 Peter 3:20–22 states that God's rescue of Noah from the flood is a picture of salvation, therefore the Noahic Fallen Creation Covenant is both preservational and redemptive.[77] The problem with this argument is that while Peter uses Noah and his family's rescue from the flood as an illustration of salvation (and baptism), Peter never refers to the post-flood covenant *itself* as portraying salvation. As well, establishing that God's works of creation and redemption are connected in a general or eschatological sense does not prove Dumbrell's contention that the historical covenant with Noah itself must then be considered salvific. Instead, the better conclusion is that the Noahic Fallen Creation Covenant, unlike the Adamic Creation Covenant, is strictly preservational and broadly providential rather than also directly offering salvation from sin. The post-flood covenant "presumes the presence of sin and evil" and "promises only to manage sin and mitigate its effects, not to eliminate it or to forgive its perpetrators."[78] Kuyper is among those who see Noah's covenant as having "only a temporal reach, promis[ing] nothing but a natural good."[79] According to Kuyper, understanding this covenant in a directly "redemptive way is therefore preposterous.

[76] John Frame, *The Escondido Theology: A Reformed Response to the Two Kingdoms Theology* (Lakeland, FL: Whitefield Media Productions, 2011), 137.

[77] Dumbrell, *Covenant and Creation* (2000), 39–41.

[78] VanDrunen, *Divine Covenants and Moral Order*, 106.

[79] Kuyper, *The Historical Section*, 35.

. . . just as impossible as it would be for you to identify creation itself as redemptive."[80] To further buttress his argument, Kuyper notes that Calvin also did not see the Noahic covenant as saving.[81] But identifying the Noahic Fallen Creation Covenant as *itself* non-redemptive does not require also postulating its complete disconnection from God's work of salvation. Instead, the covenant with Noah "creates a firm stage of history where God can work out his plan for rescuing his fallen world."[82] From the view of Scripture, this covenant "provides the biblical-theological framework within which all subsequent divine-human covenants operate."[83]

Earlier in this chapter, this book introduced the categories "common grace" and "special grace," which correspond directly to the question of the Noahic covenant's status as either redemptive or merely preservational. Taking the covenant as preservational rather than salvific, Michael Horton concludes that the Noahic Fallen Creation Covenant is the biblical covenant "most clearly related to common grace."[84] Rather than producing redemption, this common grace covenant only "defines a provisional world order under God's general kingly governance," whose "benefits were not the redemptive blessings of God's eternal kingdom" and whose "penalties were not the eternal or directly inflicted judgments of God but temporal judgments administered through the state as authorized judiciary."[85]

---

[80] Ibid., 33.

[81] Ibid., 27.

[82] Gentry and Wellum, *Kingdom through Covenant*, 169. See also Scott J. Hafemann, "The Covenant Relationship," in *Central Themes in Biblical Theology: Mapping Unity in Diversity*, eds. Scott J. Hafemann and Paul R. House (Grand Rapids: Baker, 2007), 29; Aaron Chalmers, "The Importance of the Noahic Covenant to Biblical Theology," *Tyndale Bulletin* 60, no. 2 (2009): 209; Kline, *Kingdom Prologue*, 262.

[83] Williamson, *Sealed with an Oath*, 68.

[84] Horton, *Introducing Covenant Theology*, 113. See also Arthur F. Glasser, *Announcing the Kingdom: The Story of God's Mission in the Bible* (Grand Rapids: Baker Academic, 2003), 50.

[85] Kline, *Kingdom Prologue*, 246, 261.

Therefore, the Noahic Fallen Creation Covenant is a covenant of common or universal grace through which God administers his universal reign over all creation. Despite Sailhamer's suggestion that "the idea of a covenant is far too narrow to suit its identification with the universal reign of God"[86] and though the relationship between God's works of common and special grace is often cast as "creation" *versus* "covenant," Charles Scobie counters correctly that the Bible "speaks of *a covenant belonging to the created order*" as well as of the covenant(s) of special grace.[87]

Niehaus agrees that the Noahic Fallen Creation Covenant is strictly a common grace covenant. But Niehaus also believes that the Adamic Creation Covenant is likewise only a common grace covenant.[88] In Niehaus' interpretation, after the flood "the Adamic and Noahic covenants have constituted one legal package under which all humans have lived and will continue to live until the eschaton."[89] Niehaus rightly emphasizes the discontinuity between the goals of common and special grace covenants as seen "in their provisions and in their promises."[90] Yet in labeling both the Adamic and Noahic covenants as purely common grace in orientation, Niehaus highlights only the continuity between them. As an illustration of his one-sided emphasis on continuity, Niehaus rejects the traditional Reformed distinction between the Adamic covenant as a "covenant of works" and the later covenants (including the Noahic) as "covenants of grace," in part because he believes this conception "obscures" the continuity between the Adamic and Noahic covenants.[91] A key

---

[86] Sailhamer, *The Meaning of the Pentateuch*, 582.

[87] Charles H. H. Scobie, *The Ways of Our God: An Approach to Biblical Theology* (Grand Rapids: Eerdmans, 2003), 153. VanDrunen agrees that "the natural *is* a covenantal reality." VanDrunen, *Divine Covenants and Moral Order*, 13.

[88] Hafemann appears to share Niehaus' view of the Adamic and Noahic covenants as both strictly covenants of common grace. Hafemann, "The Covenant Relationship," 29.

[89] Niehaus, *The Common Grace Covenants*, 32.

[90] Ibid., 225.

[91] Ibid., 224.

factor explaining Niehaus' singular focus on continuity is his identification of common grace covenants mainly on the basis of the
universal scope of their membership (all humanity) in contrast to
the narrowed scope of special grace covenants (a particular people).[92]
But Niehaus' categorization of the Adamic Creation Covenant as
merely common grace in orientation is inadequate if common grace
covenants are also identified by their goals of temporal preservation and general providence, in contrast to the eternal and salvific
goals additionally a part of special grace covenants. As argued above,
even though universal in scope, the goals of the Adamic Creation
Covenant also included the eternal provision of benefits similar to
those received in salvation and redemption. Therefore, the Adamic
should not be categorized as just a common grace covenant since
its "redemptive" goal distinguishes it from the merely preservational
goal of the Noahic Fallen Creation Covenant.

Humanity's Good Deeds Responsibility

The identification of the Noahic Fallen Creation Covenant
members, tasks, arena, and goals (compared and contrasted to those
of the Adamic Creation Covenant) allows us now to narrow in on
the question of humanity's ongoing good deeds responsibility under
the covenant established with Noah. Elazar believes that "Genesis 9
is one of the key chapters of the whole Bible . . . [since it describes]
the foundation for the moral obligations of all humans."[93] Though
Jonathan Burnside is correct that the basis of "moral truth" in the
biblical worldview is "presented as a matter of personal relationship
with God," his conclusion that this fact complicates "any straightforward claim to universalism" in Scripture is unnecessary since the
Noahic covenant *does* situate all humanity in a covenant relationship

[92] Ibid., 223. Niehaus slightly qualifies this position by recognizing that
the initial members of both Adam's and Noah's covenants are in some sense
simultaneously universal and particular (ibid., 34).

[93] Elazar, *Covenant and Polity*, 111.

with God, even if this common grace relationship must be distinguished from special grace covenant relationships.[94] One "good deed" that humanity is clearly responsible for under Noah's covenant is childbearing and the promotion of ongoing family life (9:1, 7). As well, the provision of food for oneself and others, including the management of animals as a food source, could also be labeled as a "good deed" for which man is responsible (9:2–4).

Genesis 9:5–6 reveals a third good deed responsibility, one described by Randall Garr as mankind's "royal duty to champion divine justice."[95] According to Gentry and Wellum, the justice expected of man under Noah's covenant is "retributive justice," which is roughly equivalent to "the *lex talionis*, the fundamental principle of retribution in the Torah."[96] Because of their ongoing identity as God's image, humanity "shares in God's own authority to punish lawlessness and, thus, curb and counteract violence. . . . [being] legally empowered to police itself. . . . [with the] divine authority to punish, correct, and protect the self and community alike. . . . [as] a sovereign power, legal guardian, and executor of justice."[97] But this responsibility to execute justice is not a vigilante justice, entrusted merely to individuals or *ad hoc* groups, but is granted to the community as a whole.[98] Kuyper therefore argues that the Noahic Fallen

---

[94] Jonathan Burnside, *God, Justice, and Society: Aspects of Law and Legality in the Bible* (Oxford: Oxford, 2011), 98. Even while sounding a stronger-than-necessary note of caution concerning the discovery of a universal moral ethic within the biblical worldview, Burnside's identification of just such universal ethics, in the Noahic covenant, Gen 1–11 as a whole, and other parts of Scripture, essentially agrees with the conclusions of this book (ibid., 76–77).

[95] W. Randall Garr, *In His Own Image and Likeness: Humanity, Divinity, and Monotheism* (Boston: Brill, 2003), 158. In addition to all humanity's general responsibility for justice, Glasser notes that rabbinic Judaism also emphasizes additional "Noachide commandments," including the demand to refrain from idolatry, incest and adultery, blasphemy, and other "inhumane conduct, such as eating flesh of a living animal." Glasser, *Announcing the Kingdom*, 50.

[96] Gentry and Wellum, *Kingdom through Covenant*, 166–67.

[97] Garr, *In His Own Image and Likeness*, 162–63.

[98] Gentry and Wellum, *Kingdom through Covenant*, 167.

Creation Covenant establishes "government and capital punishment."[99] But since the Noahic covenant provides common grace not special grace, only "justice is the concern of the state, not justification."[100] Under this covenant, humanity is responsible for the good deed of establishing and maintaining human governments which punish with proportionality the evil committed by man against man and which wisely uphold and promote the good.

Some measure of imperfect justice through the institution of human government is possible in a fallen world because, as Greg Forster claims, to varying degrees, God "equip[s] all people with a desire for natural justice."[101] According to VanDrunen, this desire for natural justice is reflective of a "natural law" which is grounded in the Noahic Fallen Creation Covenant, thereby allowing this law to be universal in relevance while also distinctly divine in origin and administration.[102] VanDrunen describes the responsibilities of this Noahic natural law (already noted above) as "a basic, minimal ethic designed for the preservation of the social order."[103] VanDrunen argues that "procreation, eating of plants and animals humanely, and pursuit of proportionate retributive justice with forbearance" are responsibilities which "people across cultural divides customarily practice . . . however imperfectly . . . evidence of an enduring human instinct toward these society-preserving activities" (128). But VanDrunen goes on to propose that the Noahic covenant "also

[99] Kuyper, *The Historical Section*, 81.

[100] Kline, *Kingdom Prologue*, 179.

[101] Greg Forster, *Joy for the World: How Christianity Lost Its Cultural Influence and Can Begin Rebuilding It* (Wheaton, IL: Crossway, 2014), 272.

[102] VanDrunen, *Divine Covenants and Moral Order*, 13. Bockmuehl clarifies that this conception of "natural law" as originating in and administered by God must be differentiated from natural law understood as an autonomously functioning "moral authority in nature that is somehow distinct from [the authority] of God himself." Markus Bockmuehl, *Jewish Law in Gentile Churches: Halakhah and the Beginning of Christian Public Ethics* (Grand Rapids: Baker Academic, 2000), 110.

[103] VanDrunen, *Divine Covenants and Moral Order*, 19.

hints at a broader cultural responsibility" (19). This implication of a wider responsibility follows from the recognition that carrying out the minimalistic ethic of Genesis 9 requires humanity to "form a broad range of social structures and engage in a range of other activities, through the exercise of wisdom" (123). This "richer and thicker ethic . . . requires social institutions such as family and state, human industry, generosity toward fellow human beings . . . [and suggests the possibility of a] penultimate human flourishing . . . through the blessing of common grace" (129). Therefore, we should conceive of this Noahic natural law not primarily as "a series of discrete rules" but instead more broadly and fundamentally as "a moral order pervading the created world and obligating human beings to live within its bounds" (187).

Later Evidence of Noahic Natural Law

Do later OT texts confirm the idea of an inherent Noahic ethic embedded in the natural world? John Barton observes that "obedience to the declared will of God" remains "probably the strongest model for ethical obligation in most books of the Hebrew Scriptures"—though these commands are largely directed toward Abraham and his descendants alone rather than toward all humanity.[104] Barton associates the rule-keeping morality of Scripture with "positive law" and "deontological ethics," a view of ethics which emphasizes the duty to obey commands (70). But while deontological ethics is the dominant OT perspective, it is "by no means the exclusive view" (43). In keeping with VanDrunen's conclusions above concerning the Noahic covenant, Barton also identifies "natural law" in the OT, a moral framework which he defines as "an accommodation of human action to principles seen as inherent in the way things are," a generalized concept "which is meant to be suggestive rather than defining" (48). Barton categorizes this

---

[104] John Barton, *Understanding Old Testament Ethics: Approaches and Explorations* (Louisville: Westminster John Knox, 2003), 47.

natural law ethic as primarily "consequentialist" (a form of "teleological" ethics) in that it emphasizes the cause and effect morality woven into created reality (70). But Barton goes on to identify another version of teleological ethics within the OT: "virtue ethics," a category variously defined by Barton as "ethics as commitment to a particular lifestyle. . . . [ethics as] moral formation and the development of the moral character over time. . . . [ethics as] a distillation from many good decisions made by virtuous people . . . [and ethics as the expression of] a moral vision" (65–66). While Barton acknowledges that "the language of 'virtue' may not be [as] well adapted to describ[ing] the Old Testament's characteristic approaches to morality" as are "deontology and consequentialism," he goes on to propose that there is indeed an implicit virtue ethic underlying OT narrative texts, an inherent morality which provides further evidence of the Noahic natural law (71).

The narratives of Abraham's life, for example, reveal indications of a shared human moral standard. When the Lord tells Abraham of his intent to destroy Sodom (Gen 18:17–21), Abraham's intercession on behalf of Sodom includes, "Far be it from you to do such a thing, to put the righteous to death with the wicked, so that the righteous fare as the wicked! Far be that from you! Shall not the Judge of all the earth do what is just?" (18:25). Niehaus notes, "being a judge in the ancient world could have connotations of both rule and juridical sentencing."[105] Carol Kaminski further argues that Genesis 18 is a "clear cut" portrayal of "judicial proceedings," as indicated by multiple textual factors, including Abraham "standing before the LORD" (18:22) as "someone standing at the 'bar of justice,' . . . making a juridical appeal," assuming the role of an attorney and "making some kind of speech for the defense."[106] In doing so, Abraham, observes Barton, appeals to "some kind of moral norm by which even God can in principle be judged, though, of course, the point of the

---

[105] Niehaus, *The Common Grace Covenants*, 239.
[106] Kaminski, *Was Noah Good?*, 144, 146.

argument is that God never deviates from this norm." Barton goes on to argue that "the very possibility of asking the question does seem to indicate that human beings may obtain their moral norms not just from what God chooses to reveal but from the perception of some ethical principle inherent in the way things are."[107] Also suggestive of natural law moral norms within the story are the "linguistic connections" and storyline similarity between the judgment of Sodom and the judgment of the world in the flood.[108] Interestingly, VanDrunen identifies the transgressions which bring God's judgment on the people of Sodom as their "egregiously violating the bare minimalistic ethic" which accompanies the Noahic Fallen Creation Covenant by their "fail[ing] to pursue procreatively fruitful sexuality and proportionate justice," Noahic ethical standards "meant to ensure the basic sustenance of human society."[109] VanDrunen then confirms this conclusion through his survey of the textual evidence of Sodom's sexual immorality and abuse of justice, both in violation of God's covenant with Noah.[110]

The narrative of Abraham's interaction with the Philistine king, Abimelech, in Genesis 20:1–18 also demonstrates an implied, natural law ethic. Abimelech takes Abraham's wife Sarah because Abraham deceives Abimelech (20:2). God confronts Abimelech directly in a dream concerning his sin of taking a married woman, warning that he would soon judge Abimelech and his family with death (20:3, 17–18). Abimelech's ensuing dream-state interaction with God is a "legal dispute," reminiscent of the judicial setting of Abraham's intercession on behalf of Sodom in Genesis 18.[111] Like Abraham, Abimelech appeals to standards of common fairness when he asks, "Lord, will you kill an innocent people? Did he not himself say to me, 'She is my sister'? And she herself said, 'He is my

---

[107] Barton, *Understanding Old Testament Ethics*, 36.
[108] Kaminski, *Was Noah Good?*, 141.
[109] VanDrunen, *Divine Covenants and Moral Order*, 137.
[110] Ibid., 138–47.
[111] Kaminski, *Was Noah Good?*, 150.

brother.' In the integrity of my heart and the innocence of my hands I have done this" (20:4–5). The word translated "innocent" (or "innocence") is the same word translated "righteous" ("righteousness") in Abraham's appeal on behalf of Sodom (Gen. 18:23, 24, 25, 26, 28) and in describing Noah before the flood (Gen. 6:9). Kaminski notes that the use of "righteous" in both Genesis 18 and 20 in reference to people who have only received God's common grace and not also God's special grace (in contrast to Noah and Abraham) means that "righteousness" here cannot mean "covenant faithfulness or covenant loyalty, since the inhabitants of Sodom [and Gerar] are not in a covenant relationship with *YHWH*."[112] Of course, if as argued above, all humanity *is* in a Noahic Fallen Creation Covenant with God, then we *can* speak of these peoples' relationship to their creator in covenantal terms, even while still distinguishing between a common grace covenant relationship and a special grace one. So while the "context for implied law in Genesis is . . . creational," Kaminski's conclusion that this natural law is therefore "not covenantal" is an unnecessary one.[113] Within the setting of the Noahic Fallen Creation Covenant, both Abraham (on behalf of Sodom) and Abimelech (on behalf of his kingdom) appeal to universal moral standards for determining innocence or guilt in a "forensic sense."[114] In spite of Abraham's intercessory legal appeal in Genesis 18, God destroys Sodom in Genesis 19, demonstrating his verdict of "unrighteous." By contrast in Genesis 20, the author "goes to great lengths to demonstrate the innocence" of Abimelech, portraying him as an example of "a righteous, even pious, Gentile"—albeit only according to the minimalistic natural law standards of the Noahic common grace covenant.[115] For instance, contrary to Abraham's mistaken assumption

---

[112] Ibid., 153.

[113] Ibid., 165.

[114] Ibid., 152.

[115] Sailhamer, *The Pentateuch as Narrative*, 175, 188. VanDrunen notes the fact that, like the stipulations of the Noahic covenant and the charges against Sodom, this episode again concerns matters of "sex and justice." VanDrunen,

that "there is no fear of God at all" among the Philistines, along with Abraham's mistaken conclusion that they would likely murder him (20:11), Abimelech is shown to be one who "fears God" and seeks to follow natural law standards implicit in creation, standards which Abimelech refers to as "things that ought not to be done" (20:9).[116]

Not only is the OT narrative world built upon an assumed universal moral foundation, so is the poetic world of OT prophecy. For example, Isaiah 13–23 consists of oracles addressed to ten foreign nations, highlighting those nations' "hubris manifest[ing] itself in injustice," in particular their rulers' attempts "to usurp the place of God and to trample the fellow human beings God appointed them to serve," transgressing the standards of the Noahic natural law.[117] Even while some nations and their rulers (such as the Philistines under Abimelech) "evidence a relative respect for this natural moral order," others show "shocking disregard for it, and on some occasions God wills to bring temporal judgments upon them."[118] Barton sees Isaiah as "our strongest evidence" for natural law in the prophets but also highlights Amos 1–2 which condemns the nations neighboring Israel for "the atrociousness of certain kinds of war crime" they have committed.[119] Barton proposes that Amos' message to the surrounding nations is best understood as an appeal to "a kind of conventional or customary law about international conduct which [Amos] at least believed to be self-evidently right and which he thought he could count on his audience's familiarity with and acquiescence in."[120] In

---

Divine Covenants and Moral Order, 157.

[116] VanDrunen argues that this narrative reveals that "two distinct notions of the fear of God inhabit the Scriptures": "the fear of the Lord," using "God's unique covenant name" and "describ[ing] the heart of true religious devotion exhibited by participants in the redemptive covenants of grace," and the more general "fear of God" which "may be found among people of various ethnic and religious origins" and which refers only to "a humane respect for just norms of decency and civility" (ibid., 160).

[117] Ibid., 179.

[118] Ibid., 207.

[119] Barton, *Understanding Old Testament Ethics*, 36, 35.

[120] Ibid., 78.

his appeal to foreign nations on the basis of "natural justice," Amos seems to be "merely echoing what he took to be popular belief and sentiment. . . . a kind of commonsense morality."[121] Armacost and Enns agree that, according to Amos, the functional moral norms operative for God's universal and providential rulership reflect "conduct that all human beings would generally deem immoral."[122] Van-Drunen concludes that Amos is addressing broadly "*human* moral obligations not limited to specific ethnic allegiance or religious affiliation" but instead rooted in the minimalistic ethic required of all people under the Noahic Fallen Creation Covenant.[123] This identification of implied Noahic natural law in the prophets as a moral standard for the nations is further confirmed by the fact that the judgment oracles addressed to the nations "never judge [them] for idolatry or other kinds of false worship," sins which are, by contrast, at the heart of the prophets' condemnation of God's special grace people, Israel.[124]

In addition to Barton's arguments for a "virtue ethic" natural law embedded in the narrative (and poetic) world of the OT, Barton also sees a "consequentialist" natural law most clearly in the wisdom literature's assumption that "the creation somehow works according to moral principles, of which God as creator is in some sense the 'source' and guarantor . . . [and which are detected] by reason."[125] Even though much of OT wisdom literature "lack[s] . . . any covenant reference"[126] and possesses an obvious similarity to "writings

---

[121] Ibid., 35, 80.

[122] Barbara E. Armacost and Peter Enns, "Crying Out for Justice: Civil Law and the Prophets," in *Law and the Bible: Justice, Mercy and Legal Institutions*, eds. Robert F. Cochran and David VanDrunen (Downers Grove, IL: IVP Academic, 2013), 126.

[123] VanDrunen, *Divine Covenants and Moral Order*, 173. Original emphasis.

[124] Ibid., 165.

[125] Barton, *Understanding Old Testament Ethics*, 29.

[126] Katherine J. Dell, "Covenant and Creation in Relationship," in *Covenant as Context: Essays in Honour of E. W. Nicholson*, eds. A. D. H. Mayes and R. B. Salters (Oxford: Oxford, 2003), 123.

from Egypt and Mesopotamia,"[127] according to Walter Kaiser, "Solomonic wisdom. . . . presupposed both Abrahamic-Davidic promise and Mosaic law," and "the fear of the Lord more than any other phrase linked together the patriarchal promise with law and wisdom."[128] But even with this organic relationship to the law and prophets, wisdom literature is, at the same time, "undoubtedly the most overtly international of all the materials in the Bible."[129] Rather than "justify[ing] right action" by reference to Israel's unique covenant and history, wisdom literature is "based more on a theology of creation. . . . draw[ing] many of its conclusions from observations of the natural world . . . . [addressing] human beings as human beings under God as creator, rather than as members of a chosen people."[130]

---

[127] Cyril S. Rodd, *Glimpses of a Strange Land: Studies in Old Testament Ethics* (Edinburgh: T&T Clark, 2001), 55.

[128] Walter C. Kaiser, *Toward an Old Testament Theology* (Grand Rapids: Zondervan, 1978), 46, 168. According to Merrill, "Proverbs breathes the spirit of the Mosaic texts." Merrill, *Everlasting Dominion*, 624. Waltke agrees that a wisdom writer in the OT "approaches the creation with the worldview expressed in Israel's historic covenants." Waltke, *An Old Testament Theology*, 898–99. Hamilton proclaims, "The fear of God so prominent in Proverbs and Ecclesiastes is informed by the holiness of Yahweh that breaks out against transgressors such as Nadab and Abihu (Leviticus 10). The voice of wisdom that cries out from these books is not spouting philosophical speculation on right and wrong; it is the song of a holy siren, wooing readers to return to the Law (Torah) and the Prophets." Hamilton, *God's Glory in Salvation through Judgment*, 272.

[129] Wright, *The Mission of God*, 443.

[130] Routledge, *Old Testament Theology*, 249. Schnabel concurs that "wisdom texts find their theological center in creation." Eckhard J. Schnabel, "Wisdom," in *New Dictionary of Biblical Theology*, ed. T. Desmond Alexander et al. (Downers Grove, IL: IVP, 2000), 843. Scobie states that OT wisdom is "based on *observation* and *experience*, and it seeks to discern the *order* that undergirds both the physical universe and human society" and can therefore be considered "the ethics of the created order." Scobie, *The Ways of Our God*, 160, 757. In a similar way, Shulz observes that numerous OT theologians have "emphasized that wisdom theology is best characterized as 'creation theology.'" R. L. Shulz, "Ecclesiastes," in *New Dictionary of Biblical Theology*, ed. T. Desmond Alexander et al. (Downers Grove, IL: IVP, 2000), 212. See also Wright, *The Mission*

Proverbs, for example, emphasizes an "empirical wisdom, which is gained through experience of life," a kind of wisdom which "assumes that the orderliness of the universe, though to some extent confused by sin, is nevertheless perceptible if people take the trouble to learn wisdom."[131] This empirical wisdom "involves the perception of a natural moral order and the skill to structure one's life effectively and fruitfully within its bounds."[132] The preamble to Proverbs makes clear that such wisdom is "exercised in the realms" of "righteousness, justice, and equity" (Prov. 1:3). Furthermore, within Proverbs, "'wisdom' and 'righteousness' are coreferential terms—that is, they are not synonyms, but they refer to the same referent. In other words, a righteous person is wise and a wise person is righteous."[133] According to Proverbs, "God anoints kings, governs nations and determines events. God gives wisdom, imparts knowledge, counsels the upright, shields the honest, guards the just, defends the poor and protects the pious."[134] Likewise, a wise and righteousness human similarly upholds justice and cares for the poor and weak. One illustration of humanity's responsibility for these good deeds is the concluding paean to the excellent wife in Proverbs 31 which encapsulates the life of wisdom promoted throughout Proverbs. Though much of the poem describes her faithful service to her own household,

---

of God, 449.

[131] Graeme Goldsworthy, "Proverbs," in *New Dictionary of Biblical Theology*, ed. T. Desmond Alexander et al. (Downers Grove, IL: IVP, 2000), 210. According to Bartholomew, Prov 1–9, in particular, is "an important biblical source for a creation ethic." Craig G. Bartholomew, "A Time for War, and a Time for Peace: Old Testament Wisdom, Creation and O'Donovan's Theological Ethics," in *A Royal Priesthood? The Use of the Bible Ethically and Politically—A Dialogue with Oliver O'Donovan*, ed. Craig G. Bartholomew et al. (Grand Rapids: Zondervan, 2002), 94.

[132] VanDrunen, *Divine Covenants and Moral Order*, 88.

[133] Waltke, *An Old Testament Theology*, 914.

[134] Roger P. Alford and Leslie M. Alford, "The Law of Life: Law in the Wisdom Literature," in *Law and the Bible: Justice, Mercy and Legal Institutions*, eds. Robert F. Cochran and David VanDrunen (Downers Grove, IL: IVP Academic, 2013), 104.

the chiastic center of the poem concerns her caring for the poor and needy beyond her household (31:20).[135] In the world revealed by Proverbs, all people are responsible to live a life of good deeds toward their fellow humans, a responsibility which the wise and righteous person fulfills.[136]

The book of Job, even more clearly than Proverbs, communicates a responsibility for good deeds which is shared by all humanity. Litfin comments, "Job is probably the least 'Jewish' of all the Old Testament books."[137] Although firmly and comfortably situated within the canonical worldview, "the literary Job is not a Hebrew and neither are his friends."[138] Waltke concludes that Job's relationship to God is like those of Noah and the line of Seth, "based on God's general revelations of his wisdom, power, and goodness in the creation and of his justice in the conscience."[139] Job speaks of his own righteous good deeds in Job 31:13–32, a self-portrayal which identifies Job as "a man whose life God approved" and as "a model for us."[140] Job's litany of good deeds includes, "his care for his own servants" (31:1–15), "his refusal to exploit the underprivileged" (31:16–23), and his "care even for those whom he did not know" (31:31–32).[141] The book of Job, along with the rest of OT wisdom literature, assumes a moral

[135] Jamie A. Grant, "'Why Bother with the Vulnerable?' The Wisdom of Social Care," in *Transforming the World: The Gospel and Social Responsibility*, eds. Jamie A. Grant and Dewi A. Hughes (Nottingham, UK: Apollos, 2009), 64–65.

[136] While Proverbs does indicate "a species of genuine wisdom [which] exists among the pagan nations," the "fear of the LORD" as "the beginning of wisdom" nonetheless means that "there is no truly wise person who does not serve the God of Israel." This "dual affirmation" leads VanDrunen to suggest two distinct kinds of wisdom in Proverbs: "a sanctified or ultimate wisdom" and "a common or proximate wisdom." VanDrunen, *Divine Covenants and Moral Order*, 397.

[137] Duane Litfin, *Word versus Deed: Resetting the Scales to a Biblical Balance* (Wheaton, IL: Crossway, 2012), 104.

[138] Grant, "Why Bother with the Vulnerable?" 59.

[139] Waltke, *An Old Testament Theology*, 931.

[140] Litfin, *Word versus Deed*, 105.

[141] Grant, "Why Bother with the Vulnerable?" 60, 61, 62.

code embedded in creation itself, which is (imperfectly) known by all humanity and which entails a responsibility for a wide variety of good deeds which accord with the minimalistic ethic of the Noahic Fallen Creation Covenant. OT wisdom, narrative, and prophetic literature each confirms and clarifies the good deeds for which all mankind bears a continuing responsibility before God.

Summary of Humanity's Good Deeds Responsibility

As part of developing a biblical theology of the good deeds mission of the New Covenant community, chapters 4 and 5 surveyed the good deeds responsibility of all humanity as communicated in Genesis 1–11. Since this book seeks to draw particular attention to the impact of one's interpretation of the Bible's covenantal structure upon one's conclusions concerning the church's good deeds mission, chapter 5 explored the relationship between Genesis 1–2 (Adamic Creation Covenant) and Genesis 9 (Noahic Fallen Creation Covenant). While there is both continuity and discontinuity between these covenants, significant differences in terms of covenant partners, tasks, arenas, and goals cause the Adamic Creation Covenant to have limited direct applicability to determining the good deeds responsibility of all humanity in a fallen world. By common grace, God allows humanity to accomplish, in an altered sense, some of Adam's original culture building responsibilities, but only by special grace do believers imperfectly realize their role as priestly worshippers and dependent children. Under the common grace of the Noahic Fallen Creation Covenant, all humanity is responsible for various good deeds that build and preserve human society, among them: raising children, providing food, establishing and maintaining just government, and caring for the poor and weak. These common grace responsibilities are reflective of the natural law woven by God into the fabric of creation, a universal ethic evident in OT narratives, prophecies, and wisdom.

6

The Good Deeds Mission of the Old Covenant Community

Chapters 4 and 5 established the uniqueness of the Adamic Creation Covenant as well as the common grace orientation of the Noahic Fallen Creation Covenant. This chapter will give exclusive attention to the subsequent special grace covenants instituted with Abraham and his descendants until the time of Christ, in particular to the good deeds mission expected of covenant members toward those outside the covenant. The three major covenants inaugurated during the era are the Abrahamic, Mosaic, and Davidic covenants. The organic continuity between these three covenants includes their shared special grace orientation, along with their corresponding limitation to only Abraham and his descendants. Concerning discontinuity and development, the Davidic covenant is only founded with David and his heir from among the rest of Abraham's descendants (though the Davidic kingdom is also intended to bless all Israel), while the Abrahamic and Mosaic covenants are made with all of Abraham's descendants. The Mosaic covenant includes extensive and detailed covenant stipulations, while the explicit stipulations attached to the Abrahamic and Davidic covenants are relatively brief. Since the Davidic covenant is only made with one royal family, its unique responsibilities have less direct application to the good deeds mission of all OT Israel. So, this book treats the Davidic mainly as an extension (and partial fulfillment) of both the Abrahamic and

Mosaic covenants. Though one can also see the Mosaic covenant as an extension of the Abrahamic covenant, a significant distinction between these two covenants concerns how one (Abrahamic) functions initially only in the anticipation of possessing the covenant land, while the other (Mosaic) is structured explicitly to function within the context of the covenant land already possessed. In inspecting the goods deeds mission of Abraham and his descendants under these special grace covenants, this book will therefore highlight how the distinction between possessing and not possessing the covenant land affects the required good deeds mission. While Scobie stresses a differentiation in the OT between the "landless period I" (from Abraham until possession of the land), "landed period I" (from possession of the land until exile), "landless period II" (exile), and "landed period II" (return from exile until the NT),[1] this book will emphasize greater continuity between Scobie's "landless period II" and "landed period II." In agreement with scholars like N. T. Wright and Stephen Dempster, this book concludes that although a remnant of Abraham's descendants returned from Babylon to the covenant land and rebuilt the temple, "the great prophecies of restoration had not yet come true," and therefore Israel was still "in exile," awaiting the coming of the promised Davidic king and his kingdom.[2]

Following Scobie only in part then, this chapter will consider Abraham and his descendants' good deeds mission as divided into three literary-historical eras: from Abraham until possession of the covenant land, from possession until exile, and from exile until Christ.[3] Abraham relates to those outside the covenant as a sojourner

---

[1] Charles H. H. Scobie, *The Ways of Our God: An Approach to Biblical Theology* (Grand Rapids: Eerdmans, 2003), 542–43.

[2] N. T. Wright, *Jesus and the Victory of God* (Minneapolis: Fortress, 1996), 126; Stephen G. Dempster, *Dominion and Dynasty: A Biblical Theology of the Hebrew Bible* (Downers Grove, IL: IVP, 2003), 224.

[3] These three eras are the same divisions which VanDrunen makes in his analysis of OT Israel. David VanDrunen, *Living in God's Two Kingdoms: A Biblical Vision for Christianity and Culture* (Wheaton, IL: Crossway, 2010), 75–97.

and resident alien living in their midst, while an Israelite possessing the land relates to those outside the covenant both as one obligated to complete separation and destruction (toward the Canaanites) and as one obligated to hospitality and care (toward resident aliens). Abraham's descendants in exile (either in Babylon or returned to the land), again follow Abraham's model of living as a sojourner among those outside the covenant, a life containing both a separating from and a sharing with Gentiles. Highlighting the distinctions between these three eras when determining the good deeds mission of Abraham and his descendants until Christ resonates with Michael Goheen's observation that "we need to trace the way Israel embodied its [mission] in the successive eras of redemptive history, in varying contexts and situations. In each setting Israel's relation and witness to the surrounding peoples differed."[4] Because of this, "A nuanced treatment of the relationships of the old covenant community to the nations will take into account the varying contexts and forms throughout Israel's history."[5] This chapter's biblical-theological survey of Israel's good deeds mission aims to be just such a "nuanced treatment."

Perhaps the key point of this chapter is the crucial recognition that the diverse commands for mutual goods deeds of love *within* the special grace covenant community of Abraham and his descendants do not simply and automatically extend to an Israelite responsibility for the same good deeds toward those *outside* the covenant community. Instead, this chapter will limit itself to the OT's more explicit commands to Israelites for good deeds toward outsiders. This essential distinction between covenant responsibilities directed inwardly

---

[4] Michael W. Goheen, *A Light to the Nations: The Missional Church and the Biblical Story* (Grand Rapids: Baker Academic, 2011), 50.

[5] Ibid., 51. Flemming agrees, "Israel lived out its mission in different ways during different periods in its history. Throughout Israel's long journey as a people, the calling to be a blessing to the nations was a constant. But the specific forms, that too, depended on the context." Dean Flemming, *Recovering the Full Mission of God: A Biblical Perspective on Being, Doing and Telling* (Downers Grove, IL: IVP Academic, 2013), 36.

and those directed outwardly is related to Israel's status, when in possession of the land, as a "unique theocracy."[6] Because Israel's covenant responsibilities in the land fuse religious and civil life (as introduced in chapter 4, "cult" and "culture"), everyone involved in the civil life/culture of the covenant (including resident aliens) is also required to participate in the religious life/cult of the covenant. Explicit covenant obedience should permeate and govern every aspect of public and private life for everyone in the society, without exception. The majority of those living in the land *should* be members of the covenant, while even the non-covenant resident aliens *must* observe the Sabbath (Deut. 5:14) and the Day of Atonement (Lev. 16:29), *may* observe circumcision (Ex. 12:48), Passover (Num. 9:14), and other sacrificial offerings (Lev. 17:8–9; Num. 15:14), and *must not* practice the idolatrous "abominations" of the Canaanites (Lev. 18:26), under pain of death (Lev. 20:2). The vast majority of Israel's covenant responsibilities are therefore oriented toward "life within the believing community."[7] By contrast, this chapter will focus primarily on Abraham and his descendants' much more restricted covenant mission toward those *outside* the believing community.

Good Deeds Mission of Abraham and His Descendants until Possession of the Covenant Land

Confirming that life under the Noahic Fallen Creation Covenant is still limited by the Genesis 3 curse of sin, immediately after exiting the ark, Noah is portrayed as sinning in a manner intentionally linked to Adam's first sin. Noah plants a garden ("a vineyard"), consumes the fruit of the garden ("wine"), and sins ("became drunk"), exposing his nakedness and resulting in a curse (Gen. 9:20–25).[8] The

---

[6] T. Desmond Alexander, *From Eden to the New Jerusalem: An Introduction to Biblical Theology* (Grand Rapids: Kregel, 2008), 80.

[7] Duane Litfin, *Word versus Deed: Resetting the Scales to a Biblical Balance* (Wheaton, IL: Crossway, 2012), 157.

[8] John Sailhamer, *The Pentateuch as Narrative: A Biblical-Theological*

vocabulary used in these verses is "reminiscent of Gen. 3–4," suggesting a "continuation, and possibly even a recapitulation" of the pattern of sin.[9] Noah's curse upon his son Ham (9:25) and blessing upon his sons Shem and Japheth (9:26–27) continues the "two seeds" storyline first introduced in Genesis 3.[10] The line of Ham (in particular, his son Canaan) represents the seed of the serpent (3:15). God's judgment on the seed of the serpent in the tower of Babel[11] narrative (11:1–9) parallels his judgment on the seed of the serpent in the flood,[12] with Genesis 6:9–11:32 recapitulating the pattern of Genesis 1:1–6:8,[13] thereby establishing the "repeating literary pattern of the book of Genesis."[14]

Commentary (Grand Rapids: Zondervan, 1992), 129.

[9] Carol M. Kaminski, *Was Noah Good? Finding Favor in the Flood Narrative* (New York: Bloomsbury T&T Clark, 2014), 102.

[10] Sailhamer, *The Pentateuch as Narrative*, 130. See also Thomas R. Schreiner, *The King in His Beauty: A Biblical Theology of the Old and New Testaments* (Grand Rapids: Baker Academic, 2013), 14.

[11] Alexander notes, "In most English versions of the Bible, the city in Gen. 11:1–9 is called Babel. This name is derived from its Hebrew name, *bābel* (11:9). However, *bābel* is also the Hebrew designation for Babylon. In English translations of the OT, the Hebrew word *bābel*, which occurs over two hundred times, is almost always consistently translated by the name 'Babylon.' In the whole OT, there are generally only two exceptions to this rule, Gen. 10:10 and 11:9, and even here a few English translations replace Babel in Gen. 10:10 with Babylon (e.g., NIV, NJPS). The use of the name Babel in Gen. 11:9 is really an anomaly and should be replaced by Babylon, as done in HCSB." T. Desmond Alexander, *From Paradise to the Promised Land: An Introduction to the Pentateuch*, 3rd ed. (Grand Rapids: Baker Academic, 2012), 152. See also Peter J. Gentry and Stephen J. Wellum, *Kingdom through Covenant: A Biblical-Theological Understanding of the Covenants* (Wheaton, IL: Crossway, 2012), 128n23.

[12] Jack M. Sasson, "The 'Tower of Babel,' as a Clue to the Redactional Structuring of the Primeval History (Genesis 1:1–11:9)," in *I Studied Inscriptions from before The Flood: Ancient Near Eastern, Literary, and Linguistic Approaches to Genesis 1–11*, eds. Richard S. Hess and David Toshio Tsumura (Winona Lake, IN: Eisenbrauns, 1994), 456.

[13] Bruce K. Waltke, *An Old Testament Theology: An Exegetical, Canonical, and Thematic Approach* (Grand Rapids: Zondervan, 2007), 307–8.

[14] Meredith G. Kline, *Kingdom Prologue: Genesis Foundations for a Covenantal*

In contrast to the line of Cain before the flood and to the gathering of humanity at the tower of Babel, the line of Shem (like the line of Seth) represents the seed of the woman (Gen. 3:15), those under God's blessing (9:26). The repeating literary pattern of Genesis 1–11 is also seen in the parallel, ten-generation genealogies of Shem (11:10–32) and of Seth (5:1–32), both genealogies performing a similar function within the narrative by picturing believing remnants in the midst of an unbelieving world.[15] Even as Noah, the tenth in Seth's line, is God's chosen channel of blessing amid the judgment of the flood, so Abraham, the tenth in Shem's line, is God's means of blessing in the midst of the judgment of Babel.[16] God's call and Abraham's

---

Worldview (Overland Park, KS: Two Age Press, 2000), 244. Toward the end of the Pentateuch, Deut. 9:15 introduces the principle "on the evidence of two or three witnesses a matter shall be confirmed." The double pattern of failure (Creation-Fall-Judgment) in Gen. 1–11 might be intended to demonstrate just this "Deuteronomic principle," establishing through the evidence of two witnesses (Gen. 3–4; 6:1–7; 9:18–11:9) that a new work of God is needed—choosing one man, Abraham, out of the nations in order to establish a holy people among the nations. A related principle is also perhaps alluded to by Joseph in Gen. 41:32, "Now as for the repeating of the dream to Pharaoh twice, it means that the matter is determined by God, and God will quickly bring it about." Clines hints in a similar direction when he states, "A sharp disjunction can then be made between universal history (Genesis 1–11) and 'salvation history' (Genesis 12 onward), with the themes of the two units being set in contrast: universal history leads only to judgment, whereas the narrowing of vision to Abraham opens the way for an era of blessing, that is, for salvation history." D. J. A. Clines, "Theme in Genesis 1–11," in *I Studied Inscriptions from before The Flood: Ancient Near Eastern, Literary, and Linguistic Approaches to Genesis 1–11*, eds. Richard S. Hess and David Toshio Tsumura (Winona Lake, IN: Eisenbrauns, 1994), 305.

[15] John H. Sailhamer, *Genesis*, in vol. 1 of *The Expositor's Bible Commentary*, eds. Tremper Longman III and David E. Garland, rev. ed. (Grand Rapids: Zondervan, 2008), 146. Sailhamer notes, "Out of the ruins of two great cities, the city of Cain and the city of Babylon, God preserves the promised 'seed'" (ibid., 147). See also Sasson, "The 'Tower of Babel,'" 456; Kline, *Kingdom Prologue*, 287.

[16] Sailhamer, *The Pentateuch as Narrative*, 139–40. Note that though Abram's name is not changed to "Abraham" within the narrative until Gen. 17:5, this

response in Genesis 12:1–7 exhibit a "striking thematic parallel [with] the picture of God's calling Noah out of the ark (8:15–20),"[17] as well as with God's original work of creation, since "the divine speech and command at Gen. 12:1 are structurally similar to the speech and implied command at the beginning of creation."[18] Abraham, like Noah, is a new Adam called to carry out a new work of God.[19]

Be a Blessing

Abraham's call includes the command to "be a blessing" (Gen. 12:2) and the promise that "in you all the families of the earth shall be blessed" (Gen. 12:3). While some translations, such as the ESV, render Genesis 12:2 as "I will bless you . . . so that you will be a blessing," implying that Abraham is more of a passive conduit of God's blessing to others, other translators take the Hebrew imperative as a straightforward command to Abraham to "be a blessing" (implying a more active sense).[20] But Gentry and Wellum recognize that adopting this interpretation still does not clarify exactly what the command to "be a blessing" means.[21] For instance, since the next verse (12:3) promises that "in [Abraham] all the families of the earth shall be blessed," does this mean that Abraham is commanded to go to those outside the covenant, actively seeking to bless them?[22] The verb in Genesis 12:3c which is translated as a passive

---

book will use "Abraham" throughout.

[17] Ibid., 128.

[18] Andreas J. Köstenberger and Peter T. O'Brien, *Salvation to the Ends of the Earth: A Biblical Theology of Mission* (Downers Grove, IL: IVP, 2001), 28n9.

[19] Gentry and Wellum, *Kingdom through Covenant*, 224.

[20] For example, see Christopher Wright—though Wright also freely acknowledges the debatable nature of this translation. Christopher J. H. Wright, *The Mission of God: Unlocking the Bible's Grand Narrative* (Downers Grove, IL: IVP Academic, 2006), 201. See also Alexander, *From Paradise to the Promised Land*, 231–32.

[21] Gentry and Wellum, *Kingdom through Covenant*, 233.

[22] Though the official covenant ceremony between God and Abraham does not occur until Gen. 15 and 17, Gentry and Wellum illustrate the relationship between Gen. 12 and Gen. 15/17 through the analogy of a marriage: "The

by the ESV ("shall be blessed") can also be translated as a reflexive ("shall bless themselves") or in a middle sense which combines the passive and reflexive ("shall win/find a blessing for themselves").[23] Gentry and Wellum reject the grammatical evidence for the reflexive translation,[24] a conclusion shared by Köstenberger and O'Brien for the additional literary reason that it "makes Abraham the model for rather than the source of blessing, and this interpretation is anticlimactic."[25] Köstenberger and O'Brien embrace the middle sense, quoting Dumbrell in support, who states that the "climactic rendering [of the middle sense] would mean that the peoples of the world would find blessing by coming to the Abrahamic descendants, rather than by later Israel's outreach. And this interpretation is consistent with the way mission is presented in the Old Testament—nations come in pilgrimage to Israel's God."[26] But Gentry and Wellum also reject the middle sense, concluding that the passive interpretation is best, referring to the observation of Chee-Chiew Lee that "nowhere in the narrative [of Genesis] do we see people actively seeking blessing for themselves by their association with Abraham or invoking his name as a formula and paradigm of blessing as a middle or direct reflexive reading would entail."[27] But, if Genesis 12:3c is a prophecy fulfilled only in reference to the "families of the earth" actively seeking blessing in Abraham's *distant* "seed" rather than also seeking blessing in Abraham during his own lifetime, then perhaps the

---

giving of the promises in chapter 12 would then represent the betrothal or engagement. The covenant making in chapter 15 and confirmation in chapter 17 would correspond to the wedding vows of the marriage covenant. After testing Abraham [in Gen. 22], God reiterates his promises by a mighty oath" (ibid., 230). For simplicity sake, this book will refer to the existence of the covenant between God and Abraham already beginning in Gen. 12.

[23] Ibid., 238–40.

[24] Ibid., 239–41.

[25] Köstenberger and O'Brien, *Salvation to the Ends of the Earth*, 30.

[26] Ibid. See also Eckhard J. Schnabel, *Jesus and the Twelve*, vol. 1 of *Early Christian Mission* (Downers Grove, IL: IVP, 2004), 62–63.

[27] Gentry and Wellum, *Kingdom through Covenant*, 240–41.

middle sense has more literary merit than Lee allows. But regardless of the validity of the middle sense, the passive element remains predominant, emphasizing that the "the promise of blessing . . . is to come from the hand of God."[28] Therefore, even if Abraham is commanded to "be a blessing," the text stresses God's initiative and sovereignty in bestowing blessing through Abraham.

Gentry and Wellum propose that "as Abraham's life unfolds, we begin to see what blessing means," defining this blessing as that which "operates in the context of a covenant relationship with God."[29] In what sense then can Abraham "be a blessing" to those who themselves still remain outside the covenant relationship with God enjoyed by Abraham? Does Genesis portray God as bestowing some sort of blessing through Abraham upon those outside the Abrahamic covenant? Alexander argues that the "most important" sense in which Genesis shows Abraham as possessing "the power to mediate God's blessing to others" is *within* the covenant family, "passed on through the chosen line of patriarchs." The heir's reception of Abraham's blessing comes both from the reigning patriarch in the "unique blessing that each father bestows on his 'firstborn' son" and from God directly in the "renewing [of God's] special relationship with the head of each generation."[30] In emphasizing this genealogical blessing, the author thereby "draws attention to the privileged position of the 'seed' of the chosen lineage" as the instrument through which Abraham's blessing to the nations would come.[31] As the Lord promised Abraham in Genesis 12:3, "I will bless those who bless you, and him who dishonors you I will curse." The Genesis narrative goes on to demonstrate repeatedly that when the covenant heir interacts with those outside the covenant (12:14–20; 14:13–16; 20:1–18; 21:22–32; 26:7–11, 26–33; 30:25–43), blessing or cursing comes upon those outside the

---

[28] Walter C. Kaiser, *Mission in the Old Testament: Israel as a Light to the Nations*, 2nd ed. (Grand Rapids: Baker Academic, 2012), 19–20.

[29] Gentry and Wellum, *Kingdom through Covenant*, 242.

[30] Alexander, *From Paradise to the Promised Land*, 155.

[31] Ibid., 159.

covenant "in direct proportion to how [they treat] the patriarchs and their 'seed.'"[32] But these blessings bestowed through Abraham on those outside the covenant in Genesis never include the blessing of actually entering into the Abrahamic covenant and receiving the special grace it offered. God's promise to bless the nations in Abraham and in his seed points toward the need of those outside the covenant to enter into Abraham's covenant with the Lord in order to obtain the blessing. For Abraham truly to "be a blessing" to the nations in more than a temporary or limited sense, the nations must share Abraham's covenant and be united with his seed.[33]

Though not special grace blessing, how through Abraham does God bestow blessing in a lesser sense upon those outside the covenant? In Egypt, because of Abraham's deception concerning his relationship to Sarah, the Lord curses Pharaoh, with Abraham's departure (and the ensuing lifting of the curse) being Abraham's only act of "blessing" toward the Egyptians (12:10–20). Abraham blesses the people of Sodom and four other neighboring cities by rescuing them from their enemies, but his motivation seems primarily the deliverance of his nephew Lot, who lives in Sodom (14:13–6). That any active effort by Abraham to bless the five cities is at best his secondary objective receives confirmation in Abraham's refusal of a reward from the king of Sodom, instead only asking the king to cover his military expenses (14:21–24). Because of his covenant loyalty to the Lord (14:22–23), Abraham keeps himself from entanglement with Sodom, a "negative response" toward the king of Sodom that the author intentionally presents in contrast to Abraham's "positive response" toward the king of Salem, Melchizedek (14:17–20).[34] In contrast to his relationship with Melchizedek (who Abraham appears

---

[32] Ibid., 157.

[33] Christopher Wright, for example, labels these two senses of "blessing" as "the general blessing of God" as distinguished from "the specifically covenantal blessing that is enjoyed by the descendants of Abraham." Wright, *The Mission of God*, 214.

[34] Sailhamer, *The Pentateuch as Narrative*, 147.

to recognize as a fellow worshipper of the true God), Abraham relates to the king of Sodom only according to a standard of general fairness, making no attempt to enter into a more significant relationship of mutual blessing, regardless of the king of Sodom's seemingly reasonable conclusion that Abraham's life-saving intervention is worthy of additional reward. Though God bestows a measure of temporary blessing upon the five cities through Abraham, still lacking is clear evidence of Abraham's sense of responsibility actively to "be a blessing" to those outside the covenant.

Later in the storyline, Abraham *does* act in a way which appears to represent a more active effort to bless the five cities. When informed of the Lord's plan to destroy the cities because of their wickedness, Abraham intercedes before the Lord, asking him to spare Sodom, even if it contains as few as ten righteous inhabitants (18:16–33). Gentry and Wellum identify Abraham's intercessory prayer as "the beginning of [Abraham] being a blessing to the nations . . . [pleading for those outside the covenant] as a priest for the nations on the basis of God's own character."[35] But even in this circumstance, Abraham's primary concern is for "the righteous" (in particular, the family of his nephew Lot) as distinct from an otherwise "wicked" populace, with any residual, temporal benefit garnered by the "wicked" hardly embodying Abraham's mission to bless them. Nonetheless, this story does begin to suggest "how the blessing to the nations of the earth might come to those who are threatened with death—it is through intercessory prayer resulting in forgiveness of the guilty and cancellation of the decision to destroy"—even though in this particular case, God responds to Abraham's plea for mercy by still carrying out judgment upon the cities.[36] This suggests that Abraham, God's chosen channel of blessing to those outside the covenant, mediates God blessing when he prays for the nations.[37]

---

[35] Gentry and Wellum, *Kingdom through Covenant*, 282–83.
[36] Kaminski, *Was Noah Good?*, 142.
[37] Wright, *The Mission of God*, 361.

This role and responsibility is confirmed in Abraham's relationship with Abimelech and the Philistines, where once again Abraham prays for Gentiles under God's judgment, this time with a result of healing rather than destruction (20:17–18).[38]

Beyond the good deed of occasional intercessory prayer, Abraham's interaction with outsiders appears otherwise to accord with the shared standards of justice and equity common in his day. Abraham enters into a covenant with Abimelech and the Philistines which establishes civil concord between them (21:22–36; later reaffirmed by Abraham's son, Isaac [26:26–33]), a covenant not to "harm" one another but only to do "good" to one another, living "in peace" (26:29).[39] Later, as a tomb for his wife, Abraham purchases a cave and its adjoining field from the Hittites at its current market value, refusing to receive it from the Hittites as a gift, but instead following the contemporary customs for establishing full legal ownership of the burial plot (23:1–20), an act which Kline describes as the willing "subordination of the patriarchal pilgrims to the temporal political powers."[40] This expectation that Abraham's covenant family would relate to those outside the covenant according to generally accepted standards of justice is also negatively illustrated when Abraham's great grandsons, Simeon and Levi, avenge Shechem's rape of their sister Dinah by slaughtering a whole city of Hivite men through the use of deception (34:1–29). Shechem and the Hivites attempted to establish an official relationship with Jacob and his family according to the conventional practice of the day (much as had Abimelech and the Philistines), but Simeon and Levi took advantage of the legal process in order to murder and plunder the Hivites, bringing upon themselves their father Jacob's condemnation for having "brought trouble on me by making me stink to the inhabitants of the land" (34:30). Yet though Abraham and his descendants appear typically

[38] Sailhamer, *The Pentateuch as Narrative*, 174.
[39] Ibid., 189.
[40] Kline, *Kingdom Prologue*, 359.

to work for the maintenance of a relative civil peace with those out-side the covenant, pursuing this goal of basic social stability seems hard to equate with obedience to the command to "be a blessing."

Doing Righteousness and Justice

Although Abraham is *described* as seeking to bless those outside the covenant through intercessory prayer for temporal deliverance, the Lord never directly *prescribes* this good deed responsibility of prayer to Abraham. But Genesis 18:19 is a passage in which the Lord speaks more directly of Abraham's covenant responsibilities, stat-ing, "I have chosen [Abraham], that he may command his children and his household after him to keep the way of the LORD by doing righteousness and justice, so that the LORD may bring to Abraham what he has promised him." Sailhamer believes that this verse is "an expansion on the ideas of 17:1 ('Walk before me and be blameless'). . . . [providing the author's most] reflective perspective on the events of the whole of the Abrahamic narratives."[41] According to Burnside, to "keep the way of the LORD by doing righteousness and justice" is a combination of three words (way, righteousness, justice) which means "to proceed in conformity with the law," giving Abraham's covenant responsibilities a "legal procedural" sense,[42] perhaps antic-ipating Abraham's courtroom pleadings before the Lord on behalf of Sodom which immediately follow (18:20–33).[43] Abraham is to do "righteousness," just as Noah was "a righteous man" (6:9), both men conforming to "agreed upon moral and ethical conventions."[44]

---

[41] Sailhamer, *The Pentateuch as Narrative*, 167. Concerning Gen. 17:1, Gen-try and Wellum state that "when people walk before God, it means that they serve as his emissary or diplomatic representative. . . . Thus the command 'walk before me' correlates directly with the command in 12:3 to be a blessing to the nations." Gentry and Wellum, *Kingdom through Covenant*, 260–61.

[42] Jonathan Burnside, *God, Justice, and Society: Aspects of Law and Legality in the Bible* (Oxford: Oxford, 2011), 88.

[43] Kaminski, *Was Noah Good?*, 142–43.

[44] Eugene H. Merrill, *Everlasting Dominion: A Theology of the Old Testament* (Nashville: B&H, 2006), 58. Concerning "righteousness," Seifrid highlights the

Concerning the second word "justice," Kaiser claims that "all concede" its basic meaning is "judicial,"[45] with Wright noting how this word can describe both more broadly "the whole process of litigation (a case)" as well as, more narrowly, only a case's "end result (the verdict and its execution)."[46] In relation to "righteousness," "justice" is "the application of righteousness, especially in situations of legal disposition. Where law is interpreted in a righteous manner, justice will prevail."[47] Together, "righteousness and justice" combine to form a "comprehensive phrase," expressing a "single complex idea" which Wright believes is best translated into English as "social justice," the characteristic quality and achievement of the just community which Abraham's ethical training is supposed to create among his covenant descendants.[48]

Waldron Scott also accepts "social justice" as the best translation of the phrase, but goes further in claiming that this means that

---

word's connation of a universal ethical standard rather than merely the more limited standard within a particular covenant relationship, such as Abraham's relationship with the Lord. Seifrid concludes that "righteousness language in the Hebrew Scriptures has to do in the first instance with God's ordering of creation" rather than a primary orientation to "covenant." The result is that "the biblical conception of kingship bears a universal dimension . . . [with a corresponding] demand for social justice . . . from God, the divine king, who has determined to secure the good and beneficial order of creation." Mark A. Seifrid, "Righteousness Language in the Hebrew Scriptures and Early Judaism," in *The Complexities of Second Temple Judaism*, vol. 1 of *Justification and Variegated Nomism*, eds. D. A. Carson, Peter T. O'Brien, and Mark A. Seifrid (Grand Rapids: Baker Academic, 2001), 425. But if, as argued in chap. 5, *both* creation (common grace preservation) *and* redemption (special grace salvation) are administered by God through covenants, then, more precisely, "righteousness language" in the OT is first rooted in God's provision of common grace administered through the Noahic Fallen Creation Covenant and only secondarily also expresses the administrative standards of God's special grace covenants.

[45] Kaiser, *Mission in the Old Testament*, 59.
[46] Wright, *The Mission of God*, 366.
[47] Merrill, *Everlasting Dominion*, 60.
[48] Wright, *The Mission of God*, 366–67.

"God's specific blessing for the nations through Abraham's descendants *is* [emphasis added] the restoration of social justice," which Abraham and his descendants are responsible to pursue actively, not only within the covenant community but also within the societies they share with those outside the covenant.[49] In considering this possible interpretation, one question is whether or not Abraham shared a common understanding of "social justice" with outsiders. In fact, this phrase ("righteousness and justice") *was* used both by ancient Israel and its ANE neighbors, commonly referring to "maintaining social justice in the society, so that equality and freedom prevail"— but, in a crucial distinction, this concept also included "a religious significance" when used within the OT.[50] For example, "Later on in the Old Testament, this word pair becomes a way of summarizing the requirements and stipulations of the Mosaic covenant,"[51] meaning that "doing righteousness and justice" within the OT is connected closely to covenant faithfulness toward the Lord within the theocratic community, rather than merely to the establishment of a measure of partial justice within the societies shared with those outside the covenant. Therefore, the biblical idea of "social justice" needs to be distinguished clearly from "how the term might commonly be used today" within contemporary societies or within other historical contexts.[52] Defined carefully, "doing social justice" *is* the covenant responsibility of Abraham and his descendants.[53]

Even defined carefully, the term "social justice" may create more confusion than clarity when used within contemporary biblical-theological deliberations. The term "social justice" might, for instance, prove to be unnecessarily provocative as a translation choice

---

[49] Waldron Scott, *Bring Forth Justice: A Contemporary Perspective on Mission* (Grand Rapids: Eerdmans, 1980), 50–52.

[50] Moshe Weinfeld, *Social Justice in Israel and in the Ancient Near East* (Minneapolis: Fortress, 1995), 5.

[51] Gentry and Wellum, *Kingdom through Covenant*, 282.

[52] Ibid.

[53] Ibid.

since within English-speaking societies there are "sharp differences of opinion about what justice actually is."[54] Too often, when people use the term "social justice," they "simply assume that when they claim that justice demands this action or that policy, everyone knows precisely what the term means."[55] The debate over how to define "justice" has a long history within the Western tradition, with Aristotle establishing many of the initial parameters of the discussion. First, Aristotle identifies "universal justice," a status which a person attains if he displays "all the proper virtues, if he is moral, if he keeps the laws."[56] According to Ronald Nash, being such a person of just character is "synonymous with personal righteousness and might be called justice as virtue."[57] As argued in chapter three, the OT *does* include this kind of "virtue ethic." Second, Aristotle establishes the category of "particular justice," describing a person who "treats other people fairly . . . [and] does not grasp after more than he is due."[58] Aristotle further divides particular justice into "corrective justice" and "distributive justice," together encapsulating the rules which "govern all impersonal [and therefore, impartial] exchanges."[59] On the one hand, corrective justice "includes criminal justice, but also encompasses the correct exchange of goods."[60] Other labels for these two subsets of corrective justice are "remedial justice" and "commercial justice," referring to courtroom fairness and economic fairness.[61] Furthermore, courtroom justice includes both a just process and a

---

[54] Timothy Keller, *Generous Justice: How God's Grace Makes Us Just* (New York: Dutton, 2010), 150.

[55] Ronald H. Nash, *Social Justice and the Christian Church* (Lanham, MD: University Press of America, 1990), 28.

[56] Ibid., 30.

[57] Ibid., 74.

[58] Ibid., 30–31.

[59] John Addison Teevan, *Integrated Justice and Equality: Biblical Wisdom for Those Who Do Good Works*, Kindle ed. (Grand Rapids: Christian's Library Press, 2014), loc. 429.

[60] Ibid., loc. 441.

[61] Nash, *Social Justice and the Christian Church*, 31.

just verdict, demonstrating the many facets of Aristotle's conception of corrective justice.[62] On the other hand, Aristotle's distributive justice refers to the idea that "people get what they are due based on merit (not rules), as opposed to the old standards of birth, status, or supposed virtue. We might call it proportional justice."[63] For Aristotle, both categories of particular justice (corrective and distributive) are "especially concerned with fairness" and, in contrast to universal justice ("justice as virtue"), can be called "justice as fairness."[64] Like Aristotle's "universal justice," his "particular justice" seems to resonate at many points with the OT picture of justice. Nevertheless, when the later OT prophets call for "righteousness and justice" in Israel, they do not merely call for fair courts, fair weights, or merit-based rewards but instead "make no distinction between failures of social justice and failures of immorality, superficial religious observance, and idolatry."[65] In contrast to Aristotle's "justice," OT "righteousness and justice" demands not only a right relationship with other people but also a right relationship with God.[66]

In recent decades, this more traditional understanding of "justice" in the West is being slowly replaced by a different version of

---

[62] Teevan, *Integrated Justice*, locs. 307–32.

[63] Ibid., loc. 441.

[64] Nash, *Social Justice and the Christian Church*, 74. What Aristotle labels "particular justice," Forster calls "natural justice," a kind of justice which is "humanly enforced" (in contrast to "theological justice," which only God can enforce). Natural justice "requires us to treat people with basic respect and play fair. . . . to be good citizens, respecting the rights of others and participating constructively in society. We might think of it as 'peace-oriented lawfulness.'" Greg Forster, *Joy for the World: How Christianity Lost Its Cultural Influence and Can Begin Rebuilding It* (Wheaton, IL: Crossway, 2014), 258–59. Sowell's term to designate what Forster labels "natural justice" and Aristotle labels "particular justice" is "traditional justice." Thomas Sowell, *The Quest for Cosmic Justice* (New York: Free Press, 2002).

[65] Teevan, *Integrated Justice*, loc. 137.

[66] From another perspective, Aristotle's "universal justice" roughly parallels the vertical (and internal) orientation of the right relationship with God that is intrinsic to OT "righteousness and justice."

"justice as fairness," where "fairness" is no longer determined primarily by equity of procedures and standards but instead by equity of outcomes. Under the particular influence of John Rawls beginning in the 1950s, this view of justice sees "all human outcomes as arbitrary" and requires "an equalization of outcomes to eliminate that unjust arbitrariness," a pursuit of "justice" typically delegated to human governments.[67] For Rawls, achieving these equal outcomes *is* "social justice," with special emphasis on "income inequality," since a "system that does not focus on the redistribution of income is fundamentally unjust."[68] Thomas Sowell argues that rather than merely pursuing equal treatment under the law, this version of "social justice" actually expresses a desire for a "cosmic justice" in which all perceived wrongs are righted and all perceived inequalities are leveled, a kind of "justice" which Sowell understandably sees as beyond mankind's power to achieve and which the attempted implementation thereof often produces more injustice than it remedies.[69] Understood according to Rawls' definition of forcibly producing equal outcomes, Abraham's call to "do social justice" would become a responsibility very different than any that he or his descendants appear to have carried out while living as sojourners among those outside the covenant. Therefore, this wide variance in how the term "social justice" is used in the contemporary world means that an alternative translation of the biblical phrase "righteousness and justice" is preferable for sake of clarity and distinction—perhaps a phrase such as "social righteousness" or "communal justice," or, even better, simply retaining the complete phrase, "righteousness and justice."

[67] Teevan, *Integrated Justice*, loc. 914.

[68] Ibid., loc. 928.

[69] Sowell, *The Quest*. From the biblical worldview, we can affirm (in a broad sense) this desire for "cosmic justice," confident that the future "new heavens and new earth" will indeed be a place of perfect justice. Nonetheless, the question remains whether or not God has given his covenant people the responsibility to pursue "cosmic justice" in this age and to attempt to implement, either within the covenant community or within broader society, a social system which operates by some standard of "cosmic justice."

In further considering Abraham's responsibility to "command his children and his household after him to keep the way of the LORD by doing righteousness and justice" (18:19), we need to make an additional differentiation between how Abraham carries out this responsibility within the covenant community and how he fulfills it within the social arena he shares with non-covenant members. Within his family, Abraham is responsible to "command" and enforce the requirement of "doing righteousness and justice," thereby keeping fully the standards of the covenant. Among those outside the covenant, Abraham is given no such responsibility or authority. Nevertheless, when Abraham interacts with those outside the covenant, his behavior still must accord with "doing justice and righteousness." But rather than attempting to impose on outsiders the more demanding standards of "justice and righteousness" found within the covenant, Abraham appears instead to relate to those outside the covenant only according to commonly accepted standards of justice, with the goal of maintaining basic social stability (as observed above). In this sense, "the Abrahamic covenant did not *directly* [emphasis added] regulate Abraham's broader social life, in its various political, legal, or economic aspects."[70] If one chooses to speak of Abraham as "doing righteous and justice" within broader society, one must distinguish it from his "doing righteousness and justice" within the covenant community. Following the categories introduced in chapter 5, this book will label Abraham's responsibility within broader society as "common grace justice" and his responsibility within the covenant community as "special grace justice."

Abraham's sense of responsibility to promote "common grace justice" in the surrounding societies appears to be carried forward by his descendants, with his great grandson Joseph's life among the Egyptians being a particularly "outstanding . . . example of the

---

[70] David VanDrunen, *Divine Covenants and Moral Order: A Biblical Theology of Natural Law* (Grand Rapids: Eerdmans, 2014), 270.

patriarchal family as agents of common grace blessing to the world of their day."[71] But until the exodus from Egypt (and the subsequent conquest of the covenant land), the covenant community's good deeds responsibility toward outsiders is always framed within the context of their living among the nations as sojourners and resident aliens. Their life among the Canaanites and the Egyptians therefore exhibits the characteristics of both a shared and a separated community, extending common grace to covenant outsiders as the opportunity allows.

Good Deeds Mission of Abraham's Descendants from Possession of the Covenant Land until the Exile

Even though Abraham and his descendants live as resident aliens in both Canaan and Egypt, they nonetheless look forward in hope to the promised time of possessing the covenant land. In Deuteronomy 3:20, the Israelites' full possession of the land is paralleled with the idea of being given "rest" by the Lord. Later, in Deuteronomy 12:9–10, being given "rest" in the covenant land is equivalent to defeating all their enemies and living in safety. Under the leadership of Joshua, Israel systematically defeats the Canaanite inhabitants and possesses the land, a result described as "the LORD gave them rest on every side" (Josh. 21:44). Israel's "resting" in the covenant land is the intended context within which the Lord designs the covenant responsibilities assigned at Sinai to be carried out. In this sense, one can label the Mosaic covenant (until the exile) as a "settled covenant of already-realized rest," in contrast to the Abrahamic covenant (until the possession) as a "sojourning covenant of not-yet-realized rest." Designed for differing contexts, these two covenants also differ in their requirements for relating to those outside the covenant. When sojourning in Canaan or Egypt, Abraham and his descendants share "common cultural space

[71] Kline, *Kingdom Prologue*, 360.

together with unbelievers in as much peace and cooperation as possible," even while remaining "radically distinct from the world in their faith and worship."[72] But when possessing the covenant land, Israel is commanded "not to maintain a common cultural life with pagans in the Promised Land."[73] Within this changed covenantal context of "settled rest," what is Israel's good deeds mission toward those outside the covenant?

Exodus-shaped Mission?

Christopher Wright argues that Israel's exodus from Egypt is the model of "God's comprehensive redemption," demonstrating God's mission to redeem the political, economic, social, and spiritual spheres.[74] Wright goes on to claim that the paradigm of God's "exodus-shaped redemption demands exodus-shaped mission" by God's covenant people.[75] But does the OT provide evidence that the Lord assigned Israel when in possession of the land an "exodus-shaped mission"? Wright's prime example that the Lord *does* require Israel to fulfill this kind of mission is the Leviticus 25 law of the jubilee, which Wright calls "God's model of restoration," encompassing both the economic and social spheres.[76] Wright recognizes that "the jubilee was intended for the survival and welfare of the families *in Israel* [emphasis added]" but proceeds to conclude that its "moral principles" ought to be applied *outside* the covenant community since these principles are "universalizable on the basis of the moral consistency of God," such that "what God required of Israel in God's land reflects what in principle he desires for humanity on

---

[72] David VanDrunen, "The Importance of the Penultimate: Reformed Social Thought and the Contemporary Critiques of the Liberal Society," *Journal of Markets and Morality* 9, no. 2 (2006): 233.

[73] VanDrunen, *Living in God's Two Kingdoms*, 89.

[74] Wright, *The Mission of God*, 268–72.

[75] Ibid., 275. Rodd is one who believes that a paradigmatic usage of the exodus "needs to be questioned." Cyril S. Rodd, *Glimpses of a Strange Land: Studies in Old Testament Ethics* (Edinburgh: T&T Clark, 2001), 183.

[76] Wright, *The Mission of God*, 289–98.

God's earth," including international debt relief and the "equitable distribution" of land, wealth, and other resources.[77] Yet, in spite of his claims for the application of the jubilee outside the covenant community, Wright simultaneously does *not* believe that *OT Israel* had a God-given mission to go to the nations outside the covenant land, including no responsibility to apply the principles of the jubilee or the exodus among the nations.[78] As those living under a "settled covenant of already-realized rest," Israel is *not* responsible before God for a mission of bringing either "exodus-shaped redemption" or "jubilee-shaped restoration" to the non-covenant peoples living outside the covenant land.

A Light to the Nations outside the Land

If OT Israel has no mission of redemption and restoration toward the nations, what *is* their responsibility toward those outside the covenant *and* outside the land? In Exodus 19:5–6, at the beginning of the process of establishing the Mosaic covenant, the Lord says to Israel, "if you will indeed obey my voice and keep my covenant, you shall be my treasured possession among all peoples, for all the earth is mine; and you shall be to me a kingdom of priests and a holy nation." According to Gentry and Wellum, "kingdom of priests" could mean "a domain of priests whom God rules," emphasizing the worship relationship between the priest and God, or could mean "the exercise of royal office by those who are in fact priests," emphasizing the mediatorial relationship between the priest and the

---

[77] Ibid., 295, 296, 298. While Skeel and Longman agree that some of the principles of the jubilee law have broader application, they express more hesitancy than Wright, believing that "the precise terms of the jubilee do not translate well into debt relief and development," since we must "recognize how far from the original context international debt relief is." David Skeel and Tremper Longman III, "Criminal and Civil Law in the Torah: The Mosaic Law in Christian Perspective," in *Law and the Bible: Justice, Mercy and Legal Institutions*, eds. Robert F. Cochran and David VanDrunen (Downers Grove, IL: IVP Academic, 2013), 96, 95.

[78] Wright, *The Mission of God*, 502.

world, or could mean both.[79] Schnabel rejects the mediatorial interpretation, seeing an "emphasis on the relationship between [Israel
and the Lord]" as the "more plausible interpretation."[80] John Davies
concludes the same, with Gentry and Wellum affirming the validity of Davies' textual arguments and his observation that "the Sinai
pericope simply contains no direct reference to Israel's responsibilities toward the nations."[81] But Gentry and Wellum go on to choose
the both/and interpretation, agreeing that though "kingdom of
priests" *does* emphasize the priestly worship relationship, centered in
"access to the divine presence" by those "consecrated and devoted to
[the Lord],"[82] this phrase *also* communicates a secondary orientation
for the priests toward the world as God's royal representatives who
mediate God's presence as a "light to the nations."[83]

[79] Gentry and Wellum, *Kingdom through Covenant*, 319.

[80] Schnabel, *Jesus and the Twelve*, 71. DeYoung and Gilbert give four reasons
for rejecting the mediatorial interpretation of "kingdom of priests": "1. The
Levitical priesthood serves a mediatorial role not in terms of incarnating God's
presence (his presence is in the glory cloud over the ark of the covenant) but
in terms of placating his anger. The primary function of the priests in the Old
Testament is to mediate between God and man by administering sacrifices. . . .
2. 'Kingdom of priests' is best understood as a designation for Israel's call to be
set apart from the world and belong to God. . . . 3. If God were giving the Israelites a missionary task to bless the non-Israelites, we might expect to see this
task specified and elaborated in the Mosaic Law. Yet the rules and regulations
of Sinai say nothing about a mission to the Gentiles. There are commands for
Israel to express care for sojourners and foreigners in its midst, but not explicit
instructions for Israel to go into the world and meet the needs of the nations.
4. The Israelites conquer the surrounding nations by military force, not by any
kind of incarnational mission. . . . The prophets never fault Israel for neglecting
its missionary or international blessing mandate." Kevin DeYoung and Greg
Gilbert, *What Is the Mission of the Church? Making Sense of Social Justice, Shalom,
and the Great Commission* (Wheaton, IL: Crossway, 2011), 35–36.

[81] Gentry and Wellum, *Kingdom through Covenant*, 321.

[82] Ibid., 320.

[83] Ibid., 319, 321. Wright agrees that the mission of Israel was "Nothing
less than to be 'a light to the nations,' the means of bringing the redemptive
blessing of God to all the nations of the world." Wright, *The Mission of God*, 31.
For references to God's servant, Israel (both to the nation as a whole and to

If one takes Israel's covenant role in the land as reflective of Adam's original covenant role in the garden, then Gentry and Wellum's interpretation fits well with this book's conclusions in chapter 4 concerning Adam's responsibilities. Therefore, like Adam, Israel as a "kingdom of priests" includes both an orientation toward their covenant Lord as priestly worshippers and an orientation toward their covenant realm as representational rulers, with the role of priest being Israel's "primary office." But in their secondary office as representational rulers, is Israel given a mission of actively going to those outside the covenant land to mediate God's presence? Kaiser believes that Exodus 19:5–6 *does* require Israel to be "God's ministers, his preachers, his prophets to their own nation as well as to other nations," to be active missionary "agents of God's blessing to all on earth," and that "nothing could be clearer."[84] Kaiser ascribes the relative lack of later textual evidence showing Israel going as missionaries to the nations to Israel's "myopically declin[ing], for the most part, to carry out her high calling as the channel through which the grace of God could come to all the nations," rather than to the Lord's not assigning this mission to Israel in the first place.[85] But Köstenberger and O'Brien find Kaiser's conclusion "unsatisfactory both exegetically and theologically," since they believe it "goes beyond the evidence."[86] They agree with Kaiser that the OT speaks often of the nations coming to Israel, but also stress that, with one or two exceptions (Isa. 66:18–24, as well as the prophet Jonah in a unique sense), the OT never speaks of Israel going to the nations.[87] As well, they observe that in the OT, the drawing of the nations (including Isa. 66:18–24) is always portrayed as an "eschatological event," rather than a contemporary mission for the

---

the Messiah, the new Israel), as "a light to the nations," see Isa. 41:8–9; 42:1–9 [42:6]; 49:1–10 [49:6]; 60:1–22 [60:1–3]; 62:1–2.

[84] Kaiser, *Mission in the Old Testament*, 22, 24.

[85] Ibid., 23.

[86] Köstenberger and O'Brien, *Salvation to the Ends of the Earth*, 35.

[87] Ibid., 42, 52.

covenant people.[88] Finally, the OT emphasizes that this eschatological ingathering of those outside the covenant is fundamentally "the work of God, not Israel."[89] Köstenberger and O'Brien's position concerning OT Israel's mission is commonly described as a strictly "centripetal" mission of attracting the nations but not actively going to those outside the covenant.[90] Kaiser's position combines this centripetal mission with a "centrifugal" responsibility for active missionary outreach beyond the covenant community. This book will follow Köstenberger and O'Brien in concluding that OT Israel living within the covenant land has only a "centripetal" mission of attraction, or as Dean Flemming describes it, a mission "mainly to show rather than tell," or primarily "a mission of presence."[91]

"Kingdom of priests" in Exodus 19:6 is parallel to the phrase "holy nation," further illustrating Israel's "mission of presence" when dwelling within the covenant land. Gentry and Wellum suggest that the "primary meaning" of the adjective "holy" refers to "the divine sphere to which the person or object relates," rather than "the sphere from which it has thereby been separated."[92] In other words, "holy" communicates firstly an emphasis on *being consecrated to* and only secondly an emphasis on *being separated from*. Israel as "a holy nation" is therefore a nation "prepared and consecrated for fellowship with God and one completely devoted to him."[93] At the same time, Israel's complete devotion to their covenant Lord also requires significant separation from outsiders as a "key function of the Law was to maintain the distinctiveness of Israel,"[94] including the obligation to

---

[88] Ibid., 42.

[89] Ibid., 42. Schnabel agrees that "the conversion of pagans is not Israel's responsibility: God himself will cause the nations to come to Zion." Schnabel, *Jesus and the Twelve*, 77.

[90] Scott, *Bring Forth Justice*, 55.

[91] Flemming, *Recovering the Full Mission of God*, 45, 57.

[92] Gentry and Wellum, *Kingdom through Covenant*, 320.

[93] Ibid., 325.

[94] Robin Routledge, *Old Testament Theology: A Thematic Approach* (Downers Grove, IL: IVP Academic, 2008), 244–45.

"studiously . . . avoid contact with the nations, except in warfare, so as not to be contaminated by them."[95] But the ultimate goal of both Israel's devotion and separation is to achieve the "attractive life . . . [of] a contrast people in the midst of the nations," a public display of "God's people living in God's way."[96] If Israel in the land keeps the way of the covenant, according to Deuteronomy 4:6–8, then "the nations would notice," and Israel's holy life would, in this way, mediate God's presence to those outside the covenant land.[97]

How do the ethical demands of Israel's consecrated life in the land correspond to the Abrahamic responsibility for "doing righteousness and justice" within the covenant family ("special grace justice")? Even though Genesis 18:19 is the only occurrence of the phrase "righteousness and justice" in the Pentateuch,[98] these words and concepts are central to many of Israel's later prophetic books, the prophets often calling Israel to repent of their unrighteousness and injustice and to keep the Abrahamic/Mosaic special grace covenants.[99] In fact, "the call to love, justice, and righteousness is sometimes used [within a prophetic book] to summarize the entire prophetic message."[100] Within the OT, "righteousness and justice" describes the foundation of God's rulership ("*Righteousness and justice* are the foundation of your throne" [Ps. 89:14; 97:2]), the rulership standard within the land for covenant kings ("O king of Judah, who sits on the throne of David . . . Thus says the LORD: *Do*

---

[95] Köstenberger and O'Brien, *Salvation to the Ends of the Earth*, 37.

[96] Goheen, *A Light to the Nations*, 40, 53.

[97] Wright, *The Mission of God*, 380.

[98] John H. Sailhamer, *The Meaning of the Pentateuch: Revelation, Composition, and Interpretation* (Downers Grove, IL: IVP Academic, 2009), 496.

[99] M. Daniel Carroll R., "Failing the Vulnerable: The Prophets and Social Care," in *Transforming the World: The Gospel and Social Responsibility*, eds. Jamie A. Grant and Dewi A. Hughes (Nottingham, UK: Apollos, 2009), 36. See also Armacost and Enns, "Crying Out for Justice," 129.

[100] Stephen G. Dempster, "Prophetic Books," in *New Dictionary of Biblical Theology*, ed. T. Desmond Alexander et al. (Downers Grove, IL: IVP, 2000), 124.

justice and righteousness" [Jer. 22:2–3]), and the perfect rulership of the promised Davidic king ("I will raise up for David a righteous Branch, and he shall reign as king and deal wisely, and shall *execute justice and righteousness* in the land" [Jer. 23:5]). For the covenant kings, "doing righteousness and justice" includes the maintenance of fair courts and fair weights (as noted above), but also refers to "acts on behalf of the poor and less fortunate classes of people," since the overall "establishment of a just society is the responsibility of the king."[101]

But within the OT, *all* God's covenant people, and not just kings, must "do justice." The prophet Micah addresses all members of the covenant, proclaiming, "He has told you, O man, what is good; and what does the LORD require of you but to do justice, and to love kindness, and to walk humbly with your God?" (Mic. 6:8). Often for the prophets, the test for determining whether or not an Israelite does justice and loves kindness is how they treat "powerless [groups who are] vulnerable to injustice, cruelty, and a general lack of concern," such as widows, orphans, resident aliens, and the poor of the land.[102] Though the king also must act on behalf of the poor and powerless, David Baker argues that within the OT, "Social care is

---

[101] Weinfeld, *Social Justice in Israel*, 8, 45.

[102] Timothy C. Tennent, *Invitation to World Missions: A Trinitarian Missiology for the Twenty-First Century* (Grand Rapids: Kregel, 2010), 394. "The poor" in the OT are not simply the economically impoverished in general. Sider notes, "The primary connotation of 'the poor' in Scripture has to do with low economic status usually due to calamity or some form of oppression," while the OT "also teach[es] that some folk are poor because they are lazy and slothful." Ronald J. Sider, *Rich Christians in an Age of Hunger: Moving from Affluence to Generosity*, 20th anniversary ed. (Dallas: Word, 1997), 41–42. Additionally, "the poor" is used to refer to God's believing covenant people as a whole. Hans Kvalbein, "Poor/Poverty," in *New Dictionary of Biblical Theology*, ed. T. Desmond Alexander et al. (Downers Grove, IL: IVP, 2000), 690. This distinction between believing poor and unbelieving poor is important since, while God certainly cares for all the oppressed, according to Merrill, "God is said to pity those in distress, almost exclusively the people of Israel in the Old Testament." Merrill, *Everlasting Dominion*, 63.

seen as the responsibility of individuals and families within the community rather than as a state provision."[103] Therefore, as a holy nation of "righteousness and justice," all Israel within the covenant land would be a light to the nations. As a contrast community displaying the glory of their covenant Lord, Israel's moral and spiritual witness would attract those outside the covenant and point them toward the true God, a responsibility to the nations which falls broadly under the category of Israel's "good deeds" mission toward those beyond the boundaries of the covenant land.

Treaties, tribute, trading, and temple. Though Israel as a light to the nations outside the covenant land is not given a mission of establishing "righteousness and justice" *in* those nations, Israel may at times have cause to war *against* those nations. In Deuteronomy 20:10–18, Moses instructs Israel that when attacking a city outside the covenant land (20:15), first "offer terms of peace" to the city and then enslave the people if the terms are accepted (20:10–11). If the terms of peace are not accepted, Israel should besiege and defeat the city, killing all adult males while taking its women, children, livestock, and other possessions as plunder (20:12–14). This standard of warring against those *outside* the covenant land contrasts to God's demand that Israel must annihilate all the Canaanite residents *within* the covenant land, "sav[ing] alive nothing that breathes . . . devot[ing] them to complete destruction" (20:16–18). While Israel must utterly destroy idolaters within the land, they should attempt to make peace treaties with idolaters outside the land.

When making treaties with those outside the covenant land, Israel is expected to be faithful to their treaty commitments. King David had received lumber and workmen from King Hiram of Tyre in order to build David's palace (2 Sam. 5:11). When David's son, Solomon, began to reign, he made a treaty with Hiram for

---

[103] David L. Baker, "Protecting the Vulnerable: The Law and Social Care," in *Transforming the World: The Gospel and Social Responsibility*, eds. Jamie A. Grant and Dewi A. Hughes (Nottingham, UK: Apollos, 2009), 31.

the lumber and workmen needed to build the temple in Jerusalem (1 Kings 5:1–12). But after twenty years of partnership with Hiram, years in which Hiram "supplied Solomon with cedar and cypress timber and gold, as much as he desired" (1 Kings 9:11), Solomon rewards Hiram with "twenty cities in the land of Galilee," an inferior gift which offends Hiram as unworthy of their long treaty relationship (1 Kings 9:12–13), a negative conclusion which the narrator seems to share when he ends by noting the vast amounts of gold which Solomon received from Hiram (1 Kings 9:14). Contrary to this portrayal, faithfulness in such treaties is required from Israel—even when the treaty is made under false pretenses. Gibeon is a city in Canaan, among the many which Israel under Joshua is supposed to conquer and destroy. In fear, the Gibeonites approach the Israelites, pretending to be a people from *outside* the covenant land who have heard of the mighty acts of the Lord and want to make a treaty with Israel (Josh. 9:3–13). Deceived, Israel makes a treaty with this city they should otherwise destroy, a treaty they must honor even upon discovering Gibeon's trickery (Josh. 9:14–10:15), a treaty in which King Saul's later unfaithfulness requires redress by the death of seven of Saul's sons (2 Sam. 21:1–14).

Particularly during the reign of Solomon, Israel interacts extensively with foreign nations. Solomon rules over all the covenant land, as well as subduing many outside kingdoms, receiving tribute from these nations (1 Kings 4:21). Beyond these kingdoms subdued by Solomon, even more distant nations come to hear Solomon's wisdom (1 Kings 4:34), also bringing great tribute (1 Kings 10:1–13). In addition to tribute relationships, Solomon establishes many trading relationships with outsiders, importing by land and sea, gold, silver, precious stones, spices, trees, animals, and weapons (1 Kings 9:26–28; 10:11, 22, 28–29). Finally, at the dedication of the temple in Jerusalem, Solomon prays that the Lord would answer the petitions of any foreigner from distant lands who comes to the temple to pray, thereby causing the report of the Lord's fame and glory to spread among the nations (1 Kings 8:41–43). Israel relates to non-covenant peoples outside the land as a just conqueror, a lucrative trading partner, and a potential mediator of God's mercy, all further enhancing Israel's role as a light to the nations.

Relationship to the Nations within the Land

As noted above, the Lord commanded Israel utterly to destroy the idolatrous Canaanite inhabitants living *in* the covenant land. This obligation contrasts sharply with the way Abraham and his descendants earlier relate to the Canaanites when living among them. The minimal good deeds responsibility of Abraham toward the Canaanites consists of living among them according to "common grace justice," pursuing together basic social stability, judicial equity, and relative peace. In addition, at times Abraham intercedes before the Lord on behalf of the Canaanites for the aversion of God's judgment and the bestowal of his mercy. But for Israel possessing the land, this "good deeds responsibility" is completely replaced by what a Canaanite might consider to be Israel's "bad deeds responsibility," showing no mercy to the Canaanites. Yet within the OT worldview, Israel's responsibility to eradicate idolatry from the covenant land is also a key component of their being a holy nation, thereby enabled to be God's light to other nations.

But righteous eradication is not the only way which Israel is to relate to non-covenant peoples living in the land. As noted above in the introduction to this chapter, Israel is to treat fairly and to care for "resident aliens." "Resident alien" is "the conventional scholarly translation" of a Hebrew word that can also be rendered as "stranger," "foreigner," "sojourner," "immigrant," or "refugee," but which this book will refer to as a "resident alien," meaning "a free person who resides outside their native country or region, being accepted by the host community and having certain rights but not regarded as a full citizen."[104] Moses describes Israel's covenant Lord as the God who "executes justice for the fatherless and the widow, and loves the

---

[104] Ibid., 19–20.

sojourner, giving him food and clothing," an example which Israel is to imitate by obeying God's command to "Love the sojourner," a command also rooted in the fact that the Israelites themselves were once "sojourners in the land of Egypt" (Deut. 10:18–19). The resident alien is likewise included in the demand for Israel to "love your neighbor as yourself" (Lev. 19:18), since Israel must "treat the stranger who sojourns with you as the native among you, and you shall love him as yourself" (Lev. 19:34). The resident alien is a vulnerable person within the ancient world, at risk of being oppressed, and Israel's covenant Lord is "concerned for the vulnerable . . . warn[ing] the Israelites of dire consequences if they do not show a similar concern."[105]

As also observed in this chapter's introduction, resident aliens are required to live in basic harmony with Israel's covenant stipulations, participating in some aspects of Israel's religious life voluntarily, some mandatorily. Generally speaking, the text portrays resident aliens as those who live within the believing community, being "largely regarded as proselyte[s]," in contrast to the idolatrous Canaanites.[106] Examples of proselytes from the OT include Rahab and her Canaanite family who confess Israel's Lord as "God in the heavens above and on the earth beneath" (Josh. 2:11), and Ruth the Moabitess, who says to Naomi the Israelite that "your people shall be my people, and your God my God" (Ruth 1:16). But even though pious resident aliens might have significant standing within the covenant community, they still have "a lower social status compared with the Israelite."[107] For example, "the laws for giving to the poor favored the fellow Israelite. . . . loans to a needy Israelite could not include interest charges, but loans to foreigners could be with interest (Deut. 23:20). . . . when debts were canceled to other Israelites [in a Sabbath year], payment could still be demanded from non-Israelites

---

[105] Ibid., 21.
[106] Schnabel, *Jesus and the Twelve*, 69.
[107] Ibid.

(Deut. 15:3)."[108] The unique status of resident aliens within Israel's covenant land means that Israel's good deeds responsibilities toward them are therefore a hybrid expression of Israel's broader good deeds mission toward foreigners. In contrast to foreigners outside the land and Canaanites within the land, resident aliens are considered partial (but not full) members of Israel's covenant community.

Good Deeds Mission of Abraham's Descendants from the Exile until Christ

After God completes the removal of his covenant people from the land in judgment (2 Kings 25:1–21), Abraham's descendants no longer possess their promised land. The original circumstances of the "settled covenant of already-realized rest" are now radically altered: the temple is destroyed, the Davidic king and his people are exiled in Babylon, and the covenant land is occupied by idolaters. As well, even after a remnant of the covenant people journeys back to the land many years later, they still remain in partial "exile," the promised return of the Davidic king and the establishment of his glorious kingdom remaining unfulfilled. How does this changed setting affect the good deeds mission of Israel toward those *outside* the covenant? In many ways, Israel's good deeds mission reverts to one very similar to Abraham's good deeds mission before the possession of the land.

An illustration of Israel's return to Abraham's original good deeds mission is found in Jeremiah 29:1–23, where Jeremiah instructs the exiles in Babylon that, contrary to the false prophets' prediction of a quick return to the covenant land, the exiles will live in Babylon for many decades before the Lord brings them back. Therefore, Jeremiah commands them to "Build houses and live in them; plant gardens and eat their produce. Take wives and have sons and

---

[108] Timothy J. Keller, *Ministries of Mercy: The Call of the Jericho Road*, 2nd ed. (Phillipsburg, NJ: P&R Publishing, 1997), 82.

daughters; multiply there, and do not decrease. But seek the welfare of the city where I have sent you into exile, and pray to the LORD on its behalf, for in its welfare you will find your welfare" (Jer. 29:5–7). The word translated here as "welfare" is the Hebrew word "shalom," a word used over 350 times in the OT, whose possible spectrum of meaning includes concepts such as "wholeness, without injury, undivided, well-being, a satisfactory condition, bodily health, and all that salvation means in its Old Testament usage."[109] Clearly the shalom which the exiles are to seek for Babylon is not eternal blessing and salvation ("special grace shalom") since, both earlier and later in the book, Jeremiah prophesies that the Lord will one day make Babylon "an everlasting waste" (25:12), "an utter desolation" (50:13), and "a horror among the nations" (51:41). Therefore, this shalom must be a "common grace shalom,"[110] which appears to correspond well with Abraham's earlier responsibility to do "common grace justice." God's covenant people in exile are indeed to seek temporal and limited flourishing for a condemned city, even if "the focus of this passage is . . . not the flourishing of Babylon but the well-being of God's people."[111] Abraham likewise lives peacefully among the Canaanites, praying for their temporal blessing while also knowing that, in the future, God will judge the Canaanites for their sin and give their land to Abraham's descendants (Gen. 15:16, 18–21). Other examples of covenant people during the times of exile living among the nations according to "common grace justice" and "common grace shalom" include: Daniel serving King Nebuchadnezzar of Babylon (Dan. 1:18–21) and King Darius of Persia (Dan. 6:1–3), Mordecai serving King Ahasuerus of Persia (Esth. 10:2–3), and Nehemiah serving King Artaxerxes of Persia (Neh. 1:11). No longer a theocracy, God's

---

[109] Arthur F. Glasser, *Announcing the Kingdom: The Story of God's Mission in the Bible* (Grand Rapids: Baker Academic, 2003), 130.

[110] DeYoung and Gilbert label the *shalom* in this passage as a "less-than-ultimate shalom." DeYoung and Gilbert, *What Is the Mission of the Church?*, 201.

[111] Litfin, *Word versus Deed*, 171.

covenant people must again learn, like Abraham, to "live faithfully when somebody else is in charge."[112] Israel in exile (whether in Babylon or returned to the land) must simultaneously live both a shared life *with* outsiders and a separated life *from* outsiders. For instance, "despite their engagement with Babylonian society, the Jews still kept the Mosaic code, so that their dress, food, and other practices continued to set them culturally apart from the Babylonians . . . Their dietary laws alone virtually dictated that Jews eat separately from pagans."[113] Though no longer dwelling in the covenant land under the Davidic king and exhibiting a more radical social separation from idolaters, the Jews still sought to be a holy nation *among* the nations, even as they promoted "common grace justice" and pursued "common grace shalom" in partnership *with* the nations.

Interrelationship of Israel's Good Deeds Mission and Humanity's Good Deeds Responsibility

In chapter 5, this book concluded that all humanity is responsible before their Creator under the Noahic Fallen Creation Covenant to participate in building and preserving human society, including by establishing just (though imperfect) governments and caring for those who are poor, weak, and vulnerable. These common grace responsibilities accord with the natural law that God has woven into the created order (although this unwritten law is imperfectly perceived and inevitably resisted by sinful humanity). Sharing a common human nature, Abraham and his descendants likewise bear these responsibilities toward other people, including those outside the covenant. When in possession of the covenant land, Abraham's

---

[112] William S. Brewbaker III and V. Philips Long, "Law and Political Order: Israel's Constitutional History," in *Law and the Bible: Justice, Mercy and Legal Institutions*, eds. Robert F. Cochran and David VanDrunen (Downers Grove, IL: IVP Academic, 2013), 76.

[113] Timothy Keller, *Center Church: Doing Balanced, Gospel-Centered Ministry in Your City* (Grand Rapids: Zondervan, 2012), 147.

descendants live a life of greater separation from outsiders, obligated to *withhold* common grace from the idolatrous Canaanites and to act instead as agents of divine judgment. Yet even while possessing the land, Israel is to continue to live according to "common grace justice," being faithful to treaties and trade agreements with the nations *outside* the covenant land. These nations are also welcome to journey to Jerusalem to pray confidently to the covenant Lord at the temple, Israel's presence thereby mediating God's mercy and fame to the nations. If faithful in their holy life in the land, Israel will function as God's light to the nations, attracting foreigners to their covenant Lord enthroned in the temple. But even after the beginning of exile (as well as before conquest), Abraham's descendants are also to do "special grace justice" *within* the covenant family in such a way as to be a contrast community before the eyes of the world. "Righteousness and justice" within the covenant should demonstrate to those outside the covenant the greatness and wisdom of Israel's God. As well, Israel should be empowered to do "common grace justice" in the world outside the covenant in such a way (with integrity, excellence, and compassion) that also contributes to Israel's effective functioning as a light to the nations. While all humanity is responsible for good deeds, Abraham's descendants bear an extra weight of responsibility, carrying out a mission of common grace justice which is undergirded by intercessory prayer, displaying the glory of God.

7

The Good Deeds Mission in the Gospels before New Covenant Inauguration

Still in exile as concerns the promises of the Davidic kingdom, the Jews awaited a new exodus as they entered the historical period of the NT documents. Like all humanity, they lived under the Noahic Fallen Creation Covenant, responsible to exercise "common grace justice" toward all people. The Jews also continued living under the Abrahamic/Mosaic special grace covenants, with the Mosaic translated from its original status as a "settled covenant of already-realized rest" to now functioning, along with the Abrahamic, as a "sojourning covenant of not-yet-realized rest." In considering the good deeds mission of Jesus the Christ and his disciples as portrayed in the Gospels, one needs to ask with N. T. Wright, "What time is it?"[1] That is, how one situates Jesus' earthly ministry within the storyline of the Bible's unfolding covenantal-historical macro-structure will significantly determine how one understands and applies the good deeds mission revealed in the Gospels. Horton describes this interpretive task as our need to "locate our place on the map of redemptive history."[2] Peter Beyerhaus employs the traditional concept of "salvation history" (*Heilsgeschichte*) to make the same point, highlighting the

---

[1] N. T. Wright, *Jesus and the Victory of God* (Minneapolis: Fortress, 1996), 467.

[2] Michael Horton, *The Gospel Commission: Recovering God's Strategy for Making Disciples* (Grand Rapids: Baker, 2011), 63.

need for "eschatological precision" when considering the "crucial distinctions between the different stages in which the divine *oikonomia*, the redemptive economy of God" unfolds within the text of Scripture and within broader human history.[3] Therefore, this chapter's survey of the good deeds mission revealed in the Gospels will seek to stay consciously within "the salvation-historical constraints of the divine economy of redemption."[4]

While there is significant continuity between the Abrahamic/ Mosaic/Davidic special grace covenants and the special grace New Covenant, the Gospels show Jesus fulfilling the old covenants in such a way that displays "massive change or discontinuity . . . an incredible epochal shift in redemptive-history . . . unlike any other time."[5] But while Jesus' birth, life, and earlier ministry already embody the beginnings of a fulfillment and a substantial development within salvation-history, the culminating inauguration of the New Covenant at the end of the Gospel narratives signifies a further development and completion of the "epochal shift." Therefore, not only is there a "distinct difference" between the Old Covenant and the New

---

[3] Peter P. J. Beyerhaus, *God's Kingdom and the Utopian Error: Discerning the Biblical Kingdom of God from Its Political Counterfeits* (Wheaton, IL: Crossway, 1992), ix.

[4] Andreas J. Köstenberger and Peter T. O'Brien, *Salvation to the Ends of the Earth: A Biblical Theology of Mission* (Downers Grove, IL: IVP, 2001), 85.

[5] Peter J. Gentry and Stephen J. Wellum, *Kingdom through Covenant: A Biblical-Theological Understanding of the Covenants* (Wheaton, IL: Crossway, 2012), 598. Gentry and Wellum state, "The new covenant supersedes all the previous covenants in redemptive-history. . . . now that Christ has come, it is important to stress that we are no longer under those previous covenants as covenants, since they have reached their fulfillment in Christ" (ibid., 604, 605). But, as noted in chap. 3, Gentry and Wellum also state, "The covenant with Noah is in effect today. . . . There is no evidence anywhere in the completed canon of Scripture as a whole that this covenant has been annulled or superseded" (ibid., 171). This tension in their argument can be resolved by seeing the Abrahamic/Mosaic/Davidic covenants as fulfilled in Christ in the *inaugurated* New Covenant while seeing the Noahic Fallen Creation Covenant as only fulfilled in Christ in the new heavens and new earth of the *consummated* New Covenant.

Covenant, there is also a "distinct difference" between Jesus' (and his disciples') pre-New Covenant ministries and their inaugurated New Covenant ministries—including potential differences in their good deeds missions.[6] Johannes Nissen agrees that (for instance, in the Gospel of Luke) these three eras—"(1) the epoch of Israel, including John the Baptist; (2) the epoch of Jesus' ministry which is seen as the middle period of salvation; and (3) the epoch of the church inaugurated by the day of Pentecost"—must be distinguished, even if not unnecessarily divided.[7] This needed distinction between eras is why the good deeds mission of Christ and his disciples before the inauguration of the New Covenant receives stand-alone treatment in this chapter.

When then *is* the New Covenant inaugurated? The Noahic Fallen Creation Covenant (Gen. 8:20–21), the Abrahamic Covenant (Gen. 15:9–17), and the Mosaic Covenant (Ex. 12:1–22; 24:5–8) (as well as, arguably, the Davidic Covenant [1 Sam. 16:1–13; 2 Sam. 7:8–17; 23:5]) are each inaugurated with blood sacrifice. As prophesied in the OT, the New Covenant is also inaugurated with blood sacrifice (Isa. 53:4–10; 42:6; 49:8; 55:3; 59:21; 61:8), the Davidic son offering himself. Christ makes clear this continued pattern of covenant inauguration by blood sacrifice in Luke 22:20 when he takes "the cup after they had eaten [the Passover meal], saying, 'This cup that is poured out for you is the new covenant in my blood.'" But does Jesus' sacrificial death and victorious resurrection *complete* the inauguration of the New Covenant? Later, Jesus' commission to his disciples in Matthew 28:18–20 includes elements of a "covenant renewal" with his disciples.[8] Christ's subsequent ascension likewise depicts his enthronement as covenant Lord.[9] The ascension in many

---

[6] J. Herbert Kane, *Christian Missions in Biblical Perspective* (Grand Rapids: Baker, 1976), 227.

[7] Johannes Nissen, *New Testament and Mission: Historical and Hermeneutical Perspectives* (New York: Peter Lang, 1999), 49.

[8] Köstenberger and O'Brien, *Salvation to the Ends of the Earth*, 102.

[9] George Eldon Ladd, *A Theology of the New Testament* (Grand Rapids:

ways therefore completes both the resurrection[10] and Jesus' sacrifice, "inaugurat[ing] his heavenly priestly ministry . . . [as] a 'minister (*leitourgos*)' in the heavenly sanctuary (Heb. 8:1–2)," a sanctuary he enters upon ascension "by means of his own blood" (Heb. 9:12).[11] Does the ascension thereby "complete the Christ event" and "inaugurate the period that extends from the Christ event to the parousia?"[12] Actually, Christ's inauguration of the New Covenant is only *fully* complete with "the giving of the Spirit."[13] The pouring forth of the Spirit at Pentecost means that "as promised by Joel, the last days have begun and the new covenant has been inaugurated."[14] The New Covenant is therefore inaugurated by the complex of events stretching from the last supper to Pentecost.

Jesus' (and his disciples') ministry on earth *before* Pentecost is thus during a unique transitional era from the Old Covenant to the New. We must then interpret the events described in the Gospels carefully, since we should not assume that "historical experiences are normative and can or should be repeated. . . . one needs to distinguish hermeneutically between what is descriptive and what is (possibly) prescriptive."[15] Even as we recognize the transitional and unique nature of the *events* of the gospels, Jonathan Pennington

---

Eerdmans, 1974), 335.

[10] Charles H. H. Scobie, *The Ways of Our God: An Approach to Biblical Theology* (Grand Rapids: Eerdmans, 2003), 455.

[11] Ibid., 457.

[12] Ibid., 465, 462.

[13] Ibid., 490.

[14] Eckhard J. Schnabel, *Jesus and the Twelve*, vol. 1 of *Early Christian Mission* (Downers Grove, IL: IVP, 2004), 404.

[15] Eckhard J. Schnabel, *Paul and the Early Church*, vol. 2 of *Early Christian Mission* (Downers Grove, IL: IVP, 2004), 1570. Goldsworthy makes a similar point: "But the various New Testament documents do not bear a uniform relationship to us in the present. This obvious fact can easily be overlooked or is often simply forgotten. Thus the words of Jesus to his disciples or to the Jews do not necessarily apply to us without qualification." Graeme Goldsworthy, *Christ-Centered Biblical Theology: Hermeneutical Foundations and Principles* (Downers Grove, IL: IVP Academic, 2012), 151.

rightly warns us not to dismiss the Gospel *texts* as merely "historical data."[16] Instead, the gospels were written with a *"post-Pentecost perspective* [including] *expert analysis and commentary.* . . . The point of a Gospel story is not *primarily* or *ultimately* to convey historical information (though history matters and the stories indeed do provide this) but to teach, explain, and exhort us God-ward, toward transformation through virtue."[17] Acknowledging with Pennington the ongoing role of the Gospels as tools for personal transformation, we nevertheless must maintain sensitivity to the descriptive/prescriptive distinction as we consider the good deeds mission of Jesus and his disciples before the New Covenant.[18]

Finally, before continuing this biblical theology of the good deeds mission of the New Covenant community, note that this book will not explore the perennial and crucial question of the

[16] Jonathan T. Pennington, *Reading the Gospels Wisely: A Narrative and Theological Introduction* (Grand Rapids: Baker Academic, 2012), 152.

[17] Ibid., 153. Original emphasis. Pennington states, "[The Gospels'] biographical nature means that in large part they exist to invite us into emulation of the good characters and avoidance of the bad; they are aretological (virture-forming)" (ibid., 144). Pennington's identification of the genre of the Gospels as virtue-forming biography also impacts how we understand their functional authority for contemporary readers since, as Hays proposes, "New Testament texts must be granted authority (or not) in the mode in which they speak. Claims about the authority of the text must respect not only its content but also its form. The interpreter should not turn narratives into law (for instance, by arguing that Acts 2:44–45 requires Christians to own all things in common) or rules into principles (for instance, by suggesting that the commandment to sell possessions and give alms [Luke 12:33] is not meant literally but that it points to the principle of inner detachment from wealth). . . . The New Testament's ethical imperatives are either normative at the level of their own claim, or they are invalid." Richard B. Hays, *The Moral Vision of the New Testament: Community, Cross, New Creation* (San Francisco: HarperSanFrancisco, 1996), 294.

[18] J. Robertson McQuilkin, "An Evangelical Assessment of Mission Theology of the Kingdom of God," in *The Good News of the Kingdom: Mission Theology for the Third Millennium*, eds. Charles Van Engen, Dean S. Gilliland, and Paul Pierson (Maryknoll, NY: Orbis, 1993), 176.

relationship between a New Covenant member's justification before God and a New Covenant member's good deeds (or works). Instead, this book will presuppose the traditional Protestant view that a person is declared righteous before God and receives Christ's imputed righteousness by grace alone through faith alone in Christ alone. Yet, while a New Covenant member's good deeds play no role in his or her justification, good deeds (including toward people outside the covenant) *are* a necessary and verifiable result that true justification and union with Christ *always* produces.[19]

Good Deeds Mission of Christ Pre-New Covenant

Any consideration of the initial good deeds mission of Christ toward those *outside* God's covenant community must begin by recognizing that the direct and primary focus of Jesus' earthly ministry is toward those *inside* the covenant. As part of Jesus' inauguration of the New Covenant, the Gospel of Matthew ends with Jesus commissioning his apostles to make disciples of all nations. But before the inauguration of the New Covenant, Jesus explicitly restricts these same men to "Go nowhere among the Gentiles and enter no town of the Samaritans, but go rather to the lost sheep of the house of Israel" (Matt. 10:5–6). Jesus also says of his own ministry, "I was sent only to the lost sheep of the house of Israel" (Matt. 15:24), exhibiting that Jesus himself works within "salvation-historical constraints." Köstenberger and O'Brien capture this restriction in Jesus' ministry by describing the storyline of the Gospels in three acts: "Jesus, the Jewish Messiah, offers the kingdom to Israel; Israel rejects Jesus, issuing in his crucifixion; the kingdom is offered universally to all those who believe in Jesus the Messiah, Jew and Gentile alike."[20]

---

[19] One recent exposition of the relationship between justification and good deeds from a distinctly biblical-theological perspective is Bradley G. Green, *Covenant and Commandment: Works, Obedience, and Faithfulness in the Christian Life* (Downers Grove, IL: IVP, 2014).

[20] Köstenberger and O'Brien, *Salvation to the Ends of the Earth*, 93.

Concerning the Gospel of Mark, Köstenberger and O'Brien note that some claim that Mark "portrays Jesus as fully and unreservedly embarking on a Gentile mission as part of his earthly ministry."[21] But Köstenberger and O'Brien believe that this reading of Mark is "demonstrably fallacious," citing three reasons in support of their conclusion: first, "one of the major instances where Jesus ministers to a Gentile, his encounter with the Syrophoenician woman, is carefully qualified by the statement regarding the Jews' primacy in salvation history." Second, "the reference to Isaiah 56:7 [which describes the nations coming to the temple to pray] in [Mark] 11:17 is eschatologically constrained." Finally, "both [Mark] 13:10 and 14:9 [both concerning the preaching of the Gospel to all the nations] refer to the church's future (not present) universal gospel proclamation."[22] Rather than an explicit focus on ministering to those outside the covenant, Christ "appears to follow the pattern of Old Testament Israel, still practiced by the Jewish synagogue in Jesus' own day, whose presence was to attract the surrounding nations to her God without going out of her way to reach them."[23] Therefore, in continuity with OT Israel, Jesus' earthly ministry (and his disciples' at that time) is almost exclusively *within* the covenant people, with only minimal, direct interaction with Gentiles.

Compassionate Love toward Gentiles

As part of the continuity between Jesus' and OT Israel's ministries toward those *outside* the covenant community (mainly separation from for the purpose of attraction), both ministries also include a category for direct ministry toward Gentiles. As noted in chapter 6, the OT Israelite when possessing the covenant land is to "love [the resident alien] as yourself," even as he or she is to "love your [Israelite] neighbor as yourself" (Lev. 19:18, 34). Jesus, likewise, tells the

---

[21] Ibid., 86.
[22] Ibid., 84.
[23] Ibid., 86.

parable of the Good Samaritan (Luke 10:25–37) to emphasize and make clear that Israel's responsibility to love their neighbor includes those outside the covenant. This love toward Gentiles is an expression of "compassion" (10:33) and "showing mercy" (10:37), which is embodied in costly actions (10:34–35) rather than merely words or sentiment.[24] As used in the Gospels, "compassion" (σπλαγχνιζομαι [splagchnizomai]) is "a strong emotion, motivated by awareness of the suffering of others, which leads to action intended to deal with that suffering."[25] Throughout the synoptic Gospels, Jesus is described as feeling "compassion" for individuals (Matt. 20:34; Mark 9:22; Luke 7:13) and for crowds (Matt. 9:36 [Mark 6:34]; 14:14; 15:32 [Mark 8:2]) and as acting to alleviate their suffering. Similarly, Jesus is portrayed as "showing mercy" (ελεεω [eleeō]) by miraculous healings and exorcisms on behalf of groups (Matt. 9:27–30; Luke 17:12–14) and individuals (Matt. 17:14–18), including occasionally toward Gentiles (Matt. 15:22–28; Mark 5:1–20), demonstrating by his own example as well as by direct admonition (Matt. 5:7; 9:13; 12:7; 18:33; Luke 15:20) that "one of the most important character qualities that Jesus seeks to inculcate in those who heed his words is the quality of *mercy*."[26] But while Jesus establishes a clear standard of responsibility for compassionate and merciful love toward all people, including those outside the covenant, his own direct ministry toward Gentiles is minimal and secondary at best, a reflection of his own restricted focus on "the lost sheep of Israel."

Jesus clearly "loves his neighbor as himself," and yet, during his earthly ministry, he simultaneously restricts his acts of love toward his *outside-the-covenant* neighbors and gives his primary time and

[24] Robert H. Stein, *The Method and Message of Jesus' Teachings*, rev. ed. (Louisville: Westminster John Knox, 1994), 104–5; John R. W. Stott, *Christian Mission in the Modern World* (Downers Grove, IL: IVP, 2008), 47.

[25] Alistair I. Wilson, "The Compassion of Christ," in *Transforming the World: The Gospel and Social Responsibility*, eds. Jamie A. Grant and Dewi A. Hughes (Nottingham, UK: Apollos, 2009), 99.

[26] Hays, *The Moral Vision of the New Testament*, 99. Original emphasis.

energy to loving his *within-the-covenant* neighbors. Jesus' "limited love" is not merely a reflection of his unique vocation within salvation history but also reveals an unavoidable constraint upon all humanity (one Jesus willingly shares during his earthly ministry): the scarcity of time and human resources in a fallen world. Facing this reality, what does it mean to "love your neighbor *as* yourself?" Augustine ponders whether or not this command means loving your neighbor "equally with yourself." If "loving a person means willing him or her some good" and if "the good which we wish or give to the other person is 'diminished by being shared with others'" [that is, if you are distributing a scarce, limited quantity good], then, according to Augustine, "it is impossible to share equally with everyone else while leaving oneself enough to survive," meaning that "we are simply unable to love all persons *equally* with ourselves when that love is expressed by the gift of scarce means."[27] Instead, Augustine proposes that Jesus' love of neighbor implies two rules: "do no harm to anyone" and "help everyone whenever possible."[28] In this interpretation, "the minimum standard of love is called 'goodwill,' and the rule about it takes a negative form: 'do no harm to anyone.'" Paired with this negative phrasing of the command to love is the positive phrasing, "'help everyone whenever possible,' contain[ing] the qualifier 'whenever possible' because helping everyone with scarce means is often not possible."[29] Aquinas follows Augustine's interpretation of Jesus' command by distinguishing between "benevolence" (goodwill or merely "wishing others a good without actually providing it") and "beneficence" (doing good or "actually providing for others out of our own scarce goods"). According to Aquinas, "As regards beneficence we are bound to observe inequality, because we cannot do good to all; but as regards benevolence, love ought not to be thus

---

[27] John D. Mueller, *Redeeming Economics: Rediscovering the Missing Element* (Wilmington, DE: Intercollegiate Studies Institute, 2014), 141. Original emphasis.

[28] Ibid.

[29] Ibid., 142.

unequal."[30] Therefore, when considering the responsibility to love neighbor which Jesus illustrates by the Good Samaritan parable, this responsibility is best seen as the expectation to love your neighbor "as a person like" yourself (benevolence always, beneficence when possible) rather than "equally with" yourself (beneficence always). The Samaritan's acts of love reflect this distinction in that they cost him the equivalent of perhaps a half week's income (beneficence when possible) rather than requiring him equally to distribute all his resources between himself and the wounded man for the rest of his life (beneficence always).[31] Jesus clearly portrays these acts of "limited love" as the Samaritan meeting his responsibility to love his neighbor. As well, the Samaritan's obligation to help this particular neighbor in need does not automatically translate into his personal "obligation to help every robbery or beating victim. That would be impossible because of scarcity."[32]

Another concept which helps clarify Jesus' own good deeds mission is the idea of "moral proximity," the principle that "our responsibilities are greatest to those who are closest to us."[33] From the perspective of those who receive our love, this principle means that "those who are closer to us have more of a claim on us than those who are distant, with proximity determined by relationships

---

[30] Ibid.

[31] Mueller estimates, "We are told that the Samaritan paid about two days' wages in cash to the innkeeper to look after the victim, and promised to pay any further costs on his return. He must have lost at least another half-day's wages stopping to help. The decision therefore cost him at least half a week's wages, or 1 percent of his annual income, on the spot (less, if as seems likely, the merchant earned more than a day laborer). For someone earning $50,000 a year today, that would be equivalent to handing out about $500 in cash for a stranger" (ibid., 190).

[32] Ibid., 194.

[33] Glenn Sunshine, "Who Are the Poor?" in *For the Least of These: A Biblical Answer to Poverty*, eds. Anne Bradley and Art Lindsley (Bloomington, IN: Westbow Press, 2014), 10. See also Kevin DeYoung and Greg Gilbert, *What Is the Mission of the Church? Making Sense of Social Justice, Shalom, and the Great Commission* (Wheaton, IL: Crossway, 2011), 183–86.

rather than geography."[34] During his earthly life (before he inaugurates the New Covenant), the Jewish man, Jesus of Nazareth, therefore, has a greater responsibility to perform acts of compassionate love toward his fellow Jews within the covenant family than toward Gentiles. Jesus, of course, always expresses *benevolence* toward all people, Jew and Gentile alike, but in the limited years of his earthly ministry before his inauguration of the New Covenant, Jesus the man primarily directs his *beneficence* toward those within the covenant community, those with whom he bears the greatest "moral proximity."

Jesus' sense of responsibility for compassionate love of neighbor extending *beyond* the covenant community is also reflected in his command to his disciples to "love your enemies and pray for those who persecute you" (Matt. 5:44), a statement in which Jesus contrasts his reference to "your enemies" with a reference to "your brothers" (Matt. 5:47). But Gerhard Lohfink asserts that this responsibility to love one's enemies cannot be "defined in an undifferentiated manner as universal philanthropy" since "Jesus stood completely on the foundation of the Old Testament, where one's neighbor is first of all one who lives nearby and who shares the same faith."[35] For Jesus, loving your neighbor (including your enemy) must begin within the covenant people, rather than becoming a "universal abstraction," precisely because "preserving this basis [of fraternal love within the people of God is what] makes it possible to go beyond the boundaries of the community."[36] Of special note is the fact that this admonition to love those outside the covenant community (enemies) also includes Jesus' command to his disciples to pray for their enemies, a responsibility reminiscent of Abraham's intercessory prayers for Canaanites and Philistines.

Jesus' miraculous healings of Gentiles in the Gospels are

[34] Sunshine, "Who Are the Poor?" 30.

[35] Gerhard Lohfink, *Jesus and Community: The Social Dimension of the Christian Faith* (Philadelphia: Fortress, 1984), 114.

[36] Ibid.

a further display of his sense of responsibility for compassionate love toward those outside the covenant. Yet even the three clearest examples of Jesus healing Gentiles indicate that these three Gentiles are distinguished from many others outside Israel's covenant community in that they possess faith in the Jewish Messiah. According to Jesus, the Roman centurion (master of a servant in need of healing) exhibits a faith in Jesus which is superior to any Jesus has yet encountered within the covenant people (Matt. 5:10), a faith which receives the healing it seeks. Likewise, Jesus affirms the Syrophoenician woman (mother of a girl in need of healing) for her great faith (Matt. 15:28), then provides healing. Finally, after receiving deliverance, the Gerasenes demoniac, though denied his plea to continue being with Jesus, obediently and enthusiastically proclaims to his neighbors "how much the Lord has done for [him], and how [the Lord] has had mercy on [him]" (Mark 5:19), also demonstrating true faith in Christ. These three are then more akin to the pious resident alien who is a partial member of the covenant community than they are to the idolatrous Canaanite who is completely excluded from the covenant community.

The identification of these three Gentiles as believers in Christ illustrates that though Jesus' miraculous healings always include the purpose of expressing his compassionate love toward Jews and Gentiles in need, they also always serve purposes beyond mere compassion. One of these purposes is to authenticate his claim to messiahship and divinity, warranting people's belief in him (John 20:30–31) (a result evident in each of the three Gentiles) as well as "anticipat[ing] the ultimate deed of Jesus by which [both Jews and Gentiles] are saved, his death and resurrection."[37] The Gospel of Matthew establishes this link between "the healing ministry of Jesus [and] his suffering and death on the cross by quoting Isaiah 53:4 [which refers to Christ's substitutionary death] in Matthew

---

[37] Graeme Goldsworthy, "Gospel," in *New Dictionary of Biblical Theology*, ed. T. Desmond Alexander et al. (Downers Grove, IL: IVP, 2000), 522.

8:17 [which refers to Christ's healing and exorcism ministry]."[38] By this connection, Matthew expects his readers to see in Jesus' healing ministry the inauguration of a greater healing still to come through the cross. Another purpose of Jesus' miracles is as "warnings to the people: they must accept Jesus as the prophet like Moses and repent and obey his words if they are to find life. Those who remain stubborn and refuse to follow him will be cut off from the covenant people."[39] The seriousness of these miraculous warnings is only heightened by the eschatological sign of Gentiles also receiving Christ's mercy through miracles. When the covenant people reject Jesus in spite of his miracles while Gentiles respond to him in faith, receiving healing, then those clinging merely to their Abrahamic lineage should know that they stand in a precarious position. Even beyond compassion, authentication, and warning, Jesus' miracles communicate the coming of a new age of "restoration to membership in Israel of those who, through sickness or whatever, had been excluded as ritually unclean."[40] In like manner, Jesus' miracles on behalf of Gentiles "bear witness to the inclusion" within God's covenant people of "those who had formerly been outside."[41] Jesus' miracles indicate that not only is God gathering Israel and returning his covenant people from exile, God is also expanding the boundaries of his covenant people to include Gentiles.[42] While Jesus clearly embraces a responsibility to show compassionate love to Gentiles, including through miraculous healing, even these miracles point forward to Christ's greatest work of compassion on behalf of those outside the covenant: inaugurating the New Covenant kingdom and inviting Gentiles to enter.

---

[38] James M. Hamilton Jr., *God's Glory in Salvation through Judgment: A Biblical Theology* (Wheaton, IL: Crossway, 2010), 370. See also Thomas R. Schreiner, *The King in His Beauty: A Biblical Theology of the Old and New Testaments* (Grand Rapids: Baker Academic, 2013), 446.

[39] Hays, *The Moral Vision of the New Testament*, 117.

[40] Wright, *Jesus and the Victory of God*, 191.

[41] Ibid., 192.

[42] Ibid., 428–37. See also Lohfink, *Jesus and Community*, 9–14.

The Scope of Jesus' Kingdom before New Covenant Inauguration

In Luke 4:18–21, before Luke records the beginning of Jesus' healing ministry, Jesus reads Isaiah 61:1–2 in the synagogue at Nazareth and proclaims himself as the fulfillment of this prophecy. These verses plainly refer to Jesus' healing ministry ("recovering of sight to the blind" [4:18]) but also include other more debated aspects of Jesus' earthly mission. In what sense did Christ before the New Covenant "proclaim liberty to the captives . . . set at liberty those who are oppressed . . . [and] proclaim the year of the Lord's favor" (4:18–19)? The "year of the Lord's favor" refers to the OT command to practice the jubilee year (Lev. 25). Robert Linthicum therefore understands Jesus' mission in Luke to be "insist[ing] upon the full implementation of jubilee so that wealth is effectively redistributed and poverty eliminated . . . reestablishing jubilee throughout Israel and perhaps even the world."[43] Flemming believes that by these verses, Jesus introduces his mission in Luke as one which "brings transformation in every dimension by every legitimate means to every person."[44] But contrary to Linthicum and Flemming, it is unconvincing to interpret Jesus' ministry in the Gospels as his attempt to institute jubilee throughout the world *at that time* or to bring transformation to every person *at that time*. As already well-established above, Jesus' mission (including his good deeds mission) before he inaugurates the New Covenant is almost solely directed to those *within* the covenant community, not to every person in the whole world. These verses therefore speak of Jesus' mission of "bring[ing] into being a restored Israel" rather than referring to a mission to both Jews and Gentiles.[45]

But what about *within* the covenant people? According to Luke, is Jesus' mission at that time fully to implement the OT

[43] Robert C. Linthicum, *Transforming Power: Biblical Strategies for Making a Difference in Your Community* (Downers Grove, IL: IVP, 2003), 68.

[44] Dean Flemming, *Recovering the Full Mission of God: A Biblical Perspective on Being, Doing and Telling* (Downers Grove, IL: IVP Academic, 2013), 111.

[45] Hays, *The Moral Vision of the New Testament*, 124.

jubilee *within* Israel, redistribute wealth, eliminate poverty, and transform every dimension of life *within* Israel by every legitimate means? This literalistic interpretation is not supported by the rest of Luke's Gospel. Rather than literal release from prison or alleviation of political oppression, subsequently in Luke, "Jesus most frequently brings relief from *demonic* [emphasis added] oppression (4:33–37; 6:18–19; 7:21; 8:2, 26–39; 9:37–43; 11:14–23; 13:10–17, 32)," demarcating within the gospel narratives that his mission of "set[ting] at liberty those who are oppressed" is a ministry of spiritual liberation rather than political liberation.[46] As confirmation of this, Luke 4:18–19 describes not Jesus' political action but his "eschatological proclamation," a powerful message of good news which is "the means by which release and liberty are achieved."[47] As well, it seems that if Jesus *is* tasked to free those unjustly imprisoned in his day, this mission would surely begin with his cousin and forerunner, John the Baptist, but instead John is executed in prison as Jesus makes no attempt to free him.[48] Concerning a mission of literally implementing jubilee, N. T. Wright observes that "at no point in the rest of Jesus' ministry do we find such an agenda."[49] Wright also notes that "the fact that Luke has Jesus quote from Isaiah [61] rather than from Leviticus [25] may suggest that Jesus' program, like Isaiah's, made use of Jubilee *imagery* rather than the fully-blown legislation itself."[50] Jesus' ministry of jubilee within the covenant people is therefore best understood not as "a political program that human beings can implement" but instead as "the promised eschatological action of God."[51]

---

[46] William J. Larkin Jr., "Mission in Luke," in *Mission in the New Testament: An Evangelical Approach*, eds. William J. Larkin Jr. and Joel F. Williams (Maryknoll, NY: Orbis, 1998), 162. See also Schnabel, *Jesus and the Twelve*, 229; Donald G. Bloesch, *The Invaded Church* (Waco, TX: Word, 1975), 105.

[47] Goldsworthy, "Gospel," 523.

[48] Beyerhaus, *God's Kingdom and the Utopian Error*, 76.

[49] Wright, *Jesus and the Victory of God*, 295.

[50] Ibid. Original emphasis.

[51] Hays, *The Moral Vision of the New Testament*, 203.

But even if Jesus' own good deeds mission *is* primarily to Jews and even if that mission within the Gospel narratives does *not* include his own active efforts at political, economic, and structural transformation within Israel, does Jesus' proclamation of the "kingdom of God" nonetheless still demand a broader, more comprehensive and holistic understanding of Jesus' mission? After all, as Schnabel notes, "the kingdom of God is the *cantus firmus*, the heart, of Jesus' proclamation."[52] Johannes Verkuyl believes that Jesus' message within the Gospels ("the gospel of the Kingdom") *does* "address itself to all immediate human need, both physical and mental. It aims to right what is wrong on earth. It enjoins engagement in the struggle for racial, social, cultural, economic and political justice." For Verkuyl, any attempt to make distinctions between "individual and corporate *shalom*, vertical and horizontal reconciliation, word proclamation and [a] comprehensive approach, witness and service, [and] micro- and macro-structural concerns" creates "sham dilemmas" and "unbiblical dichotomies."[53] One could add to Verkuyl's list the distinctions this book has made above between mission responsibilities *within* the covenant community and *outside* the covenant community and between those *before* and *after* the inauguration of the New Covenant. Others join Verkuyl in rejecting these kinds of distinctions and embracing a broader conception of Jesus' kingdom work. Sugden, for instance, claims that "the Lordship of Christ and the activity of his Kingdom" is not "confined to where he is consciously acknowledged" since "wherever he acts in the world it is as redeemer and Lord, not just creator."[54] Sugden understands the kingdom to "fulfill God's

---

[52] Schnabel, *Jesus and the Twelve*, 210.

[53] Johannes Verkuyl, "The Biblical Notion of Kingdom: Test of Validity for Theology of Religion," in *The Good News of the Kingdom: Mission Theology for the Third Millennium*, eds. Charles Van Engen, Dean S. Gilliland, and Paul Pierson (Maryknoll, NY: Orbis, 1993), 73.

[54] Chris Sugden, "A Presentation of Concern for Kingdom Ethics," in *Mission as Transformation: A Theology of the Whole Gospel*, eds. Vinay Samuel and Chris Sugden (Oxford: Regnum Books International, 1999), 212.

will in creation," and therefore "social good done by those who have neither repented nor center their activity on Christ" is also "kingdom activity" since "the [spiritual] state of agents is irrelevant."[55] Sugden (and Samuel) not only see God's "kingdom building activity" occurring within his covenant people but also see it happening within "the history of all the nations and human society" since "there are many activities, structures, and movements in the world that already share in God's saving work by his grace."[56] McKnight describes this view of "kingdom work" as "good deeds done by good people (Christians or not) in the public sector for the common good."[57] If one follows the views of Sugden, Samuel, and Verkuyl, Jesus' mission to proclaim the "gospel of the Kingdom" appears to be a much broader and more comprehensive mission which includes a greatly expanded responsibility for good deeds toward those outside the covenant community.

In determining accurately the scope of Jesus' kingdom proclamation in the Gospels, we must begin by recognizing that "kingdom" (βασιλεια [basileia]) is "a multivalent term" whose "semantic range" and "map of meaning" extends beyond any one "core idea" and is instead used in "different ways . . . in different contexts."[58] D. A. Carson describes "kingdom" as "a tensive symbol that is decisively shaped by the surrounding contexts," requiring us to "constantly struggle with the tension inherent in [the uses of 'kingdom']."[59] This should caution us against any tendency to adopt a monolithic definition of "kingdom." As well, the OT revelation of God's rule

[55] Ibid., 217, 218.

[56] Vinay Samuel and Chris Sugden, "God's Intention for the World," in *The Church in Response to Human Need*, eds. Vinay Samuel and Chris Sugden (Grand Rapids: Eerdmans, 1987), 135, 141.

[57] Scot McKnight, *Kingdom Conspiracy: Returning to the Radical Mission of the Local Church* (Grand Rapids: Brazos, 2014), 4.

[58] Jonathan T. Pennington, *Heaven and Earth in the Gospel of Matthew* (Grand Rapids: Baker Academic, 2007), 282.

[59] D. A. Carson, *Christ and Culture Revisited* (Grand Rapids: Eerdmans, 2008), 53.

should also inform our interpretation of "kingdom" in the Gospels. Briefly in chapter 5, for instance, this book noted that in the OT, God rules all people providentially as an expression of his common grace administered through the Noahic Fallen Creation Covenant. But this book also noted that God rules his chosen people salvifically as an expression of his special grace administered through the Abrahamic, Mosaic, and Davidic covenants. Following this interpretation, one can speak either of God's two kingdoms or of God's one kingdom administered through two distinct covenants. Along with these two distinct (though not disconnected) OT conceptions of God's kingdom ("the universal kingship of God" and "the covenant kingship of God with Israel"), McKnight identifies one more conception within the OT: a fully realized "future universal rule," an era which most agree has yet to arrive, leaving only the other two OT expressions of God's rule as possible aspects realized in Jesus' proclamation of the "kingdom of God" during his earthly ministry.[60] Wolters and Goheen, though, reject any attempts to "restrict the scope of the kingdom" by "find[ing] new variants of a two-realm theory" which in any way limit "the scope of Christ's lordship."[61] But this unwillingness to allow for distinctions or variations within our definition of "kingdom" soon becomes untenable. For example, Stott asserts that "the kingdom of God in the New Testament is a fundamentally *Christological* concept," a kingdom which "may be said to exist only where Jesus Christ is consciously acknowledged as Lord."[62] Stott immediately pairs this statement with an affirmation of Christ's present, universal lordship over *all* things, but nonetheless still maintains the differentiation between Christ's lordship over those who consciously submit to him and those who do not. This

[60] McKnight, *Kingdom Conspiracy*, 45.

[61] Albert M. Wolters and Michael W. Goheen, *Creation Regained: Biblical Basics for a Reformational Worldview*, 2nd ed. (Grand Rapids: Eerdmans, 2005), 78, 79.

[62] John R. W. Stott, "The Response," in *Evangelism, Salvation and Social Justice* (Nottingham, UK: Grove Books, 1977), 23. Original emphasis.

necessary distinction within Christ's present rulership requires some version of a two kingdoms conception.[63]

Even when recognizing this distinction between the two ways God administers his rule in a fallen world, the question remains, when Jesus refers to the "kingdom of God" in the Gospels, is he referring to the kingdom of God's common grace rule, to the kingdom of God's special grace rule, or to both? Thomas Schreiner responds by stating, concerning the kingdom in the Gospel of Mark,

---

[63] Those who agree that there is an unavoidable theological necessity to distinguish between the two ways God presently rules include Carson, *Christ and Culture Revisited*, 63, 211; Peter Beyerhaus, "A Biblical Encounter with Some Contemporary Philosophical and Theological Systems," in *In Word and Deed: Evangelism and Social Responsibility*, ed. Bruce J. Nicholls (Grand Rapids: Eerdmans, 1986), 182; Scobie, *The Ways of Our God*, 460; Bloesch, *The Invaded Church*, 60; Roger E. Hedlund, *The Mission of the Church in the World: A Biblical Theology* (Grand Rapids: Baker, 1991), 45–46; Charles E. Van Engen, *God's Missionary People: Rethinking the Purpose of the Local Church* (Grand Rapids: Baker, 1991), 110; and Russell P. Shedd, "Social Justice: Underlying Hermeneutical Issues," in *Biblical Interpretation and the Church: Text and Context*, ed. D. A. Carson (Exeter, UK: Paternoster, 1984), 207. Keller likewise embraces the need to make distinctions in defining how God rules his fallen creation, but nonetheless goes on to reject a "two kingdoms model" because he perceives it as "teach[ing] that it is possible for human life to be conducted on a religiously neutral basis" and as "produc[ing] a form of 'social quietism.'" Timothy Keller, *Center Church: Doing Balanced, Gospel-Centered Ministry in Your City* (Grand Rapids: Zondervan, 2012), 213, 215. As well, Keller interprets a two kingdoms model as underemphasizing "the pervasive effects of the fall into sin on all of life, on the antithesis between belief and unbelief, and on the idols at the heart of every culture," therefore "being naïve about how people truly need the Scripture and the gospel, not just general revelation, to guide their work in the world" (ibid., 225–26). While Keller may be accurately portraying the position of some who hold a version of a two kingdoms model, Keller's depiction does not represent the two kingdoms model of this book or of many others, such as VanDrunen. See John A. Wind, "The Keys to the Two Kingdoms: Covenantal Framework as the Fundamental Divide between VanDrunen and His Critics," *Westminster Theological Journal* 77, no. 1 (Spring 2015): 15–34. Ironically, Keller's own view, which he positions as "biblically balanced," is actually very similar to the two kingdoms position of VanDrunen and of this book. Keller, *Center Church*, 226–32.

that "when Mark declares that the kingdom of God has arrived in Jesus Christ, he is not merely saying that God rules over all things everywhere. The kingdom of God in Mark refers especially to God's saving rule, to the fulfillment of his saving promises."[64] Bauckham and Hart likewise believe that "Jesus was at pains to avoid the implication that God rules in the way that earthly kings rule. Much of Jesus' teaching seems designed precisely to show how God's rule differs from earthly rule."[65] Further emphasizing that the kingdom Jesus proclaims is heavenly in character and eternal rather than earthly in character and temporal, I. Howard Marshall observes that within the Gospel of John, "the language of the kingdom of God has all but disappeared" and is "in effect . . . replaced by the concept of eternal life"—though "the concept of Jesus as king and therefore the ruler of a kingdom (John 18:36) is powerfully present."[66] All these interpreters seem to recognize that the "kingdom of God" Jesus proclaims refers to God's eternal rule over his special grace covenant people rather than merely God's temporal rule over all humanity (including through the agency of human governments).

Pennington provides further evidence through his study of the Gospel of Matthew that the kingdom proclaimed by Jesus during his earthly ministry refers only to God's rule over his unique covenant people. Though Matthew's characteristic phrase, the "kingdom of heaven," is often interpreted as reflecting a decision on his part to replace the word "God" by "heaven" in order not to offend Jewish sensitivities, Pennington argues that Matthew actually uses "heaven" in order to emphasize that the kingdom Jesus proclaims is "from heaven and heavenly" and therefore is "not like earthly kingdoms, stands over against them, and will eschatologically replace them (on

---

[64] Schreiner, *The King in His Beauty*, 455.

[65] Richard Bauckham and Trevor Hart, *Hope Against Hope: Christian Eschatology at the Turn of the Millennium* (Grand Rapids: Eerdmans, 1999), 164.

[66] I. Howard Marshall, *New Testament Theology: Many Witnesses, One Gospel* (Downers Grove, IL: IVP, 2004), 581.

earth)."[67] According to Pennington, "heaven" for Matthew functions "mainly as a foil for earth, as a means of critiquing what is wrong with the way humans live on the earth, by contrasting the two realms and by looking forward to the eschaton when the tension between the two realms will be resolved."[68] Pennington's case for a two realms conception in Matthew seems to accord well with the conclusion above that the kingdom Jesus proclaims is only the special covenant kingdom of salvation and not also a reference to God's present providential rule over all creation.

But even if Jesus' kingdom as portrayed in the Gospel narratives *begins* with a more limited scope, do Jesus' parables describing the growth of the kingdom (as seeds growing [Matt. 13:24–32] and leaven spreading [Matt. 13:33]) provide warrant for concluding that now, after almost 2000 years of growth, the kingdom has expanded beyond its original, more restricted scope, perhaps allowing a legitimately broadened use of the "kingdom" concept today? Bauckham and Hart believe that any interpretation of these parables which sees them as "depicting an incremental expansion of the kingdom from

---

[67] Pennington, *Heaven and Earth in the Gospel of Matthew*, 298, 321. While most uses of the word pair "heaven and earth" in the OT and in the rest of the NT function in a "merismatic sense" (using two contrasting words to refer to one comprehensive entity), Pennington proposes that most of the uses of "heaven and earth" in Matthew have an "antithetic sense" (communicating a contrast, tension, and antithesis between the pair) (ibid., 199–201). For example, when Jesus proclaims that "all authority in heaven and on earth has been given to me" (Matt. 28:18), he *is* communicating his universal authority, but is saying it by antithesis (authority in *both* the realm of heaven *and* the realm of earth) rather than simply by merism (in all things). Put another way, in the context of Matthew's narrative, Jesus is saying that in addition to the authority "on earth" which he had previously demonstrated (as witnessed by the disciples and revealed in the text [7:29; 8:26–27; 9:6–8; 12:8; 17:5; 21:23–27]), upon his death and resurrection, Jesus also now possesses authority "in heaven," thereby "complet[ing] Jesus' earlier assertions about having authority 'on earth'" (ibid., 204). For Matthew, Christ is now Lord of both realms (heaven *and* earth), but, at this time, the two realms continue to exist in eschatological tension.

[68] Ibid., 333.

small beginnings to universal reality" is mistaken. Instead, Jesus is making a "contrast between the easily unnoticed present reality of the kingdom and its eschatological universality," meaning that rather than being inheritors of 2000 years of progress beyond the initial seed or leaven of the kingdom, the status of those within the New Covenant remains that of those faced with the ongoing hiddenness and mystery of the kingdom.[69] As Bauckham says in another place, "We should not, as it were, place ourselves at some point in the seed's steady growth to world tree proportions. The church is never far from the insignificance of Jesus and his band of unimpressive followers."[70]

Jesus' proclamation of the kingdom of God/heaven in the Gospel narratives therefore provides no warrant for concluding that his own good deeds mission to those outside the covenant is actually an extensive and comprehensive one. Instead, Jesus' good deeds are primarily *within* the covenant community since

---

[69] Bauckham and Hart, *Hope Against Hope*, 162.

[70] Richard Bauckham, *Bible and Mission: Christian Witness in a Postmodern World* (Grand Rapids: Baker Academic, 2003), 18. See also Ken Gnanakan, *Kingdom Concerns: A Biblical Theology of Mission Today* (Leicester, UK: IVP, 1993), 123; Tim Chester, *Good News to the Poor: Social Involvement and the Gospel* (Wheaton, IL: Crossway, 2013), 85–90. One area where we *do* see development and progression is in the content of the phrase "the gospel of the kingdom" (Matt. 4:23; 9:35; 24:14). Though Jesus proclaims "the gospel of the kingdom" during the era of Matt. 4:23 and 9:35 (literary bookends to his Galilee ministry before he sends out the Twelve to announce the same gospel on his behalf [10:1–42]), this message clearly does not yet include a proclamation of Christ's death, resurrection, ascension, and pouring out of the Spirit for the salvation of sinners. Within Matthew's narrative, only later does Jesus reveal to his (uncomprehending) disciples that "he must go to Jerusalem and suffer many things from the elders and chief priests and scribes, and be killed, and on the third day be raised" (16:21; repeated in 17:22–23 and 20:17–19). After this revelation but just before his crucifixion, Jesus again directs his disciples' attention to "this gospel of the kingdom" (24:14), a message with additional content in comparison to the message earlier in Jesus' Galilee ministry. This indicates that even within the literary course of Matthew's Gospel, the concept "gospel of the kingdom" develops and progresses, gradually designating for the disciples a message of expanded content.

according to the Gospel narratives, "kingdom refers to a people governed by a king," rather than merely to God's providential rule over all people.[71] For Jesus, the concept of "kingdom" does not designate "something elusive and unattached" but is "bound to a concrete people, the people of God."[72] In the Gospels, the kingdom is consequently only inaugurated within the Old Covenant people (later, more fully, only within the New Covenant people). Jesus' proclamation of the kingdom in no way implies a realization of the kingdom *beyond* the covenant people since only "to the degree that the kingdom has been inaugurated" can it "be realized in our world today."[73] Therefore, "the righteousness and justice of the messianic order cannot be found, in the present age, in the arenas of the political, social, economic, or academic orders. Instead, the reign of Christ is focused in this age solely on His reign as Messiah over the people called into the Kingdom."[74] As established above, Christ

[71] McKnight, *Kingdom Conspiracy*, 74.

[72] Lohfink, *Jesus and Community*, 72. In contrast, many evangelicals in recent years have followed Ladd in concluding that "the Kingdom of God is not a *realm* or a *people*, but it is God's *reign*." George Eldon Ladd, "The Gospel of the Kingdom," in *Perspectives On The World Christian Movement: A Reader*, eds. Ralph D. Winter and Steven C. Hawthorne, 4th ed. (Pasadena, CA: William Carey Library, 2009), 85. Original emphasis. France, for example, claims that the kingdom of God is not "a definable empirical entity," but is instead "the abstract idea of God being king, his sovereignty, his control of his world and its affairs." Therefore, according to France, "the phrase 'kingdom of God' is telling us something about God (the fact that he reigns), not describing something called 'the kingdom.'" R. T. France, "The Church and the Kingdom of God: Some Hermeneutical Issues," in *Biblical Interpretation and the Church: Text and Context*, ed. D. A. Carson (Exeter, UK: Paternoster, 1984), 31, 32. But contrary to Ladd and France, this book concludes that "kingdom of God" is not only the fact of God's reign but also refers to the particular people and realm over which God rules, a people who willingly submit to his rule—which, at this time, is the inaugurated New Covenant community of the church or, as we might term it, "the inaugurated kingdom of God."

[73] McKnight, *Kingdom Conspiracy*, 11.

[74] Russell Moore, *The Kingdom of Christ: The New Evangelical Perspective* (Wheaton, IL: Crossway, 2004), 151–52.

during the era of the Gospels *does* have a good deeds mission to those outside the covenant community, but this good deeds mission is *not* Jesus' comprehensive attempt to inaugurate the kingdom of God/heaven beyond the covenant community within all arenas of human society.

Summary of Christ's Good Deeds Mission before New Covenant Inauguration

Before Jesus inaugurated the New Covenant, his good deeds mission to those outside the covenant community is limited. Christ demonstrates a sense of responsibility to show compassionate love toward Gentiles when confronted with opportunities to do so, but does not appear actively to seek those outside the covenant for the purpose of doing them good. One can characterize Jesus' posture toward Gentiles as *always* expressing "benevolence" and good will while only demonstrating "beneficence" or good deeds *when possible*. Christ's personal responsibility for "beneficence" toward Gentiles is necessarily limited by the principle of "moral proximity," giving him (along with all humans) a greater obligation to provide active care for those with whom he has a closer relationship and more clearly defined duty. On occasion, Jesus extends compassionate love to those outside the covenant by miraculous healings. Yet even in these cases, the miracles convey more than just Christ's compassion, also authenticating his identity, warranting faith in him, warning Israel not to reject him, and indicating the inclusion within the covenant people of those previously excluded. Within the scope of the Gospels, Jesus' mission is not to bring *political* liberation to all people in his day but only a message of *spiritual* liberation for the covenant people. The kingdom Jesus proclaims concerns only God's special grace rule over his covenant people, not also his common grace rule over all people. Therefore, the good deeds of Jesus toward Gentiles are not displays of Jesus' working to inaugurate God's kingdom within all aspects of human society but are only expressions of his compassionate love and beneficence.

Good Deeds Mission of Disciples Pre-New Covenant

Christopher Little states that "any missiological paradigm which does not distinguish [the mission of] Jesus from [the mission of] His disciples in any age is not credible."[75] While Christ's divinity and unique mission as savior make Little's claim generally true, within the age of the disciples' ministry *before* the inauguration of the New Covenant, the missions of Jesus and his disciples to do good deeds to those outside the covenant community are significantly similar. Like Christ, his disciples are primarily responsible for good deeds toward those within the covenant. But also like Christ, the disciples are to extend love of neighbor to Gentiles, bestowing beneficence when possible. Even as their heavenly Father "makes his sun rise on the evil and on the good, and sends rain on the just and on the unjust" (Matt. 5:45), so the disciples are to offer their compassion and mercy to both Jews and Gentiles, demonstrating that they are sons of their perfect heavenly Father (Matt. 5:45–48). Like Jesus, the disciples, when sent out to proclaim the kingdom, also perform attesting miracles that extend compassion to people in need—though the disciples before the inauguration of the New Covenant are never portrayed as healing Gentiles. But since the disciples' mission within the Gospels is "an integral part of Jesus' own mission,"[76] and since they are "given the authority of Jesus himself for their task,"[77] it is possible that the disciples at that time also heal some Gentiles who seek them as they proclaim the kingdom.

[75] Christopher R. Little, "What Makes Mission Christian?" *International Journal of Frontier Missiology* 25, no. 2 (Summer 2008): 68.

[76] Köstenberger and O'Brien, *Salvation to the Ends of the Earth*, 119.

[77] I. Howard Marshall, "Luke's 'Social' Gospel: The Social Theology of Luke-Acts," in *Transforming the World: The Gospel and Social Responsibility*, eds. Jamie A. Grant and Dewi A. Hughes (Nottingham, UK: Apollos, 2009), 121.

Light of the World, City on a Hill, Salt of the Earth

According to Jesus, his disciples *are* "the salt of the earth," "the light of the world," and "a city set on a hill" (Matt. 5:13–14). As salt, they are responsible to maintain their "taste" and their "saltiness" (5:13). As light, they are tasked to "let your light shine before others, so that they may see your good works and give glory to your Father who is in heaven" (5:16). As a city, they must not "be hidden" (5:14). Jesus employs the "traditional images of Israel as salt and light" in order to describe the disciples' mission assignment, images which "refer explicitly to the prophetic hope of gathering the nations to Mount Zion."[78] In the world of Second Temple Judaism, the motif of "the light of the world" was "well-known and usually interpreted as a reference to Israel's task of proving to the nations that Yahweh—the God of the Jews—reigned over all."[79] In invoking this motif, Christ indicates that in his (and his disciples') mission, "Israel is being restored to its original calling: to be a light to the nations."[80] As concluded in chapter 6, OT Israel is responsible, as God's royal representatives, to mediate God's presence in the world by being consecrated and devoted priestly worshippers who are both distinct from and attractive to the world. They will achieve this by "doing righteousness and justice"—both "special grace justice" *within* the covenant community and "common grace justice," as they have opportunity, *outside* the covenant community. Jesus and his community of disciples are clearly taking up this OT mantle. Because of this, "Jesus spends a great deal of time teaching his disciple community a distinctive way of life that will stand as a contrast to the surrounding culture and make clear that the day of God's kingdom has dawned."[81]

---

[78] Michael W. Goheen, *A Light to the Nations: The Missional Church and the Biblical Story* (Grand Rapids: Baker Academic, 2011), 90.

[79] John Dickson, *The Best Kept Secret of Christian Mission: Promoting the Gospel with More Than Our Lips* (Grand Rapids: Zondervan, 2010), 87.

[80] Goheen, *A Light to the Nations*, 85.

[81] Ibid., 88.

As "a model community living in obedience to God," the covenant community of Jesus' disciples is to be "a demonstration plot in which God's will can be exhibited."[82]

As argued above, Jesus in the Gospels gives the disciples a mission that includes a responsibility for good deeds of love toward Gentiles when possible. Jesus confirms the disciples' good deeds mission in Matthew 5:16 by indicating that their task of "let[ting] your light shine before others" is equivalent to letting others "see your good works." Since Israel being a "light to the nations" in the OT (Isa. 42:6; 49:6; 60:1–3; 62:1–2) includes their being observed by those outside the covenant, Jesus' disciples being the "light of the world" also includes their good works being done in such a way that Gentiles notice, and furthermore, probably includes their doing good deeds on behalf of Gentiles. This emphasis on the public and unconcealed nature of the disciples' good deeds is also reinforced by Jesus' use of the image of a "city set on a hill that cannot be hidden" (Matt. 5:14). The disciples are to be "a community of light" which, through their evident good works, "embod[ies] and express[es] the new life of the kingdom amongst themselves and outward to others."[83] The concept of "good works" (or good deeds) in verse 16 "carries the same meaning it does throughout the New Testament. It means *acts of kindness/goodness*."[84] Yet, as Jesus makes clear, the disciples' good

---

[82] Hays, *The Moral Vision of the New Testament*, 97.

[83] Melvin Tinker, "The Servant Solution: The Coordination of Evangelism and Social Action," in *Transforming the World: The Gospel and Social Responsibility*, ed. Jamie A. Grant and Dewi A. Hughes (Nottingham, UK: Apollos, 2009), 161.

[84] Dickson, *The Best Kept Secret of Christian Mission*, 89. Original emphasis. Perman claims that Matt 5:13–16 and the command to do good for others sums up "the entire purpose [of the Christian life]." Perman's conclusion seems somewhat reductionistic and does not make the necessary distinctions between the differing responsibilities for good deeds within and outside the covenant community nor between the responsibilities to evangelize and to do good deeds for those outside the covenant community. Perman goes on to define Christian "productivity" as "to be fruitful in good works," since "productive things . . . are things that do good." Matthew Perman, *What's Best Next: How the Gospel*

deeds mission to Gentiles is *not* an end in itself but is ultimately for the purpose of helping those outside the covenant to come to "give glory to your Father who is in heaven" (Matt. 5:16). As John Piper notes, this result can only occur if our good deeds are accompanied both by "a word of testimony concerning the truth and beauty of Jesus" and by "the Spirit mercifully blow[ing] on the hearts of those who see the evidence of that beauty in our lives."[85] With the ultimate goal of all people coming to glorify God, "Followers of Jesus are not do-gooders with no eternal aims for those they love. They know exactly what the greatest and highest and most joyful good is: seeing and savoring God in Jesus forever. This is their aim and they are unashamed of it. They think any lesser aim is a failure of love."[86] Hence, the disciples' good deeds mission is never to be strictly compartmentalized or separated from their responsibility to proclaim the verbal message of the kingdom and to pray that the Spirit might work to draw those not yet united with their covenant Lord.

Not only are disciples "the light of the world" and "a city set on a hill" which is to let the light of their good deeds shine before others, they are also "the salt of the earth" which must retain its "taste"

Transforms the Way You Get Things Done (Grand Rapids: Zondervan, 2014), 74. The danger in defining biblical good deeds according to a (potentially modern) idea of "productivity" is that we might subtly adopt a truncated view of "the good," a view which is more culturally-determined than biblically-determined. For instance, in the rest of the book, Perman focuses on efficiency in scheduling, daily routines, time and project management, delegation, and other facets of what is often addressed in modern business management literature. Much of this is wise advice, particularly for those serving within administrative and office settings. But, this conception of "productivity" tends to be more task-oriented rather than relationship-oriented and might actually cause a person to misunderstand what *is* truly the appropriate good deed to do in certain times, settings, and cultures. Therefore, while "productivity" in the sense employed by Perman *may* be a legitimate expression of "doing good deeds," it is better not to conceive of the biblical category of "good deeds" too narrowly.

[85] John Piper, *What Jesus Demands from the World* (Wheaton, IL: Crossway, 2006), 358.

[86] Ibid., 359.

and "saltiness" in order to be "good for anything" in the world (Matt. 5:13). Schnabel interprets the disciples' identity as salt to mean that "just as salt is an indispensable ingredient" in food, so the witness and presence of the disciples in the world is "essential and irreplaceable." Likewise, just as "salt exists for food," so the disciples are a community of servants who "live not for their own benefit or advantage but for the sake of the earth."[87] Stott believes that Jesus intends by his use of "salt of the earth" to indicate that the disciples are responsible to "permeate . . . [and] penetrate deeply into secular society" for the purpose of preserving the communities which disciples share with those outside the covenant, keeping the communities from "deteriorate[ing] . . . [and] going bad."[88] Melvin Tinker disagrees with Stott's interpretation, believing that "it is doubtful that this is the way Jesus intended these metaphors to function in the context of the address given from the mountain."[89] Instead, Tinker emphasizes the need to interpret these verses (and the whole Sermon on the Mount) against the background of Isaiah 40–66. When read against this background, according to Tinker, Jesus' kingdom instructions on the mountain fulfill Isaiah's portrait of the "Servant of the Lord" who "heralds good tidings from the mountain" (Isa. 40:9; 52:7), a message that "the exile is ended and restoration begins for the people of God" (155). In keeping with the themes of the rest of Isaiah 40–66, Isaiah 60–62 portrays the eschatological era of the "elevation of a new Jerusalem" (Isa. 60:1–20; 62:1–12) and of "the formation of a people of righteousness who will become a light to the nations" (Isa. 60:21–61:3) as also "a time of unprecedented covenant fidelity" (Isa. 61:4–11) (156). Israel, as the covenant people, is the original servant of the Lord, tasked to be a light to the nations. But Israel fails in this responsibility, becoming "blind" and "deaf" (Isa. 42:18). Now the new "Servant of the Lord," the new "Israel"

---

[87] Schnabel, *Jesus and the Twelve*, 314.
[88] Stott, *Christian Mission in the Modern World*, 50.
[89] Tinker, "The Servant Solution," 150.

(Isa. 49:3), will be "a [new] covenant for the people, a light for the nations" (Isa. 42:6). Within the vision of Isaiah 40–66, the light of God's people shines forth eschatologically to the nations "on the basis of the covenant renewal," forming a new covenant community which faithfully shines its light—a vision which Jesus and his disciples fulfill within the Gospel narratives. Tinker continues by arguing that if he is correct to identify the covenant renewal of Isaiah 40–66 as the proper background for understanding Jesus' designation of his disciples as the "light of the world," then "salt of the earth," against this same background, is best understood as "a symbolic reference to maintaining the covenant." Tinker believes this interpretation is also "justified by a consideration of the Old Testament use of 'salt' in covenantal agreements" (Lev. 2:13; 2 Chron. 13:5) (157). In contrast to Stott's conclusion that Jesus' disciples are to preserve and uphold *secular society*, "salt of the earth" then refers to the disciples' responsibility to preserve and uphold *the covenant*. Lohfink likewise interprets "salt of the earth" as a metaphor emphasizing the need for the covenant people to maintain their "contrast character" as a "holy people . . . do[ing] the will of God."[90]

If "salt of the earth" *does* refer to the disciples' responsibility to maintain covenant fidelity, then the relationship between this metaphor and the "light of the world" metaphor fits neatly within the OT parameters discussed in chapters 4 and 6. In chapter 4, we saw that Adam and Eve are created to be priestly worshippers dwelling in God's presence. On the basis of this faithful covenant devotion (as it were, maintaining the salt of the covenant), they are to reflect the light of their heavenly Father's glory out to creation as representational rulers (as the light of the world). In chapter 6, this book identified the establishment of this same pattern for OT Israel, a chosen people called to maintain covenant fidelity in order to function properly in their vocation as a light to the nations. In this regard, before the inauguration of the New Covenant, the good

---

[90] Lohfink, *Jesus and Community*, 67.

deeds mission of Christ's disciples toward those outside the covenant is largely in keeping with that of OT Israel. In order for the nations accurately to see the reflected glory of Israel's holy God, the disciples must first maintain covenant fidelity as priestly worshippers. Such covenant-keeping will then produce abundant and unmistakable good deeds (including toward those outside the covenant) which will accomplish the goal of displaying the glory of Israel's covenant Lord and drawing the nations to his light.

Summary of Pre-New Covenant Good Deeds Mission

Before he inaugurated the New Covenant, Christ's and his disciples' good deeds missions toward those outside the covenant represent their assumption of OT Israel's original assignment to be a light to the nations. While they bestow most of their good deeds upon those within the covenant community, even these good deeds are a part of their demonstration of the light of God's presence before watching Gentiles. As well, when possible and opportunities arise, Jesus and his disciples are also responsible to extend active love of neighbor to Gentiles in need. While their "moral proximity" to the covenant people and the unavoidable scarcity of time and resources (along with the "salvation-historical constraints" of Jesus' unique mission to "the lost sheep of Israel") requires Jesus and his disciples to prioritize good deeds of compassionate love to those within the covenant community, Jesus' miraculous healings of Gentiles who seek him indicate that a new age is dawning when many previously excluded from the covenant kingdom will be included. Within the Gospels, the special grace covenant kingdom proclaimed by Christ and his disciples provides spiritual liberation from demonic oppression and sin while at the same time indicating no attempt to inaugurate the kingdom of God/heaven beyond the boundaries of the covenant community, thereby in any way establishing the kingdom within the various spheres of general human society shared with those outside the covenant community. But even if the kingdom of

God/heaven in this age and the good deeds mission of Jesus and his disciples that flows from it are not comprehensive within human society in this way, they are comprehensive in the sense that Jesus and his disciples are responsible to be themselves permeated by the salt of covenant faithfulness and to shine the light of God's glory by good deeds done within every sphere and activity of their lives.

8

The Good Deeds Mission of the New Covenant Community

At the beginning of the Gospel narratives, the new day of God's covenant kingdom begins to dawn, but, as proposed in chapter 7, the New Covenant and its community are not fully inaugurated until the bestowal of the Spirit on the day of Pentecost.[1] Even while recognizing significant continuity between the good deeds mission of the disciples before and after the inauguration of the New Covenant, one must nevertheless separately consider the good deeds mission of the disciples *after* Pentecost because of the unprecedented development and shift which takes place within the covenant relationship. But what about *Christ's* good deeds mission? Does the resurrected and ascended covenant Lord continue to have a good deeds mission to those outside the inaugurated New Covenant community?

Good Deeds Mission of Christ in the Inaugurated New Covenant

Because Christ bodily sits at the right hand of the Father (Acts 2:33–35), ruling as New Covenant Lord, he cannot perform good

---

[1] Lunde agrees that "the inaugurated [and only partially realized] nature of the kingdom implies a similar inauguration of the covenant that is associated with it." Jonathan Lunde, *Following Jesus, The Servant King: A Biblical Theology of Covenantal Discipleship*, Kindle ed. (Grand Rapids: Zondervan, 2010), locs. 4151–155.

deeds for those outside the covenant in the same way he did within the Gospel narratives, providing miraculous healings for Gentiles in face-to-face encounters.[2] When Jesus healed them at that time, the Gentile recipients of Jesus' miracles readily acknowledged that these acts of compassion and provision were bestowed upon them through the man, Jesus of Nazareth. Within the era of the inaugurated New Covenant, this same man continues to extend compassion and make provision for those outside the covenant but is unrecognized and uncredited by those receiving the aid. Christ does these good deeds for unbelievers in his role as providential ruler over all creation. After his resurrection, Jesus proclaims that "all authority in heaven and on earth has been given to me" (Matt. 28:18). By being seated at the Father's right hand, Christ is seated "far above all rule and authority and power and dominion, and above every name that is named not only in this age but also in the one to come" (Eph. 1:21). Christ, "in this age," possesses all rulership and power, a "power that enables him even to subject all things to himself" (Phil. 3:21). As Lord of all, Jesus also provides for all creation (which was originally created "by him," "through him," and "for him" [Col. 1:16]) because "all things [presently] hold together" in Christ (Col. 1:17). The book of Hebrews also confirms (after first declaring that the world was created "through" Christ [Heb 1:2]) that Jesus "upholds the universe by the word of his power" (Heb. 1:3). According to Grudem, the word translated as "upholds" includes more than merely the static idea of "sustains" but instead contains the dynamic idea of "carrying" or "bearing" something from one location to another, communicating

---

[2] In regard to the Pentecost narratives in particular, Goldsworthy observes, "While the new experience of the Spirit indwelling the church continues, we can never again experience the transition from the old context (Jesus present in the flesh) to the new context (Jesus absent in the flesh but present in the Spirit). To be aware that this is *transition*, and not an ongoing event, does affect our hermeneutics and qualifies our application of the Pentecost narratives." Graeme Goldsworthy, *Christ-Centered Biblical Theology: Hermeneutical Foundations and Principles* (Downers Grove, IL: IVP Academic, 2012), 151–52.

the sense that the one doing the "upholding" has an "active, purposeful control over the thing being carried."[3] That which Christ himself said of the Father, "he makes his sun rise on the evil and on the good, and sends rain on the just and on the unjust" (Matt. 5:45), can likewise be said of the now-exalted God-man, Jesus of Nazareth, who is the providential Lord over all creation, doing abundant (though temporal) good to those who are still "separated from Christ, alienated from the commonwealth of Israel and strangers to the covenants of promise, having no hope and without God in the world" (Eph. 2:12).

Not only does Christ continue his good deeds mission directly through his work as providential Lord over all creation, he also continues to do good deeds indirectly through his spiritual body on earth. All members of the New Covenant are indwelt by the Spirit of God, which is "the Spirit of Christ" (Rom. 8:9). In receiving this "one Spirit," all members of the covenant are "baptized into one body (1 Cor. 12:13). This "one body" is "the body of Christ," and all those within the New Covenant are "individually members of [Christ's body]" (1 Cor. 12:27). For members of Christ's body on earth, all their good deeds are ultimately the result of God himself "work[ing] in [them], both to will and to work for his good pleasure" (Phil. 2:13). Christ himself by the Spirit indwells, compels, and empowers his New Covenant community to desire and to do good deeds. The church itself *is* Christ's "workmanship, created in Christ Jesus for good works, which God prepared beforehand, that we should walk in them" (Eph 2:10). Though the resurrected Lord himself no longer walks the earth, his good deeds mission has been vastly expanded as each person, both within and outside the New Covenant, daily receives from his hand unmeasured mercy and provision, either directly from him as providential Lord or indirectly from him through his spiritual body, the church.

[3] Wayne A. Grudem, *Bible Doctrine: Essential Teachings of the Christian Faith*, ed. Jeff Purswell (Grand Rapids: Zondervan, 1999), 143.

Good Deeds Mission of Disciples
in the Inaugurated New Covenant

Christ's spiritual body on earth, the inaugurated New Covenant community, continues the pattern of OT Israel and of Jesus and his disciples before Pentecost in bearing a greater responsibility for doing good deeds toward those within the covenant than toward those outside. Paul admonishes believers "as we have opportunity, let us do good to everyone, and especially to those who are of the household of faith" (Gal. 6:10), demonstrating this order of priority and expressing the principle of "moral proximity" as discussed in chapter 7. When considering the good deed of providing financial assistance to people in need, Schreiner describes the order of priority in terms of "circles of responsibility" in which members of the New Covenant should "first support their own family members and fellow believers" and second, "if funds permit . . . should support others."[4] The phrase "if funds permit" acknowledges the unavoidable scarcity of resources in a fallen world (also discussed in chapter 7) which means that the believer is not responsible equally to bestow his or her "beneficence" on all people—since that would be impossible. Bruce Longenecker notes that there was a "huge number of destitute and poor within the ancient urban context" while the early urban churches had "relatively limited resources."[5] The first New Covenant communities "simply did not have the resources to do much beyond alleviating some of the needs of their own members. . . . To have done much more would have been to spread their very limited resources more thinly than they already were."[6] While those within the church *are* to "do good to everyone" as they "have opportunity," Keller affirms that, nonetheless, "the Christian's first responsibility

---

[4] Thomas R. Schreiner, *Paul, Apostle of God's Glory in Christ: A Pauline Theology* (Downers Grove, IL: IVP Academic, 2006), 441.

[5] Bruce W. Longenecker, *Remember the Poor: Paul, Poverty, and the Greco-Roman World* (Grand Rapids: Eerdmans, 2010), 291.

[6] Ibid., 292.

for mercy is to other believers, to those with whom he or she is in closest covenant."[7] Keller therefore describes the church's "ministry of mercy" as "primarily a covenantal blessing" rather than simply a work of general philanthropy.[8] Yet even the covenantal character of the church's good deeds mission does not "exclude the possibility of extending care to others beyond the community,"[9] as we "must not mistake Paul's emphasis on care-within-the-church as *rejection* of various kinds of beneficence outside the ecclesial sphere,"[10] since "our obligation does not stop with those who are our spiritual kin."[11] While the responsibility of members of the inaugurated New Covenant community to do good deeds for those outside the covenant is clear, there is a common temptation to stretch various NT texts beyond their obvious meaning in order to provide additional warrant for this responsibility. Passages sometimes used to bolster the case for the responsibility to do good deeds for unbelievers include, 1 John 3:17 ("if anyone has the world's goods and sees his brother in need, yet closes his heart against him, how does God's love abide in him?"); James 2:15–16 ("If a brother or sister is poorly clothed and lacking in daily food, and one of you says to them, 'Go in peace, be warmed and filled,' without giving them the things needed for the body, what good is that?"); and Matthew 25:31–46 ("'And when did we see you sick or in prison and visit you?' And the King will answer them, 'Truly, I say to you, as you did it to one of the least of these my brothers, you did it to me.'" [25:39–40]). However, as Keller rightly points out, these passages "all make reference to [helping] a brother

---

[7] Timothy J. Keller, *Ministries of Mercy: The Call of the Jericho Road*, 2nd ed. (Phillipsburg, NJ: P&R Publishing, 1997), 82.

[8] Ibid., 81.

[9] Longenecker, *Remember the Poor*, 292.

[10] Jason Hood, "Theology in Action: Paul and Christian Social Care," in *Transforming the World: The Gospel and Social Responsibility*, eds. Jamie A. Grant and Dewi A. Hughes (Nottingham, UK: Apollos, 2009), 141. Original emphasis.

[11] Craig Blomberg, *Neither Poverty nor Riches: A Biblical Theology of Material Possessions* (Downers Grove, IL: IVP, 1999), 246.

or sister" within the New Covenant community and not simply to helping any person in need.[12] Claiming these particular verses as divinely-inspired and authoritative warrant for a good deeds mission beyond the church is questionable and runs the risk of distracting from the more solid textual basis provided by the NT for this responsibility.

Another verse also at times claimed as support for a mission of good deeds to the poor outside the covenant community is Galatians 2:10 where Paul recounts how when he (accompanied by Barnabas) first met with Peter, James, John, and the other leaders of the Jerusalem church, "they asked us to remember the poor, the very thing I was eager to do." But rather than a reference to "remembering the poor" generically considered, Jason Hood argues that this is most likely concerning "*Christians* [emphasis added] in a state of material want due to some combination of natural or political disaster (food shortages could be caused by both) and loss of inheritance and family structure as social punishment for believing in Jesus as Messiah and joining his followers."[13] Schnabel believes that this verse is regarding "financial support for the poor Christians in Jerusalem (and Judea)."[14] Longenecker concurs that the poor within the covenant community *are* the referent, but believes that rather than a geographically-specific reference *only* to poor believers in Jerusalem or Judea, the verse actually "demarcates caring for the poor [within the church] without geographical restriction or specificity."[15] In either case, while there *are* good NT reasons for Christians to take responsibility for caring for poor people in general, this verse does not provide direct support for that good deeds mission. The disciples in the post-Pentecost era continue to have a responsibility for good deeds toward those outside the covenant, but this mission also continues

[12] Keller, *Ministries of Mercy*, 82.

[13] Hood, "Theology in Action," 130.

[14] Eckhard J. Schnabel, *Paul and the Early Church*, vol. 2 of *Early Christian Mission* (Downers Grove, IL: IVP, 2004), 997.

[15] Longenecker, *Remember the Poor*, 182.

to be secondary to the first priority of mutual love within the New Covenant community.[16]

[16] Another textual reason to maintain a clear distinction between the Christian's weightier responsibility to do good to fellow believers and his or her comparatively less weighty responsibility toward those outside the covenant is the restricted use of the word "love" within the NT epistles. Lohfink claims that within these letters, "interpersonal love almost without exception means love for one's brother in the faith . . . [and] that the New Testament letters normally use terms completely different from *agape/agapan* (love/to love) to designate concern for people outside the church." Gerhard Lohfink, *Jesus and Community: The Social Dimension of the Christian Faith* (Philadelphia: Fortress, 1984), 110. One example is 1 Peter 2:17, "Honor everyone. Love the brotherhood. Fear God. Honor the emperor." Lohfink notes that this "fourfold admonition, so carefully constructed . . . shows that a different terminology is suited for conduct within the community (second and third parts) than for conduct which extends beyond the community (first and fourth parts)." The key counter example to Lohfink's claim is 1 Thess. 3:12, "may the Lord make you increase and abound in love for one another and for all." Lohfink asserts that this is the only place in the NT epistles "where the object of *agape* also includes non-Christians." But he observes that later in the same letter, Paul also "distinguishes more precisely" between how he speaks of the two distinct responsibilities to love. When speaking of conduct within the church in 4:9–10, Paul "formulates as follows: 'But concerning love of the brethren (*philadelphia*) you have no need to have any one write to you, for you yourselves have been taught by God to love one another; and indeed you do love all the brethren throughout Macedonia. But we exhort you, brethren, to do so more and more.'" But when Paul addresses "conduct which transcends the churches" in 5:15, "he formulates differently: 'See that none of you repays evil for evil, but always seek to do good to one another and to all.'" Lohfink finds this same "striking distinction between 'loving' and 'doing good'" in Gal. 5–6 (ibid., 111). Paul uses the command to "love your neighbor as yourself" in Gal. 5:14 only to refer to "the conduct of members of the community among themselves" as "here, as elsewhere in Paul, the 'neighbor' is one's fellow believer." When later in the letter (Gal. 6:9–10) Paul addresses the covenant members' responsibilities toward those outside the covenant, his discussion "takes place under the rubric 'doing good,' not under that of 'love'" (Gal. 6:9–10) (ibid., 112). Further, Lohfink notes that a restricted use of "love/ to love" has "always been recognized" within the Johannine literature, "simply reflect[ing] with particular clarity what is true of the entire New Testament" (ibid., 114). Lohfink's observations concerning the distinct terminology employed by the apostolic authors when referring to love/good deeds within

The Church as the Light of the World

The inaugurated New Covenant community continues the earlier identity of Jesus' disciples as the "light of the world" and "a city set on a hill," publically displaying good deeds for the observance of those outside the covenant. The church's light only shines outward properly "when God's love is realized in their midst,"[17] as "the holiness of God's people" is "a major factor in their larger vocation to be the lights of the world."[18] The New Covenant community must continue to maintain the salt of the covenant in order to be a distinct and attractive contrast community before the watching world. While the church also has an "active witness" of evangelizing and doing good deeds toward those outside the covenant, Robert Plummer describes the church's responsibility to maintain holiness, mutual love, and overall covenant fidelity as the church's "passive witness," living "carefully regulated" lives in order to "avoid giving any offense to potential converts."[19] Through their "new-creational life,"[20] believers "authenticate the gospel,"[21] creating "communities that prefigure and embody the reconciliation and healing of the world."[22]

---

the covenant community and love/good deeds toward those outside the community provide additional evidence for the need to distinguish between these two responsibilities, including the greater weight of duty accompanying love within the covenant.

[17] Schnabel, *Paul and the Early Church*, 1475.

[18] N. T. Wright, *After You Believe: Why Christian Character Matters* (New York: HarperOne, 2012), 246.

[19] Robert L. Plummer, *Paul's Understanding of the Church's Mission: Did the Apostle Paul Expect the Early Christian Communities to Evangelize?* (Waynesboro, GA: Paternoster, 2006), 96.

[20] G. K. Beale, *A New Testament Biblical Theology: The Unfolding of the Old Testament in the New* (Grand Rapids: Baker, 2011), 835.

[21] Plummer, *Paul's Understanding of the Church's Mission*, 98.

[22] Richard B. Hays, *The Moral Vision of the New Testament: Community, Cross, New Creation* (San Francisco: HarperSanFrancisco, 1996), 32.

Good Deeds Mission in Acts

In considering the whole scope of the book of Acts, Marshall concludes that the disciples are portrayed as "engaged in God's mission to bring salvation to people everywhere," a salvation whose "primarily spiritual character . . . is evident."[23] In Marshall's interpretation, the "central emphasis" for the New Covenant community in Acts "lies upon making known the word and calling people to repentance, belief, and baptism. No other mission is given to the church."[24] Yet, Marshall also notes that the "spiritual changes" brought about by this salvation "entail changes in people that affect their social life, and hence a social element is built into the gospel and its effects."[25] When people truly "repent and turn to God," the result is always "performing deeds in keeping with their repentance" (Acts 26:20), demonstrating that those "who accept the call to repent live differently from the way that they did previously."[26] The disciple Tabitha (Dorcas) in Joppa, for instance, is "full of good works and acts of charity" (Acts 9:36), confirming that "the lives of believers are ideally filled with good works."[27] Jesus himself is held up by Peter within Acts when speaking to Gentiles as one who, during his earthly ministry, "went about doing good and healing all who were oppressed by the devil" (Acts 10:38). When Paul addresses Gentiles, he describes God as one who "did good by giving you rains from heaven and fruitful seasons, satisfying your hearts with food and gladness" (Acts 14:17), with "the implicit point being that [God's] people should follow [God's] example" in also doing good for Gentiles.[28] These verses make clear that within Acts "doing good to others by caring

---

[23] I. Howard Marshall, "Luke's 'Social' Gospel: The Social Theology of Luke-Acts," in *Transforming the World: The Gospel and Social Responsibility*, eds. Jamie A. Grant and Dewi A. Hughes (Nottingham, UK: Apollos, 2009), 114.

[24] Ibid.

[25] Ibid.

[26] Ibid.

[27] Ibid.

[28] Ibid., 116.

for their needs is recognized and practiced as good behavior by both Jews and Gentiles, and therefore all the more it is to be practiced by Christian believers."[29]

But even regarding Acts, the temptation persists to claim more textual warrant for a mission of good deeds beyond the covenant community than legitimately exists. For instance, Stott includes the "ministry of tables" to widows *within* the church (Acts 6:1–6) as support for the responsibility of social action on behalf of non-Christians.[30] But Marshall counters that within Acts, evidence of a New Covenant community "social program that went wider [than the church] . . . is not indicated," with any possible concept of pursuing broader social transformation being "unusual in the ancient world" and "possibly beyond [the church's] horizon."[31] Acknowledging with Marshall the need for caution when adducing which data within Acts supports (or does not support) a good deeds mission beyond the church, we can also conclude with Marshall that even within those early covenant communities "the boundaries cannot have been set tightly," as a local church's "charitable care would surely extend to . . . the unbelieving husband of a believing wife."[32] When taken as a whole, Acts therefore confirms that in the post-Pentecost world, just as revealed by the Gospels in the pre-Pentecost world, disciples of Christ *are* tasked with a clear though limited mission of good deeds toward those outside the covenant community.

Good Deeds Mission in the Pauline Epistles

In his epistle to the Romans, Paul includes multiple exhortations to the New Covenant community for good deeds toward those outside the church. Paul calls them to "bless those who persecute you; bless and do not curse them" (12:14). Even when being persecuted,

[29] Ibid.

[30] John R. W. Stott, *Christian Mission in the Modern World* (Downers Grove, IL: IVP, 2008), 45.

[31] Marshall, "Luke's 'Social' Gospel," 119.

[32] Ibid., 124–25.

215

"repay no one evil for evil, but give thought to *do what is honorable in the sight of all*" (12:17), indicating that their good deeds are often recognized as such by those outside the covenant community.[33] Not only must the church be a fellowship of harmony, "if possible, so far as it depends on [the believers]," they are to "live peaceably *with all*" (12:18). This includes actively serving non-believers, including persecutors, since "if your enemy is hungry, feed him; if he is thirsty, give him something to drink" (12:20). Regardless of how the world treats them, New Covenant members must strive to "not be overcome by evil, but overcome evil *with good*" (12:21). Even though at times, the government itself may be the church's persecutor, Christians are nonetheless to "be subject to the governing authorities" (13:1), with Paul's encouragement that usually if believers "*do what is* [generally recognized as] *good*," they "will receive [the ruler's] approval (13:3).[34] N. T. Wright describes Paul's exhortations for good deeds in Romans as expressing the Christian obligation to "practice the art of living as good citizens, celebrating what can be celebrated in the wider world and grieving over what has brought sadness into people's lives."[35]

The good deeds mission toward non-Christians so evident in Paul's letter to the Romans is also clear in his other letters. In 2 Corinthians, Paul characterizes God's will for the New Covenant community as "abound[ing] in *every good work*" (9:8). In Ephesians,

[33] This in no way implies that those outside the New Covenant community are to serve as the final arbiters for determining what is a "good deed" and what is not. An action which Scripture clearly reveals as a good deed (such as protecting unborn human life) may actually be considered "unloving" and "intolerant" by the society of which the church is a part.

[34] One should not assume that Paul's command here requires a strictly pacifist position as regards the Christian's relationship to government. For instance, early within the Protestant Reformation, Calvin, Beza, Knox, the Huguenots, and others developed "Reformed Resistance Theory," which argued for the place of legitimate Christian resistance against established governmental powers. See David VanDrunen, *Natural Law and the Two Kingdoms: A Study in the Development of Reformed Social Thought* (Grand Rapids: Eerdmans, 2010), 119–48.

[35] Wright, *After You Believe: Why Christian Character Matters*, 237.

Christ creates the church as his new creation "for *good works*, which God prepared beforehand, that we should walk in them" (2:10). Later in Ephesians, concerning a converted thief, Paul commands him to "no longer steal, but rather let him labor, doing honest work with his own hands, so that he may have something to share *with anyone in need*" (4:28), demonstrating that Christian financial sharing is to extend beyond the covenant community when possible to "anyone in need." In Colossians, "walk[ing] in a manner worthy of the Lord" and being "fully pleasing to him" includes "bearing fruit in *every good work*" (1:10). Finally, as highlighted in the title of this book, in Galatians, Paul admonishes the New Covenant community to "not grow weary of *doing good* . . . [but instead] as we have opportunity, let us *do good to everyone*, and especially to those who are of the household of faith" (6:9–10). Litfin describes these verses in Galatians as Paul's "classic statement of the Christian's broader social obligations."[36] Longenecker affirms that Paul's exhortation here "sums up in a general way, and in the form of a firm appeal, what the Apostle regards as the ethical task of the Christian community," these verses "hold[ing] a key structural position in the unfolding of Paul's Galatian letter" and "representing the end result or ultimate outcome of his theological reflections."[37]

Paul's Thessalonian epistles provide additional evidence of the New Covenant community's good deeds mission. Paul exhorts the Thessalonian church with similar language as the Colossian letter when he commands them to "walk in a manner worthy of God" (1 Thess. 2:12). Such "walk[ing] properly" is to be done consciously *"before outsiders,"* letting the light of Christ shine in such a way that those outside the covenant community see it (1 Thess. 4:12). As in the epistle to the Romans, rather than vengeance on persecutors, the church is to "see that no one repays anyone evil for evil, but

---

[36] Duane Litfin, *Word versus Deed: Resetting the Scales to a Biblical Balance* (Wheaton, IL: Crossway, 2012), 90.

[37] Longenecker, *Remember the Poor*, 141, 142.

always seek to *do good* to one another and *to everyone*" (1 Thess. 5:15), an admonition occurring close to the end of Paul's first letter. In his second letter to the Thessalonians, Paul reveals that he and his apostolic band "always pray for you that our God may . . . fulfill every resolve *for good* and every work of faith by his power" (2 Thess. 1:11). Later in the letter, Paul directly prays for the Thessalonian church that "our Lord Jesus Christ himself, and God our Father . . . comfort your hearts and establish them in *every good work* and word" (2 Thess. 2:16–17). Paul then concludes this second letter by encouraging the Thessalonians one more time not to "grow weary in *doing good*" (2 Thess. 3:13). Longenecker observes that, similarly to Galatians, Paul brings both Thessalonian letters to "a close with an emphasis on doing good works."[38]

According to Plummer, perhaps "the densest concentration of Pauline texts which have the opinion of outsiders in view," including as regards Christians doing good deeds, is "found in the Pastoral epistles."[39] Within 1 Timothy, one important good deed toward non-Christians, one in keeping with the example of Abraham, the command of Jeremiah to the exiles in Babylon, and the command of Jesus to his disciples before Pentecost, is Paul's insistence that believers make "supplications, prayers, intercessions, and thanksgivings . . . for *all people*, for kings and all who are in high positions" for the goal of Christians being able to "lead a peaceful and quiet life, godly and dignified in every way," an experience of social stability which also better enables a second goal of "all people [having the opportunity] to be saved and to come to the knowledge of the truth" by freely hearing the gospel message (2:1–4). This demonstrates that the church's prayers for social stability are not for "maintaining a quietistic life in a private corner of society" but for "the intention of safeguarding continued missionary activity and effectiveness"[40] since

---

[38] Ibid., 149.

[39] Plummer, *Paul's Understanding of the Church's Mission*, 98.

[40] Schnabel, *Paul and the Early Church*, 1470.

"a peaceful environment is judged to be conducive to the spreading of the gospel."[41] As Christians consider their responsibility to do good to all, Harvie Conn proposes that "intercessory prayer [ought to be seen] as the first and constant component" of, what he calls, "our 'social evangelism.'"[42] Paul also highlights the responsibility of believing women to "adorn themselves . . . with what is proper for women who profess godliness—with *good works*" (2:9–10). This female Christian responsibility is particularly non-negotiable for widows who desire to be supported financially by the covenant community, as only a widow "having a reputation for *good works . . .* [and who] has devoted herself to *every good work*" (5:9–10) is qualified to receive the church's assistance. When a widow (or any other Christian) has gained a "reputation for good works," it is because, according to Paul, "*good works* are conspicuous, and even those that are not cannot remain hidden" (5:25). Paul concludes 1 Timothy by insisting that Timothy instruct "the rich [Christians] in this age . . . to *do good*, to be rich in *good works*, to be generous and ready to share" (6:18). Just as in the Galatian and Thessalonian letters, Paul ends 1 Timothy with an admonishment to good deeds.[43]

2 Timothy continues Paul's emphasis on the New Covenant community's good deeds mission when he declares that believers who are "cleanse[d] . . . from what is dishonorable . . . [and are] a vessel for honorable use, set apart as holy, useful to [their] master" are thereby those who are "ready for *every good work*" (2:21). Later, Paul reveals the ultimate source enabling a believer to be "ready for every good work" when he describes "all Scripture" as "breathed out by God and profitable for teaching, for reproof, for correction, and for training in righteousness" (3:16). The training in righteousness that Scripture provides is for the greater purpose of "the man of God [being] complete, equipped for *every good work*" (3:17).

[41] Hays, *The Moral Vision of the New Testament*, 67.

[42] Harvie M. Conn, *Evangelism: Doing Justice and Preaching Grace* (Grand Rapids: Zondervan, 1982), 80.

[43] Longenecker, *Remember the Poor*, 149.

Within his letter to Titus, Paul contrasts the good example that Titus is to set for the church with the bad example set by false teachers who "profess to know God, but they deny him by *their works. They are detestable, disobedient, unfit for *any good work*" (1:16). In contrast, Titus is to "show yourself in all respects to be a model of *good works*" (2:7). But this standard also applies to all members of the New Covenant community, including "bondservants" who are to "be submissive to their own masters in everything," being "well-pleasing, not argumentative, not pilfering, but showing all good faith" (2:9–10). By this good behavior, these Christians will "adorn the doctrine of God our Savior" (2:10). Plummer notes that the semantic range of the verb translated as "adorn" allows for a meaning of "to honor" (as in "to honor the faith they profess by acting in accordance with it") or a meaning of "to make attractive" (as in "to make Christian teaching attractive to their masters" by their good deeds).[44] But Plummer goes on to state that the verb's "overwhelming use . . . in the NT and LXX conveys the sense of adorning in an attractive fashion."[45] Strikingly, this Greek verb (κοσμεω [*kosmeō*]) is the source for "the English word *cosmetic*," communicating the idea of Christians "beautifying the doctrine of God our Savior" by their good deeds.[46] Paul then repeats the idea that Christians are saved in order to do good deeds when he declares that "our great God and Savior Jesus Christ . . . gave himself for us to redeem us from all lawlessness and to purify for himself a people for his own possession who are *zealous for good works*" (2:13–14). Paul continues his avalanche of admonitions to good deeds when he instructs Titus to "remind [the church] to be submissive to rulers and authorities, to be obedient, to be ready for *every good work*, to speak evil of *no one*, to avoid quarreling, to be gentle, and to show perfect courtesy *toward all people*" (3:1–2). Again, Paul repeats that "those who have believed in God"

[44] Plummer, *Paul's Understanding of the Church's Mission*, 99.

[45] Ibid., 100.

[46] John Dickson, *The Best Kept Secret of Christian Mission: Promoting the Gospel with More Than Our Lips* (Grand Rapids: Zondervan, 2010), 106.

must "be careful to devote themselves to *good works*" (3:8). Finally, Paul's ends the letter by urging Titus one last time to "let our people learn to devote themselves to *good works*, so as to help cases of urgent need, and not be unfruitful" (3:14). Longenecker notes Paul's literary pattern for a final time: just as in the epistles to the Galatians, the Thessalonians, and Timothy, Paul ends his letter to Titus with "an emphasis on doing good to those in need."[47] Towner asserts that the three key concepts describing the model Christian life in the Pastoral epistles (faith, godliness, and good works), along with other terms Paul uses (prudence, moderation, discretion, self-control, seriousness or respectability, love, patience, endurance, and hope), are all "Hellenistic vocabulary . . . well known in [the] secular ethics [of that day] to describe the outward life."[48] For Paul, members of the New Covenant community must be those whose lives are so filled with conspicuous good deeds that even non-Christians who are hostile to the gospel will nonetheless recognize an undeniable embodiment of godliness and moral goodness.

Good Deeds Mission in the General Epistles

Within the General Epistles, the two key letters regarding the good deeds mission of the New Covenant community are Hebrews and 1 Peter. Though James 1:27 ("Religion that is pure and undefiled before God, the Father, is this: to visit orphans and widows in their affliction and to keep oneself unstained from the world") is a powerful statement of the Christian duty to care for those who are weak and vulnerable, Köstenberger is nevertheless correct in recognizing that, overall, "James emphasizes internal congregational matters" rather than relationships with non-Christians.[49] Likewise,

---

[47] Longenecker, *Remember the Poor*, 150.

[48] P. H. Towner, "The Pastoral Epistles," in *New Dictionary of Biblical Theology*, ed. T. Desmond Alexander et al. (Downers Grove, IL: IVP, 2000), 333–34.

[49] Andreas J. Köstenberger, "Mission in the General Epistles," in *Mission in the New Testament: An Evangelical Approach*, eds. William J. Larkin Jr. and Joel F. Williams (Maryknoll, NY: Orbis, 1998), 190.

"2 Peter and Jude are concerned for the most part with combating false teachers; 1 John primarily seeks to refute a proto-gnostic heresy; [and] 2 John and 3 John are brief personal letters."[50] In contrast, both Hebrews and 1 Peter are written to call persecuted believers to "work out their Christian faith in adverse circumstances through submission to authority; non-retaliation; love of enemies; harmonious, loving, and unified relationships within the church; recognition of the heavenly calling of believers; and perseverance," the authors exhibiting "a concern for believers' witness by way of a godly life in the midst of a largely hostile environment."[51] Because of their great salvation in Christ, the believers addressed in the book of Hebrews are to renew their efforts to "stir up one another to love and *good works*" (10:24). One expression of their good works is their responsibility to "strive for peace *with everyone*" (12:14). Finally, the letter ends with the reminder, "do not neglect to *do good* and to share what you have, for such sacrifices are pleasing to God" (13:16). As a community in the midst of being persecuted by those outside the covenant, the brothers and sisters are to respond with renewed efforts to bless non-Christians by doing good for them, sharing with them, and striving to live in peace with them.

First Peter also addresses a New Covenant community under duress (1:6; 3:13–17; 4:1, 12–19; 5:9–10). Within trying circumstances, Peter exhorts the Christians to "keep your conduct among the Gentiles honorable, so that when they speak against you as evildoers, they may see your *good deeds* and glorify God on the day of visitation" (2:12). John Dickson notes that Peter "was present when Jesus first uttered the words, 'let your light shine before others, that they may see your good deeds and glorify your Father in heaven,'" indicating that Peter's words in 2:12 are probably a paraphrase of Jesus' original teaching.[52] One good deed that shines out to the world is being

---

[50] Ibid.

[51] Ibid., 192.

[52] Dickson, *The Best Kept Secret of Christian Mission*, 99. Christopher Wright concurs that "Peter's phraseology in 1 Pet 2:12" is "almost certain[ly] . . . a

"subject for the Lord's sake to every human institution, whether it be to the emperor as supreme, or to governors as sent by him to punish those who do evil and to praise those who *do good*. For this is the will of God, that by *doing good* you should put to silence the ignorance of foolish people" (2:13–15). Like Paul, Peter urges Christians to perform good deeds that are recognized as such by those outside the covenant community as Peter is "sensitive to the way in which the Christian lifestyle is perceived in public life."[53] Peter again makes this clear with the concise instructions, "Honor *everyone*. Love the brotherhood. Fear God. Honor *the emperor*" (2:17), illustrating that New Covenant members must be attentive to exhibiting public conduct which accords with generally accepted standards of honor and respect. Also like Paul, Peter commands the community not to respond in kind to their persecutors, "not repay[ing] evil for evil or reviling for reviling, but on the contrary, bless[ing], for to this you were called" (3:9). As a brotherhood called to bestow blessing on those outside the covenant, they are to "keep [their] tongue[s] from evil and [their] lips from speaking deceit" and to "turn away from evil and *do good* . . . seek[ing] peace and pursu[ing] it," a people who are "zealous for *what is good*" (3:10–11, 13). In spite of the hostility they are experiencing, Christians are to maintain "an outgoing, positive attitude toward life in society" and to do good faithfully to all people as a witness to those outside the covenant, including those persecuting the church.[54]

Peter addresses those within the inaugurated New Covenant community as "sojourners" like Abraham (2:11) and "exiles" like the Jews in Babylon (1:1). Schreiner proposes that it is "quite

---

conscious echo of the teaching [Peter] once heard from the lips of Jesus." Christopher J. H. Wright, *The Mission of God: Unlocking the Bible's Grand Narrative* (Downers Grove, IL: IVP Academic, 2006), 390.

[53] Bruce W. Winter, *Seek the Welfare of the City: Christians as Benefactors and Citizens* (Grand Rapids: Eerdmans, 1994), 13.

[54] I. Howard Marshall, *New Testament Theology: Many Witnesses, One Gospel* (Downers Grove, IL: IVP, 2004), 656.

improbable" that Peter is writing to those who were "actually political exiles" but is rather focusing attention on "their alienation from life in this world."[55] Peter's use of the terminology of "sojourners" and "exiles" fits well with the conclusions of this book in chapters 6 and 7 concerning the status of the covenant people in the world. This identity as outsiders and resident aliens situates the New Covenant people as those who, though they *are* to engage faithfully in general human society and to do good, are nonetheless always looking beyond this present age to the age to come. Bruce Winter effectively captures this dual orientation when he observes, "Eschatologically, for [the believers addressed in 1 Peter] 'every home was a foreign land,' but in terms of their social ethics 'every foreign land was their home.'"[56] A social ethic of doing good is a necessary expression of the church's vocation as "a chosen race, a royal priesthood, a holy nation" (2:9), which "declare[s] the virtues or characteristics of the One who called them out of darkness into his marvelous light."[57] In order to continue to be the light of the world which directs people's attention to the world to come, the church must maintain New Covenant fidelity by "be[ing] holy in all [their] conduct," even as their covenant Lord is holy (1:15–16).

Inaugurated New Covenant

The good deeds of the New Covenant community, on the one hand, express a genuine concern for general human flourishing, a desire that all people might experience provision, care, and peace within their daily lives. On the other hand, these same good deeds reveal a hope which transcends the passing circumstances of this life and which, even gladly, relinquishes temporal goods in order to take hold of eternal ones. Such a hope empowers those united to Christ in the New Covenant to give freely as those whose eternal

---

[55] Thomas R. Schreiner, *The King in His Beauty: A Biblical Theology of the Old and New Testaments* (Grand Rapids: Baker Academic, 2013), 604.

[56] Winter, *Seek the Welfare of the City*, 209.

[57] Ibid., 20.

inheritance is secure, abundant, and freely received. Life within the inaugurated New Covenant is to be lived constantly in anticipation of the fullness still to come, a future orientation which paradoxically creates a people dedicated to doing good in the present. As Hays describes it, the church "hang[s] in suspense between Jesus' resurrection and parousia," an intermediate age within which "all the New Testament writers work out their understandings of God's will for the community."[58] This "tension between the 'already' and the 'not yet' of God's reign . . . should not be resolved," but the New Covenant community must instead learn to live and serve within "this creative tension."[59] James Davison Hunter agrees that this tension is "inevitable and irresolvable" in this age and acknowledges that, even though "living with it is finally unsatisfying," embracing this life in two worlds is "the only option for the church and its people."[60] N. T. Wright designates the church's calling as being those who live "the kingdom-in-advance life," embodying the reality of the coming kingdom within a world still groaning under the weight of sin.[61] As the inaugurated New Covenant kingdom, even while investing all *ultimate* hope in the not-yet-arrived consummation, believers nonetheless are able also to work for "intermediate hope"[62] in this world, an "idealism without illusions,"[63] which is abundant in doing good

[58] Hays, *The Moral Vision of the New Testament*, 198.

[59] David J. Bosch, *Transforming Mission: Paradigm Shifts in Theology of Mission* (Maryknoll, NY: Orbis Books, 1991), 32. Moore notes how "the gradual consensus developing within several significant quarters of American evangelicalism sees the eschatological Kingdom in terms of a tension between the 'already' of initial fulfillment and the 'not yet' of future consummation." Russell Moore, *The Kingdom of Christ: The New Evangelical Perspective* (Wheaton, IL: Crossway, 2004), 36.

[60] James Davison Hunter, *To Change the World: The Irony, Tragedy, and Possibility of Christianity in the Late Modern World* (New York: Oxford, 2010), 230.

[61] Wright, *After You Believe*, 124.

[62] N. T. Wright, *Surprised by Hope: Rethinking Heaven, the Resurrection, and the Mission of the Church* (New York: HarperOne, 2008), 192.

[63] George Weigel, *Idealism without Illusions: U.S. Foreign Policy in the 1990s* (Grand Rapids: Eerdmans, 1994).

deeds for the temporal blessing of others, even while holding loosely to the actual experience of temporal health, wealth, and peace.

Eschatological Incentives for Good Deeds

In "The Grand Rapids Report on Evangelism and Social Responsibility" (1982), a statement produced by a consultation co-convened by the Lausanne Committee for World Evangelism and the World Evangelical Fellowship, participants in the consultation identify three different "eschatological incentives" for Christian social responsibility (that is, the good deeds mission of the New Covenant community). Firstly, they identify the motivating factor of the judgment to come since "though we are judged by grace alone through faith alone, we shall be judged by those good works of love through which our secret faith is made public."[64] Secondly, the participants in the consultation assert that the Bible's "eschatological vision" is a reality which should "give both direction and inspiration to our present duty."[65] Finally, they identify the fact that there is some measure of continuity between this earth and the future new heavens and new earth as an additional incentive for doing good deeds in this age.[66]

Future judgment according to good deeds. While this book continues to presuppose that members of the New Covenant community enter into saving union with Christ solely by trusting in his work of grace on their behalf, Scripture nonetheless also indicates a vital relationship between good works and final salvation. For instance, Peter, in addressing those "who *have* [already] obtained a faith of equal standing with ours by the righteousness of our God

[64] International Consultation on the Relationship between Evangelism and Social Responsibility, "The Grand Rapids Report on Evangelism and Social Responsibility: An Evangelical Commitment," in *Making Christ Known: Historic Mission Documents from the Lausanne Movement, 1974–1989*, ed. John R. W. Stott (Grand Rapids: Eerdmans, 1997), 193.

[65] Ibid.

[66] Ibid., 194–95.

and Savior Jesus Christ" (2 Peter 1:1), proclaims that "for this very reason," Christians *must* "make every effort to supplement your faith with virtue, and virtue with knowledge, and knowledge with self-control, and self-control with steadfastness, and steadfastness with godliness, and godliness with brotherly affection, and brotherly affection with love" (1:5–7). Peter continues that "if [and only if] these qualities are yours and are increasing" will believers be kept "from being ineffective or unfruitful in the knowledge of our Lord Jesus Christ" (1:8). But Peter goes further in asserting that by diligent growth in godly character and the practice of good deeds that accompanies it, members of the New Covenant are able to "confirm [their] calling and election . . . [and] will never fall" but instead will "be richly provided . . . an entrance into the eternal kingdom of our Lord and Savior Jesus Christ" (1:10–11). Schreiner and Caneday determine that the phrase "will never fall" does *not* mean "if you practice these virtues, you will never sin," an interpretation which they see as "quite improbable."[67] Instead, the correct interpretation is that Christians displaying growing godliness and good deeds "will never fall, that is, they will obtain final salvation," with "fall" here referring to "apostasy" (291). Peter therefore encourages virtuous living not merely "because it makes life on earth more fulfilling" or "will lead to greater rewards in heaven" but because it is "*necessary* [emphasis added] to obtain entrance into the kingdom of Jesus Christ" (290). According to Peter, "Final salvation is at stake in [the] call to obedience. . . . Godly living, in other words, ensures that one will enter the kingdom of our Lord Christ in the future" (291). Not only does Peter hold up evident holiness of character and deeds as necessary for those who desire to experience final salvation, he also commends virtuous living as a means of those same people experiencing "subjective assurance that [their] faith is genuine, that [they]

---

[67] Thomas R. Schreiner and Ardel B. Caneday, *The Race Set before Us: A Biblical Theology of Perseverance and Assurance* (Downers Grove, IL: IVP, 2001), 291.

are not deceiving [themselves] about [their] relationship with God" (292). Schreiner and Caneday conclude that "neither Peter nor any other biblical writer believes entrance into the eternal kingdom is obtained apart from good works" (318). Consequently, the reality of eschatological judgment and the hope of final salvation provide members of the New Covenant community with ongoing motivation for their good deeds mission.

Eschatological vision. A second incentive for the good deeds mission is the eschatological vision which Scripture holds before the church. As those who are "looking forward to the city that has foundations, whose designer and builder is God" (Heb. 11:10) and who have been empowered by the inbreaking presence of the Spirit, the New Covenant people in their "mission are able and called to erect *signs of the Kingdom*."[68] These signs are the individual sign of "renewed human lives" and the corporate sign of "the indigenous church, [which is] an eschatological community,"[69] "a proleptic reality . . . [and] the vanguard of God's new world."[70] Within the New Covenant community, believers are "called to anticipate their full liberation through an eschatological ethic permeating the present life of the church," thereby "reflect[ing] and anticipat[ing] [the] new creation moral dynamic."[71] Churches "uniquely embody" this anticipatory ethic by displaying a "forgiving love [which] transcends the claims of retributive justice."[72]

But while it is clear that the eschatological vision of Scripture compels good deeds of love *within* the New Covenant community, does this vision also incentivize a good deeds mission toward those

---

[68] Peter P. J. Beyerhaus, *God's Kingdom and the Utopian Error: Discerning the Biblical Kingdom of God from Its Political Counterfeits* (Wheaton, IL: Crossway, 1992), 19. Original emphasis.

[69] Ibid.

[70] Bosch, *Transforming Mission*, 169.

[71] David VanDrunen, *Divine Covenants and Moral Order: A Biblical Theology of Natural Law* (Grand Rapids: Eerdmans, 2014), 430, 449.

[72] Ibid., 461.

still *outside* the covenant? In the Apostle Paul's case, Bosch argues that "precisely because of his concern for the 'ultimate,' [Paul] is preoccupied with the 'penultimate,'" as "authentic hope thus compels ethical seriousness . . . [and produces] an ethic that strains and labors to move God's creation toward the realization of God's promise in Christ."[73] According to Bosch, "our hope for a fundamentally new future" therefore should spur the church to good deeds beyond the covenant community, even if the impact of those good deeds on surrounding societies produces results which "conform . . . only to a very limited degree, to the 'blueprint' of God's reign."[74] VanDrunen agrees that the "new creation moral dynamic" must be "expressed in various ways by individual Christians' conduct in broader society."[75] While Christians must continue to "support the administration of justice in civil life," the eschatological ethic of the New Covenant community also "penultimizes their support of the pursuit of retributive justice" and causes believers to be known as those who consistently "exercise a merciful, reconciling, and restorative love that transcends the claims of retributive justice."[76] But the actual, ongoing realization of life lived within this tension is a constant challenge which involves, in some measure, upholding the ethic of the new creation (embodied in the eschatological institution of the church) within the boundaries of the still-existing old creation (and its "protological institutions"). As VanDrunen states, "Determining how to witness to the new moral order while honoring the present moral order is perhaps *the* central issue of Christian ethics."[77]

Not maintaining this tension can cause believers to "confuse the ultimate hope of a new creation with proximate hopes, hopes of change in our neighborhood, society, or world."[78] But, as Tim

[73] Bosch, *Transforming Mission*, 150.
[74] Ibid., 154.
[75] VanDrunen, *Divine Covenants and Moral Order*, 449.
[76] Ibid., 469.
[77] Ibid., 478.
[78] Tim Chester, *Good News to the Poor: Social Involvement and the Gospel*

Chester points out, the New Covenant community's "eschatological future hope is certain and arises from the promise of God. It does not disappoint us (Rom. 5:5). Historical hopes [by contrast] *are* susceptible to disappointment."[79] Chester warns the church not to conflate its ultimate hope with "penultimate possibilities," using "the language of eschatology . . . to describe hope for change in history through social involvement," thereby reducing "ultimate hope . . . to proximate expectation."[80] Instead, disciples of Christ must clearly recognize that "the expectation of historical change—which can be a powerful motive for action—is not the same as the eschatological hope of the New Testament," since "change in history is provisional" and "subject to reversals," while "Christian hope is certain."[81] Eric Voegelin asserts that many of the totalitarian political ideologies of modern times resulted from a gradual effort by some in the West to "immanentiz[e] the Christian eschaton," making it possible for ideologues to "endow [general human] society in its natural existence with a meaning which [the biblical vision of] Christianity denied to it."[82] Such potential pitfalls are part of what causes some theologians, like Bavinck, to "dismiss . . . New Testament eschatology as a platform for social transformation."[83] Chester agrees that "the incentive for social transformation" must be "established on other grounds," such as "faith in God and love for others."[84] While acknowledging with Chester the danger in employing eschatology as a motivation

---

(Wheaton, IL: Crossway, 2013), 89.

[79] Ibid.

[80] Tim Chester, "Eschatology and the Transformation of the World: Contradiction, Continuity, Conflation and the Endurance of Hope," in *Transforming the World: The Gospel and Social Responsibility*, eds. Jamie A. Grant and Dewi A. Hughes (Nottingham, UK: Apollos, 2009), 239.

[81] Ibid., 239, 240.

[82] Eric Voegelin, *The New Science of Politics: An Introduction* (Chicago: University of Chicago, 1952), 163.

[83] John Bolt, *Economic Shalom: A Reformed Primer on Faith, Work, and Human Flourishing* (Grand Rapids: Christian's Library Press, 2013), 16.

[84] Chester, "Eschatology and the Transformation of the World," 241.

for any Christian efforts at widespread social transformation, in regards to a less ambitious and more general mission of good deeds, the Bible's eschatological vision *does* provide a measure of limited and qualified incentive for doing good deeds, even if the relationship between eschatology and social involvement "remains [unavoidably] ambiguous."[85]

Continuity between this world and the next. The third eschatological incentive for the church's good deeds mission suggested by "The Grand Rapids Report" is continuity between the current earth and the future new earth. In considering the question whether, and in what way, our present good deeds last into eternity, Jeff Van Duzer groups the most common answers into three categories: agnosticism, annihilation, and adoption. Van Duzer describes the "agnosticism" group as those who do not think Scripture provides enough data clearly to answer the question, believing that "given the highly symbolic language used to describe the end times, it is better to simply acknowledge that there are questions that God has not chosen to answer at this time. We can hope for a certain state of affairs, but we cannot preach it as God's revealed truth."[86] If one adopts this view, the use of continuity between the ages as an incentive for the good deeds mission seems highly questionable.

The "annihilation" group, by comparison, is more certain concerning "the radical discontinuity between this world and the next." In Van Duzer's interpretation, for the annihilation group, Christian work, good deeds, and the products thereof do not have "intrinsic theological meaning" but only "instrumental theological meaning" since, for this group, "in the end, what we make will not last."[87]

---

[85] Ibid. See also Hays who detects an "'eschatological reservation' that constantly qualifies Paul's understanding of Christian existence on this side of the parousia. . . . the ambiguity of life between the times." Hays, *The Moral Vision of the New Testament*, 24, 25.

[86] Jeff Van Duzer, *Why Business Matters to God (And What Still Needs to Be Fixed)* (Downers Grove, IL: IVP, 2010), 89.

[87] Ibid., 90–91.

Moltmann, for example, is one who "emphasizes the radical contradiction of present existence by the promise of God," with an insistence that "the future is entirely new," and that "only the *ex nihilo* acts of resurrection and new creation can truly correspond to the promise."[88] In the "annihilation" view, eschatological continuity is also an unlikely incentive for good deeds in the present.

The "adoption" group believes that there *is* continuity between a Christian's work/good deeds in this creation and in the new creation, with the result that "work done in the world will be redeemed along with creation."[89] According to Van Duzer, the adoption group claims that "the material world not only counts now but also has some (albeit ill-defined) eternal significance . . . [with] some part of this material world last[ing] into eternity," since "the material world of work and things matters to God," a view of the value of the material world which Van Duzer does not believe the annihilation group can consistently hold.[90] The adoption group argues that "annihilation implies that the material world is either bad or insignificant," and for God to require Christians to do work with "no eternal significance would be cruel and therefore inconsistent with God's loving nature."[91] The adoption group finds its strongest support for their claim of continuity in Christ's bodily resurrection, arguing that the continuity displayed in his resurrection body points to further continuity in the new creation.[92] Van Duzer describes himself as a "cautious adopter."[93]

The adoption group's claim that a *lack* of continuity in our work and good deeds would render the material world and our works as ultimately insignificant and without "intrinsic theological meaning" is not a convincing argument. The presupposition that eternal

---

[88] Chester, "Eschatology and the Transformation of the World," 229–30.
[89] Ibid., 233.
[90] Van Duzer, *Why Business Matters to God*, 92.
[91] Ibid., 93.
[92] Ibid.
[93] Ibid., 94.

significance or meaning requires eternal existence is easily refuted.[94] The obvious example is human marriage, which Jesus says will not continue "in the resurrection" (Matt. 22:30). Yet, throughout Scripture, human marriage is consistently presented as one of the most significant and meaningful human realities in this temporary age, including its having been designed by God as a revelation of the eternal relationship between Christ and his church (Eph. 5:22–33). Also questionable is Van Duzer's assertion that the possession of "intrinsic theological meaning" by a Christian's work and good deeds in this world necessitates, what amounts to, an "ontological continuity" of those works into the next world, making no distinction between a continuity of nature/essence/matter and a "moral continuity" (the eternal ethical results of our good deeds).[95] Calling into question the claim of ontological continuity for a Christian's good deeds in no way denies the larger vision of ontological continuity which Jesus' resurrected body and the new heavens and new earth reveals. As Horton states, biblical eschatology does *not* present an ontologically dualistic picture of creation (unlike "Platonic-Cartesian-Kantian dualism"), but rather reveals an "ethical" dualism ("righteousness/unrighteousness; sin/grace; justice/injustice") and a "historical" dualism ("this present age" and "the age that is to come").[96] The biblical realities of ethical and historical dualism are "the result of concrete historical breaches in the divine-human relationship, not the product of the structures of created reality itself," affirming a fundamentally positive view of the creation and its future renewal and transformation.[97]

---

[94] Oliver O'Donovan, for instance, states, "Just because we can say that [government or other realities in this age] have a valuable role, we should not conclude that they are for eternity." Oliver O'Donovan, "Response to James W. Skillen," in *A Royal Priesthood? The Use of the Bible Ethically and Politically—A Dialogue with Oliver O'Donovan*, ed. Craig G. Bartholomew et al. (Grand Rapids: Zondervan, 2002), 420.

[95] Chester, "Eschatology and the Transformation of the World," 233.

[96] Michael S. Horton, *Covenant and Eschatology: The Divine Drama* (Louisville: Westminster John Knox, 2002), 28.

[97] Ibid., 29.

Nonetheless, a specific ontological continuity between the original body of Christ (and those in Christ) and their resurrected bodies as well as a general ontological continuity between the fallen and redeemed creations does *not* provide adequate textual warrant for the stronger claim of the continued ontological existence of our works and good deeds into eternity.

When pressed, even those who confidently embrace a vision of fuller continuity between the two ages recognize that it is difficult to determine exactly what this continuity will look like. N. T. Wright, for example, asserts that

> Every act of love, gratitude, and kindness; every work of art or music inspired by the love of God and delight in the beauty of his creation; every minute spent teaching a severely hand-icapped child to read or to walk; every act of care and nur-ture, of comfort and support, for one's fellow human beings and for that matter one's fellow nonhuman creatures . . . all of this will find its way, through the resurrecting power of God, into the new creation that God will one day make.[98]

But after making this fairly comprehensive claim, Wright then acknowledges that "I have no idea what precisely this will mean in practice," a laudable note of caution that raises the question as to whether Wright's earlier confidence is adequately warranted.[99] Cos-den, as noted in chapter 2, is likewise an enthusiastic proponent of the motivation provided to Christians by the belief that their works last into eternity—or, as he puts it, the "salvation" of their works. But even Cosden hedges his bets by shying away from "proposing too simplistic or too literalistic a view of our work's salvation or glorifica-tion."[100] Bauckham, who typically emphasizes greater discontinuity

[98] Wright, *Surprised by Hope*, 208.

[99] Ibid., 209.

[100] Darrell Cosden, *The Heavenly Good of Earthly Work* (Peabody, MA: Hen-drickson, 2006), 114.

between the ages, nonetheless posits that "the new creation of all things will be a taking, through transformation, into eternity, of all that has ever happened throughout the aeons of this world's time." But Bauckham quickly qualifies this expansive claim by adding, "Needless to say, it is absurd to suppose we could understand how this unprecedented act can happen."[101] In light of such statements of eschatological agnosticism, Stephen Williams wonders "how meaningful it is to speak of human achievements being taken up into the new creation" or of such hoped-for continuity providing motivation for Christian good deeds since "at best the incentive seems to be that of a possibility, not that of a promise."[102] Even if a Christian's knowledge of precisely how God will transform his or her works is not necessary for this hope to function as an incentive, "the deeper our agnosticism goes . . . the more we should be inclined to ask whether we are on the right track as regards incentives for social responsibility."[103] As Chester observes, "the more specific one tries to be in pinning down the nature of continuity the more abstract one is forced to be! And yet the more abstract one is, the less concrete becomes the motive for social or cultural action at a practical level."[104] Oliver O'Donovan shares this "apophatic and reserved" posture toward the idea of eschatological continuity in good deeds because he believes a proper "epistemology for eschatology" requires the church's vision of the eschaton to remain within the boundaries of "scriptural depiction" and to avoid unwarranted speculation.[105] While the *ethical* continuity between our good deeds in this life

[101] Richard Bauckham and Trevor Hart, *Hope Against Hope: Christian Eschatology at the Turn of the Millennium* (Grand Rapids: Eerdmans, 1999), 132.

[102] Quoted in Chester, "Eschatology and the Transformation of the World," 236.

[103] Ibid.

[104] Ibid., 238.

[105] Oliver O'Donovan, "Response to Daniel Carroll R.," in *A Royal Priesthood? The Use of the Bible Ethically and Politically—A Dialogue with Oliver O'Donovan*, ed. Craig G. Bartholomew et al. (Grand Rapids: Zondervan, 2002), 144.

and their results in the age to come *should* provide incentives for doing good deeds, any *ontological* continuity of our good deeds into eternity is a speculative concept which is, finally, unnecessary as a motivator for good deeds.

Interrelationship of the Disciples Mission and Humanity's Responsibility

In chapter 5, this book proposed that all humanity, as those still living under the Noahic Fallen Creation Covenant, are responsible for a "common grace cultural mandate," performing various good deeds that build and preserve human society, such as raising children, providing food, establishing and maintaining just government, and caring for the poor and weak. These shared human responsibilities allow for the possibility of cultural progress in limited and temporary ways, expressing God's general providence, establishing a measure of "common grace justice," and permitting a degree of "penultimate human flourishing." God administers his universal sovereignty over all people in this age by means of a natural law (a shared, though imperfect, human ethic) woven by God into the fabric of creation, including into the very nature of humanity. Through this universal rulership, God restrains the effects of sin and erects a stage for the drama of redemption but does not provide salvation, which is only available through membership in his special grace covenants.

How then does the New Covenant community's mission to do good deeds to those outside the covenant relate to the shared human responsibility to do good deeds under the Noahic Fallen Creation Covenant? In one sense, the church's good deeds mission is simply an expression of the common human duty for good deeds. Since good deeds are required of all and are inherently (though only temporally) good, as well as being acts in keeping with God's providential will, Christian good deeds need not always be explicitly connected to evangelism, even if they are nonetheless unavoidably a part of the Christian's larger lifestyle of witness. Doing good on behalf of other human beings created as the image of God is a God-honoring activity which requires no additional justification. Yet in another sense, the good deeds of the New Covenant community will always remain distinct from the good deeds performed by non-Christians, since the virtuous actions of believers are governed by the clearer and non-negotiable revealed moral standards of Scripture, standards which may at times be out of step with the common ethical norms and priorities of a given society. New Covenant acts of love are also empowered by the indwelling Spirit and are done consciously for the glory of God in a way which is impossible for those not in Christ. As well, the Christian's good deeds mission always maintains second place behind the believer's greater responsibility to express mutual, brotherly love within the covenant community, a love by which Christ says, "all people will know that you are my disciples" (John 13:35). Additionally, Christian love is never finally satisfied to express care and make provision for others merely in this passing age, but also longs for all people to come personally to know the eternal care and provision of God in Christ Jesus. Therefore, even as members of the New Covenant are to be "zealous for what is good," doing good to all as they have the opportunity, believers are also to be "always . . . prepared to make a defense to anyone who asks you for a reason for the hope that is in you" (1 Peter 3:13, 15). The good deed of evangelism is truly the "greatest good deed," even though often rejected by unbelievers as anything but a "good deed." While many non-Christians do various good deeds (as they should), only Christians can (and must) do the "greatest good deed" of verbally proclaiming the gospel message.

Because the church has the unique duty of evangelism, a responsibility with dramatic and eternal ramifications, the New Covenant community must be careful not to allow the special grace mandate of evangelism to be lost amidst the common grace mandate of good deeds. To help avoid this problem, some, like Kuyper, make a distinction between the church as "an organism" and the church as "an institution," or the church as believers dispersed throughout society and the church as officially functioning through pastors and deacons teaching, administering ordinances, and leading corporate initiatives.[106] As Kuyper declares, "Only through the institution can the church offer us that unique life sphere where the ground we tread, the air we breathe, the language we speak, and the nourishment of our spirit are not those of the world but of the Holy Spirit."[107] In Kuyper's conception of the church, the church as organism is more fundamental than the church as institution.[108] At one level, Kuyper's emphasis seems intuitively correct, for the believer is united to Christ and his universal body upon new birth, and only subsequently united to a particular local, institutional church. This priority of relationship is also analogous to the recognition that the individual's prior relationship to his or her birth family is more fundamental than that individual's relationship to a particular earthly government. But, at another level, Kuyper's decision to give priority to the work of the organic[109] church over the institutional church is problematic, since it tends toward downplaying the unique and vital work of the church gathered.[110] Better to affirm Kuyper's distinction between the organic and institutional church, while maintaining a priority for the work of the church in its institutional form. As this book argued above, the covenant community's first responsibility is to maintain internal covenant fidelity, only in this way being enabled to function properly as the "light of the world."

---

[106] Abraham Kuyper, *Rooted & Grounded: The Church as Organism and Institution*, Kindle ed. (Grand Rapids: Christian's Library Press, 2013), locs. 125–26. Horton describes this distinction as "the church as organism" and "the church as organization," or "the church-as-scattered" and "the church-as-gathered." Michael Horton, *The Gospel Commission: Recovering God's Strategy for Making Disciples* (Grand Rapids: Baker, 2011), 284, 287.

[107] Kuyper, *Rooted & Grounded*, locs. 508–11.

[108] VanDrunen, *Natural Law and the Two Kingdoms*, 297–98.

[109] Kuyper's use of "organic church" must be distinguished from some contemporary uses of the term to designate a "house church" or "simple church" model of local church life.

[110] David VanDrunen, "Abraham Kuyper and the Reformed Natural Law and Two Kingdom Traditions," *Calvin Theological Journal* 42 (2007): 304.

In general, this book suggests that the New Covenant community's good deeds mission should be carried out by the "organic church" while the "institutional church" should focus its energies on its unique tasks of shepherding those within the covenant and evangelizing those still outside the covenant.[111] As clarification, this distinction in no way limits Christians outside the auspices of the local church from banding together in for-profit or non-profit organizations in order to do various good deeds within society, including ones done explicitly in the name of Christ.[112] The need for making this distinction also results from the recognition that the institutional church's direct involvement in doing various good deeds within society "run[s] the risk of exceeding the competence of the church, of talking and acting pretentiously on matters about which Christians have [little] expertise."[113] Another reason to maintain this distinction between "the forms of ministry and service in which the church *as a church* engages and the forms of ministry and service in which Christians belonging to those churches engage" is that this distinction guards the institutional church from becoming too entangled in the complex, and often contentious, debates of politics, economics, and other matters of public policy, issues concerning which mature Christians within the same local church

---

[111] Other possible terms to describe what Kuyper designates as the "organic church" include "non-institutional church," "dispersed church" (contrasted to "assembled church"), "unofficial church (contrasted to "official church"), and "informal/non-formal church" (contrasted to "formal church"). Regardless of which term is used, the key point is to maintain the underlying distinction between the roles and responsibilities of the local church as expressed through the direct leadership of its elders and deacons and the roles and responsibilities of individual Christians acting apart from the official sanction and oversight of the local church.

[112] Keller favors just such a general distinction in mission responsibilities. See Timothy Keller, *Center Church: Doing Balanced, Gospel-Centered Ministry in Your City* (Grand Rapids: Zondervan, 2012), 294; Keller, *Ministries of Mercy*, 189.

[113] Bosch, *Transforming Mission*, 387.

might reasonably disagree.[114] Nevertheless, at times, the New Covenant community in its institutional form *must* "bring a distinctly Christian witness to bear on . . . social situations," causing "the lines between the cultural and spiritual mandates of the church" to "become somewhat hazy."[115] For example, extreme matters of moral crisis, such as speaking out against abortion or slavery, require the institutional church to be willing to proclaim the pertinent teachings of Scripture clearly and publically, regardless of the surrounding society's receptivity to the message.[116]

Summary of Good Deeds Mission of the Inaugurated New Covenant Community

The good deeds mission of the disciples after Pentecost toward those still *outside* the New Covenant community always occupies a secondary position behind the church's weightier responsibility of good deeds *within* the covenant community. Each Christian is surrounded by concentric circles of relational responsibility, the closer the relationship, the greater the "moral proximity." The church continues the vocation once possessed by OT Israel to be "the light of the world," an identity and function only realized by first maintaining covenant fidelity and holy living. Beyond this mission of

---

[114] D. A. Carson, *Christ and Culture Revisited* (Grand Rapids: Eerdmans, 2008), 153.

[115] Donald G. Bloesch, *The Invaded Church* (Waco, TX: Word, 1975), 56–57.

[116] In contrast, James Henley Thornwell, well-known American Presbyterian theologian of the nineteenth century, did not believe that the institutional church should ever "speak into the affairs of state which were outside its immediate purview," since the church is "an essentially spiritual organization." Charles Hodge agreed with Thornwell on the need to distinguish the institutional and organic church, including their respective responsibilities, but Hodge also believed that the church has the "duty to speak the truth of God's law in the public arena." Therefore, Hodge advocated for the institutional church to "openly and boldly make formal pronouncements on issues of public morality, all the while avoiding pronouncements on political matters." Gary Steward, *Princeton Seminary (1812–1929): Its Leaders' Lives and Works* (Phillipsburg, NJ: P&R Publishing, 2014), 181–82.

"passive witness" (and along with the responsibility for active verbal proclamation of the Gospel), the New Covenant people must also be "zealous for good deeds," a mission amply evident throughout Acts, the Pauline epistles, and the General epistles, making clear the church's duty to "do good to all people" as they "have the opportunity." Believers continue to be sojourners and exiles, resident aliens living within the already/not yet tension of the inaugurated New Covenant. The Christian community's expectation of the future consummation of the New Covenant creates additional eschatological incentives for the good deeds mission, including the necessity of exhibiting a life of good deeds in order to experience final salvation, the ethical continuity between our good deeds and eternal results, and the demand to bring the "new creation moral dynamic" to bear within broader society, even while resisting the pull toward "immanentizing the eschaton." While the good deeds mission of believers should generally be carried out by the "church as organism" rather than the "church as institution," if necessary, the institutional church must also be ready to do good to those outside the covenant by addressing moral matters within broader society, even if some of these ethical stances will be perceived as intolerant and hateful rather than as good deeds expressing the truth in love.

Good Deeds Responsibility of Christ and His Disciples in the Consummated New Covenant

Like Adam and Eve's good deeds responsibility before sin, the good deeds responsibility of Christ and the disciples within the consummated New Covenant cannot technically be labeled a "mission" according to the definition of this book. Within this book, "mission" means the responsibilities of those *within* the special grace covenant community toward those *outside* the covenant. Yet in the consummation, just as in Eden before sin, everyone within the world *is* a member of the special grace covenant community, the New Covenant. Therefore, "mission" ceases in the new heavens and new earth. What will continue will be humanity's renewed and transformed responsibility to be priestly worshippers in God's presence, dependent sons and daughters, and representational rulers over all creation, who will perfectly reflect the glory of God in the face of Christ within a community of mutual love.

9

Conclusions

Defining Debated Terms

The literature review in chapters 2 and 3 identified how, in the debate over properly understanding the relationship between the church's evangelism and good deeds missions, the use of different definitions for key terms illustrates the division between the equal priority and evangelistic priority sides. Those key debated terms include kingdom, gospel, evangelism, incarnational, salvation, redemption, and reconciliation. This book also suggested that a biblical-theology of the good deeds mission which highlights the importance of the covenantal macro-structure of Scripture can help bring clarity to this definitional debate. With the biblical-theological survey complete, we can now test this earlier claim.

Kingdom

Many adopt an expansive definition of "kingdom" (as they perceive it to be used in the NT), as well as a correspondingly broadened concept of "kingdom work." Wolters and Goheen suggest that whenever some aspect in human society "grows in obedience and conformity to God's creational law, there the kingdom advances and the world is pushed back."[1] Sugden claims that

---

[1] Albert M. Wolters and Michael W. Goheen, *Creation Regained: Biblical Basics for a Reformational Worldview*, 2nd ed. (Grand Rapids: Eerdmans,

"kingdom activity empowers *society* [emphasis added] as Christians and others willing to follow it move in the direction of the Kingdom, counteracting the moral disablement evil brings to *society*. The Holy Spirit works in *society* strengthening the wills of people who may not be Christians to turn God's way. [Kingdom activity] conserves *society*."[2] Van Engen describes one of the roles of the church as being "a force to transform society to more closely resemble the kingdom of God."[3]

But as argued in chapters 7 and 8, "kingdom" in the NT (and in the present age) is better understood more narrowly as equivalent to the inaugurated New Covenant community, that is, the inaugurated kingdom. While the resurrected and ascended covenant Lord *does* rule as the providential Lord of creation over all things, including general human society, this rulership must be kept distinct from his rulership over the inaugurated kingdom, that is, the church. Christ administers his rule over the church through the New Covenant, while administering his rule over all humanity through the Noahic Fallen Creation Covenant. "Kingdom work," then, is *not* work that can be done by non-Christians but can *only* be done by members of the inaugurated kingdom. This "kingdom work" is also limited to mutual service *within* the inaugurated New Covenant community (thereby strengthening the inaugurated kingdom) as well as limited to evangelistic efforts to invite others to *enter* the New Covenant (thereby expanding the

---

2005), 81.

[2] Chris Sugden, "A Presentation of Concern for Kingdom Ethics," in *Mission as Transformation: A Theology of the Whole Gospel*, eds. Vinay Samuel and Chris Sugden (Oxford: Regnum Books International, 1999), 213.

[3] Charles E. Van Engen, *God's Missionary People: Rethinking the Purpose of the Local Church* (Grand Rapids: Baker, 1991), 115. Peter Kuzmic proposes that those living the kingdom lifestyle should aim to see "that which has been inaugurated more and more realized here and now as it approaches its consummation." Peter Kuzmic, "History and Eschatology: Evangelical Views," in *In Word and Deed: Evangelism and Social Responsibility*, ed. Bruce J. Nicholls (Grand Rapids: Eerdmans, 1986), 157.

membership of the inaugurated kingdom). In both cases, "kingdom work" is a special grace work of God, not merely the common grace that the Lord extends to all under the Noahic Covenant. The good deeds done by all people, Christian or non-Christian, therefore are *not* inherently works of the inaugurated kingdom. Christians, like non-Christians, are responsible before God to do various good works, with Christian good deeds also being distinctly empowered by the Holy Spirit, done in accordance with the moral norms of Scripture, and consciously seeking to beautify the gospel and glorify God. The Christian good deeds mission, therefore, has an ambiguous relationship with "kingdom work." In one sense, in all his or her good works toward those outside the covenant, a Christian is not merely aiming to bring penultimate blessing and flourishing into the lives of non-Christians but also always seeking to adorn the gospel in such a way that those on the outside looking in might desire to enter in as well, receiving ultimate and eternal blessing. In another sense, Christian good deeds have stand-alone validity, apart from any explicit connection to the proclamation of the verbal message of salvation. On their own, these good deeds, in no sense, can be labeled "kingdom work," as though merely by doing good in society a Christian is "building the kingdom." As McKnight notes, "To disconnect the biblical idea of kingdom from social activism . . . does not entail withdrawal" by Christians from society, even as this book has shown that believers have an ongoing responsibility before God to be active within society, doing good and promoting "common grace human flourishing."[4] Likewise, the Christian responsibility for upholding "common grace *shalom*" in society is not equivalent to the "special grace *shalom*" that comes only through membership in the inaugurated New Covenant kingdom.

---

[4] Scot McKnight, *Kingdom Conspiracy: Returning to the Radical Mission of the Local Church* (Grand Rapids: Brazos, 2014), 111.

Gospel

Along with a broadened understanding of "kingdom," many also promote an expanded definition of the "gospel of the kingdom." In this view, the "gospel" is not merely the message of what God has done in Christ to inaugurate the New Covenant, allowing people to enter in and live this New Covenant life, with all its attendant blessings. Instead, according to Costas, "the gospel cannot be reduced to being merely a verbal message" but also can be "incarnated in a given situation" in such a way that the "incarnational witness may be thought of as a legitimate interpretation of the *meaning* [emphasis added] of the gospel."[5] Costas believes that, in defining "gospel," it is illegitimate to make a distinction "between the 'essence' of the gospel and its 'application.'"[6] "Gospel" is therefore defined not merely as the message proclaimed but also the life it produces, in such a way that a changed life itself can be called "the gospel."

In contrast, this book agrees with Goldsworthy that "the gospel is the proclamation of what God has done in Christ, and needs always to be distinguished from the fruit of the gospel, which is God's work in those who believe."[7] While the good deeds which the gospel produces within a believer's life are a necessary and normal fruit of receiving the gospel message, these results should not themselves be labeled "the gospel." One important reason why this distinction must be maintained is the fact that many non-Christians do (as they ought to) various good deeds, many times exceeding the good works of Christians within society. But even as non-Christian good deeds within society should not be labeled "the gospel," so Christian good works are not themselves "the gospel." In the same way that "kingdom work" is not equivalent to all human good deeds within society, so the "gospel" cannot be defined as good deeds themselves. While

[5] Orlando E. Costas, *The Church and Its Mission: A Shattering Critique from the Third World* (Wheaton, IL: Tyndale, 1974), 141.

[6] Ibid., 193.

[7] Graeme Goldsworthy, "Gospel," in *New Dictionary of Biblical Theology*, ed. T. Desmond Alexander et al. (Downers Grove, IL: IVP, 2000), 523.

the saying "preach the gospel at all times, and if necessary use words" is a popular one, it is a misleading one, since it is "simply not possible to preach the gospel without words. The gospel is inherently a *verbal* thing, and preaching the gospel is inherently a *verbal* behavior."[8] As Pennington observes, "consistently throughout the New Testament Epistles the 'gospel' refers to the *oral proclamation* about Jesus the Christ."[9] Plummer agrees that "Paul most frequently uses the term 'gospel' (or synonymous expressions) to describe the *content* of his message or the *act of proclaiming* that message," while going on to add that for Paul, the "gospel" can also refer to "a *powerful, effective, and dynamic force. . . the effective decree or power* of accomplishing God's will."[10] Acknowledging with Plummer that the "gospel" is *both* a message *and* its inherent power, the good works produced by that power are not themselves part of the definition of "gospel." Instead, the "gospel" is the Spirit-empowered message of the new creation, accomplished by Christ in the inaugurational acts of the New Covenant, a message which, though producing lives filled with good deeds, must always be distinguished from the good deeds themselves.

Evangelism

Those who tend to define the "gospel" as *both* a powerful verbal message *and* the good deeds it produces, therefore also tend to promote an enhanced definition of "evangelism." Tennent, for example, suggests "broaden[ing] our understanding of evangelism" to include "summoning the *entire culture* to the inbreaking realities of the New

---

[8] Duane Litfin, *Word versus Deed: Resetting the Scales to a Biblical Balance* (Wheaton, IL: Crossway, 2012), 12–13. Original emphasis.

[9] Jonathan T. Pennington, *Reading the Gospels Wisely: A Narrative and Theological Introduction* (Grand Rapids: Baker Academic, 2012), 5. Original emphasis.

[10] Robert L. Plummer, *Paul's Understanding of the Church's Mission: Did the Apostle Paul Expect the Early Christian Communities to Evangelize?* (Waynesboro, GA: Paternoster, 2006), 51–52. Original emphasis.

Creation. Evangelism is the permeation of the whole gospel into every aspect of a culture and demonstrating, through word and deed, what it means to be 'in Christ.'"[11] James Gustafson agrees with the idea that "evangelism" includes good deeds permeating into all spheres of culture, declaring that "evangelism is about enabling the gospel of grace in Jesus Christ to be born into our lives, our cultures, our societies, our organizations, and our traditions. . . . Evangelism *is* transformation, transformation *is* development [of human society], and development *is* evangelism in a very real sense."[12]

But, if the "evangel" (ευαγγελιον [*euangelion*]) is a Spirit-empowered verbal message of what God in Christ has accomplished in inaugurating the New Covenant (and will later complete in consummating the New Covenant), then "to evangelize"(ευαγγελιζομαι [*euangelizomai*]) is to proclaim that verbal message, inviting those still outside the inaugurated New Covenant kingdom to enter in, not also referring to the good deeds within society which necessarily *result from* entering the kingdom. Flemming agrees that "to evangelize," within the context of the ancient world, only "described the verbal announcement of good news."[13] Dickson concurs that the noun "gospel" ("evangel") and the verb "to evangelize" were "media terms . . . always referr[ing] to the announcement of happy or important events. . . . [with the] modern media term 'newsflash' probably com[ing] closest in meaning to the ancient word *gospel*."[14] Therefore, Stott concludes that "evangelism may and must be

---

[11] Timothy C. Tennent, *Invitation to World Missions: A Trinitarian Missiology for the Twenty-First Century* (Grand Rapids: Kregel, 2010), 404–5. Original emphasis.

[12] James W. Gustafson, "The Integration of Development and Evangelism," *Missiology* 26, no. 2 (April 1998): 133. Original emphasis.

[13] Dean Flemming, *Recovering the Full Mission of God: A Biblical Perspective on Being, Doing and Telling* (Downers Grove, IL: IVP Academic, 2013), 160.

[14] John Dickson, *The Best Kept Secret of Christian Mission: Promoting the Gospel with More Than Our Lips* (Grand Rapids: Zondervan, 2010), 112. While "evangelism" is clearly an act of verbal proclamation, Scripture also uses it to refer to verbal proclamation beyond communicating the message

defined only in terms of *the message*," designating the act of "evangelism" as the Spirit-empowered proclamation of this greatest of good news, not also as the doing of good deeds.[15] Again, in maintaining this narrower definition of "evangelism," this book in no way downplays the importance of the "evangelist" possessing a virtuous character and a life of abundant good deeds. For instance, within the cultural context of the Greco-Roman world, "Personal credibility is an important factor when an orator visits a city for the first time and seeks to establish contact with the citizens, and it is an important factor for missionaries who start to preach the gospel in a city as well as for the leaders of the Christian community who continue to evangelize among their fellow citizens."[16] But while high character and good deeds are a vital and necessary accompaniment to effective evangelism, they are not themselves "evangelism." Dickson makes

---

to non-Christians. According to Köstenberger and O'Brien, "although ['to evangelize'] is often taken to include only initial or primary evangelism, Paul employs the *euangelion* word-group to cover the whole range of evangelistic and teaching ministry—from the initial proclamation of the gospel to the building up of believers and grounding them firmly in the faith." Andreas J. Köstenberger and Peter T. O'Brien, *Salvation to the Ends of the Earth: A Biblical Theology of Mission* (Downers Grove, IL: IVP, 2001), 183. Schnabel agrees that the oral proclamation of the gospel includes both "missionary preaching" to those outside the New Covenant and "the instruction of believers" within the New Covenant. Eckhard J. Schnabel, *Paul and the Early Church*, vol. 2 of *Early Christian Mission* (Downers Grove, IL: IVP, 2004), 961.

[15] John R. W. Stott, *Christian Mission in the Modern World* (Downers Grove, IL: IVP, 2008), 63. Bosch agrees that "others confuse a 'prophetic' or 'holistic' ministry with evangelism. Principalities and powers, societies and nations can be challenged through the church's prophetic ministry, which is thus valuable, but they cannot as such repent and come to faith. . . . I do not deny that authentic evangelism has profound significance for development, liberation, justice, and peace, but this does not mean that one can turn it around and claim that these activities of social relief can somehow together constitute the comprehensive concept of evangelism." David J. Bosch, "Toward Evangelism in Context," in *The Church in Response to Human Need*, eds. Vinay Samuel and Chris Sudgen (Grand Rapids: Eerdmans, 1987), 185.

[16] Schnabel, *Paul and the Early Church*, 1362.

the helpful distinction between "proclaiming the gospel" with words ("evangelism") and "promoting the gospel" with our deeds.[17] While both are crucial, both are not "evangelism."[18]

Incarnational

Related to the idea of "proclaiming the gospel in deeds," the concept of the church being entrusted by Christ with an "incarnational" mission also blurs important distinctions. Tennent believes that "from the vantage point of the Incarnation" (within which "God's word and God's deed are one"), the church's mission must also exhibit a "fundamental unity between word and deed," meaning that we cannot separate evangelism and social action since they can only be separated "in the rarified air of theological discourse, not in the actual engagement of the church in the world."[19] Robert Webber agrees that Christ's incarnation "provide[s] the theological thrust for Christian social action."[20] Even as Christ's mission was "incarnational," so the New Covenant community's mission is to be "incarnational," exhibiting "all the dimensions and scope of Jesus' own ministry."[21] Rather than making any distinction between the church's mission of verbal proclamation and her mission of good deeds, believers must reject this "unbiblical dichotomy" and "return to the gospel and mission in the way of Jesus," that is, an incarnational, holistic mission which blends good news and good deeds, making no differentiation or order of priority.[22]

[17] Dickson, *The Best Kept Secret of Christian Mission*, 23.

[18] Sider gives six reasons why evangelism and social action must be kept distinct in Ronald J. Sider, *Good News and Good Works: A Theology for the Whole Gospel* (Grand Rapids: Baker, 1999), 159–62.

[19] Tennent, *Invitation to World Missions*, 399.

[20] Robert E. Webber, *The Church in the World: Opposition, Tension, or Transformation?* (Grand Rapids: Zondervan, 1986), 270.

[21] Michael W. Goheen, *A Light to the Nations: The Missional Church and the Biblical Story* (Grand Rapids: Baker Academic, 2011), 117.

[22] Michael W. Goheen, *Introducing Christian Missions Today: Scripture, History, and Issues* (Downers Grove, IL: IVP, 2014), 236.

But as this book has attempted to make clear, the New Covenant community's mission of evangelism to those outside the covenant *must* be kept distinct from (though not unrelated to) the mission of good deeds to non-Christians. As well, this biblical theology of the good deeds mission has emphasized covenantal-historical distinctions when seeking to discern the church's God-assigned mission from Scripture. One distinction is the unavoidable discontinuity (along with areas of continuity) between the unique mission of Jesus and the mission of his disciples. For instance, in his study of the Gospel of John, Köstenberger draws attention to John's portrayal of Jesus' "ontological uniqueness . . . [a] fundamental dissimilarity in person, role, and function" between Jesus and his disciples.[23] Because of this, Köstenberger proposes that "incarnational" language should be reserved for Jesus uniquely. Rather than imitating Jesus in his incarnation, the disciples are to imitate "the nature of Jesus' relationship with his sender" (the Father) by displaying "obedience and utter dependence" toward *their* sender (the Son).[24] In fact, according to Jesus himself, when "the age of the Spirit" arrives after Jesus' death, resurrection, and ascension, the disciples' mission will actually *exceed* Jesus' mission with respect to their "gather[ing] [of] the eschatological harvest" produced by Jesus' inauguration of the New Covenant, the disciples thereby "perform[ing] 'greater works'" than Jesus in his earthly mission because of their works being done in "a different, more advanced phase of God's economy of salvation" and being accomplished by "the *exalted* Christ through believers."[25] But even so, these "greater works" should *not* be described as "incarnational" since this refers to the unique act of God himself in taking on full humanity, a mission which is *not* analogous to the church's mission task. As Schnabel declares, "The event of the coming of Jesus

---

[23] Andreas J. Köstenberger, *The Mission of Jesus and the Disciples according to the Fourth Gospel: With Implications for the Fourth Gospel's Purpose and the Mission of the Contemporary Church* (Grand Rapids: Eerdmans, 1998), 74.

[24] Ibid., 217.

[25] Ibid., 173, 175.

into the world is unique, unrepeatable and incomparable."[26] As Jesus himself declares, he came into the world "to give his life as a ransom for many" (Matt. 20:28), a mission that the New Covenant community is *not* called to imitate. While in the church's missions, both of evangelism and good deeds, they should *identify with* the circumstances, suffering, and common humanity of the fellow sinners to whom they minister (even as the sinless Christ identified himself with humanity through his unique incarnation), the church's mission should not thus be described as "incarnational." As well, the concept of "incarnational" does *not* provide warrant for eliminating a distinction between the church's evangelism and good deeds missions.

Salvation, Redemption, and Reconciliation

Along with the idea that Christian good deeds can, in some sense, "bring the kingdom to broader society" or "incarnate the gospel within culture," is the idea that such good deeds can bring to present human society some measure of the "salvation," "redemption," and "reconciliation" of which the NT speaks. Costas defines the church's work of "salvation" to include "active commitment toward world peace, understood in the broadest terms—as *shalom*—and equally strong commitment to the struggles for justice," with the result that Christian "participation in the contemporary struggles for justice can be regarded as legitimate manifestations (glimpses, if you wish) of salvation," since part of the already-manifest presence of "God's coming salvation" is "God's action in secular history."[27] Concerning the related term "redemption," Costas also claims that "refusing to relate [the church's present advocacy of justice and peace in society] to messianic salvation" is an illegitimate effort at "limiting the scope of redemption."[28] Samuel and Sugden agree that we can find "some evidence of redemption outside the church" *if* we properly

---

[26] Schnabel, *Paul and the Early Church*, 1575.
[27] Costas, *The Church and Its Mission*, 203, 205, 298.
[28] Ibid., 204.

define "redemption" more broadly as "God's activity in fulfilling his intention for the world."[29] Webber posits that already in the age of the inaugurated kingdom, "Everything that is affected by sin is now affected by redemption. Healing is now possible between man and God, man and himself, man and other men, and man and nature. The disintegrating power of sin has been reversed by redemption."[30] According to Van Duzer, this means that "like Jesus, Christians have been anointed (called and empowered) to redeem" every realm of society, including the business world, such that "business must concern itself with redemptive as well as creative work. . . . Those goods and services that enable a community to flourish will now often take on a redemptive quality. . . . [producing products which] reach back and help to redeem broken situations. . . . [and] work[ing] to redeem the character of the jobs assigned to company employees."[31] Per Wolters and Goheen, Christ's (and the church's) work of "redemption" in the present includes "the progressive removal of [sin's] effects everywhere," resulting in "the recovery of creational goodness."[32]

These broad interpretations of NT "salvation" and "redemption" in the present age are joined by equally expansive uses of the term "reconciliation." For example, Ott and Strauss claim that

[29] Vinay Samuel and Chris Sugden, "God's Intention for the World," in *The Church in Response to Human Need*, eds. Vinay Samuel and Chris Sugden (Grand Rapids: Eerdmans, 1987), 153.

[30] Robert E. Webber, *The Secular Saint: A Case for Evangelical Social Responsibility* (Grand Rapids: Zondervan, 1979), 182. Litfin, who mainly shares the interpretational conclusions and concerns of this book, nonetheless claims that "in Christ God is [now] redeeming every dimension of his creation and every aspect of human experience, and he calls his redeemed people [now] to serve him by joining sacrificially in that process, extending God's healing touch to every individual and every community—indeed, to the very cosmos itself through our creation care." Litfin, *Word versus Deed*, 119. In contrast, this book concludes that this expansive definition of God (and the church's) work of "redemption" in this age is textually unwarranted.

[31] Jeff Van Duzer, *Why Business Matters to God (And What Still Needs to Be Fixed)* (Downers Grove, IL: IVP, 2010), 112, 114.

[32] Wolters and Goheen, *Creation Regained*, 83.

"reconciliation is more than merely a task of missions; it is central to the overarching purpose and nature of missions," by which claim they go on to merge the tasks of evangelism/church planting ("vertical reconciliation") with the tasks of philanthropy/justice ("horizontal reconciliation"), both under the larger rubric of "reconciliation."[33] Douglas Moo suggests that Colossians 1:20 (God the Father working "through [Christ] to reconcile to himself all things, whether on earth or in heaven, making peace by the blood of his cross") implies that "the reconciliation secured by Christ means that nature is 'already' restored in principle to that condition in which it can fulfill the purpose for which God created it and thereby praise its Creator," as well as implying that Christians, "in light of the 'not yet' side of reconciliation, are to work toward the goal of creation's final transformation."[34] Moo thus suggests a broader definition for God's (and the church's) work of "reconciliation" in the present age, an expanded definition which matches similar enlargements in defining the NT's portrayal of the extent to which "salvation" and "redemption" are already inaugurated (and being progressively realized) in the broader world today.

In contrast to these expanded definitions, this book argues that the good deeds of Christians toward those outside the covenant should *not* be understood, in a NT sense, to be bringing "salvation," "redemption," or "reconciliation" to either general human society or the natural world. These gifts in the age of the inaugurated kingdom are instead *only* experienced (and progressively though imperfectly realized) by the members of the New Covenant community, not human society as a whole nor the natural world. As

---

[33] Craig Ott and Stephen J. Strauss, *Encountering Theology of Mission: Biblical Foundations, Historical Developments, and Contemporary Issues* (Grand Rapids: Baker Academic, 2010), 97.

[34] Douglas J. Moo, "Eschatology and Environmental Ethics: On the Importance of Biblical Theology to Creation Care," in *Keeping God's Earth: The Global Environment in Biblical Perspective*, eds. Noah J. Toly and Daniel I. Block (Downers Grove, IL: IVP Academic, 2010), 38.

Sider concludes, "the dominant connotation of the words 'save' and 'salvation' throughout the New Testament does not encourage the adoption of a broad definition of salvation."[35] Similarly, Sider determines that "redemption" is *not* "something that happens to secular economic and political structures now. It is something that happens to persons as they are in Christ."[36] Hunter agrees that "while the activity of culture-making has validity before God, this work is not, strictly speaking, redemptive or salvific in character. Where Christians participate in the work of world-building they are not, in any precise sense of the phrase, 'building the kingdom of God.'"[37] While the salvation and redemption which *will be* experienced by believers in the consummated New Covenant *are* cosmic and comprehensive in scope, this future reality should not obscure the fact that "salvation" and "redemption" in the present can *only* be experienced within the inaugurated New Covenant community. This means that the church's current works of "salvation" and "redemption" concern the entrance into and the growth unto maturity of the New Covenant community, requiring the church to emphasize "the priority of personal regeneration" in her mission out to the world.[38] Sharing this concern for definitional distinctions, Howard Peskett and Vinoth Ramachandra propose that "probably it would be more helpful to talk of 'reforming' rather than 'redeeming' society," reflecting the distinction Barth made in "picture[ing] God's activity in the world as two concentric circles: the inner circle is the 'kingdom of God,' centered on and inaugurated by Jesus Christ; the outer circle is the realm of God's providential rule over all things."[39] Likewise, God's

[35] Ronald J. Sider, "Evangelism, Salvation and Social Justice," in *Evangelism, Salvation and Social Justice* (Nottingham, UK: Grove Books, 1977), 16.

[36] Ibid.

[37] James Davison Hunter, *To Change the World: The Irony, Tragedy, and Possibility of Christianity in the Late Modern World* (New York: Oxford, 2010), 233.

[38] Russell Moore, *The Kingdom of Christ: The New Evangelical Perspective* (Wheaton, IL: Crossway, 2004), 110.

[39] Howard Peskett and Vinoth Ramachandra, *The Message of Mission: The Glory of Christ in All Time and Space* (Downers Grove, IL: IVP, 2003), 255–56.

(and the church's) work of "reconciliation" only occurs now within the inaugurated New Covenant community, not broader society. As Sider asserts, "the only time Paul used language about salvation and redemption, for anything other than the justification and regeneration and reconciliation occurring now in the church, is when he discussed the *eschatological* restoration at our Lord's return."[40] Horton concludes, "One does not have to 'bless' work or secular institutions with the adjective 'Christian,' or 'redemptive,' or 'kingdom' for [them] to be honorable to God."[41] In fact, doing so not only goes beyond biblical categories, but also produces unintended ill effects, including what VanDrunen calls "an eschatological burdening of cultural work."[42] Instead, as this book has sought to demonstrate, Christian good deeds in broader society are required and important, extending God's common grace to a sin-sick world and adorning the gospel message and the life of the New Covenant community in attractive garb, but these good deeds do not themselves bring salvation, redemption, or reconciliation.

Biblical Dualism Requires Evangelistic Priority

A common reason given for rejecting the evangelistic priority position is the claim that this position reflects an unbiblical dualism between the spiritual and material worlds, giving the spiritual a false priority over the material.[43] In contrast, since Wolters and

---

[40] Sider, "Evangelism, Salvation, and Social Justice," 11. Original emphasis.

[41] Michael S. Horton, *Where in the World Is the Church? A Christian View of Culture and Your Role in It* (Phillipsburg, NJ: P&R Publishing, 2002), 187.

[42] David VanDrunen, *Natural Law and the Two Kingdoms: A Study in the Development of Reformed Social Thought* (Grand Rapids: Eerdmans, 2010), 384.

[43] Among the authors who largely dismiss the evangelistic priority position as a form of misguided dualism are David J. Bosch, *Transforming Mission: Paradigm Shifts in Theology of Mission* (Maryknoll, NY: Orbis Books, 1991), 262–345; James F. Engel and William A. Dyrness, *Changing the Mind of Missions: Where Have We Gone Wrong?* (Downers Grove, IL: IVP, 2000), 58–66; Goheen, *Introducing Christian Missions Today*, 228–33; Andrew Kirk, *The Good News*

Goheen believe that the church is "called to promote renewal in every department of creation," therefore, they also believe the church cannot adopt an "invisible dividing line within creation [which] limits the applicability of such basic biblical concepts as reconciliation, redemption, salvation, sanctification, renewal, the kingdom of God, and so on."[44] Instead of an "invisible dividing line within creation," Goheen asserts that the New Covenant community must "overcome the inherent dualisms of the past—individual and society, soul and body, present and future, vertical and horizontal, evangelism and seeking justice, word and deed."[45] This conscious effort to overcome dualisms is necessary because, according to Goheen, "there often remains [in popular evangelicalism] a deep dichotomy between eternity and time, kingdom and history, salvation and social action, church and society, soul and body, spiritual and physical, heaven and earth, word and deed, with the former given priority in each case." Goheen is convinced that a "fundamental dualism continues to percolate below the surface of much evangelical thought and action," implying that at some level, this dualism is akin to a form of "false consciousness" which needs to be deconstructed and dismissed.[46] In other words, those who sincerely hold the evangelistic priority position do not fully realize that their position, rather than being a reflection of what Scripture actually reveals, is in truth a function of

---

of the Kingdom Coming: The Marriage of Evangelism and Social Responsibility (Downers Grove, IL: IVP, 1983), 88–89; J. Richard Middleton, *A New Heaven and A New Earth: Reclaiming Biblical Eschatology* (Grand Rapids: Baker Academic, 2014), 5–11; Johannes Verkuyl, "The Biblical Notion of Kingdom: Test of Validity for Theology of Religion," in *The Good News of the Kingdom: Mission Theology for the Third Millennium*, eds. Charles Van Engen, Dean S. Gilliland, and Paul Pierson (Maryknoll, NY: Orbis, 1993), 73–74; Michael E. Wittmer, *Heaven Is a Place on Earth: Why Everything You Do Matters to God* (Grand Rapids: Zondervan, 2004), 42–45, 54–68; N. T. Wright, *Surprised by Hope: Rethinking Heaven, the Resurrection, and the Mission of the Church* (New York: HarperOne, 2008), 213–21.

[44] Wolters and Goheen, *Creation Regained*, 73.

[45] Goheen, *Introducing Christian Missions Today*, 160.

[46] Ibid., 233.

their (perhaps unconscious) embrace of a dualistic (Platonic- and Enlightenment-influenced) view of the world.

Hopefully, this book has demonstrated that, even if *some* evangelicals who hold an evangelistic priority position *may perhaps* hold to a biblically-invalid form of dualism, the evangelistic priority position cannot thereby be dismissed as merely a function of a pre-commitment to a mistakenly dualistic worldview. Instead, this book has provided a rigorous biblical-theological survey of the good deeds mission of the New Covenant community which holds to a high view of the church's good deeds in society, deeds which seek to achieve "common grace justice" and "penultimate human flourishing" in this age, even while holding to a clear priority for evangelism in the institutional church's mission out to the world. One goal of this book is to encourage those on the equal priority side of the debate to engage with the biblical-theological arguments provided in this book rather than merely to dismiss the evangelistic priority position as the misbegotten child of Enlightenment dualism. Interestingly, in spite of also claiming that the evangelistic priority position embodies a falsely dualistic orientation, J. Richard Middleton acknowledges that "admittedly, few contemporary Christians are still trapped in a radical sort of dualism, denigrating this world as purely evil and hoping for escape to heaven."[47] Recognizing this, the question of "dualism" should cease to be the primary lens through which many approach the question of the relationship between the church's missions of evangelism and good deeds. As Pennington observes

> 'Dualism' is a term and concept that has been so widely appealed to in religious studies that inevitably, it has been abused and misapplied. For example, Second Temple apocalyptic literature, the Qumran community, and the Gospel of John have all been summarily labeled (and often vilified, especially John) as 'dualistic.' The problem with this is not that

[47] Middleton, *A New Heaven and A New Earth*, 274.

258

these documents do not manifest any dualistic polarities—
they do—but that the *label* 'dualism' is too vague to be used
so freely. The term is used to encompass such a wide variety
of different views that it ceases to be reliable. Moreover, as
Miroslav Wolf has observed, 'dualism' often serves simply as
a convenient term of opprobrium, applied derisively to 'any
duality deemed unacceptable' by the scholar using it.[48]

Pennington goes on to note how N. T. Wright points out that "many
elements in Jewish and Christian literature that are labeled as 'dualistic' are in reality 'perfectly normal features of most if not all biblical
theology' and do not indeed reflect Iranian Zoroastrianism or any
other type of dualism."[49]

Instead of reflecting an erroneous dualism, this book advocates
for the priority of evangelism in the church's mission because of "the
priority of the future," that is, the fact that "blessing in God's future is
more important than blessing in this life."[50] Chester recognizes that
this priority of the future over the present is sometimes "dismissed
as dualism, but that is a mistake. Dualism has become something of
a bogey word that is used to dismiss arguments without true engagement with the issues. . . . to say that physical and spiritual belong
together is very different from saying that the temporal is as important as the eternal."[51] This "biblical dualism," which distinguishes
between the value/duration of the present and of the future, means
that "all [of this present] creation cannot be identified in monistic
fashion with the kingdom-realm of God."[52] As O'Donovan declares,

[48] Jonathan T. Pennington, *Heaven and Earth in the Gospel of Matthew*
(Grand Rapids: Baker Academic, 2007), 331.

[49] Ibid., 332.

[50] Tim Chester, *Good News to the Poor: Social Involvement and the Gospel*
(Wheaton, IL: Crossway, 2013), 56, 57.

[51] Ibid., 57, 58.

[52] Meredith G. Kline, *Kingdom Prologue: Genesis Foundations for a Covenantal Worldview* (Overland Park, KS: Two Age Press, 2000), 171.

"The doctrine of 'the two' must not be collapsed into a doctrine of the one."[53] Carl Braaten agrees that "a monistic model is inadequate both to the self-transcending dynamics of human existence and to the transcendent revelation of a fulfilling destiny in the life of the world to come." Instead, "any eschatology worth its salt contains a two-dimensional reference, first to human existence in the world as it is and secondly to that eschatological dimension which holds the key to salvation."[54] Therefore, Horton correctly asserts that the act of "distinguishing clearly between the common and the holy, the kingdoms of this age and the kingdom of Christ, culture and the gospel, general and special revelation" is "not engaging in Platonic dualism," but is rather a "biblical dualism" which is required by the picture of the world revealed in the text of Scripture.[55]

Christopher Wright objects to "the language of priority and primacy" when discussing the place of evangelism within the church's mission, because he believes such language "quickly tends to imply singularity and exclusion" and to communicate the idea that evangelism is "the *only* real mission."[56] Again, hopefully, this book has demonstrated that Wright's fear is biblically unfounded (and certainly not a sufficient cause for dismissing the language of "priority" or "primacy"), since this book holds high the mandatory mission of good deeds in society, even while maintaining a clear priority for the institutional church's mission of evangelism. As well, Wright attempts to bypass the question of priorities in the church's mission by proposing the use of the idea of "ultimacy," rather than of "primacy," in regards to evangelism, part of his attempt to promote

[53] Oliver O'Donovan, "Response to Gerrit de Kruijf," in *A Royal Priesthood? The Use of the Bible Ethically and Politically—A Dialogue with Oliver O'Donovan*, ed. Craig G. Bartholomew et al. (Grand Rapids: Zondervan, 2002), 239.

[54] Carl E. Braaten, *The Flaming Center: A Theology of Christian Mission* (Philadelphia: Fortress, 1977), 58.

[55] Michael Horton, *The Gospel Commission: Recovering God's Strategy for Making Disciples* (Grand Rapids: Baker, 2011), 103.

[56] Christopher J. H. Wright, *The Mission of God: Unlocking the Bible's Grand Narrative* (Downers Grove, IL: IVP Academic, 2006), 317. Original emphasis.

a holistic approach to missions.[57] But as Little observes, "issues of 'ultimacy' imply 'primacy.'"[58] Once the need for priorities is recognized, then, according to Hesselgrave, the model of holistic missions becomes dubious since, "The frame of the 'holistic cradle' is constructed out of one fiber—namely, the notion that no priorities are allowable."[59] Little, by contrast, believes that "priorities in Christian mission are unavoidable and non-negotiable."[60] Mike Barnett agrees and proclaims, "Woe unto Evangelicals if our next 'inheritance' subjugates the priority of proclamation."[61]

One evangelical who once embraced a holistic missions paradigm but now questions its wisdom is Ajith Fernando, a native of Sri Lanka who continues to minister primarily within that comparatively impoverished nation. Fernando acknowledges that in the past, "I have always been reluctant to use the language of priority," a reluctance he still partially possesses.[62] But Fernando goes on to declare, "we need clarity" (44). This clarity is lacking because of what he identifies as a "tendency among some evangelicals to downplay verbal proclamation" in favor of good deeds (45). One dynamic behind this phenomenon, according to Fernando, is the fact that, while broader society generally affirms Christians' involvement in good deeds such as "AIDS ministry and social development," the world will never affirm Christians for doing evangelism, a distinction

---

[57] Ibid., 319.

[58] Christopher R. Little, "In Response to 'The Future of Evangelicals in Mission.,'" in *Missionshift: Global Mission Issues in the Third Millennium*, eds. David J. Hesselgrave and Ed Stetzer (Nashville: B&H Academic, 2010), 217.

[59] David J. Hesselgrave, *Paradigms in Conflict: 10 Key Questions in Christian Missions Today* (Grand Rapids: Kregel, 2005), 123.

[60] Christopher R. *Little, Polemic Missiology for the 21st Century: In Memoriam of Roland Allen* Kindle ed. (Colombia, SC: Christopher R. Little, 2013), locs. 367–68.

[61] Mike Barnett, "The Missing Key to the Future of Evangelical Mission," in *Missionshift: Global Mission Issues in the Third Millennium*, eds. David J. Hesselgrave and Ed Stetzer (Nashville: B&H Academic, 2010), 227.

[62] Ajith Fernando, "Getting Back on Course: It's Time to Return to the Priority of Evangelism," *Christianity Today* 51, no. 11 (2007): 43, 44.

in social cost/benefit analysis which makes doing good deeds more attractive and doing evangelism less attractive (42). Therefore, in Fernando's estimation, "if talk of priority will help the church to a fresh commitment [to verbal evangelism], then so be it. Christ certainly seems to share that priority: 'For what will it profit a man if he gains the whole world and forfeits his life? Or what shall a man give in return for his life?' (Matt. 16:26)" (45). So, while Fernando's hesitant embrace of priority language for evangelism at first appears to be mainly a strategic posture in reaction to the neglect of evangelism, by the end of the article, Fernando seems to recognize that a priority for evangelism in the church's mission is demanded by the text and worldview of Scripture itself. While all humans can (and should) do good deeds, Kane also helps to clarify this priority by rightly stating that the New Covenant community is "the one institution to which Jesus Christ delegated the responsibility for the evangelization of the world," an exalted and unique mission which must retain clear operational priority in the institutional church's allocation of its resources of personnel, time, prayer, money, and other capital.[63]

This biblical theology of the good deeds mission of the New Covenant community has sought to bring particular attention to the impact of an interpreter's larger conception of the covenantal macro-structure of Scripture upon how he or she answers the evangelistic priority or equal priority question. Tinker agrees that "answers to questions of priority and motivation in evangelism and social action are inevitably shaped by the theological framework in which they are viewed."[64] One result of this covenantal framework-focused study is the formulation of an additional way in which evangelism has primacy. Chapter 3 noted how Sider identifies five facets of how

[63] J. Herbert Kane, *Christian Missions in Biblical Perspective* (Grand Rapids: Baker, 1976), 265.

[64] Melvin Tinker, "The Servant Solution: The Coordination of Evangelism and Social Action," in *Transforming the World: The Gospel and Social Responsibility*, eds. Jamie A. Grant and Dewi A. Hughes (Nottingham, UK: Apollos, 2009), 149.

one can speak more precisely of the "priority" of evangelism: logical, ontological, vocational, temporal, and resource allocation-related— all distinct facets of evangelistic priority. This book identifies a sixth: salvation-historical priority. In earlier salvation history, both OT Israel and Jesus/his disciples before the resurrection did *not* have an evangelizing mission outside Israel and only a very limited good deeds mission beyond the covenant community. In the phase of salvation history still to come, the New Covenant community after the consummation *will* experience the comprehensive and cosmic salvation of the kingdom, including the transformation of all human society. All humanity in the new heavens and new earth will be members of the covenant community—salvation will be complete and evangelism will be unnecessary. But in the present phase of salvation history (the age of the inaugurated New Covenant), the church *is* given an extensive mission to those *outside* the covenant, with a priority for evangelism. That mission also includes doing good to all people as Christians have the opportunity, but the weight of responsibility for the institutional church toward the world during this age is *not* reforming or transforming broader human society but is instead proclaiming the gospel message and inviting people to enter the inaugurated New Covenant community. We can therefore describe evangelism within the institutional church's mission out to the world as possessing a "salvation-historical priority" over the mission of good deeds.

Doing Good through Macroeconomics and Politics

When considering the many ways in which members of the New Covenant community can do good within broader society (mainly apart from the official efforts of the institutional church at the local level), many distinguish between works of relief, development, and social reform. "Relief" meets the immediate and pressing needs of people, often in emergency circumstances, such as natural disaster, sickness, or political upheaval. Particularly at the local level, these are efforts in which the involvement of the institutional church in an official capacity *may* be more appropriate. But while "relief" is a vital way to do good in society, relief typically only "deals with symptoms, not with causes."[65] In contrast, "development" or "community development" is "the attempt to provide long-term solutions to chronic problems like floods, famines, and earthquakes, most often by assisting community members to help themselves through cooperative action."[66] We can also understand "community development" more broadly as not merely efforts to assist the least developed and neediest communities but instead *all* efforts that contribute to the general building up of human communities and to the expression within those communities of "common grace justice" and "penultimate human flourishing." This includes people's everyday work responsibilities and how each person has the opportunity to contribute in their own way to the positive development of human society in this world.[67] Such broader works of community building are likewise legitimate ways through which Christians can do good

---

[65] Waldron Scott, *Bring Forth Justice: A Contemporary Perspective on Mission* (Grand Rapids: Eerdmans, 1980), 267.

[66] Ibid.

[67] Some recent books on the theology of work and vocation include Steve Garber, *Visions of Vocation: Common Grace for the Common Good* (Downers Grove, IL: IVP, 2014); Os Guinness, *The Call: Finding and Fulfilling the Central Purpose of Your Life* (Nashville: Thomas Nelson, 1998); Bill Heatley, *The Gift of Work: Spiritual Disciplines for the Workplace* (Colorado Springs, CO: NavPress, 2008); Timothy Keller, *Every Good Endeavor: Connecting Your Work to God's Work* (New York: Riverhead Books, 2012); Tom Nelson, *Work Matters: Connecting Sunday Worship to Monday Work* (Wheaton, IL: Crossway, 2011); William C. Placher, ed., *Callings: Twenty Centuries of Christian Wisdom on Vocation* (Grand Rapids: Eerdmans, 2005); R. Paul Stevens, *The Other Six Days: Vocation, Work, and Ministry in Biblical Perspective* (Grand Rapids: Eerdmans, 2000); Sebastian Traeger and Greg Gilbert, *The Gospel at Work: How Working for King Jesus Gives Purpose and Meaning to Our Jobs* (Grand Rapids: Zondervan, 2013); Gene Veith, *God at Work: Your Christian Vocation in All of Life* (Wheaton, IL: Crossway, 2002); Miroslav Volf, *Work in the Spirit: Toward a Theology of Work* (Eugene, OR: Wipf & Stock, 2001); Gustaf Wingreen, *Luther on Vocation* (Eugene, OR: Wipf & Stock, 2004).

within society. The more debated questions concern how Christians should do good within society at a macro-level, the level of "social reform," the realm of macroeconomics[68] and politics. These are complex topics of consideration and the fairly brief comments below are intended to be suggestive of further areas of potential research prompted by the conclusions of this book.

Doing Good through Macroeconomics

Some Christians believe that the Bible supports an approach to macroeconomics which emphasizes central government planning and extensive redistribution of wealth, and consequently, if Christians want to do good through macroeconomics, then they should advocate for such economic systems. For example, Kirk believes that the "overwhelming weight of biblical evidence suggests that private accumulation of wealth is not to be tolerated beyond the enjoyment of a frugal, adequate lifestyle, when substantial sectors of society (in our world hundreds of millions) do not have the basic necessities of their existence met."[69] Therefore, Kirk proposes that it is a "biblical imperative to redistribute wealth on a regular basis. Ideally, this would happen voluntarily. Left to themselves, however, most people would not make the connection between maximizing their own advantages and increasing the disadvantage of others."[70] Because most will continue to maximize their own economic advantage without recognizing how doing so inherently disadvantages others (Kirk claims), therefore, government must impose wealth redistribution. In arguing this, Kirk embraces a "zero sum" view of

[68] Macroeconomics is the facet of the larger discipline of economics which specifically considers large-scale economic systems and generalized economic theories.

[69] Kirk, *The Good News of the Kingdom Coming*, 74. Of note is the fact that Kirk writes in 1983, before the fall of Soviet communism.

[70] Ibid., 82. Kirk even suggests that James 5:1–6 "anticipat[es] Marx's discussion of surplus-value, the value added in the manufacturing process which is not returned to the worker but kept as profit, either to be reinvested in the business or paid to the shareholders." Ibid., 107.

economics which sees every gain made by one person or group as necessarily meaning an equal loss by another person or group, a view which Kirk adopts because he is persuaded that "socialism points to the considerable historical evidence which shows that one cannot maximize one's advantage without causing deprivation and suffering to another."[71] Kirk also rejects the idea that the "basic economic problem is . . . one of scarcity," instead merely assuming the ongoing and sufficient production of the goods and services needed by all humanity while then asserting that "the basic problem is how to achieve a fair distribution of wealth so that everyone's basic needs are adequately met."[72] Kirk concludes then that Christians should support goals such as "the fixing of both minimum and maximum incomes for different jobs" and "the state . . . own[ing] the means of production of all activities that have genuinely social implications—road systems, railways, communications and primary products (oil, gas, coal and, to a greater extent than present, land)."[73] Scott agrees that "the present [capitalist] international economic order . . . [is a system which] takes from the poor and gives to the rich."[74] Christopher Wright seems to concur concerning the Bible's demand for an economic system which redistributes wealth (coercively if necessary), including (apparently) *between* nation-states. On the basis of his argument from the paradigm of OT Israel, Wright proposes, "If in our day the rich—individuals or nations—cannot be *persuaded* [original emphasis] to make the sacrifices necessary to enable a more equitable deal for the poor, we face the moral and political question of whether they should be *compelled* to do so, whether by radical revolutionary means or by the more gentle process of redistributive taxation."[75]

[71] Ibid., 62.

[72] Ibid., 63.

[73] Ibid., 84.

[74] Scott, *Bring Forth Justice*, 136. Scott writes in 1980, like Kirk's book, before the fall of Soviet communism.

[75] Christopher J. H. Wright, *God's People in God's Land: Family, Land, and*

In contrast to macroeconomic perspectives like these, other Christians are convinced that some version of a free market system best coheres with the biblical worldview and is, therefore, the best way for Christians to do good through macroeconomics. Sider once advocated views similar to Kirk, Scott, and Wright, but now acknowledges that "my thinking has also changed. I've learned more about economics. And I have continued to study the Scriptures. When the choice is communism or democratic capitalism, I support democratic government and market economies."[76] Sider is convinced that "a market-oriented economy is clearly better than any alternative framework we now know" and that "private property is so good that everybody ought to have some."[77] Sider now believes that the Bible does *not* "support a communist economic system" or other approaches which centralize economic power, but instead, "Biblical principles point in the direction of decentralized private ownership that allows families to control their economic destinies."[78] Sider has also changed his interpretation of what the Bible reveals about the proper distribution of wealth within a particular society.

Property in the Old Testament (Grand Rapids: Eerdmans, 1990), 179. Newbigin seems to resonate with the weight of Wright's concerns when he states, "The ideology of the free market . . . is a form of idolatry . . . [responding to which must be recognized as] probably [the church's] most urgent missionary task during the [twenty-first] century." Lesslie Newbigin, *The Open Secret: An Introduction to the Theology of Mission*, rev. ed. (Grand Rapids: Eerdmans, 1995), 95. For further consideration of Wright's paradigmatic approach to OT ethics as applied to the socio-economic realm, see John A. Wind, "Not Always Right: Critiquing Christopher Wright's Paradigmatic Application of Scripture to the Socio-economic Realm," *Southern Baptist Journal of Theology* 19, no. 2 (Summer 2015): 81–104. For further consideration of Wright's paradigmatic approach to OT ethics as applied to creation care, see John A. Wind, "Does the Old Testament 'Authorize' a Creation Care Mission of the Church? Examining Christopher Wright's Claims," *Journal of Global Christianity* 2, no. 1 (2016): 33–47.

[76] Ronald J. Sider, *Rich Christians in an Age of Hunger: Moving from Affluence to Generosity*, 20th anniversary ed. (Dallas: Word, 1997), xiii.

[77] Ibid., xiv.

[78] Ibid., 94.

Sider shares, "I never thought biblical revelation demanded absolute equality of income and wealth. But I used to be more concerned than I am today with the proportion of income and wealth that different groups possess."[79]

Others concur with Sider's advocacy of the free market system as the best means for Christians to do good through macroeconomics. John Bolt promotes a free market economic model "within the framework of a legal order that secures property rights" as the best macroeconomic system in a fallen world. Bolt believes that such an economic system has been "unquestionably" shown by "empirical historical comparisons with other economic orders" to be the best "engine for economic growth and the hope for the world's poor."[80] Yet, Bolt cautions Christians not to see "free-market polity" within a society of "ordered liberty" as anything more than a "penultimate good," requiring Christians to maintain "eschatological reserve" concerning any economic hopes and expectations in this life.[81] VanDrunen agrees that a "free-market economy is (or at least has a strong claim to be) the best form of economic organization for a fallen world upheld by God's common grace under the covenant with Noah," even while simultaneously "fall[ing] radically short of capturing the economic relationships that characterize the eschatological kingdom of Christ."[82] Because of this, Christians "ought to

[79] Ibid., xiv.

[80] John Bolt, *Economic Shalom: A Reformed Primer on Faith, Work, and Human Flourishing* (Grand Rapids: Christian's Library Press, 2013), 94.

[81] Ibid., 95.

[82] David VanDrunen, "The Market Economy and Christian Ethics: Refocusing Debate through the Two-Kingdoms Doctrine," *Journal of Markets and Morality* 17, no. 1 (Spring 2014): 13. VanDrunen's (and Bolt's) "eschatological reserve" is in contrast to some who claim that Christians "should expect God to bring forth every kind of blessing [in this age], such as economies that flourish with justice and righteousness, agricultures and industries that abound with plenty for all, and peace throughout communities and between peoples and races. We can expect that God will enable His people to wage war with disease, to break the vicious cycles of poverty, to provide water in desert lands, and to be present with healing in the midst of catastrophe. . . . we are right to expect

keep the profound limitations of the market economy always before them . . . mak[ing] [Christians] ever eager to sacrifice their worldly gains in the market as a testimony to the economic abundance of the coming kingdom."[83]

This unavoidable eschatological tension between the ages, as well as the profound complexity of competing macroeconomic theories, all attempting to make sense of the billions of daily economic decisions and counter-decisions made freely by individuals and groups within an increasingly globalized commercial system, should cause Christians to avoid dogmatism and to embrace humility when considering how best to do good through macroeconomics. For instance, we should not oversimplify the question of how best to help the financially impoverished, either within our own countries or in other countries. Within Scripture, poverty is presented as a complex phenomenon with diverse causes. David Kotter, for example, notes how the NT reveals poverty as typically resulting from one or a combination of four factors: oppression by others, moral failure and foolishness, external calamities, and the reality of living in a fallen world.[84] Myers concurs that "poverty is a complex,

---

that our mission will lead to social and material change or transformation." Sarita D. Gallagher and Steven C. Hawthorne, "Blessings as Transformation," in *Perspectives on The World Christian Movement: A Reader*, 4th ed., eds. Ralph D. Winter and Steven C. Hawthorne (Pasadena, CA: William Carey Library, 2009), 39–40.

[83] VanDrunen, "The Market Economy and Christian Ethics, 13. Other Christians who advocate some version of a free-market economic system as the best way for Christians to do good through macroeconomics include Chad Brand and Tom Pratt, *Seeking the City: Wealth, Poverty, and Political Economy in Christian Perspective* (Grand Rapids: Kregel, 2013); Wayne Grudem and Barry Asmus, *The Poverty of Nations: A Sustainable Solution* (Wheaton, IL: Crossway, 2013); Austin Hill and Scott Rae, *The Virtues of Capitalism: A Moral Case for Free Markets* (Chicago: Northfield Publishing, 2010).

[84] David Kotter, "Remember the Poor: A New Testament Perspective on the Problems of Poverty, Riches, and Redistribution," in *For the Least of These: A Biblical Answer to Poverty*, eds. Anne Bradley and Art Lindsley (Bloomington, IN: Westbow Press, 2014), 70.

multifaceted phenomenon . . . unlikely [to provide] any simple answers" but instead requiring a "multidisciplinary" approach which uses "the tools of anthropology, sociology, social psychology, spiritual discernment, and theology, all nicely integrated"—though Myers glaringly neglects to mention the tool of economics.[85]

The danger of neglecting proven economic insight can lead to the sad result of "when helping hurts."[86] Too often, well-intended financial, material, or service aid, distributed by Christians either domestically or internationally, ends up economically hurting the very people it intends to help. As Nash proposes, "When 'aid' is grounded on bad economics, it will usually make any bad situation worse."[87] International aid, in particular, presents many pitfalls for Christians. For example, Jim Harries notes concerning "holistic missions" aid to Africa and other third world countries that "people's problems are complex, so finding solutions is complex," but rather than helping, outside mission aid has ended up merely "giving license to western people to force their solutions onto African (and other Third World) communities using money and technology."[88] The actual (though unintended) result of "holistic missions" in Africa has been "serious problems, especially unhealthy dependency of African churches and communities on the west, and a serious impeding of local African initiatives and ecclesial or social/economic development."[89] The danger of "when helping hurts" encourages us to consider the principle of "subsidiarity," a principle closely related the principle of "moral proximity" introduced in chapter 7.

[85] Bryant L. Myers, *Walking with the Poor: Principles and Practices of Transformational Development* (Maryknoll, NY: Orbis, 1999), 86.

[86] See Steve Corbett and Brian Fikkert, *When Helping Hurts: How to Alleviate Poverty without Hurting the Poor . . . and Yourself* (Chicago: Moody, 2012).

[87] Ronald H. Nash, *Social Justice and the Christian Church* (Lanham, MD: University Press of America, 1990), 3.

[88] Jim Harries, "'Material Provision' or Preaching the Gospel: Reconsidering 'Holistic' (Integral) Mission," *Evangelical Review of Theology* 32, no. 3 (2008): 267.

[89] Ibid., 270.

According to Glenn Sunshine, whereas moral proximity "looks at problems and asks where I am personally responsible to act given my finite time and resources," subsidiarity considers "problems and asks who is best equipped to deal with them."[90] The general principle of subsidiarity is the assertion that "solutions are best found on as local a level as possible, with higher level institutions becoming involved only when the problems are too big for lower levels to handle."[91] Therefore, in seeking to do good to others through international aid and macro-economic development, Christians should wisely defer as much as possible to local initiatives which are contextualized for each unique circumstance. This decentralized economic approach to Christian aid is more complicated than merely writing a big check, but in seeking to do good through economics and macroeconomic systems, Christians must not be satisfied with simply good intentions but with actual results.

Doing Good through Politics

One of the primary ways that Christians have the opportunity to do macroeconomic good to others (again, mainly apart from the official actions of the institutional church) is through the legal, policy, and macroeconomic decisions they support through their political choices (if they live within a nation with some form of participative democracy). Like with economics, perspectives vary on the relationship between the work of the church and politics. James Skillen believes that the church is called to participate in God's kingdom work of now "redeeming" human government,[92] whereas McKnight

---

[90] Glenn Sunshine, "Who Are the Poor?" in *For the Least of These: A Biblical Answer to Poverty*, eds. Anne Bradley and Art Lindsley (Bloomington, IN: Westbow Press, 2014), 31–32.

[91] Ibid., 32.

[92] James W. Skillen, "Acting Politically in Biblical Obedience?" in *A Royal Priesthood? The Use of the Bible Ethically and Politically—A Dialogue with Oliver O'Donovan*, ed. Craig G. Bartholomew et al. (Grand Rapids: Zondervan, 2002), 413.

sees the church's involvement in politics as "a colossal distraction from kingdom mission."[93] Agreeing with McKnight that Christian political involvement is *not* "kingdom work," the political realm is nonetheless a realm within which Christians (within participative democracies) should consider how best to do good.[94] Like macroeconomic considerations, Christians should beware of too much dogmatism in the realm of politics. Also like economics, Christians should be modest about the possibility of doing political good in cross-cultural settings, likewise applying the principle of subsidiarity in recognizing that any attempts by Christians to bring a measure of reform to a society through the political process should "most often come from indigenous believers and churches" rather than outside or foreign Christians.[95]

Even while willingly (as opportunity allows) seeking to do good through the political process, Christians must also consider that though "change in political systems and economic conditions *can* occur relatively quickly," a deeper influence upon culture "typically takes place over the course of multiple generations."[96] From

[93] McKnight, *Kingdom Conspiracy*, 102.

[94] One recent evangelical consideration of how best to do good in the political realm is Wayne A. Grudem, *Politics According to the Bible: A Comprehensive Resource for Understanding Modern Political Issues in Light of Scripture* (Grand Rapids: Zondervan, 2010).

[95] Doug Coleman, "The Agents of Mission: Humanity," in *Theology and Practice of Mission: God, the Church, and the Nations*, ed. Bruce Riley Ashford (Nashville: B&H Academic, 2011), 45.

[96] Hunter, *To Change the World*, 45. For example, O'Donovan believes that Christianity impacted European society over centuries by cultivating the values of "freedom, merciful judgment, natural right, and openness to speech," values which undergirded the gradual rise of a "Christian constitutionalism" in Europe. Jonathan Chaplin, "Political Eschatology and Responsible Government: Oliver O'Donovan's 'Christian Liberalism,'" in *A Royal Priesthood? The Use of the Bible Ethically and Politically—A Dialogue with Oliver O'Donovan*, ed. Craig G. Bartholomew et al. (Grand Rapids: Zondervan, 2002), 272, 283. David Hall also believes that Calvinism made a distinctive contribution to European forms of government by promoting five tenets: "1. Depravity as a perennial human variable to accommodate; 2. Accountability for leaders via a

this perspective, Hunter encourages believers desiring to do good through politics not to lose sight of the fact that, in the long run, "faithful presence . . . irrespective of influence" is more vital to doing good in a society than mere short-term political activism.[97] This also illustrates why the institutional church must always prioritize evangelism in its mission beyond the covenant community since any political attempts to replace "unjust structures with more equitable ones will finally be crowned with failure unless a far more profound transformation is wrought in the men who establish them and wield their power."[98] This truth has long been recognized by Christians when considering the political realm. John Witherspoon, pastor, president of Princeton University,[99] and signer of the Declaration of Independence, declared in 1776, "A good form of government may hold the rotten materials [of a corrupt people] together for some time, but beyond a certain pitch, even the best constitution will be ineffectual, and slavery must ensue." According to Witherspoon, even more important than the form of government is whether or not "the manners of a nation are pure" and "true religion [biblical

collegium; 3. Republicanism as the preferred form of government; 4. Constitutionalism needed to restrain both the rulers and the ruled; 5. Limited government, beginning with the family, as foundational," quoted in R. Michael Allen, *Reformed Theology* (Edinburgh: T&T Clark, 2010), 156. Concerning Christianity's impact on European culture in general, Keller notes how "Christianity permanently altered the old honor-based European cultures in which pride was valued rather than humility, dominance rather than service, courage rather than peaceableness, glory more than modesty, loyalty to one's own tribe rather than equal respect for all individuals. Even though there is today some slippage in Western society back toward that pagan worldview, today's secular Europeans are still influenced far more by the Christian ethic than by the old pagan ones. And by and large, Western societies are more humane places to live because of it. In other words, Christianity transformed a pagan culture." Timothy Keller, *Center Church: Doing Balanced, Gospel-Centered Ministry in Your City* (Grand Rapids: Zondervan, 2012), 207.

[97] Hunter, *To Change the World*, 95.

[98] Shedd, "Social Justice," 201.

[99] The school was called the College of New Jersey until 1896 when the name was changed to Princeton University.

Christianity] and internal principles maintain their vigor."[100] Almost a hundred years earlier (1682), William Penn, founder of the Pennsylvania colony, stated similarly, "Let men be good, and the government cannot be bad; if it be ill, they will cure it. But, if men be bad, let the government be never so good, they will endeavor to warp and spoil it to their turn."[101] True change in politics ultimately requires true change in citizens, an internal work which only the Spirit-empowered gospel of the New Covenant kingdom can produce in any lasting way. Therefore, even in seeking to do good through politics, Christians must remain ever sensitive to the great limitations of the political realm and remain steadfastly committed to their more fundamental missions of evangelism and "faithful presence" within each society as "the light of the world."

Summary of the Good Deeds Mission
of the New Covenant Community

This book has demonstrated the crucial impact of one's conception of Scripture's overall covenantal framework upon the question of the proper relationship between the church's missions of evangelism and good deeds. With an in-depth literature review of the competing biblical-theological arguments offered by the equal priority and evangelistic priority positions since 1974, this book showed the need for its own unique contribution. By first tracing humanity's good deeds responsibility (both before and after sin) and Abraham/his descendants' good deeds mission (both when possessing and not possessing the covenant land), this book properly situated the New

---

[100] John Witherspoon, "The Dominion of Providence over the Passions of Men," in *Political Sermons of the American Founding Era, 1730–1805*, ed. Ellis Sandoz, 2nd ed. (Indianapolis: Liberty Fund, 1998), 1:553.

[101] William Penn, "Charter of Liberties and Frame of Government of the Province of Pennsylvania in America," in *Colonial Origins of the American Constitution: A Documentary History*, ed. Donald S. Lutz (Indianapolis: Liberty Fund, 1998), 274.

Covenant community's good deeds mission (both before and after covenant inauguration) within a salvation-historical plotline which recognizes both continuity and discontinuity between these covenantal epochs. The church, along with all humanity, continues to live under the Noahic Fallen Creation Covenant of common grace preservation, responsible to do good deeds which promote "common grace justice" and "penultimate human flourishing" within society. But the New Covenant community, like the Abrahamic/Mosaic Covenant communities before, also lives under the covenant of God's special grace. Like the Abrahamic/Mosaic communities, the church continues to be the light of the world, responsible to maintain the salt of covenant fidelity and to attract those outside the covenant by her good deeds. But unlike the earlier covenants, the New Covenant community also has a responsibility to proclaim the gospel message of how Christ has inaugurated the New Covenant (and will consummate it) and of how this covenant Lord invites sinners to enter into eternal union with him. This mission of evangelism (in comparison to the mission of good deeds) must retain operational priority within the institutional church's ministry beyond the covenant community, both because of evangelism's "salvation-historical priority" and because of the priority of the future, rather than because of any form of mistaken dualism. In highlighting the covenantal relationships between the Adamic Creation Covenant and Noahic Fallen Creation Covenant, between the Abrahamic Covenant of not-yet-realized rest and the Mosaic Covenant of already-realized-rest, and between the not-yet-inaugurated New Covenant of the Gospels, the inaugurated New Covenant of Acts and the Epistles, and the consummated New Covenant of the new heavens and the new earth, this book provided a template of key interpretive questions which each evangelical must consider when developing a biblical theology of the good deeds mission of the New Covenant community. While *rejecting* a more expansive understanding of the church's good deeds mission in society as "kingdom work" which brings some measure of what the NT labels as "salvation," "redemption," and "reconciliation," this book nevertheless sought to offer a positive portrayal of the Christian responsibility for abundant good deeds. While justification and entrance into the New Covenant is solely on the basis of Christ's work and not the believer's, all who are truly in Christ will live a faithful covenant life displaying good deeds as the fruit of their covenant Lord's indwelling presence. Therefore, all members of the New Covenant *must* seek to "do good to all people as you have the opportunity."

Bibliography

Books

Alexander, T. Desmond. *From Eden to the New Jerusalem: An Introduction to Biblical Theology*. Grand Rapids: Kregel, 2008.

_____. *From Paradise to the Promised Land: An Introduction to the Pentateuch*. 3rd ed. Grand Rapids: Baker Academic, 2012.

Allen, R. Michael. *Reformed Theology*. Edinburgh: T&T Clark, 2010.

Allert, Craig D. *A High View of Scripture? The Authority of the Bible and the Formation of the New Testament Canon*. Grand Rapids: Baker Academic, 2007.

Arnold, Bill T. *Genesis*. New York: Cambridge, 2009.

Ashford, Bruce Riley, ed. *Theology and Practice of Mission: God, the Church, and the Nations*. Nashville: B&H Academic, 2011.

Balentine, Samuel E. *The Torah's Vision of Worship*. Minneapolis: Fortress, 1999.

Barth, Karl. *Church Dogmatics*. Edited by G. W. Bromiley and T. F. Torrance. Vol. 3, *The Doctrine of Creation*. Pt. 1. Translated by J. W. Edwards, O. Bussey, and H. Knight. London: T&T Clark International, 2004.

Bartholomew, Craig G., and Michael W. Goheen. *The Drama of Scripture: Finding Our Place in the Biblical Story*. Grand Rapids: Baker Academic, 2004.

Barton, John. *Understanding Old Testament Ethics: Approaches and Explorations*. Louisville: Westminster John Knox, 2003.

Bauckham, Richard. *The Bible and Ecology: Rediscovering the Community of Creation*. Waco, TX: Baylor, 2010.

_____. *Bible and Mission: Christian Witness in a Postmodern World*. Grand
Rapids: Baker Academic, 2004.

_____. *Living with Other Creatures: Green Exegesis and Theology*. Waco, TX: Baylor, 2011

Bauckham, Richard, and Trevor Hart. *Hope Against Hope: Christian Eschatology at the Turn of the Millennium*. Grand Rapids: Eerdmans, 1999.

Beale, G. K. *A New Testament Biblical Theology: The Unfolding of the Old Testament in the New*. Grand Rapids: Baker, 2011.

_____. *The Temple and the Church's Mission: A Biblical Theology of the Dwelling Place of God*. Downers Grove, IL: IVP, 2004.

Beckwith, Roger. *The Old Testament Canon of the New Testament Church*. Eugene, OR: Wipf & Stock, 2008.

Beisner, E. Calvin. *Where the Garden Meets Wilderness: Evangelical Entry into the Environmental Debate*. Grand Rapids: Acton Institute/Eerdmans, 1997.

Beyerhaus, Peter. *God's Kingdom and the Utopian Error: Discerning the Biblical Kingdom of God from Its Political Counterfeits*. Wheaton, IL: Crossway, 1992.

_____. *Shaken Foundations: Theological Foundations for Mission*. Grand Rapids: Zondervan, 1972.

Blocher, Henri. *In the Beginning: The Opening Chapters of Genesis*. Downers Grove, IL: IVP, 1987.

Block, Daniel I. *For the Glory of God: Recovering a Biblical Theology of Worship*. Grand Rapids: Baker Academic, 2014.

Bloesch, Donald G. *The Invaded Church*. Waco, TX: Word, 1975.

Blomberg, Craig L. *Neither Poverty nor Riches: A Biblical Theology of Material Possessions*. Grand Rapids: Eerdmans, 1999.

Bockmuehl, Markus. *Jewish Law in Gentile Churches: Halakhah and the Beginning of Christian Public Ethics*. Grand Rapids: Baker Academic, 2000.

Bolt, John. *Economic Shalom: A Reformed Primer on Faith, Work, and Human Flourishing*. Grand Rapids: Christian's Library Press, 2013.

Bosch, David J. *Transforming Mission: Paradigm Shifts in Theology of Mission*. Maryknoll, NY: Orbis, 1991.

Bouma-Prediger, Steven. *For the Beauty of the Earth: A Christian Vision for Creation Care*. 2nd ed. Grand Rapids: Baker Academic, 2010.

Braaten, Carl E. *The Flaming Center: A Theology of Christian Mission*. Philadelphia: Fortress, 1977.

Brand, Chad, and Tom Pratt. *Seeking the City: Wealth, Poverty, and Political Economy in Christian Perspective*. Grand Rapids: Kregel, 2013.

Burnside, Jonathan. *God, Justice, and Society: Aspects of Law and Legality in the Bible*. Oxford: Oxford, 2011.

Carson, D. A. *Christ and Culture Revisited*. Grand Rapids: Eerdmans, 2008.

Cassuto, Umberto. *A Commentary on the Book of Genesis: Part 1, From Adam to Noah*. Jerusalem: Magnes, 1961.

Chester, Tim. *Good News to the Poor: Social Involvement and the Gospel*. Wheaton, IL: Crossway, 2013.

Childs, Brevard S. *The Book of Exodus: A Critical, Theological Commentary*. Philadelphia: Westminster, 1974.

Conn, Harvie M. *Evangelism: Doing Justice and Preaching Grace*. Grand Rapids: Zondervan, 1982.

Corbett, Steve, and Brian Fikkert. *When Helping Hurts: How to Alleviate Poverty without Hurting the Poor . . . and Yourself*. Chicago: Moody, 2012.

Cosden, Darrell. *The Heavenly Good of Earthly Work*. Peabody, MA: Hendrickson, 2006.

Costas, Orlando E. *The Church and Its Mission: A Shattering Critique from the Third World*. Wheaton, IL: Tyndale, 1974.

Dempster, Stephen G. *Dominion and Dynasty: A Biblical Theology of the Hebrew Bible*. Downers Grove, IL: IVP, 2003.

DeYoung, Kevin, and Greg Gilbert. *What is the Mission of the Church? Making Sense of Social Justice, Shalom, and the Great Commission.* Wheaton, IL: Crossway, 2011.

Dickson, John. *The Best Kept Secret of Christian Mission: Promoting the Gospel with More Than Our Lips.* Grand Rapids: Zondervan, 2010.

Dowsett, Rose. *The Cape Town Commitment: A Confession of Faith and a Call to Action—Study Edition.* Peabody, MA: Hendrickson, 2012.

Dumbrell, William J. *Covenant and Creation: An Old Testament Covenant Theology.* Carlisle, UK: Paternoster, 2013.

_____. *Covenant and Creation: A Theology of the Old Testament Covenants.* Carlisle, UK: Paternoster, 2000.

Dyrness, William A. *Let the Earth Rejoice!: A Biblical Theology of Holistic Mission.* Westchester, IL: Crossway, 1983.

Elazar, Daniel J. *Covenant & Polity in Biblical Israel: Biblical Foundations & Jewish Expressions.* New Brunswick, NJ: Transaction, 1995.

Engel, James F., and William A. Dyrness. *Changing the Mind of Missions: Where Have We Gone Wrong?* Downers Grove, IL: IVP, 2000.

Erickson, Millard J. *Christian Theology.* 2nd ed. Grand Rapids: Baker, 1998.

Evans, Craig A., and Emanuel Tov, eds. *Exploring the Origins of the Bible: Canon Formation in Historical, Literary, and Theological Perspective.* Grand Rapids: Baker Academic, 2008.

Fesko, J. V. *Last Things First: Unlocking Genesis 1–2 with the Christ of Eschatology.* Fearn, Scotland: Christian Focus Publications, 2007.

Fielding, Charles. *Preach and Heal: A Biblical Model for Missions.* Richmond, VA: International Mission Board, 2008.

Flemming, Dean. *Recovering the Full Mission of God: A Biblical Perspective on Being, Doing and Telling.* Downers Grove, IL: IVP Academic, 2013.

Forster, Greg. *Joy for the World: How Christianity Lost Its Cultural Influence and Can Begin Rebuilding It.* Wheaton, IL: Crossway, 2014.

Frame, John M. *Salvation Belongs to the Lord: An Introduction to Systematic Theology.* Phillipsburg, NJ: P&R Publishing, 2006.

_____. *The Escondido Theology: A Reformed Response to the Two Kingdoms Theology.* Lakeland, FL: Whitefield Media Productions, 2011.

Frei, Hans W. *The Eclipse of Biblical Narrative: A Study in Eighteenth and Nineteenth Century Hermeneutics.* New Haven, CT: Yale, 1974.

Fretheim, Terence E. *The Book of Genesis: Introduction, Commentary, and Reflections.* In vol. 1 of *The New Interpreter's Bible.* Edited by Leander E. Keck, 319–674. Nashville: Abingdon Press, 1994.

Garber, Steve. *Visions of Vocation: Common Grace for the Common Good.* Downers Grove, IL: IVP, 2014.

Garr, W. Randall. *In His Own Image and Likeness: Humanity, Divinity, and Monotheism.* Boston: Brill, 2003.

Gentry, Peter J., and Stephen J. Wellum. *Kingdom through Covenant: A Biblical-Theological Understanding of the Covenants.* Wheaton, IL: Crossway, 2012.

Glasser, Arthur F. *Announcing the Kingdom: The Story of God's Mission in the Bible.* Grand Rapids: Baker Academic, 2003.

Gnanakan, Ken. *Kingdom Concerns: A Biblical Theology of Mission Today.* Downers Grove, IL: IVP, 1993.

Goheen, Michael W. *Introducing Christian Missions Today: Scripture, History, and Issues.* Downers Grove, IL: IVP, 2014.

_____. *A Light to the Nations: The Missional Church and the Biblical Story.* Grand Rapids: Baker Academic, 2011.

Goldsworthy, Graeme. *Christ-Centered Biblical Theology: Hermeneutical Foundations and Principles.* Downers Grove, IL: IVP Academic, 2012.

Green, Bradley G. *Covenant and Commandment: Works, Obedience, and Faithfulness in the Christian Life.* Downers Grove, IL: IVP, 2014.

Grudem, Wayne A. *Bible Doctrine: Essential Teachings of the Christian Faith*. Edited by Jeff Purswell. Grand Rapids: Zondervan, 1999.

_____. *Business for the Glory of God: The Bible's Teaching on the Moral Goodness of Business*. Wheaton, IL: Crossway, 2003.

_____. *Politics According to the Bible: A Comprehensive Resource for Understanding Modern Political Issues in Light of Scripture*. Grand Rapids: Zondervan, 2010.

Grudem, Wayne, and Barry Asmus. *The Poverty of Nations: A Sustainable Solution*. Wheaton, IL: Crossway, 2013.

Guinness, Os. *The Call: Finding and Fulfilling the Central Purpose of Your Life*. Nashville: Thomas Nelson, 1998.

Hafemann, Scott J. *The God of Promise and the Life of Faith: Understanding the Heart of the Bible*. Wheaton, IL: Crossway, 2001.

Hahn, Scott W. *Kinship by Covenant: A Canonical Approach to the Fulfillment of God's Saving Promises*. New Haven, CT: Yale, 2009.

Hamilton, Victor P. *The Book of Genesis: Chapters 1–17*. Grand Rapids: Eerdmans, 1990.

Hamilton, James M., Jr. *God's Glory in Salvation through Judgment: A Biblical Theology*. Wheaton, IL: Crossway, 2010.

Hays, Richard B. *The Moral Vision of the New Testament: Community, Cross, New Creation*. San Francisco: HarperSanFrancisco, 1996.

Heatley, Bill. *The Gift of Work: Spiritual Disciplines for the Workplace*. Colorado Springs, CO: NavPress, 2008

Hedlund, Roger E. *The Mission of the Church in the World: A Biblical Theology*. Grand Rapids: Baker, 1991.

Henry, Carl F. H. *The Uneasy Conscience of Modern Fundamentalism*. Grand Rapids: Eerdmans, 2003.

Heschel, Abraham J. *The Sabbath: Its Meaning for Modern Man*. New York: Farrar, Straus & Giroux, 1951.

Hesselgrave, David J. *Paradigms in Conflict: 10 Key Questions in Christian Missions Today*. Grand Rapids: Kregel, 2005.

Hill, Austin, and Scott Rae. *The Virtues of Capitalism: A Moral Case for Free Markets*. Chicago: Northfield Publishing, 2010.

Hirsch, E. D. *Validity in Interpretation*. New Haven, CT: Yale, 1967.

Hoekema, Anthony A. *Created in God's Image*. Grand Rapids: Eerdmans, 1986.

Horton, Michael S. *Covenant and Eschatology: The Divine Drama*. Louisville: Westminster John Knox, 2002.

_____. *The Gospel Commission: Recovering God's Strategy for Making Disciples*. Grand Rapids: Baker, 2011.

_____. *Introducing Covenant Theology*. Grand Rapids: Baker, 2006.

_____. *Where in the World is the Church? A Christian View of Culture and Your Role in It*. Phillipsburg, NJ: P&R Publishing, 2002.

Hunter, James Davison. *To Change the World: The Irony, Tragedy, and Possibility of Christianity in the Late Modern World*. New York: Oxford, 2010.

Kaiser, Walter C. *Mission in the Old Testament: Israel as a Light to the Nations*. 2nd ed. Grand Rapids: Baker Academic, 2012.

_____. *Toward an Old Testament Theology*. Grand Rapids: Zondervan, 1978.

Kaiser, Walter C., and Moisés Silva. *An Introduction to Biblical Hermeneutics: The Search for Meaning*. Grand Rapids: Zondervan, 1994.

Kaminski, Carol M. *Was Noah Good? Finding Favor in the Flood Narrative*. New York: Bloomsbury T&T Clark, 2014.

Kane, J. Herbert. *Christian Missions in Biblical Perspective*. Grand Rapids: Baker, 1976.

Kato, Byang H. *Theological Pitfalls in Africa*. Kisumu, Kenya: Evangel Publishing House, 1975.

Keller, Timothy. *Center Church: Doing Balanced, Gospel-Centered Ministry in Your City*. Grand Rapids: Zondervan, 2012.

_____. *Every Good Endeavor: Connecting Your Work to God's Work*. New York: Riverhead Books, 2012.

_____. *Generous Justice: How God's Grace Makes Us Just*. New York: Dutton, 2010.

_____. *Ministries of Mercy: The Call of the Jericho Road*. 2nd ed. Phillipsburg, NJ: P&R Publishing, 1997.

Kelly, Stewart E. *Truth Considered and Applied: Examining Postmodernism, History, and Christian Faith*. Nashville: B&H Academic, 2011.

Kirk, Andrew. *The Good News of the Kingdom Coming: The Marriage of Evangelism and Social Responsibility*. Downers Grove, IL: IVP, 1983.

_____. *What Is Mission? Theological Explorations*. Minneapolis: Fortress, 2000.

Klein, William W., Craig Blomberg, and Robert L. Hubbard, Jr. *Introduction to Biblical Interpretation*. Dallas: Word, 1993.

Kline, Meredith G. *Images of the Spirit*. Grand Rapids: Baker, 1980.

_____. *Kingdom Prologue: Genesis Foundations for a Covenantal Worldview*. Overland Park, KS: Two Age Press, 2000.

Klink, Edward W., and Darian R. Lockett. *Understanding Biblical Theology: A Comparison of Theory and Practice*. Grand Rapids: Zondervan, 2012.

Köstenberger, Andreas J. *The Missions of Jesus and the Disciples According to the Fourth Gospel: With Implications for the Fourth Gospel's Purpose and the Mission of the Contemporary Church*. Grand Rapids: Eerdmans, 1998.

Köstenberger, Andreas J., and Peter T. O'Brien. *Salvation to the Ends of the Earth: A Biblical Theology of Mission*. Downers Grove, IL: IVP, 2001.

Kuyper, Abraham. *The Historical Argument: Part 1, Noah–Adam*. Part 1 in vol. 1 of *Common Grace*. Grand Rapids: CLP Academic, 2013.

_____. *Rooted and Grounded: The Church as Organism and Institution*. Kindle ed. Grand Rapids: Christian's Library Press, 2013.

Ladd, George Eldon. *A Theology of the New Testament*. Grand Rapids: Eerdmans, 1974.

Lim, Timothy H. *The Formation of the Jewish Canon*. New Haven, CT: Yale, 2013.

Linthicum, Robert C. *Transforming Power: Biblical Strategies for Making a Difference in Your Community*. Downers Grove, IL: IVP, 2003.

Lints, Richard. *The Fabric of Theology: A Prolegomenon to Evangelical Theology*. Grand Rapids: Eerdmans, 1993.

Litfin, Duane. *Word Vs Deed: Resetting the Scales to a Biblical Balance*. Wheaton, IL: Crossway, 2012.

Little, Christopher R. *Mission in the Way of Paul: Biblical Mission for the Church in the Twenty-first Century*. New York: Peter Lang, 2005.

_____. *Polemic Missiology for the 21st Century: In Memoriam of Roland Allen*. Kindle ed. Colombia, SC: Christopher R. Little, 2013.

Lohfink, Gerhard. *Jesus and Community: The Social Dimension of the Christian Faith*. Philadelphia: Fortress, 1984.

Longenecker, Bruce W. *Remember the Poor: Paul, Poverty, and the Greco-Roman World*. Grand Rapids: Eerdmans, 2010.

Lunde, Jonathan. *Following Jesus, The Servant King: A Biblical Theology of Covenantal Discipleship*. Kindle ed. Grand Rapids: Zondervan, 2010.

Marshall, I. Howard. *New Testament Theology: Many Witnesses, One Gospel*. Downers Grove, IL: IVP, 2004.

Mathews, Kenneth A. *Genesis 1–11:26*. The New American Commentary, vol. 1A. Nashville: B&H, 1996.

McDonald, Lee Martin. *Formation of the Bible: The Story of the Church's Canon*. Peabody, MA: Hendrickson, 2012.

McGavran, Donald A. *The Clash Between Christianity and Cultures*. Washington, DC: Canon, 1974.

McGoldrick, James E. *Abraham Kuyper: God's Renaissance Man*. Auburn, MA: Evangelical Press, 2000.

McKnight, Scot. *Kingdom Conspiracy: Returning to the Radical Mission of the Local Church*. Grand Rapids: Brazos, 2014.

Merrill, Eugene H. *Everlasting Dominion: A Theology of the Old Testament*. Nashville: B&H, 2006.

Middleton, J. Richard. *A New Heaven and A New Earth: Reclaiming Biblical Eschatology*. Grand Rapids: Baker Academic, 2014.

Moore, Russell. *The Kingdom of Christ: The New Evangelical Perspective*. Wheaton, IL: Crossway, 2004.

Mueller, John D. *Redeeming Economics: Rediscovering the Missing Element.* Wilmington, DE: Intercollegiate Studies Institute, 2014.

Myers, Bryant L. *Walking with the Poor.* Maryknoll, NY: Orbis, 1999.

Naselli, Andrew David, and Collin Hansen, eds. *Four Views on the Spectrum of Evangelicalism.* Grand Rapids: Zondervan, 2011.

Nash, Ronald H. *Social Justice and the Christian Church.* Lanham, MD: University Press of America, 1990.

Nelson, Tom. *Work Matters: Connecting Sunday Worship to Monday Work.* Wheaton, IL: Crossway, 2011.

Newbigin, Lesslie. *The Open Secret: An Introduction to the Theology of Mission.* Revised ed. Grand Rapids: Eerdmans, 1995.

Niehaus, Jeffrey J. *The Common Grace Covenants.* Vol. 1 of *Biblical Theology.* Wooster, OH: Weaver Book Company, 2014.

Nissen, Johannes. *New Testament and Mission: Historical and Hermeneutical Perspectives.* New York: Peter Lang, 1999.

Ott, Craig, and Stephen J. Strauss. *Encountering Theology of Mission: Biblical Foundations, Historical Developments, and Contemporary Issues.* Grand Rapids: Baker Academic, 2010.

Payne, Don J. *The Theology of the Christian Life in J. I. Packer's Thought: Theological Anthropology, Theological Method, and the Doctrine of Sanctification.* Bletchey, UK: Paternoster, 2006.

Pennington, Jonathan T. *Heaven and Earth in the Gospel of Matthew.* Grand Rapids: Baker Academic, 2007.

_____. *Reading the Gospels Wisely: A Narrative and Theological Introduction.* Grand Rapids: Baker Academic, 2012.

Perman, Matthew. *What's Best Next: How the Gospel Transforms the Way You Get Things Done.* Grand Rapids: Zondervan, 2014.

Peskett, Howard, and Vinoth Ramachandra. *The Message of Mission: The Glory of Christ in All Time and Space.* Downers Grove, IL: IVP, 2003.

Peters, George W. *A Biblical Theology of Missions.* Chicago: Moody, 1972.

Piper, John. *What Jesus Demands from the World.* Wheaton, IL: Crossway, 2006.

Placher, William C., ed. *Callings: Twenty Centuries of Christian Wisdom on Vocation*. Grand Rapids: Eerdmans, 2005.

Plummer, Robert L. *Paul's Understanding of the Church's Mission: Did the Apostle Paul Expect the Early Christian Communities to Evangelize?* Waynesboro, GA: Paternoster, 2006.

Postell, Seth D. *Adam as Israel: Genesis 1–3 as the Introduction to the Torah and Tanakh*. Eugene, OR: Wipf & Stock, 2011.

Reno, R. R. *Genesis*. Grand Rapids: Brazos, 2010.

Richter, Sandra L. *The Epic of Eden: A Christian Entry into the Old Testament*. Downers Grove, IL: IVP Academic, 2008.

Robinson, Gnana. *The Origin and Development of the Old Testament Sabbath*. Frankfurt: Peter Lang, 1987.

Rodd, Cyril S. *Glimpses of a Strange Land: Studies in Old Testament Ethics*. Edinburgh: T&T Clark, 2001.

Routledge, Robin. *Old Testament Theology: A Thematic Approach*. Downers Grove, IL: IVP Academic, 2008.

Sailhamer, John H. *Genesis*. In vol. 1 of *The Expositor's Bible Commentary*. Rev. ed. Edited by Tremper Longman III and David E. Garland, 21–332. Grand Rapids: Zondervan, 2008.

_____. *Genesis Unbound: A Provocative New Look at the Creation Account*. 2nd ed. Colorado Springs, CO: Dawson Media, 2011.

_____. *Introduction to Old Testament Theology: A Canonical Approach*. Grand Rapids: Zondervan, 1995.

_____. *The Meaning of the Pentateuch: Revelation, Composition, and Interpretation*. Downers Grove, IL: IVP Academic, 2009.

_____. *The Pentateuch as Narrative: A Biblical-Theological Commentary*. Grand Rapids: Zondervan, 1992.

Scalise, Charles J. *Hermeneutics as Theological Prolegomena: A Canonical Approach*. Macon, GA: Mercer, 1994.

Schnabel, Eckhard J. *Jesus and the Twelve*. Vol. 1 of *Early Christian Mission*. Downers Grove, IL: IVP, 2004.

_____. *Paul and the Early Church*. Vol. 2 of *Early Christian Mission*. Downers Grove, IL: IVP, 2004.

Schreiner, Thomas R. *The King in His Beauty: A Biblical Theology of*

287

the Old and New Testaments. Grand Rapids: Baker Academic, 2013.

_____. *Paul, Apostle of God's Glory in Christ: A Pauline Theology*. Downers Grove, IL: IVP Academic, 2006.

Schreiner, Thomas R., and Ardel B. Caneday. *The Race Set before Us: A Biblical Theology of Perseverance and Assurance*. Downers Grove, IL: IVP, 2001.

Scobie, Charles H. H. *The Ways of Our God: An Approach to Biblical Theology*. Grand Rapids: Eerdmans, 2003.

Scott, Waldron. *Bring Forth Justice: A Contemporary Perspective on Mission*. Grand Rapids: Eerdmans, 1980.

Seitz, Christopher R. *The Goodly Fellowship of the Prophets: The Achievement of Association in Canon Formation*. Grand Rapids: Baker Academic, 2009.

Sider, Ronald J. *Good News and Good Works: A Theology for the Whole Gospel*. Grand Rapids: Baker, 1999.

_____. *Rich Christians in an Age of Hunger: A Biblical Study*. New York: Paulist Press, 1977.

_____. *Rich Christians in an Age of Hunger: Moving from Affluence to Generosity*. 20th anniversary ed. Dallas: Word, 1997.

Sills, M. David. *Reaching and Teaching: A Call to Great Commission Obedience*. Chicago: Moody, 2010.

Smith, Mark S. *The Priestly Vision of Genesis 1*. Minneapolis: Fortress, 2010.

Sowell, Thomas. *The Quest for Cosmic Justice*. New York: Free Press, 2002.

Stein, Robert H. *The Method and Message of Jesus' Teachings*. Rev. ed. Louisville: Westminster John Knox, 1994.

_____. *Playing by the Rules: A Basic Guide to Interpreting the Bible*. Grand Rapids: Baker, 1994.

Sterns, Richard. *The Hole in Our Gospel: What Does God Expect of Us? The Answer that Changed My Life and Might Just Change the World*. Nashville: Thomas Nelson, 2009.

Stevens, R. Paul. *The Other Six Days: Vocation, Work, and Ministry in Biblical Perspective*. Grand Rapids: Eerdmans, 2000

Steward, Gary. *Princeton Seminary (1812–1929): The Leaders' Lives and Works.* Phillipsburg, NJ: P&R Publishing, 2014.

Stott, John R. W. *Christian Mission in the Modern World.* Downers Grove, IL: IVP, 2008.

Tate, W. Randolph. *Biblical Interpretation: An Integrated Approach.* Peabody, MA: Hendrickson, 1991.

Teevan, John Addison. *Integrated Justice and Equality: Biblical Wisdom for Those Who Do Good Works.* Kindle ed. Grand Rapids: Christian's Library Press, 2014.

Tennent, Timothy C. *Invitation to World Missions: A Trinitarian Missiology for the Twenty-First Century.* Grand Rapids: Kregel, 2010.

Towner, W. Sibley. *Genesis.* Louisville: Westminster John Knox, 2001.

Traeger, Sebastian, and Greg Gilbert. *The Gospel at Work: How Working for King Jesus Gives Purpose and Meaning to Our Jobs.* Grand Rapids: Zondervan, 2013.

Van Duzer, Jeff. *Why Business Matters to God (And What Still Needs to Be Fixed).* Downers Grove, IL: IVP, 2010.

Van Engen, Charles. *God's Missionary People: Rethinking the Purpose of the Local Church.* Grand Rapids: Baker, 1991.

_____. *Mission on the Way: Issues in Mission Theology.* Grand Rapids: Baker Books, 1996.

Van Til, Henry R. *The Calvinistic Concept of Culture.* Grand Rapids: Baker, 1959.

VanDrunen, David. *Divine Covenants and Moral Order: A Biblical Theology of Natural Law.* Grand Rapids: Eerdmans, 2014.

_____. *Living in God's Two Kingdoms: A Biblical Vision for Christianity and Culture.* Wheaton, IL: Crossway, 2010.

_____. *Natural Law and the Two Kingdoms: A Study in the Development of Reformed Social Thought.* Grand Rapids: Eerdmans, 2010.

Vanhoozer, Kevin J. *Is There a Meaning in This Text? The Bible, the Reader, and the Morality of Literary Knowledge.* Grand Rapids: Zondervan, 1998.

Veith, Gene Edward. *God at Work: Your Christian Vocation in All of Life*. Wheaton, IL: Crossway, 2002.

Voegelin, Eric. *The New Science of Politics: An Introduction*. Chicago: University of Chicago, 1952.

Volf, Miroslav. *Work in the Spirit: Toward a Theology of Work*. Eugene, OR: Wipf & Stock, 2001.

Von Rad, Gerhard. *Genesis*. London: SCM, 1961.

Wagner, C. Peter. *Church Growth and the Whole Gospel: A Biblical Mandate*. New York: Harper & Row, 1981.

Waltke, Bruce K. *An Old Testament Theology: An Exegetical, Canonical, and Thematic Approach*. Grand Rapids: Zondervan, 2007.

Watson, Francis. *Text and Truth: Redefining Biblical Theology*. Grand Rapids: Eerdmans, 1997.

Webber, Robert E. *The Church in the World: Opposition, Tension, or Transformation?* Grand Rapids: Zondervan, 1986.

_____. *The Secular Saint: A Case for Evangelical Social Responsibility*. Grand Rapids: Zondervan, 1979.

Weigel, George. *Idealism without Illusions: U. S. Foreign Policy in the 1990s*. Grand Rapids: Eerdmans, 1994.

Weinfeld, Moshe. *Social Justice in Israel and in the Ancient Near East*. Minneapolis: Fortress, 1995.

Wenham, Gordan J. *Genesis 1–15*. Word Biblical Commentary, vol. 1. Dallas: Word, 1987.

_____. *Genesis 16–50*. Word Biblical Commentary, vol. 2. Dallas: Word, 1994.

Williamson, Paul R. *Sealed with an Oath: Covenant in God's Unfolding Purpose*. Downers Grove, IL: IVP, 2007.

Wingreen, Gustaf. *Luther on Vocation*. Eugene, OR: Wipf & Stock, 2004.

Winter, Bruce W. *Seek the Welfare of the City: Christians as Benefactors and Citizens*. Grand Rapids: Eerdmans, 1994.

Wittmer, Michael E. *Heaven Is a Place on Earth: Why Everything You Do Matters to God*. Grand Rapids: Zondervan, 2004.

Wolters, Albert M., and Michael W. Goheen. *Creation Regained:*

Biblical Basics for a Reformational Worldview. 2nd ed. Grand Rapids: Eerdmans, 2005.

Wright, Christopher J. H. *God's People in God's Land: Family, Land, and Property in the Old Testament*. Grand Rapids: Eerdmans, 1990.

_____. *The Mission of God: Unlocking the Bible's Grand Narrative*. Downers Grove, IL: IVP Academic, 2006.

_____. *The Mission of God's People: A Biblical Theology of the Church's Mission*. Grand Rapids: Zondervan, 2010.

_____. *Old Testament Ethics for the People of God*. Downers Grove, IL: IVP, 2004.

Wright, N. T. *After You Believe: Why Christian Character Matters*. New York: HarperOne, 2012.

_____. *Jesus and the Victory of God*. Minneapolis: Fortress, 1997.

_____. *Surprised by Hope: Rethinking Heaven, the Resurrection, and the Mission of the Church*. New York: HarperOne, 2008.

Articles and Chapters

Alford, Roger P., and Leslie M. Alford. "The Law of Life: Law in the Wisdom Literature." In *Law and the Bible: Justice, Mercy and Legal Institutions*, edited by Robert F. Cochran and David Van-Drunen, 101–20. Downers Grove, IL: IVP Academic, 2013.

Armacost, Barbara E., and Peter Enns. "Crying Out for Justice: Civil Law and the Prophets." In *Law and the Bible: Justice, Mercy and Legal Institutions*, edited by Robert F. Cochran and David Van-Drunen, 121–50. Downers Grove, IL: IVP Academic, 2013.

Baker, David L. "Protecting the Vulnerable: The Law and Social Care." In *Transforming the World: The Gospel and Social Responsibility*, edited by Jamie A. Grant and Dewi A. Hughes, 17–34. Nottingham, UK: Apollos, 2009.

Barnett, Mike. "The Missing Key to the Future of Evangelical Mission." In *Missionshift: Global Mission Issues in the Third Millennium*, edited by David J. Hesselgrave and Ed Stetzer, 223–32. Nashville: B&H Academic, 2010.

Bartholomew, Craig G. "A Time for War, and a Time for Peace: Old Testament Wisdom, Creation and O'Donovan's Theological Ethics." In *A Royal Priesthood? The Use of the Bible Ethically and Politically—A Dialogue with Oliver O'Donovan*, edited by Craig G. Bartholomew, Jonathan Chaplin, Robert Song, and Al Wolters, 91–112. Grand Rapids: Zondervan, 2002.

Beuttler, Fred W. "Evangelical Missions in Modern America." In *The Great Commission: Evangelicals and the History of World Missions*, edited by Martin I. Klauber and Scott M. Manetsch, 108–32. Nashville: B&H Academic, 2008.

Beyerhaus, Peter. "A Biblical Encounter with Some Contemporary Philosophical and Theological Systems." In *In Word and Deed: Evangelism and Social Responsibility*, edited by Bruce J. Nicholls, 165–87. Grand Rapids: Eerdmans, 1985.

Bird, Phyllis A. "Male and Female He Created Them: Genesis 1:27b in the Context of the Priestly Account of Creation." In *I Studied Inscriptions from before The Flood: Ancient Near Eastern, Literary, and Linguistic Approaches to Genesis 1–11*, edited by Richard S. Hess and David Toshio Tsumura, 329–61. Winona Lake, IN: Eisenbrauns, 1994.

Block, Daniel I. "To Serve and to Keep: Toward a Biblical Understanding of Humanity's Responsibility in the Face of the Biodiversity Crisis." In *Keeping God's Earth: The Global Environment in Biblical Perspective*, edited by Noah J. Toly and Daniel I. Block, 116–40. Downers Grove, IL: IVP Academic, 2010.

Bosch, David J. "Toward Evangelism in Context." In *The Church in Response to Human Need*, edited by Vinay Samuel and Chris Sudgen, 180–92. Grand Rapids: Eerdmans, 1987.

Brewbaker, William S., III, and V. Philips Long. "Law and Political Order: Israel's Constitutional History." In *Law and the Bible: Justice, Mercy and Legal Institutions*, edited by Robert F. Cochran and David VanDrunen, 49–79. Downers Grove, IL: IVP Academic, 2013.

Brisson, E. Carson. "The Gates of Dawn: Reflections on Genesis

1:1–10; 2:1–4a." In *God Who Creates: Essays in Honor of W. Sibley Towner*, edited by William P. Brown and S. Dean McBride Jr., 53–58. Grand Rapids: Eerdmans, 2000.

Brower, Kent E. "Eschatology." In *New Dictionary of Biblical Theology*, edited by T. Desmond Alexander, Brian S. Rosner, D. A. Carson, and Graeme Goldsworthy, 459–64. Downers Grove, IL: IVP, 2000.

Bullmore, Michael A. "The Four Most Important Biblical Passages for a Christian Environmentalism." *Trinity Journal* 19, no. 2 (Fall 1998): 139–62.

Campbell, Evvy Hay, ed. *Holistic Mission: Occasional Paper No. 33*. Pattaya, Thailand: Lausanne Committee for World Evangelization, 2004.

Carroll R. (Rodas), M. Daniel. "Failing the Vulnerable: The Prophets and Social Care." In *Transforming the World: The Gospel and Social Responsibility*, edited by Jamie A. Grant and Dewi A. Hughes, 35–50. Nottingham, UK: Apollos, 2009.

——————. "The Power of the Future in the Present: Eschatology and Ethics in O'Donovan and Beyond." In *A Royal Priesthood? The Use of the Bible Ethically and Politically—A Dialogue with Oliver O'Donovan*, edited by Craig G. Bartholomew, Jonathan Chaplin, Robert Song, and Al Wolters, 116–43. Grand Rapids: Zondervan, 2002.

Carson, D. A. "Love." In *New Dictionary of Biblical Theology*, edited by T. Desmond Alexander, Brian S. Rosner, D. A. Carson, and Graeme Goldsworthy, 646–50. Downers Grove, IL: IVP, 2000.

——————. "Unity and Diversity in the New Testament: The Possibility of Systematic Theology." In *Scripture and Truth*, edited by D. A. Carson and John D. Woodbridge, 65–95. Grand Rapids: Baker, 1992.

Chalmers, Aaron. "The Importance of the Noahic Covenant to Biblical Theology." *Tyndale Bulletin* 60, no. 2 (2009): 207–16.

Chaplin, Jonathan. "Political Eschatology and Responsible Government: Oliver O'Donovan's 'Christian Liberalism.'" In *A Royal*

Priesthood? The Use of the Bible Ethically and Politically—A Dialogue with Oliver O'Donovan, eds. Craig G. Bartholomew, Jonathan Chaplin, Robert Song, and Al Wolters, 265–308. Grand Rapids: Zondervan, 2002.

Chester, Tim. "Eschatology and the Transformation of the World: Contradiction, Continuity, Conflation and the Endurance of Hope." In *Transforming the World: The Gospel and Social Responsibility*, edited by Jamie A. Grant and Dewi A. Hughes, 225–45. Nottingham, UK: Apollos, 2009.

Clines, D. J. A. "The Image of God in Man." *Tyndale Bulletin* 19 (1968): 53–103.

_____. "Theme in Genesis 1–11." In *I Studied Inscriptions from before The Flood: Ancient Near Eastern, Literary, and Linguistic Approaches to Genesis 1–11*, edited by Richard S. Hess and David Toshio Tsumura, 285–309. Winona Lake, IN: Eisenbrauns, 1994.

Coleman, Doug. "The Agents of Mission: Humanity." In *Theology and Practice of Mission: God, the Church, and the Nations*, edited by Bruce Riley Ashford, 36–47. Nashville: B&H Academic, 2011.

Cordell, Sean. "The Gospel and Social Responsibility." In *Theology and Practice of Mission: God, the Church, and the Nations*, edited by Bruce Riley Ashford, 92–108. Nashville: B&H Academic, 2011.

Dell, Katherine J. "Covenant and Creation in Relationship." In *Covenant as Context: Essays in Honour of E. W. Nicholson*, edited by A. D. H. Mayes and R. B. Salters, 111–33. Oxford: Oxford, 2003.

Dempster, S. "Prophetic Books." In *New Dictionary of Biblical Theology*, edited by T. Desmond Alexander, Brian S. Rosner, D. A. Carson, and Graeme Goldsworthy, 122–26. Downers Grove, IL: IVP, 2000.

Dressler, Harold H. P. "The Sabbath in the Old Testament." In *From Sabbath to Lord's Day*, edited by D. A. Carson, 21–42. Grand Rapids: Zondervan, 1982.

Dumbrell, William J. "Genesis 2:1–17: A Foreshadowing of the New Creation." In *Biblical Theology: Retrospect and Prospect*, edited by Scott J. Hafemann, 53–65. Downers Grove, IL: IVP, 2001.

Eitel, Keith E. "On Becoming Missional: Interacting with Charles Van Engen." In *Missionshift: Global Mission Issues in the Third Millennium*, edited by David J. Hesselgrave and Ed Stetzer, 30–40. Nashville: B&H Academic, 2010.

Erickson, Millard J. "Foundationalism: Dead or Alive?" *Southern Baptist Journal of Theology* 5, no. 2 (Summer 2001): 20–32.

Feinberg, John S. "Systems of Discontinuity." In *Continuity and Discontinuity: Perspectives on the Relationship Between the Old and New Testaments*, edited by John S. Feinberg, 63–86. Wheaton, IL: Crossway, 1988.

Fernando, Ajith. "Getting Back on Course: It's Time to Return to the Priority of Evangelism." *Christianity Today* 51, no. 11 (2007): 40–45.

France, R. T. "The Church and the Kingdom of God: Some Hermeneutical Issues." In *Biblical Interpretation and the Church: Text and Context*, edited by D. A. Carson, 30–44. Exeter, UK: Paternoster, 1984.

Gallagher, Sarita D., and Steven C. Hawthorne. "Blessings as Transformation." In *Perspectives On The World Christian Movement: A Reader*, 4th ed., edited by Ralph D. Winter and Steven C. Hawthorne, 34–41. Pasadena, CA: William Carey Library, 2009.

Geisler, Norman L. "A Response to Paul G. Hiebert 'The Gospel in Human Contexts: Changing Perceptions of Contextualization' and to Darrell Whiteman and Michael Pocock." In *Missionshift: Global Mission Issues in the Third Millennium*, edited by David J. Hesselgrave and Ed Stetzer, 129–43. Nashville: B&H Academic, 2010.

Gentry, Peter J. "Kingdom through Covenant: Humanity as the Divine Image." *Southern Baptist Journal of Theology* 12, no. 1 (Spring 2008): 16–42.

Goldsworthy, Graeme. "Gospel." In *New Dictionary of Biblical*

Theology, edited by T. Desmond Alexander, Brian S. Rosner, D. A. Carson, and Graeme Goldsworthy, 521–24. Downers Grove, IL: IVP, 2000.

_____. "Proverbs." In *New Dictionary of Biblical Theology*, edited by T. Desmond Alexander, Brian S. Rosner, D. A. Carson, and Graeme Goldsworthy, 208–11. Downers Grove, IL: IVP, 2000.

Grant, Jamie A. "'Why Bother with the Vulnerable?' The Wisdom of Social Care." In *Transforming the World: The Gospel and Social Responsibility*, edited by Jamie A. Grant and Dewi A. Hughes, 51–67. Nottingham, UK: Apollos, 2009.

Gustafson, James W. "The Integration of Development and Evangelism." *Missiology* 26, no. 2 (April 1998): 131–42.

Hafemann, Scott J. "The Covenant Relationship." In *Central Themes in Biblical Theology: Mapping Unity in Diversity*, edited by Scott J. Hafemann and Paul R. House, 20–65. Grand Rapids: Baker, 2007.

Harries, Jim. "'Material Provision' or Preaching the Gospel: Reconsidering 'Holistic' (Integral) Mission." *Evangelical Review of Theology* 32, no. 3 (2008): 257–70.

Harvey, John D. "Mission in Jesus' Teaching." In *Mission in the New Testament: An Evangelical Approach*, edited by William J. Larkin Jr. and Joel F. Williams, 30–49. Maryknoll, NY: Orbis, 1998.

Hasel, Gerhard. "Sabbath in the Pentateuch." In *The Sabbath in Scripture and History*, edited by Kenneth A. Strand, 21–43. Washington, DC: Review and Herald, 1982.

Hesselgrave, David J. "Conclusion: A Scientific Postscript—Grist for the Missiological Mills of the Future." In *Missionshift: Global Mission Issues in the Third Millennium*, edited by David J. Hesselgrave and Ed Stetzer, 256–93. Nashville: B&H Academic, 2010.

Hinkson, Jon. "Mission Among Puritans and Pietists." In *The Great Commission: Evangelicals and the History of World Missions*, edited by Martin I. Klauber and Scott M. Manetsch, 23–43. Nashville: B&H Academic, 2008.

Hirsch, E. D. "Coming with Terms to Meaning." *Critical Inquiry* 12, no. 3 (Spring 1986): 627–30.

_____. "Meaning and Significance Reinterpreted." *Critical Inquiry* 11, no. 2 (December 1984): 202–25.

_____. "Transhistorical Intentions and the Persistence of Allegory." *New Literary History* 25, no. 3 (Summer 1994): 549–67.

Hood, Jason. "Theology in Action: Paul and Christian Social Care." In *Transforming the World: The Gospel and Social Responsibility*, edited by Jamie A. Grant and Dewi A. Hughes, 129–46. Nottingham, UK: Apollos, 2009.

International Congress on World Evangelization. "The Lausanne Covenant." In *Making Christ Known: Historic Mission Documents from the Lausanne Movement, 1974–1989*, edited by John R. W. Stott, 1–35. Grand Rapids: Eerdmans, 1997.

_____. "The Manila Manifesto: An Elaboration of the Lausanne Covenant 15 Years Later." In *Making Christ Known: Historic Mission Documents from the Lausanne Movement, 1974–1989*, edited by John R. W. Stott, 225–48. Grand Rapids: Eerdmans, 1997.

International Consultation on the Relationship between Evangelism and Social Responsibility. "The Grand Rapids Report on Evangelism and Social Responsibility: An Evangelical Commitment." In *Making Christ Known: Historic Mission Documents from the Lausanne Movement, 1974–1989*, edited by John R. W. Stott, 165–213. Grand Rapids: Eerdmans, 1997.

Kline, Meredith G. "Creation in the Image of the Glory-spirit." *Westminster Theological Journal* 39, no. 2 (Spring 1977): 250–72.

Köstenberger, Andreas J. "Mission in the General Epistles." In *Mission in the New Testament: An Evangelical Approach*, edited by William J. Larkin Jr. and Joel F. Williams, 189–206. Maryknoll, NY: Orbis, 1998.

_____. "Twelve Theses on the Church's Mission in the Twenty-First Century: In Interaction with Charles Van Engen, Keith Eitel, and Enoch Wan." In *Missionshift: Global Mission Issues in the Third Millennium*, edited by David J. Hesselgrave and Ed Stetzer, 62–70. Nashville: B&H Academic, 2010.

Kotter, David. "Remember the Poor: A New Testament Perspective on the Problems of Poverty, Riches, and Redistribution." In *For the Least of These: A Biblical Answer to Poverty*, edited by Anne Bradley and Art Lindsley, 60–91. Bloomington, IN: Westbow Press, 2014.

Kuzmic, Peter. "History and Eschatology: Evangelical Views." In *In Word and Deed: Evangelism and Social Responsibility*, edited by Bruce J. Nicholls, 135–64. Grand Rapids: Eerdmans, 1985.

Kvalbein, Hans. "Poor/Poverty." In *New Dictionary of Biblical Theology*, edited by T. Desmond Alexander, Brian S. Rosner, D. A. Carson, and Graeme Goldsworthy, 687–91. Downers Grove, IL: IVP, 2000.

Ladd, George Eldon. "The Gospel of the Kingdom." In *Perspectives On The World Christian Movement: A Reader*, 4th ed., edited by Ralph D. Winter and Steven C. Hawthorne, 83–95. Pasadena, CA: William Carey Library, 2009.

Larkin Jr., William J. "Introduction." In *Mission in the New Testament: An Evangelical Approach*, edited by William J. Larkin Jr. and Joel F. Williams, 1–7. Maryknoll, NY: Orbis, 1998.

_____. "Mission in Acts." In *Mission in the New Testament: An Evangelical Approach*, edited by William J. Larkin Jr. and Joel F. Williams, 170–86. Maryknoll, NY: Orbis, 1998.

_____. "Mission in Luke." In *Mission in the New Testament: An Evangelical Approach*, edited by William J. Larkin Jr. and Joel F. Williams, 152–69. Maryknoll, NY: Orbis, 1998.

Little, Christopher R. "In Response to 'The Future of Evangelicals in Mission.'" In *Missionshift: Global Mission Issues in the Third Millennium*, edited by David J. Hesselgrave and Ed Stetzer, 203–22. Nashville: B&H Academic, 2010.

_____. "What Makes Mission Christian?" *International Journal of Frontier Missiology* 25, no. 2 (Summer 2008): 65–73.

Marshall, I. Howard. "Luke's 'Social' Gospel: The Social Theology of Luke-Acts." In *Transforming the World: The Gospel and Social Responsibility*, edited by Jamie A. Grant and Dewi A. Hughes, 112–28. Nottingham, UK: Apollos, 2009.

Maxwell, Ian Douglas. "Civilization or Christianity? The Scottish Debate on Mission Method, 1750–1835." In *Christian Missions and the Enlightenment*, edited by Brian Stanley, 123–40. Grand Rapids: Eerdmans, 2001.

McBride Jr., S. Dean. "Divine Protocol: Genesis 1:1–2:3 as Prologue to the Pentateuch." In *God Who Creates: Essays in Honor of W. Sibley Towner*, edited by William P. Brown and S. Dean McBride Jr., 3–41. Grand Rapids: Eerdmans, 2000.

McQuilkin, J. Robertson. "An Evangelical Assessment of Mission Theology of the Kingdom of God." In *The Good News of the Kingdom: Mission Theology for the Third Millennium*, edited by Charles Van Engen, Dean S. Gilliland, and Paul Pierson, 172–80. Maryknoll, NY: Orbis, 1993.

Moo, Douglas J. "Eschatology and Environmental Ethics: On the Importance of Biblical Theology to Creation Care." In *Keeping God's Earth: The Global Environment in Biblical Perspective*, edited by Noah J. Toly and Daniel I. Block, 23–43. Downers Grove, IL: IVP Academic, 2010.

Nelson, Kurt. "The Priority of Jesus' Command." *Occasional Bulletin* 20, no. 3 (Fall 2007): 5–6.

_____. "The Universal Priority of Proclamation." *Occasional Bulletin* 20, no. 1 (Winter 2007): 3–6.

O'Brien, P. T. "Principalities and Powers: Opponents of the Church." In *Biblical Interpretation and the Church: Text and Context*, edited by D. A. Carson, 110–50. Exeter, UK: Paternoster, 1984.

O'Donovan, Oliver. "Response to Daniel Carroll R." In *A Royal Priesthood? The Use of the Bible Ethically and Politically—A Dialogue with Oliver O'Donovan*, edited by Craig G. Bartholomew, Jonathan Chaplin, Robert Song, and Al Wolters, 144–46. Grand Rapids: Zondervan, 2002.

_____. "Response to Gerrit de Kruijf." In *A Royal Priesthood?*

The Use of the Bible Ethically and Politically—A Dialogue with Oliver O'Donovan, edited by Craig G. Bartholomew, Jonathan Chaplin, Robert Song, and Al Wolters, 238–40. Grand Rapids: Zondervan, 2002.

_____. "Response to James W. Skillen." In *A Royal Priesthood? The Use of the Bible Ethically and Politically—A Dialogue with Oliver O'Donovan*, edited by Craig G. Bartholomew, Jonathan Chaplin, Robert Song, and Al Wolters, 418–20. Grand Rapids: Zondervan, 2002.

Padilla, C. Rene. "The Biblical Basis for Social Ethics." In *Transforming the World: The Gospel and Social Responsibility*, edited by Jamie A. Grant and Dewi A. Hughes, 187–204. Nottingham, UK: Apollos, 2009.

_____. "Holistic Mission." In *A New Vision, A New Heart, A Renewed Call: Lausanne Occasional Papers From the 2004 Forum for World Evangelization*, edited by William Claydon, 11–23. Pasadena, CA: William Carey Library, 2005.

Penn, William. "Charter of Liberties and Frame of Government of the Province of Pennsylvania in America." In *Colonial Origins of the American Constitution: A Documentary History*, edited by Donald S. Lutz, 271–86. Indianapolis: Liberty Fund, 1998.

Richter, Sandra. "A Biblical Theology of Creation Care." *The Asbury Journal* 62, no. 1 (Spring 2007): 67–76.

Rosner, Brian S. "Biblical Theology." In *New Dictionary of Biblical Theology*, edited by T. Desmond Alexander, Brian S. Rosner, D. A. Carson, and Graeme Goldsworthy, 3–11. Downers Grove, IL: IVP, 2000.

Russell, Mark L. "A Brief Apology for Holistic Mission: My Response to 'The Universal Priority of Proclamation' by Kurt Nelson." *Occasional Bulletin* 20, no. 3 (Fall 2007): 3–4.

_____. "Christian Mission Is Holistic." *International Journal of Frontier Missiology*. 25, no. 2 (Summer 2008): 93–98.

Samuel, Vinay, and Chris Sugden. "Evangelism and Social Responsibility: A Biblical Study on Priorities." In *In Word and Deed:*

Evangelism and Social Responsibility, edited by Bruce J. Nicholls, 189–214. Grand Rapids: Eerdmans, 1986.

————. "God's Intention for the World." In *The Church in Response to Human Need*, edited by Vinay Samuel and Chris Sudgen, 128–160. Grand Rapids: Eerdmans, 1987.

Sasson, Jack M. "The 'Tower of Babel' as a Clue to the Redactional Structuring of the Primeval History (Genesis 1:1–11:9)." In *I Studied Inscriptions from before The Flood: Ancient Near Eastern, Literary, and Linguistic Approaches to Genesis 1–11*, edited by Richard S. Hess and David Toshio Tsumura, 448–57. Winona Lake, IN: Eisenbrauns, 1994.

Schnabel, Eckhard J. "Scripture." In *New Dictionary of Biblical Theology*, edited by T. Desmond Alexander, Brian S. Rosner, D. A. Carson, and Graeme Goldsworthy, 34–43. Downers Grove, IL: IVP, 2000.

————. "Wisdom." In *New Dictionary of Biblical Theology*, edited by T. Desmond Alexander, Brian S. Rosner, D. A. Carson, and Graeme Goldsworthy, 843–48. Downers Grove, IL: IVP, 2000.

Seifrid, Mark A. "Righteousness, Justice, and Justification." In *New Dictionary of Biblical Theology*, edited by T. Desmond Alexander, Brian S. Rosner, D. A. Carson, and Graeme Goldsworthy, 740–45. Downers Grove, IL: IVP, 2000.

————. "Righteousness Language in the Hebrew Scriptures and Early Judaism." In *The Complexities of Second Temple Judaism*, 415–42. Vol. 1 of *Justification and Variegated Nomism*. Edited by D. A. Carson, Peter T. O'Brien, and Mark A. Seifrid. Grand Rapids: Baker Academic, 2001.

Shead, A. G. "Sabbath." In *New Dictionary of Biblical Theology*, edited by T. Desmond Alexander, Brian S. Rosner, D. A. Carson, and Graeme Goldsworthy, 745–50. Downers Grove, IL: IVP, 2000.

Shedd, Russell P. "Social Justice: Underlying Hermeneutical Issues." In *Biblical Interpretation and the Church: Text and Context*, edited by D. A. Carson, 195–233. Exeter, UK: Paternoster, 1984.

Shulz, R. L. "Ecclesiastes." In *New Dictionary of Biblical Theology*, edited by T. Desmond Alexander, Brian S. Rosner, D. A. Carson, and Graeme Goldsworthy, 211–15. Downers Grove, IL: IVP, 2000.

Sider, Ronald J. "Evangelism, Salvation and Social Justice." In *Evangelism, Salvation and Social Justice*, 1–18. Nottingham: Grove Books, 1977.

Sider, Ronald J., and James Parker III. "How Broad is Salvation in Scripture." In *In Word and Deed: Evangelism and Social Responsibility*, edited by Bruce J. Nicholls, 85–108. Grand Rapids: Eerdmans, 1985.

Skeel, David, and Tremper Longman III. "Criminal and Civil Law in the Torah: The Mosaic Law in Christian Perspective." In *Law and the Bible: Justice, Mercy and Legal Institutions*, edited by Robert F. Cochran and David VanDrunen, 80–100. Downers Grove, IL: IVP Academic, 2013.

Skillen, James W. "Acting Politically in Biblical Obedience?" In *A Royal Priesthood? The Use of the Bible Ethically and Politically—A Dialogue with Oliver O'Donovan*, edited by Craig G. Bartholomew, Jonathan Chaplin, Robert Song, and Al Wolters, 398–417. Grand Rapids: Zondervan, 2002.

Stetzer, Ed. "Responding to '"Mission" Defined and Described' and the Four Responders." In *Missionshift: Global Mission Issues in the Third Millennium*, edited by David J. Hesselgrave and Ed Stetzer, 71–81. Nashville: B&H Academic, 2010.

Stott, John R. W. "The Response." In *Evangelism, Salvation and Social Justice*, 19–24. Nottingham, UK: Grove Books, 1977.

Strauss, Steve. "A Single Priority or Two Commands to Be Obeyed?" *Occasional Bulletin* 20, no. 3 (Fall 2007): 1–2, 6.

Sugden, Chris. "A Presentation of Concern for Kingdom Ethics." In *Mission as Transformation: A Theology of the Whole Gospel*, edited by Vinay Samuel and Chris Sudgen, 208–35. Oxford: Regnum Books International, 1999.

Sunshine, Glenn. "Who Are the Poor?" In *For the Least of These: A*

Biblical Answer to Poverty, edited by Anne Bradley and Art Lindsley, 3–34. Bloomington, IN: Westbow Press, 2014.

Tinker, Melvin. "The Servant Solution: The Coordination of Evangelism and Social Action." In *Transforming the World: The Gospel and Social Responsibility*, edited by Jamie A. Grant and Dewi A. Hughes, 147–67. Nottingham, UK: Apollos, 2009.

Towner, P. H. "The Pastoral Epistles." In *New Dictionary of Biblical Theology*, edited by T. Desmond Alexander, Brian S. Rosner, D. A. Carson, and Graeme Goldsworthy, 330–36. Downers Grove, IL: IVP, 2000.

Twelftree, G. H. "Signs and Wonders." In *New Dictionary of Biblical Theology*, edited by T. Desmond Alexander, Brian S. Rosner, D. A. Carson, and Graeme Goldsworthy, 775–81. Downers Grove, IL: IVP, 2000.

Vander Hart, Mark D. "Creation and Covenant Part One: A Survey of the Dominion Mandate in the Noahic and Abrahamic Covenants." *Mid-America Journal of Theology* 6, no. 1 (Fall 1990): 3–18.

VanDrunen, David. "Abraham Kuyper and the Reformed Natural Law and Two Kingdom Traditions." *Calvin Theological Journal* 42 (2007): 283–307.

_____. "Bearing Sword in the State, Turning Cheek in the Church: A Reformed Two-Kingdoms Interpretations of Matthew 5:38–42." *Themelios* 34, no. 3 (November 2009): 322–34.

_____. "Calvin, Kuyper, and 'Christian Culture.'" In *Always Reformed: Essays in Honor W. Robert Godfrey*, edited by R. Scott Clark and Joel E. Kim, 135–53. Escondido, CA: Westminster Seminary California, 2010.

_____. "The Importance of the Penultimate: Reformed Social Thought and the Contemporary Critiques of the Liberal Society." *Journal of Markets and Morality* 9, no. 2 (2006): 219–49.

_____. "The Market Economy and Christian Ethics: Refocusing Debate through the Two-Kingdoms Doctrine." *Journal of Markets and Morality* 17, no. 1 (Spring 2014): 11–45.

_____. "The Reformed Two Kingdoms Doctrine: An Explanation and Defense." *The Confessional Presbyterian* 8 (2012): 177–90.

_____. "A System of Theology? The Centrality of Covenant for Westminster Systematics." In *The Pattern of Sound Doctrine: Systematic Theology at the Westminster Seminaries*, edited by David VanDrunen, 195–220. Phillipsburg, NJ: P&R Publishing, 2004.

_____. "The Two Kingdoms: A Reassessment of the Transformationist Calvin." *Calvin Theological Journal* 40 (2005): 248–66.

_____. "The Two Kingdoms and the Ordo Salutis: Life Beyond Judgment and the Question of the Dual Ethic." *Westminster Theological Journal* 70 (2008): 207–24.

_____. "The Two Kingdoms and the Social Order: Political and Legal Theory in Light of God's Covenant with Noah." *Journal of Markets and Morality* 14, no. 2 (Fall 2011): 445–62.

VanDrunen, David, and R. Scott Clark. "The Covenant before the Covenants." In *Covenant, Justification, and Pastoral Ministry: Essays by the Faculty of Westminster Seminary California*, edited by R. Scott Clark, 167–96. Phillipsburg, NJ: P&R Publishing, 2007.

Vanhoozer, Kevin. "A Drama of Redemption Model." In *Four Views on Moving Beyond the Bible to Theology*, edited by Gary T. Meadors, 161–63. Grand Rapids: Zondervan, 2009.

Verkuyl, Johannes. "The Biblical Notion of Kingdom: Test of Validity for Theology of Religion." In *The Good News of the Kingdom: Mission Theology for the Third Millennium*, edited by Charles Van Engen, Dean S. Gilliland, and Paul Pierson, 71–81. Maryknoll, NY: Orbis, 1993.

Walton, J. H. "Eden, Garden of." In *Dictionary of the Old Testament: Pentateuch*, edited by T. Desmond Alexander and David W. Baker, 202–7. Downers Grove, IL: IVP, 2003.

Wellum, Stephen J. Unpublished class notes for *Contemporary Issues in Evangelical Theological Formulation*. Spring 2013.

Wenham, Gordon J. "Sanctuary Symbolism in the Garden of Eden Story." In *I Studied Inscriptions from before The Flood: Ancient Near Eastern, Literary, and Linguistic Approaches to Genesis 1–11*, edited by Richard S. Hess and David Toshio Tsumura, 399–404. Winona Lake, IN: Eisenbrauns, 1994.

Williams, Joel F. "Conclusion." In *Mission in the New Testament: An Evangelical Approach*, edited by William J. Larkin Jr. and Joel F. Williams, 239–47. Maryknoll, NY: Orbis, 1998.

Williamson, Paul R. "Covenant." In *New Dictionary of Biblical Theology*, edited by T. Desmond Alexander, Brian S. Rosner, D. A. Carson, and Graeme Goldsworthy, 419–29. Downers Grove, IL: IVP, 2000.

Wilson, Alistair I. "The Compassion of Christ." In *Transforming the World: The Gospel and Social Responsibility*, edited by Jamie A. Grant and Dewi A. Hughes, 94–111. Nottingham, UK: Apollos, 2009.

Wind, John A. "Does the Old Testament 'Authorize' a Creation Care Mission of the Church? Examining Christopher Wright's Claims." *Journal of Global Christianity* 2, no. 1 (2016): 33–47.

_____. "The Keys to the Two Kingdoms: Covenantal Framework as the Fundamental Divide Between VanDrunen and His Critics." *Westminster Theological Journal*: 77, no. 1 (Spring 2015): 15–34.

_____. "Not Always Right: Critiquing Christopher Wright's Paradigmatic Application of Scripture to the Socio-economic Realm." *Southern Baptist Journal of Theology* 19, no. 2 (Summer 2015): 81–104.

Winter, Ralph D. "The Mission of the Kingdom." In *Perspectives On The World Christian Movement: A Reader*, 4th ed., edited by Ralph D. Winter and Steven C. Hawthorne, 572–73. Pasadena, CA: William Carey Library, 2009.

_____. "Three Mission Eras: And the Loss and Recovery of Kingdom Mission." In *Perspectives On The World Christian Movement: A Reader*, 4th ed., edited by Ralph D. Winter and

Steven C. Hawthorne, 263–78. Pasadena, CA: William Carey Library, 2009.

_____. "The Two Structures of God's Redemptive Mission." In *Perspectives On The World Christian Movement: A Reader*, 4th ed., edited by Ralph D. Winter and Steven C. Hawthorne, 244–62. Pasadena, CA: William Carey Library, 2009.

Witherspoon, John. "The Dominion of Providence over the Passions of Men." In Vol. 1 of *Political Sermons of the American Founding Era, 1730–1805*, 2nd ed., edited by Ellis Sandoz, 533–58. Indianapolis: Liberty Fund, 1998.

World Evangelical Fellowship Consultation on the Church in Response to Human Need.

"Transformation: The Church in Response to Human Need—The Wheaton '83 Statement." In *The Church in Response to Human Need*, edited by Vinay Samuel and Chris Sudgen, 254–65. Grand Rapids: Eerdmans, 1987.

Wright, Christopher J. H. "According to the Scriptures': The Whole Gospel in Biblical Revelation." *Evangelical Review of Theology* 33, no. 1 (January 2009): 4–18.

_____. "The Authority of Scripture in an Age of Relativism: Old Testament Perspectives." In *The Gospel in the Modern World: A Tribute to John Stott*, edited by Martyn Eden and David F. Wells, 31–48. Downers Grove, IL: IVP, 1991.

_____. "Christ and the Mosaic of Pluralisms." In *Global Missiology For The 21st Century: The Iguassu Dialogue*, edited by William D. Taylor, 71–100. Grand Rapids: Baker Academic, 2000.

_____. "The Earth Is the Lord's: Biblical Foundations for Global Ecological Ethics and Mission." In *Keeping God's Earth: The Global Environment in Biblical Perspective*, edited by Noah J. Toly and Daniel I. Block, 216–41. Downers Grove, IL: IVP Academic, 2010.

_____. "The Ethical Authority of the Old Testament: A Survey of Approaches, Part 1." *Tyndale Bulletin* 43, no. 1 (May 1992): 101–20.

_____. "The Ethical Authority of the Old Testament: A Survey of Approaches, Part 2." *Tyndale Bulletin* 43, no. 2 (November 1992): 203–31.

_____. "Family, Covenant, and Kingdom of God: Biblical Reflections." *Transformation* 19, no. 1 (January 2002): 11–19.

_____. "God or Mammon: Biblical Perspectives on Economies in Conflict." *Mission Studies* 12, no. 2 (1995): 145–56.

_____. "'Prophet to the Nations': Missional Reflections on the Book of Jeremiah." In *A God of Faithfulness: Essays in Honour of J. Gordon McConville on His 60th Birthday*, edited by Jamie A. Grant, Alison Lo, and Gordon J. Wenham, 112–29. New York: T&T Clark, 2011.

_____. "Response to Gordon McConville." In *Canon and Biblical Interpretation*, edited by Craig G. Bartholomew, Scott Hahn, Robin Parry, Christopher Seitz, and Al Wolters, 282–92. Grand Rapids: Zondervan, 2006.

_____. "The Righteous Rich in the Old Testament." *Evangelical Review of Theology* 35, no. 3 (July 2011): 255–64.

_____. "The Whole Church: A Brief Biblical Survey." *Evangelical Review of Theology* 34, no. 1 (January 2010): 14–28.

Index of Scripture

313

Index of Subjects and Names

John Anthony Wind (Adv.M.Div, Ph.D., The Southern Baptist Theological Seminary) is assistant professor of theology at Colorado Christian University in Lakewood, Colorado. He also served with his family for eight years in Asia.

Also from P&R Publishing

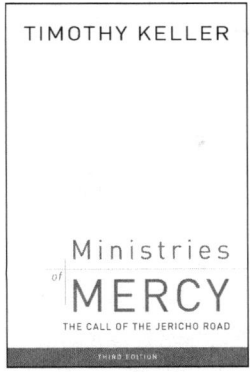

The Good Samaritan didn't ignore the battered man on the Jericho road. Like him, we're aware of people in need around us—the widow next door, the family strapped with medical bills, the homeless man outside our church. God calls us to help them, whether they need shelter, assistance, medical care, or just friendship.

Tim Keller shows that caring for these people is the job of every believer, as fundamental to Christian living as evangelism, discipleship, and worship. But he doesn't stop there. He shows *how* we can carry out this vital ministry as individuals, families, and churches.

Join Keller as he explores the biblical way to participate in compassion ministries and deals perceptively with thorny issues of balancing the cost of meeting needs with the limits of time and resources, giving material aid vs. teaching responsibility, meeting needs within the church vs. outside the church, and more.

"There was a point in my pastoral ministry when I looked for a steady hand on mine as I tried to navigate the swirling waters of mercy ministries in an urban setting while remaining deeply committed to heralding God's Word through the exposition of Scripture. Not surprisingly, I found it in Tim Keller's *Ministries of Mercy*."
—John Piper